Lecture Notes in Computer Sci

Commenced Publication in 1973
Founding and Former Series Editors:
Gerhard Goos, Juris Hartmanis, and Jan van Leeuwen

Jean-Michel Bruel (Ed.)

Satellite Events at the MoDELS 2005 Conference

MoDELS 2005 International Workshops
Doctoral Symposium, Educators Symposium
Montego Bay, Jamaica, October 2-7, 2005
Revised Selected Papers

 Springer

Volume Editor

Jean-Michel Bruel
Université de Pau
LIUPPA
64012 Pau, P.O. Box , France
E-mail: Jean-Michel.Bruel@univ-pau.fr

Library of Congress Control Number: 2005938812

CR Subject Classification (1998): D.2, D.3, I.6, K.6

LNCS Sublibrary: SL 2 – Programming and Software Engineering

ISSN	0302-9743
ISBN-10	3-540-31780-5 Springer Berlin Heidelberg New York
ISBN-13	978-3-540-31780-7 Springer Berlin Heidelberg New York

Springer is a part of Springer Science+Business Media

springer.com

© Springer-Verlag Berlin Heidelberg 2006
Printed in Germany

Typesetting: Camera-ready by author, data conversion by Scientific Publishing Services, Chennai, India
Printed on acid-free paper   SPIN: 11663430   06/3142   5 4 3 2 1 0

Preface

It was a tradition in the previous UML series to host a number of workshops. Workshops provide the opportunity for a small group of people to exchange recent or preliminary results and to conduct intensive discussions on a particular topic. They complement in a sense the main conference and are generally very appreciated by attendees, most of them also attending the main conference.

For this new 2005 edition, it has been decided to host 12 one-day satellite events, during the 3 first days of the conference. The 2003 conference held 9 workshops, last year one held 9 workshops and a new Doctorial Symposium. This year, we have chosen to hold the successful Doctorial Symposium and to add a novelty, mainly related to the broader scope of the new series, a Symposium dedicated to models education.

The selection committee that helped me reviewing the proposals and that was formed by the following researchers:

- Elisa Baniassad, Chinese University of Hong Kong
- Siobhán Clarke, Trinity College Dublin, Ireland
- Gregor Engels, U. of Paderborn, Germany
- Ana Moreira, Universidade Nova de Lisboa, Lisbon, Portugal
- Ivan Porres, Åbo Akademi University, Turku, Finland
- Ambrosio Toval, U. of Murcia, Spain

We have selected 10 workshops which are detailed in the following section. Among the selected workshops, four have been previously held in the previous edition of the conference, one is the merging of two successful workshops from last year, and five are new to the conference series. This novelty has been particularly interesting and we hope that the community will also appreciate it. It reflects the changes at the main conference level itself.

These twelve events have been, both in terms of registration or in discussions and interest, a very pleasant success. The reader will find in this proceedings an abstract of each workshops, written by their organizers, as well as an improved version of a selection of the 2 best papers of each workshops. An exception has been made for the Doctorial Symposium, were all the Ph.D. papers have been included as 2-pages summary of their work. We hope that this will provide a good idea of the workshops discussions and results.

I would like to thank the workshop organizers, the selection committee members for the help and advices they have provided, and also Geri Georg, conference chair of the MODELS 2005 conference, for her support and her friendship.

November 2005

Jean-Michel Bruel
Workshop Chair
MODELS'2005

Sponsors

ACM Special Interest Group on
Software Engineering

IEEE Computer Society

Corporate Donors

Microsoft Corporation

IBM

Digicel Jamaica

Air Jamaica

Springer

Academic Supporters

Knowledge to Go Places

Colorado State University

Canada's Capital University
Carleton University

University of North Dakota

University of Technology, Jamaica

French National Science Funds

Table of Contents

W4 – Aspect-Oriented Modeling

W5 – MTiP

W6 – WiSME

W7 – MDDAUI

W8 – NfC

W9 – MDD for Product-Lines

W10 – WUsCaM

Educator's Symposium

Doctorial Symposium

Tool Support for OCL and Related Formalisms – Needs and Trends

Thomas Baar[1], Dan Chiorean[2], Alexandre Correa[3],
Martin Gogolla[4], Heinrich Hußmann[5], Octavian Patrascoiu[6],
Peter H. Schmitt[7], and Jos Warmer[8]

[1] École Polytechnique Fédérale de Lausanne (EPFL), Switzerland
[2] "Babes-Bolyai" University of Cluj-Napoca, Romania
[3] University of Rio de Janeiro, Brazil
[4] University of Bremen, Germany
[5] LMU Munich, Germany
[6] University of Kent, United Kingdom
[7] Universität Karlsruhe, Germany
[8] Ordina, The Netherlands

Abstract. The recent trend in software engineering to model-centered methodologies is an excellent opportunity for OCL to become a widely used specification language. If the focus of the development activities is shifted from implementation code to more abstract models then software developers need a formalism to provide a complete, unambiguous and consistent model at a very detailed level. OCL is currently the only language that can bring this level of detail to UML models. The purpose of the workshop was to identify future challenges for OCL and to discuss how OCL and its current tool support can be improved to meet these challenges. The workshop gathered numerous experts from academia and industry to report on success stories, to formulate wishes to the next generation of OCL tools, and to identify weaknesses in the language, which make OCL sometimes cumbersome to use. The workshop could also attract numerous people whose aim was to get an overview on the state of the art of OCL tool support and on how OCL can efficiently be applied in practice.

1 Motivation and Goals

Model-centric methodologies see modeling artifacts as the primary output of development activities and not implementation code, as it is currently the case in most software development projects. These new methodologies were triggered by recent standardizations of meta-modeling technologies, which have facilitated the syntactic and semantic specification of modeling languages. It has been reported in numerous case studies how model-centric approaches can yield a productivity leap and thus dramatically reduce development costs. Model-centric methodologies could, however, not become mainstream yet, because this would require a matured, seamless tool support for all development phases. One of today's great

J.-M. Bruel (Ed.): MoDELS 2005 Workshops, LNCS 3844, pp. 1–9, 2006.

challenges is to make modeling tools as powerful and easy to use as current Integrated Development Environments (IDEs) for programming languages.

The Object Constraint Language (OCL) is a standardized, versatile, multi-purpose specification language. It can bring a degree of preciseness to graphical models that is needed if the graphical models should become the *primary* arti-facts in the development process. The pressure to improve the tool support for OCL goes along with the overall challenge to improve the quality of modeling tools in general. Improved tool support is just one thing that has to be addressed in order to increase the popularity of OCL. There are plenty of other questions this workshop was devoted to. The following list is a (surely incomplete) classi-fication of questions that need to be answered.

Technical Questions on How to Improve Tool Support for OCL.   There is a technical dimension how the community can effectively provide better OCL tool support. How can we facilitate the development of new tools? Which features should an OCL tool offer to encourage the usage of OCL in practice? Is it feasible to make OCL executable and to provide an animator for OCL? Should we strive for a common architecture of OCL tools which would enable us to reuse standard components, such as a parsing component?

These and similar questions are discussed in the workshop papers [5–8]. The project described in [6] provides a new grammar for OCL that can be used as a starting point to build a parser (actually, the grammar has been already 'implemented' in form of a parser). This is a remarkable step forward since the official grammar given in the OCL 2.0 language specification intentionally abstracts from 'implementation glitches'.

Language Issues.   The language specification for OCL has certainly improved over the last years, but there are still some debatable points in the OCL seman-tics. Furthermore, OCL is missing some constructs, e.g. a modifies clause, that are widely accepted in the specification language community and that are offered by other specification languages such as the Java Modeling Language (JML).

The paper [9] strives to find a solution for the frame problem that has been highly neglected in OCL so far. The papers [8, 5] discuss besides the semantics of certain constructs also the general architecture of OCL. They try to classify the concepts according to their importance from the language architecture's point of view. Based on this concept classification, the definition of OCL in syntax and semantics could be reorganized to make it more flexible and to define OCL rather as a family of languages than one, entirely fixed language.

Usability Questions and Application Examples.   Besides improved tool support and a clear and concise language description, OCL would also bene-fit from more convincing examples and application scenarios.

The paper [3] applies OCL to make the terminology used by meta-modeling experts much more precise. So far, there was a rudimental common agreement among meta-modelers on what basic meta-modeling concepts are supposed to mean but this agreement has never been formalized beforehand.

The paper [4] describes an approach to guide the user when writing OCL constraints. The paper shows how a widely-used class of OCL constraints can actually be generated by instantiating a schematic OCL constraint. This technique is especially suitable for software developers who write their first constraints and want to become familiar with the language.

1.1 Organization

The workshop continued a series of OCL workshops held at previous UML conferences: York, 2000, Toronto 2001, San Francisco, 2003, and Lisbon, 2004. The workshop was organized by the authors of this article, some of them where already involved in the organization of previous OCL workshops and some of them joint the organization team for the first time.

The organizing team formed also the programme committee of the workshop. Each workshop submission received 2-4 reviews written by the members of the organizing team. Based on the reviews, the decision on the paper acceptance was taken unanimously. For papers that were co-authored by one of the workshop organizers, the review process, of course, ensured that the authors had no influence on the acceptance/rejection decision for papers written by themselves.

2 Accepted Papers

All papers accepted at the workshop are published in [1], what can be downloaded either from EPFL's publication archive http://infoscience.epfl.ch or from the workshop's website [2]. For the convenience of the reader, we have included here the abstract of each paper.

Title: *On Squeezing M0, M1, M2, and M3 into a Single Object Diagram*
Authors: Martin Gogolla, Jean-Marie Favre, Fabian Büttner
Abstract: We propose an approach for the integrated description of a metamodel and its formal relationship to its models and the model instantiations. The central idea is to use so-called layered graphs permitting to describe type graphs and instance graphs. A type graph can describe a collection of types and their relationships whereas an instance graph can represent instances belonging to the types and respecting the relationships required by the type graph. Type graphs and instance graphs are used iteratively, i.e., an instance graph on one layer can be regarded as a type graph of the next lower layer. Our approach models layered graphs with a UML class diagram, and operations and invariants are formally characterized with OCL and are validated with the USE tool. Metamodeling properties like strictness or well-typedness and features like potency can be formulated as OCL constraints and operations. We are providing easily understandable definitions for several metamodeling notions which are currently used in a loose way by modelers. Such properties and features can then be discussed on a rigorous, formal ground. This issue is also the main purpose of the paper, namely, to provide a basis for discussing metamodeling topics.

Title: *Formal Description of OCL Specification Patterns for Behavioral Specification of Software Components*
Author: Jörg Ackermann
Abstract: The Object Constraint Language (OCL) is often used for behavioral specification of software components. One current problem in specifying behavioral aspects comes from the fact that editing OCL constraints manually is time consuming and error-prone. To simplify constraint definition we propose to use specification patterns for which OCL constraints can be generated automatically. In this paper we outline this solution proposal and develop a way how to formally describe such specification patterns on which a library of reusable OCL specifications is based.

Title: *Supporting OCL as part of a Family of Languages*
Authors: David H. Akehurst, Gareth Howells, Klaus D. McDonald-Maier
Abstract: With the continued interest in Model Driven techniques for software development more and more uses are found for query or expression languages that navigate and manipulate object-oriented models. The Object Constraint Language is one of the most frequently used languages; however, its original intended use as a constraint expression language has been succeeded by its frequently proposed use as a basis for a more general model query language, model transformation language and potential action language. We see a future where OCL forms a basis for a family of languages related in particular to Model Driven Development techniques; as a consequence we require an appropriate tool suite to aid in the development of such language families. This paper proposes some important aspects of such a tool suit.

Title: *Generation of an OCL 2.0 Parser*
Authors: Birgit Demuth, Heinrich Hussmann, Ansgar Konermann
Abstract: The OCL 2.0 specification defines explicitly a concrete and an abstract syntax. The concrete syntax allows modelers to write down OCL expressions in a textual way. The abstract syntax represents the concepts of OCL using a MOF compliant metamodel. OCL 2.0 implementations should follow this specification. In doing so emphasis is placed on the fact that at the end of the processing a tool should produce the same well-formed instance of the abstract syntax as given in the specification. This offers the possibility to implement OCL-like languages with the same semantics that are for example easier to use for business modelers. Therefore we looked for a parser technique that helps us to generate an OCL parser to a large extent. In this paper we present the technique we developed and proved within the scope of the Dresden OCL Toolkit. The resulting Dresden OCL2 parser is especially characterized by using a generation approach not only based on a context-free grammar but on an attribute grammar to create the required instance of the abstract syntax of an OCL expression.

Title: *Lessons Learned from Developing a Dynamic OCL Constraint Enforcement Tool for Java*
Authors: Wojciech J. Dzidek, Lionel C. Briand, Yvan Labiche

Abstract: Analysis and design by contract allows the definition of a formal agreement between a class and its clients, expressing each partys rights and obligations. Contracts written in the Object Constraint Language (OCL) are known to be a useful technique to specify the precondition and postcondition of operations and class invariants in a UML context, making the definition of object-oriented analysis or design elements more precise while also helping in testing and debugging. In this article, we report on the experiences with the development of ocl2j, a tool that automatically instruments OCL constraints in Java programs using aspect-oriented programming (AOP). The approach strives for automatic and efficient generation of contract code, and a non-intrusive instrumentation technique. A summary of our approach is given along with the results of an initial case study, the discussion of encountered problems, and the necessary future work to resolve the encountered issues.

Title: *Proposals for a Widespread Use of OCL*
Authors: Dan Chiorean, Maria Bortes, Dyan Corutiu
Abstract: In spite of the fact that OCL and UML evolved simultaneously, the usage of the constraint language in modeling real-world applications has been insignificant compared to the usage of the graphical language. Presently, OCL is requested in new modeling approaches: Model Driven Architecture, Model Driven Development, Domain Specific Languages, Aspect Oriented Modeling, and various emerging technologies: Semantic Web, Business Rules. In this context, the question What has to be done for OCL to become the rule, not the exception, in the modeling domain? is more pressing than ever. The purpose of this paper is to propose an answer to this question, although not a complete one. Our work is an attempt to synchronize the language specification and its understanding, straight related to the language implementation in CASE tools, by proposing solutions for incomplete or non-deterministic OCL specifications. In order to manage the new extensions required for the constraint language, a new language structure is suggested.

Title: *OCL and Graph Transformations – A Symbiotic Alliance to Alleviate the Frame Problem*
Author: Thomas Baar
Abstract: Many popular methodologies are influenced by Design by Contract. They recommend to specify the intended behavior of operations in an early phase of the software development life cycle. In practice, software developers use most often natural language to describe how the state of the system is supposed to change when the operation is executed. Formal contract specification languages are still rarely used because their semantics often mismatch the needs of software developers. Restrictive specification languages usually suffer from the frame problem: It is hard to express which parts of the system state should remain unaffected when the specified operation is executed. Constructive specification languages, instead, suffer from the tendency to make specifications deterministic.

This paper investigates how a combination of OCL and graph transformations can overcome the frame problem and can make constructive specifications less deterministic. Our new contract specification language is considerably more expressive than both pure OCL and pure graph transformations.

3   Workshop Results

The workshop attracted 38 registered attendees. The motivation was rather divers; some of them wanted to learn OCL and to get acquainted with it, others came to discuss specific problems in depth.

3.1   Spontaneous Tool Overview Session

Since the workshop attracted many people from academia and industry who were not OCL experts but wanted to get an overview on OCL technology, Martin Gogolla made, after every workshop participant has introduced himself, the suggestion to devote the first session to present briefly some of the currently existing OCL tools. This was especially attractive since some of the tool developers were sitting in the workshop room. The following tools were informally presented to the audience:

Martin Gogolla: USE Tool. The USE tool (UML-based Specification Environment)[1] supports analysts, designers and developers in executing UML models and checking OCL constraints and thus enables them to employ model-driven techniques for software production. USE allows the validation of UML models and OCL constraints based on animation and certification. USE permits analyzing the model structure (classes, associations, attributes, and invariants) and the model behavior (operations and pre- and postconditions) by generating typical snapshots (system states) and by executing typical operation sequences (scenarios). Developers can formally check constraints (invariants and pre- and postconditions) against their expectations and can, to a certain extent, derive formal model properties.

Heinrich Hußmann: Dresden OCL2 Toolkit. The Dresden OCL2 Toolkit[2] is a set of tools for processing OCL specifications. The heart of the toolkit is a recently redesigned parser for OCL 2.0. The Abstract Syntax Tree (AST) produced by the parser conforms with the official metamodel of OCL 2.0. Other tools in the toolkit can translate OCL specifications into SQL queries or into Java code, which is able to check the correctness of OCL assertions at runtime.

Behzad Bordbar: UML2Alloy. UML2Alloy[3] allows to translate UML class diagrams enriched with OCL expressions into models written in Alloy. Class diagrams are used to depict the static structure of the system. OCL statements are used to both define behavior through pre- and postconditions, and invariants on the UML class diagrams. The tool accepts a UML model of the system in

---

[1] See http://www.db.informatik.uni-bremen.de/projects/USE/
[2] See http://dresden-ocl.sourceforge.net
[3] See http://www.cs.bham.ac.uk/~bxb/UML2Alloy.html

XMI format and guides the user step by step through the translation of the UML model to a corresponding Alloy model. Users can then use Alloy Analyzer on the produced Alloy model to conduct analysis. Alloy Analyzer provides the ability of Analysis. This includes simulation of the system, which provides examples of instances that conform to the model. This is particularly helpful in checking if the model is overconstrained and to increase the confidence in correctness of the model. It is also possible to check the correctness of logical statements, assertions, about the model.

Thomas Baar: KeY Tool and Grammatical Framework (GF). The KeY tool[4] is not primarily an OCL tool but has an OCL front end (in fact, it uses the OCL parser from the Dresden OCL toolkit) for behavioral specification of operations in a UML class diagram. The KeY tool allows the user to verify the correctness of operation implementations written in Java in respect to an OCL specification given as a pair of pre- and postcondition (contract). Otherwise stated, using KeY one can statically prove that whenever the operation's implementation is invoked in a state in which the pre-condition holds, the execution of the implementation will terminate and yield to a state in which the postcondition holds.

The Grammatical Framework (GF) is designed as a stand-alone tool but has been fully integrated into the KeY tool. The Grammatical Framework offers translations of OCL specifications into natural language. Most developers appreciate if OCL constraints are presented in natural language since – as for any other formal specification language – it is time consuming to read and to understand formal OCL constraints. Languages, currently supported by GF as a target language, are English, Swedish, Finnish, German. Also the opposite direction of translation, from natural language to OCL, is prototypically realized.

3.2   Discussion

The last session of the workshop was devoted to discussion on OCL issues raised during the paper presentation sessions as well as other issues that are of common interest. The following list captures the main points of the discussion. Many problems remained unsolved and it was not always possible to come to an agreement among all participants.

OCL Must Be Supported by Better Tools. Most of the current OCL tools are academic tools and were developed by a team of a single university. Although the quality of tools has improved considerably over the last years, it is not a surprise that these OCL tools cannot compete in terms of usability and the functionality they offer with integrated development environments for writing implementation code.

One trap a lot of OCL tool development teams fall into is to capture every possible application scenario for OCL by their tool. Instead of a one-fits-it-all-tool we need rather a component-oriented approach where specialized tools

---

[4] See http://www.key-project.org

provide services using standardized interfaces and other tools can take advantages of them. Examples for such services could be: parse a constraint, evaluate a constraint, pretty print a constraint, find counterexample that constraint always holds, generate implementation code, etc. A first step towards this goal could be to define a list of functionalities a user would expect from a matured OCL tool. The list should also clarify in which scenario the functionality would be useful.

Applying OCL Yields to Better Software and Saves Valuable Time. Based on the current examples and case studies it is hard to convince software developers on the usefulness of applying OCL in practice. There are even experiences reported in the literature where an OCL specification of a Java framework is considered to be less informative than other ways to specify the framework, e.g. by a reference implementation or carefully written informal comments. On the other hand, a few controlled experiments conducted in academic settings have reported positive results on using OCL in UML based developments.

Developers might be convinced more easily once we had compelling results from more experiments available. For instance, it would be interesting to set up two teams developing the same application in parallel and measure the effort and the quality of the resulting artifacts. One team uses OCL assertions whereas the other tries to model and implement the application the traditional way without OCL assertions. Such an experiment can hardly be done in real software industry but it is possible to run it at universities with two groups of students (trained in OCL and without any knowledge on OCL).

Promising Application Areas for OCL Have to Be Identified. We need a clear idea on what are the most promising application scenarios for OCL. If OCL is used at the very detailed level of implementation models to describe the behavior of implemented methods, then it competes for instance with JML. In this case, OCL is often not chosen as the specification language because it's semantics is not aligned enough with this application area. For instance, the type system of OCL refers to that of UML and do not take the peculiarities of Java's type system into account (however, the Java type system could be made available to OCL via a Java profile).

But weaknesses on one side are strengths on the other side. Since OCL is fully integrated into the UML metamodel, it can specify properties directly at any level of abstraction. As another advantage, OCL provides powerful mechanisms for reflection and allows the user to explore the metamodel within a constraint.

OCL Is a Family of Languages. The application scenarios of OCL are very divers and require sometimes to adapt the semantics of certain constructs to the current scenario or to add new, scenario-specific constructs. This gives rise to treat OCL as a family of languages instead of a fixed one. The OCL language specification should be rewritten according to this fact and should allow the user to customize the currently needed dialect of OCL. The possibility to customize the language has of course to be backed by the tools that support OCL. Either a tool can be customized by the user, i.e. the tool is tailored to the OCL dialect the user has in mind, or the tool clearly states which of OCL's dialects it supports.

More Teaching Modules on the Art of Specification Are Needed. There is still a lack of good teaching modules for OCL and the diversity among the illustrating examples for OCL constraints is rather low. Also case studies on bigger projects would help many potential users to find out whether or not OCL is the proper formalism to describe the problems they have.

It was decided on the workshop to launch a new website as an archive of existing teaching modules, experience reports, etc. This website is already available under `http://www-st.inf.tu-dresden.de/ocl/`. Everybody is encouraged to contribute!

Acknowledgement

The authors are grateful to Behzad Bordbar and Dave Akehurst for their comments on earlier drafts of this workshop report.

References

1. Thomas Baar, editor. *Tool Support for OCL and Related Formalisms - Needs and Trends, MoDELS'05 Conference Workshop, Montego Bay, Jamaica, October 4, 2005, Proceedings*, Technical Report LGL-REPORT-2005-001. EPFL, 2005.
2. Homepage of OCL Workshop 2005. `http://lgl.epfl.ch/members/baar/oclws05`.
3. Martin Gogolla, Jean-Marie Favre, and Fabian Büttner. On squeezing M0, M1, M2, and M3 into a single object diagram.
4. Jörg Ackermann. Formal description of OCL specification patterns for behavioral specification of software components.
5. David H. Akehurst, Gareth Howells, and Klaus D. McDonald-Maier. Supporting OCL as part of a family of languages.
6. Birgit Demuth, Heinrich Hussmann, and Ansgar Konermann. Generation of an OCL 2.0 parser.
7. Wojciech J. Dzidek, Lionel C. Briand, and Yvan Labiche. Lessons learned from developing a dynamic OCL constraint enforcement tool for Java.
8. Dan Chiorean, Maria Bortes, and Dyan Corutiu. Proposals for a widespread use of OCL.
9. Thomas Baar. OCL and graph transformations – a symbiotic alliance to alleviate the frame problem.

Lessons Learned from Developing a Dynamic OCL Constraint Enforcement Tool for Java

Wojciech J. Dzidek[2], Lionel C. Briand[1,2], and Yvan Labiche[1]

[1] Software Quality Engineering Laboratory,
Department of Systems and Computer Engineering – Carleton University,
1125 Colonel By Drive, Ottawa, ON, K1S 5B6, Canada
{briand, labiche}@sce.carleton.ca
[2] Simula Research Laboratory, Lysaker, Norway
dzidek@simula.no

Abstract. Analysis and design by contract allows the definition of a formal agreement between a class and its clients, expressing each party's rights and obligations. Contracts written in the Object Constraint Language (OCL) are known to be a useful technique to specify the precondition and postcondition of operations and class invariants in a UML context, making the definition of object-oriented analysis or design elements more precise while also helping in testing and debugging. In this article, we report on the experiences with the development of ocl2j, a tool that automatically instruments OCL constraints in Java programs using aspect-oriented programming (AOP). The approach strives for automatic and efficient generation of contract code, and a non-intrusive instrumentation technique. A summary of our approach is given along with the results of an initial case study, the discussion of encountered problems, and the necessary future work to resolve the encountered issues.

1 Introduction

The usefulness of analysis and design by contract (ADBC) has been recognized by current and emerging software paradigms. For example, in [1], a book on component software, an entire chapter is devoted to the subject of contracts, and the author argues that using a formal language to specify them would be ideal except for the disadvantage of the complexity associated with the usage of a formal language. However, recent experiments have shown that OCL provides a number of advantages in the context of UML modeling [2], thus suggesting its complexity to be manageable by software engineers. Likewise in [3], a book discussing distributed object-oriented technologies, Emmerich argues that the notion of contracts is paramount in distributed systems as client and server are often developed autonomously. Last, model driven architecture (MDA), also known as model driven development (MDD), is perceived by many as a promising approach to software development [4]. In [4], the authors note that the combination of UML with OCL is at the moment probably the best way to develop high-quality and high-level models, as this results in precise, unambiguous, and consistent models. Having discussed the advantages of OCL, it comes as a surprise that the language is not used more widely for ADBC. One reason

J.-M. Bruel (Ed.): MoDELS 2005 Workshops, LNCS 3844, pp. 10–19, 2006.

for this might be the well-established prejudices against any formal elements among software development experts and many influential methodologists. Another reason for the unsatisfactory utilization of OCL is the lack of industrial strength tools, e.g., tools to generate code assertions from OCL contracts.

The benefits of using contract assertions in source code is shown in [5], where a rigorous empirical study showed that such assertions detected a large percentage of failures and thus can be considered acceptable substitutes to hard-coded oracles in test drivers. This study also showed that contract assertions can be used to significantly lower the effort of locating faults after the detection of a failure, and that the contracts need not be perfect to be highly effective. Based on such results, the next step was therefore to address the automation of using OCL contracts to instrument Java systems. This paper reports on our experience with the development and use of *ocl2j*, a tool for the automated verification of OCL contracts in Java systems [6]. These verifications are dynamic, i.e., are performed during the execution of the application.

The paper briefly starts with background information, motivation, and related work. Then we go through an overview of our approach, followed by a discussion of some of the main technical and methodological issues with respect to transformation of constraints from OCL to Java. Next, an initial case study, aimed at showing the feasibility of the ocl2j approach, is presented. Finally, difficulties with using OCL for this purpose are outlined, conclusions are then provided.

2   Motivation and Related Work

Currently, two tools exist for the purpose of dynamic enforcement of OCL constraints in Java systems: the Dresden OCL toolkit (DOT) [7, 8] and the Object Constraint Language Environment (OCLE) [9]. We decided to implement our own solution as DOT did not fulfill all of our requirements and OCLE did not exist at the time, though it doesn't fully address our needs either.

Our aim was to have a tool that would: (1) support all the core OCL 1.4 functionality, (2) correctly enforce constraints, (3) instrument (insert the contract checking and enforcement code) program code at the bytecode level (as opposed to altering the source-code), (4) allow for optional dynamic enforcement to the Liskov Substitution Principle (LSP) [10], (5) support for separate compilation (i.e., allowing modifications of the application source code without recompiling assertion code or vice-versa), (6) correctly check constraints when exceptions are thrown, (7) have the ability for assertion code to use private members, (8) have the option to use either compile-time or load-time instrumentation (with load-time instrumentation constraint checking code can be installed or removed without requiring recompilation), and (9) have the ability to add assertions to classes for which the source-code is not available.

DOT was the pioneering work for this problem and is open-source software. It relies on the following technical choices. First, the instrumentation occurs at the source code level: original methods are renamed and wrapped, and supplementary code is added. OCL types are implemented in Java and Java variables (attributes, method parameters or return value) used in assertions are wrapped with equivalent OCL types. Last, the generated code is constructed in such a way that it uses Java reflection mechanisms at runtime to determine implementation details. Additional logic is inserted that tries to minimize the checking of invariants. Those technical decisions result in a large memory and performance penalty as a direct consequence of the virtual cloning (of all objects) and the wrapping (of all objects involved in OCL constraints). Support for OCL is also incomplete as, for example, query operations are not supported. Furthermore, constraints on elements in collections are not properly enforced as changes to elements in the collection can go unnoticed [6]. (Source-code level instrumentation suffers from two main disadvantages: it makes the developer deal with two versions of the source-code and it makes it much harder to debug the application, e.g., when single stepping through the source-code.)

OCLE is a UML CASE tool offering OCL support both at the UML metamodel and model level, though we only look at the latter: i.e., support for dynamic OCL constraint enforcement. Like DOT, OCLE instruments the source code and is limited in its support of OCL (e.g. the @pre keyword is not supported). Furthermore, it cannot instrument existing (reverse-engineered) source code.

Note that although other tools exist that add design by contract support to Java [11, 12], they are not discussed in this paper as they do not address the transformation of OCL expressions into assertions.

3   The ocl2j Approach

This section presents our approach (ocl2j) towards the automatic generation and instrumentation of OCL constraints in Java. Our approach consists of Java code being created from OCL expressions and the target system then being instrumented: (1) The necessary information is retrieved from the target system's UML model and source code; (2) Every OCL expression is parsed, an abstract syntax tree (AST) is generated [7], and the AST is used to create the assertion code (the OCL to Java transformation rules were defined as semantic actions associated with production rules of the OCL grammar [13]. The generation of Java assertions from OCL constraints is thus rigorously defined and easily automated.); (3) The target system is then instrumented with the assertion code, using AspectJ which is the main Java implementation of Aspect Oriented Programming (AOP) [14]. The techniques involved in step (3) are omitted as they're already described in [15]. It is important to emphasize that this strategy played a large role in helping us achieve the goals outlines in Section 2.

The section starts (Section3.1) with a discussion of how OCL types are transformed in Java types. Next, Section 3.2 discusses the topic of equality with respect to OCL and Java. Section 3.3 shows how the OCL @pre construct is addressed. Finally, Section 3.4 shows how we were able to use AspectJ to provide clean and efficient support for oclAny::oclIsNew().

3.1   OCL to Java Transformations

The checking of contracts at runtime slows down the execution of the program. If this slowdown is too great the developers will not use the technology. For this reason it is important to focus on techniques that enable faster checking of contracts. One of these techniques is to translate OCL expressions directly into Java using the types retrieved from the target system (through reflection) at the assertion-code generation stage, instead of wrapping Java types and operations with OCL-like types and operations [7, 8]. The translation time is thus spent during instrumentation rather than execution. This distinction becomes critical during maintenance of large systems since changes to the system only occur to the subsystem under development. For this reason it is both unnecessary and inefficient to perform the OCL to Java type resolution over the whole system every time the system is executed.

Our OCL to Java type resolution relies on the following principles. First, whenever a simple mapping exists between OCL and Java types/operations, the translation is straightforward. For instance, OCL collection operation `size()` maps directly to the `size()` operation of the `java.util.Collection` interface (which every collection class in Java implements). When OCL types/operations cannot be directly converted to types/operations from standard Java libraries, the instrumentation code (aspect code) provides the functionality that is "missing" in the libraries. This ensures that no wrapping is necessary, and no additions to the target system are required. The instrumentation code (i.e., the aspect) contains inner classes with operations that provide additional functionality to complete the mapping to Java such as the `collection->count(obj):Integer` operation, that counts the number of times object `obj` occurs in `collection` and does not have any counterpart in Java collection classes/interfaces. The aspect code thus contains inner class `OclCollection` with a `count()` static operation that takes two arguments: the collection on which to count, and the object that needs to be counted.

Next, OCL, unlike Java, has no notion of primitive types (e.g., `int`) as everything is considered an object. Java, on the other hand, supports primitive types and corresponding primitive value wrapper classes, or simply wrapper classes (e.g., `Integer`). OCL provides four, so-called, basic types: `Boolean`, `Integer`, `Real` and `String`. There is one exception to these differences in OCL and Java type systems: strings are objects in both OCL and Java. Having both primitive types and wrapper classes has a major impact on the process of OCL to Java transformation (unless the system is written in Java 1.5 where the autoboxing feature is available). For example, consider the following OCL constraint: `someCollection->includes(5)`. When transforming the OCL expression into Java source code, 5 has to be transformed into either primitive value 5 or an instance of wrapper class Integer (`new Integer(5)`). As Java collections only take objects as elements, the latter is the correct choice. A general, trivial solution to this problem would be to convert every literal value into an object, but as already discussed, this is inefficient. A more efficient solution consists in analyzing the types used in the OCL expression, the types required in the corresponding Java source code, as well as the characteristics of the expression, and converting objects to their primitive types when possible (i.e. values used in logical, addition, multiplication, and unary operations).

OCL has three collection types, namely `Set`, `Bag`, and `Sequence`, whereas, Java only has two main collection interfaces, namely `java.util.Set` and `java.util.List` (we assume that user-define collections directly or indirectly implement `java.util.Collection`). There is a direct mapping between OCL `Set` and `java.util.Set` and between OCL `Sequence` and `java.util.List`. However, OCL `Bag` does not have a direct Java counterpart. A bag is a collection in which duplicates are allowed [16]. `java.util.Set` cannot be used to implement an

OCL `Bag` as it does not allow duplicates. The only possible alternative, which is assumed in the ocl2j approach, is to implement OCL `Bag` with `java.util.List`.

The following 3 scenarios are encountered when translating a collection operation:

1. There is a direct mapping between the OCL operation and a Java operation.
2. The OCL operation does not have a direct counterpart but its functionality can easily be derived from existing Java operations.
3. OCL operations that iterate over collections and evaluate an OCL expression (passed as a parameter to the operation) on elements in the collection are more complex. They do not have a direct Java counterpart and cannot be simply implemented using the operations provided by `java.util.Set` or `java.util.List`. These OCL operations are `exists`, `forAll`, `isUnique`, `sortedBy`, `select`, `reject`, `collect`, and `iterate`. They require more attention as the parameter is an OCL expression which requires to be instrumented as well in the aspect code. Templates and transformation rules are used to generate a unique method (residing in the aspect) for every distinct use of these operations [6].

3.2 Testing for Equality

Assertion code that tests for equality can take any one of three forms. First, if the values to be compared are of primitive type then the Java "==" construct is used in the equality test. Next, if the values being compared (or just one of them) are of reference type wrapping a primitive then the primitive value is extracted from the object using the appropriate method (e.g., `intValue()` for an object of type `Integer`) and again the values are tested for equality using the Java "==" construct. In other cases, objects are tested for equality using their `equals(o:Object):boolean` method. This is done as equality in OCL is defined at the object level, not the reference level. For example, let's take a look at the `java.awt.Point` class which has two attributes: `x:int` and `y:int`. Given two points `Point a = new Point(5, 5)` and `Point b = new Point(5, 5)`. If we compare these points at a "reference level" they will not be equal (`a == b` evaluates to `false`), even though they the two objects a and b do represent the same point. Thus, `Point`'s `equals` method must be used to evaluate their equality (`a.equals(b)` evaluates to `true`).

We assume that the `equals()` method is properly implemented [17] so that objects are deemed equal when their key attributes are equal. We define *key attributes* as attributes that define an object's identity (e.g., attributes x and y in the case of the `Point` class). Sometimes each instance of a class is unique (no clones are possible) in which case the default `equals()` functionality (i.e., inherited from `java.lang.Object`, considers each instance only equal to itself) will suffice as this functionality only compares reference values for equality, but when this is not the case the `equals()` method must be overridden. Note that this last point is often neglected by developers of Java-based systems [17].

3.3 Using Previous Property Values in OCL Postconditions

This section discusses the practical implementation of the OCL language construct `@pre`, used in postconditions to access the value of an object property at the start of the execution of the operation. Depending on the property that the @pre is associated with different values and amount of data must be stored temporarily until the constrained method finishes executing so that the postcondition can be checked. @pre can be used with respect to one of the following:

1. *Java types corresponding to OCL Basic types or query methods that return a value of such a type.* The mapping between these types is discussed in Section 3.1. In the case of a primitive type, the primitive value is stored in a temporary variable. In the case of an object, the reference to the object is stored in a temporary variable. Only the reference is stored as these types are immutable and thus they cannot change (during the execution of the constrained method).

2. *Query methods that return an object.* In this case the objects are handled in the same way as described above, only the reference to that object is stored in a temporary variable (duplicated), the object itself is not cloned. The object is not cloned as we assume that the target system is written with proper encapsulation techniques, meaning that query methods that return an object to which the context class (the class containing the query method) is related via composite aggregation return a clone of the object, not the object itself. This is standard practice as discussed in Item 24 of [17]. Note that this is a necessary requirement as the following example will demonstrate: Consider a query method returning a reference to an object X, used in a method M's postcondition with the @pre keyword (i.e., we are interested in the value of X at precondition-time): i.e., the postcondition reads ...=...query()@pre. Further assume that M modifies X during its execution. Once M finishes execution the postcondition is verified. Since the query method returns a reference to X (instead of a clone of X), the postcondition will use the new version of X, as opposed to the original version at precondition-time.

3. *Objects (references to objects).* The object types in this discussion exclude the ones discussed in the points above. In this case a clone of the object is taken and stored in a temporary variable. We assume that the programmer properly implements cloneability support (as will be discussed).

4. *Collections.* A collection's identity is defined by the elements in that collection, thus a clone of a collection contains a clone of every element in the original collection. Using @pre on a collection will result in such a duplication of the collection in most cases. When the OCL collection operation being invoked on someCollection@pre   is   size():Integer,   isEmpty():Boolean, notEmpty():Boolean, or sum():T then only the result of the operation is stored in the temporary variable. We note that in a lot of cases it may not be necessary to duplicate the collection in such a manner to enforce the postcondition correctly, but this is a subject for future work.

For a guide to providing support for cloneability see Item 10 in [17]. Essentially, two types of cloning methods exist. In a shallow copy, the fields declared in a class and its parents (if any) will have values identical to those of the object being cloned. In the case of a class exhibiting one or more composite relationships the shallow copy is not sufficient and a deep copy must be used. In a deep copy, all the objects in the composition hierarchy must also be cloned. To understand why, recall our objective: We need access to the objects, as they were, before the constrained method executed. Objects are uniquely identified by their key attributes (key attributes are discussed in Section 3.2). If these objects have composite links to other objects (i.e., their class has composite relationships), thus forming a hierarchy of objects, the key attributes may be located anywhere in the hierarchy. A deep copy is therefore necessary.

3.4 `oclAny::oclIsNew()` Support

Any OCL type in a UML model, including user-defined classes, is an instance of `OclType`: it allows access to meta-level information regarding the UML model. In addition, every type in OCL is a child class of `OclAny`, i.e., all model types inherit the properties of `OclAny`. Among those properties is operation `oclAny::oclIsNew()` that can only be used in a postcondition: It evaluates to `true` if the object on which it is called has been created during the execution of the constrained method.

The ocl2j solution to the problem of implementing operation `oclAny::oclIsNew()` is the following. If this operation is used on a type in an OCL expression, a collection is added to an AspectJ aspect. This collection will store references to all the instances of the type created during the execution of the constrained method (as `oclAny::oclIsNew()` can only be used in the context of a postcondition): This is easily achieved with AspectJ as it only requires that the aspect comprises an advice to add, at the end of the execution of any constructor of the type of interest or its subtypes, the reference of the newly created instance. This raises the question of the choice of the Java data structure to store those references and the impact of aspect code on object garbage collection in Java: Objects in the instrumented program should be garbage collected if they are not used in the application code, even though they may be referenced by the aspect code. A solution to this problem is to use class `java.util.WeakHashMap` to store these references in the aspect. This collection was specifically designed so as to store references that would not be accounted by the garbage collector. It is based on a hash map where the keys are weak references to the objects we are monitoring. The garbage collector can get rid of an object, even when this object is still referenced, provided that these references are only used in instances of class `WeakHashMap`. When this is the case, the object is garbage collected and any reference to it removed from instances of the `WeakHashMap`.

Determining whether an object was created during the execution of the constrained method involves checking the `WeakHashMap` collection for the presence of the object in question. Finally, after the constrained method finishes executing and the postcondition is checked, the collection of instances (created during the execution of that method) is discarded.

Please note that this solution is not easily mapped to a solution that enables the use of the `oclAny::allInstances()` construct as there is no way to *force* the JVM to run the garbage collection operation (though `Runtime.getRuntime().gc()` can be used to *suggest* this to the JVM). Thus, such an implementation of `oclAny::allInstances()` could, in certain instances, return a collection of objects including ones that are designated for garbage collection (no longer referenced).

4 Preliminary Case Study

The case study is based on the system presented in [16]: The "Royal and Loyal" system example. Though modest in size, this system was chosen due to the large number of diverse constraints being already defined for it, including some quite complex ones. It should then provide initial evidence that ocl2j works for a wide variety of constraints. The UML model in [16] was expanded in this work to the system shown in [6] in order to be implementable. Once expanded, it was implemented in Java and consisted of 381 LOCs, including 14 classes, 47 OCL constraints, 53 attributes, and 46 operations.

The original version of the R&L system and the version with the assertion code (instrumented) are compared for a set of scenarios where various numbers of customers are added and various amounts of purchases are made. We use the following three criteria for comparison: (1) bytecode size of the classes, (2) time it takes to execute the program (in various scenarios), and (3) memory footprint (again, in various scenarios). From the case study we conclude that programs that have relatively large collections with many complicated constraints associated with these collections can expect, as a ballpark figure, a degradation in execution time of 2 to 3 times. Otherwise, the degradation in performance is smaller as the execution speed is slowed down by roughly 60%. This is significant but does not prevent the use of instrumented contracts in most cases during testing, unless the system's behavior is extremely sensitive to execution deadlines. The sources of degradation in performance have been further investigated in [6] where solutions are proposed for optimization. With respect to criteria (1), the target system grew 2.5 times in size, and (3), the maximum overhead percentage observed for the above scenarios were 14% and 10.5%, respectively.

5 Future Challenges

While developing ocl2j we ran into several non-trivial issues that require significant work to address. Among others:

- Providing support for the `@pre` keyword leaves a lot of room for performance optimizations. For example, to properly evaluate the postcondition `self.aCollection@pre = self.aCollection` in every scenario, one must create a new collection (say `tempCollection`) that holds a clone of every element present in `self.aCollection`. If `aCollection` is large or if the elements in that collection are expensive to clone, then the evaluation of this postcondition becomes very expensive. Furthermore, this potentially expensive operation is not even necessary if all the designer intended to check was whether `self.aCollection@pre` and `self.aCollection` point to the same object (i.e. hold the same reference). In such a situation the designer should be allowed to distinguish weather a deep or shallow copy is meant by the `@pre`. One way of addressing this would be by adding the keyword `@preShallow` to OCL.
- The use of `@pre` may lead to un-computable expressions. As shown in [18], the expression `self.b.c@pre` with respect to the example in Section 7.5.15 in [20]

is not computable: "Before invocation of the method, it is not yet known what the future value of the b property will be, and therefore it is not possible to store the value of `self.b.c@pre` for later use in the postcondition!".

- Our experience revealed that, by far, the largest performance penalties (execution time overhead) of checking the OCL constraints during the execution of the system came from OCL collection operations [6]. For this reason we have started working on an approach to minimize these performance penalties. In general the strategy involves checking a constraint on a collection whenever the state of the collection changes in such a way that it could invalidate the constraint. For example, consider the constraint `aCollection->forAll(anExpression)`. If this constraint is an invariant then it will be checked before and after any public method executes, even if neither the state of `aCollection` nor its elements changes. An alternative to this would be to check that `anExpression` holds for a newly added element to `aCollection`, and that `anExpression` holds for elements in the collection that undergo changes that may invalidate it. This alterative will be more efficient on a large, often-checked, collection that does not undergo large changes. Note that this kind of strategy is facilitated by the use of AOP as the instrumentation technology.

- The implementation of the `OclAny::allInstances():Set(T)` functionality in Java is challenging since Java uses automatic garbage collection, i.e., objects do not have to be explicitly destroyed. Thus, the only way to know whether an object is ready to be garbage collected (and therefore not be in the `allInstances` set) is to run the garbage collection operation (costly execution-wise) after every state change in the system involving the destruction of a reference.

6 Conclusions

We have presented a methodology, supported by a prototype tool (ocl2j), to automatically transform OCL constraints into Java assertions. The user of ocl2j can then specify whether a runtime exception is thrown or an error message is printed to the standard error output upon the falsification of an assertion during execution. This has shown, in past studies [5], to be extremely valuable during testing to detect failures and help debugging.

Transformation rules to translate OCL constraints into Java assertions have been derived in a systematic manner with the goal that upon instrumentation the generated assertion code will be efficient in terms of execution time and memory overhead. This was largely achieved thanks to the systematic definition of efficient semantic actions on production rules in the OCL grammar, and the minimization of reflection use at runtime. An initial case study has shown that the overhead due to instrumentation compares very well to previous approaches [8] and is likely to be acceptable in most situations, at least as far as testing is concerned. More empirical studies are however required. Furthermore, we have shown how we dealt with aspects of the OCL specification that present serious instrumentation challenges (e.g. providing support for @pre and `oclIsNew()`) and reported on issues that we feel require future work (e.g. refinement of the OCL syntax and advanced optimization techniques).

References

1. Szyperski, C., *Component Software*. 2nd ed. 2002: ACM Press.
2. Briand, L.C., et al. *A Controlled Experiment on the Impact of the Object Constraint Language in UML-Based Development*. In *IEEE ICSM* 2004. p. 380-389.
3. Emmerich, W., *Engineering Distributed Objects*. 2000: Wiley.
4. Kleppe, A., J. Warmer, and W. Bast, *MDA Explained - The Model Driven Architecture: Practice and Promise*. 2003: Addison-Wesley.
5. Briand, L.C., Y. Labiche, and H. Sun, *Investigating the Use of Analysis Contracts to Improve the Testability of Object-Oriented Code*. Software - Practice and Experience, 2003. **33**(7): p. 637-672.
6. Briand, L.C., W. Dzidek, and Y. Labiche, *Using Aspect-Oriented Programming to Instrument OCL Contracts in Java*. 2004. SCE-04-03. http://www.sce.carleton.ca/squall.
7. Finger, F., *Design and Implementation of a Modular OCL Compiler*. 2000, Dresden University of Technology.
8. Wiebicke, R., *Utility Support for Checking OCL Business Rules in Java Programs*. 2000, Dresden University of Technology.
9. LCI, *Object Constraint Language Environment (OCLE)*. http://lci.cs.ubbcluj.ro/ocle/.
10. Liskov, B., *Data Abstraction and Hierarchy*. SIGPLAN Notices, 1988. **23**(5).
11. Plösch, R., *Evaluation of Assertion Support for the Java Programming Language*. Journal Of Object Technology, 2002. **1**(3).
12. Lackner, M., A. Krall, and F. Puntigam, *Supporting Design by Contract in Java*. Journal Of Object Technology, 2002. **1**(3).
13. Appel, A.W., *Modern Compiler Implementation in Java*. 2nd ed. 2002: Cambridge University Press.
14. Elrad, T., R.E. Filman, and A. Bader, *Aspect-oriented programming: Introduction*. Communications of the ACM, 2001. **44**(10): p. 29-32.
15. Briand, L.C., W.J. Dzidek, and Y. Labiche. *Instrumenting Contracts with Aspect-Oriented Programming to Increase Observability and Support Debugging*. In *IEEE International Conference on Software Maintenance*. 2005.
16. Warmer, J. and A. Kleppe, *The Object Constraint Language*. 1999: Addison-Wesley.
17. Bloch, J., *Effective Java: Programming Language Guide*. 2001: Addison Wesley.
18. Hussmann, H., F. Finger, and R. Wiebicke. *Using Previous Property Values in OCL Postconditions - An Implementation Perspective*. in *<<UML>>2000 Workshop - "UML 2.0 - The Future of the UML Constraint Language OCL"*. 2000.

OCL and Graph-Transformations – A Symbiotic Alliance to Alleviate the Frame Problem*

Thomas Baar

École Polytechnique Fédérale de Lausanne (EPFL),
School of Computer and Communication Sciences,
CH-1015 Lausanne, Switzerland
`thomas.baar@epfl.ch`

Abstract. Many popular methodologies are influenced by Design by Contract. They recommend to specify the intended behavior of operations in an early phase of the software development life cycle. Formal contract specification languages, however, are still rarely used because their semantics often mismatch the needs of software developers. Restrictive specification languages usually suffer from the "frame problem": It is hard to express which parts of the system state should remain unaffected when the specified operation is executed. Constructive specification languages, instead, suffer from the tendency to make specifications deterministic. This paper investigates how a combination of OCL and graph transformations can overcome the frame problem and can make constructive specifications less deterministic. Our new contract specification language is considerably more expressive than both pure OCL and pure graph transformations.

Keywords: Design by Contract, Behavior Specification, Graph Grammars, OCL, QVT.

1 Motivation

Design by Contract (DbC) [1, 2] encourages software developers to specify the behavior of class operations in an early phase of the software development life cycle. Precise descriptions of the intended behavior of operations can be of great help to grasp design decisions and to understand the responsibilities of classes identified in the design. The specification of behavior is given in form of a *contract* consisting of a pre- and a postcondition, which clarify two things: The pre-condition explicates all conditions that are expected to hold whenever the operation is invoked. The post-condition describes how the system state looks like upon termination of the operation's execution.

There are many specification languages available to define contracts formally. Despite their differences at the surface level, all languages can be divided into only two classes. The classification is based on the technique to specify the

---

* This work was supported by HASLER-Foundation, project DICS-1850.

J.-M. Bruel (Ed.): MoDELS 2005 Workshops, LNCS 3844, pp. 20–31, 2006.

post-condition of a contract. *Restrictive specification languages* formulate the post-condition in form of a predicate, i.e. a Boolean expression, which restricts the allowed values for properties in the post-state. Well-known examples for restrictive languages are OCL, JML, Z, and Eiffel. *Constructive specification languages* interpret post-conditions not as restrictions on the post-state but – conceptually completely different – as updates, which transform the pre-state into the post-state. In many cases, an update denotes a deterministic contract: for a pre-state that satisfies the pre-condition the post-state can be computed deterministically. Well-known examples for constructive languages are B, ASM, graph transformations, and UML's Action Language.

This paper investigates how the expressive power of constructive languages – as an example we consider one form of graph transformations – can be improved to master non-deterministic contracts. In Sect. 3, the basic elements of graph transformations are extended with restrictive specification elements (OCL clauses). In its extended version, graph transformations are more powerful but still not powerful enough to formalize all contracts that are relevant in practice. Thus, a second extension is discussed in Sect. 4, which allows to simulate the loose semantics of restrictive languages. To summarize, the proposed extensions of graph transformations enable software developers to write formal contracts that (1) do not suffer from the frame problem, (2) are non-deterministic, and (3) allow to change a state freely.

Related Work. The idea to use graph transformations to formalize contracts is not novel. There are even already tools for this purpose available [3, 4]. The examples we found in the literature, however, are always deterministic contracts, which do not require to extend graph transformations with restrictive specification elements.

The idea to extend graph transformations with OCL clauses has been adopted from the Query/Views/Transformations proposal (QVT) [5], which is a response on a corresponding request for proposals by the OMG. In Sect. 3, the QVT approach is put into a broader context by providing the link from model transformation (the original application domain of QVT) to formal contract specification.

Extending graph transformation rules with OCL also means to combine OCL with object diagrams, what has been explored in the literature also for a different target than contract formalization. The language VOCL (Visual OCL) uses collaborations to represent OCL constraints in a visual format for better readability [6]. Similarly, the proposal made by Schürr in [7] is inspired by Spider diagrams and aims at a more readable, graphical depiction of OCL constraints. The approaches described in [6, 7] cannot be compared with the approach presented in this paper because they have a fundamentally different goal. Firstly, [6, 7] do not use OCL in order to improve the expressive power of a graphical formalism. Instead, the graphical formalism is merely used as an alternative to OCL's textual standard syntax. Secondly, our approach targets only operation contracts whereas [6, 7] aim at a visualization of any kind of OCL constraints including invariants.

2   Restrictive Languages and the Frame Problem

2.1   Example: CD Player

The main purpose of CD players is to entertain people and to play the content of compact discs (CDs). The content of a CD is organized by tracks that are burned in a certain order on the CD. We want to assume that a CD can be played in two modes. In the normal mode, all tracks on the CD are played in the same order as they appear on the CD. In addition, the CD player can work in a shuffle mode in which the tracks are played in a randomized order. Finally, we want to assume that a CD player has a display on which, depending on the chosen display mode, the elapsed or remaining time for the current track is shown. This CD player scenario is modeled straightforwardly by the class diagram shown in Fig. 1.

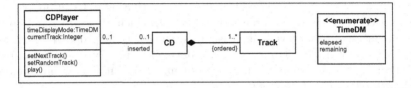

Fig. 1. Static model of CD player scenario

In the next subsection, we will focus on the formal behavior specification for the operations `setNextTrack()` whose intended semantics is to determine the next track to be played if the CD player is working in the normal mode. The operation `setRandomTrack()` will be specified in Sect. 3 and determines the next track if the CD player works in the shuffle mode.

2.2   Complexity of the Frame Problem

The intended semantics of operation `setNextTrack()` is to move one track forward on the CD and to increase the value of attribute `currentTrack` by one. The formalization of this behavior in a restrictive language such as OCL seems to be straightforward but there are some traps one can fall into.

context CDPlayer :: setNextTrack ()
    pre: self . inserted –>notEmpty ()
    post: self . currentTrack = (self . currentTrack@pre mod
    self . inserted . track –>size ()) + 1

This contract has some merits since it resolves ambiguities that were hidden in the informal description of the behavior. The first important information is expressed by the pre-condition saying that the CD player assumes to have a CD inserted whenever the operation `setNextTrack()` is invoked. Note that this assumption is indeed necessary because the post-condition navigates over the currently inserted CD. The second merit of the contract is to make explicit the behavior of `setNextTrack()` when the current track is the last one on the CD. Reasonable variants might be to set `currentTrack` to zero (and thus to stop playing) or to continue with the first track on the CD as it is stipulated by our OCL constraint.

Although the OCL contract clarifies the informally given specification in some respects, it does not capture completely the intended behavior. According to the formal semantics of OCL in [8], an implementation still fulfills the contract even if it would not only change the value of `currentTrack` but also the display mode (attribute `timeDisplayMode`). Or the implementation could create/delete other objects, or could change the state of other objects, or could change the connections (links) between objects.

3   Constructive Languages and Non-deterministic Contracts

Graph transformations are introduced as a constructive specification language. It is discussed, why pure graph transformations are able to specify the operation `setNextTrack()` but fail to specify `setRandomTrack()` correctly. To overcome this problem, we finally discuss a combination of constructive and restrictive specification style.

3.1   Non-deterministic Contracts

Non-deterministic contracts are necessary when not all details of the operation behavior should be fixed in time of writing the contract.

The intended behavior of `setRandomTrack()` is a typical example for a non-deterministic contract. The operation name set*Random*Track might be misleading as it might set up the expectation that our contract will enforce a true randomized behavior of the implementation in the sense that invoking the operation twice in the same state will most likely result in different post-states. Note that this kind of randomness cannot be expressed by a contract (neither in OCL nor in any other contract language) because it would require to describe formally the behavior of multiple invocations whereas a contract can specify only the behavior of a single invocation.

The specification of `setRandomTrack()` in OCL looks as follows:

```
context  CDPlayer :: setRandomTrack ()
    pre:  self . inserted ->notEmpty ()
    post: Set { 1 .. self . inserted . track ->size ()}
            ->includes ( self . currentTrack )
```

This contract suffers again from the frame problem but, if this is ignored for a while, the post-condition keeps intentionally the exact post-state open and thus allows many different implementations. Even, an implementation that constantly sets attribute `currentTrack` to 1 was possible and would conform to this contract.

3.2   Graph Transformations as a Constructive Language

A graph transformation rule consists of two graph patterns called left-hand side (LHS) and right-hand side (RHS). Graph patterns are normal graphs whose elements, i.e. nodes and links connecting some nodes, are identified by labels.

Besides this basic version of graph transformation rules, modern graph transformation systems offer much more sophisticated elements to describe patterns such as typed nodes, multiobjects, negative application conditions (NACs), parameters, etc. (see [9]). In the rest of the paper, we will use the graph transformation system QVT submitted as a proposal to the OMG for the standardization of model transformations. For details on the syntax/semantics of this formalism, the interested reader is referred to [5]. A bigger example on how QVT can be used as a contract specification language is given in [10].

As a simple example for a behavioral specification using graph transformations, Fig. 2 shows a rule specifying the intended behavior of `setNextTrack()`.

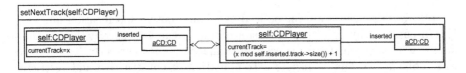

Fig. 2. Specification of `setNextTrack` with QVT

The graph patterns LHS, RHS use typed nodes (e.g. `self:CDPlayer`) that must conform to the system description given in Fig. 1. The LHS of the rule serves two things. First, it imposes restrictions that must hold in order to make the rule applicable for the given state. For `setNextTrack()`, the effective restriction is that the CD player `self` has a CD inserted (expressed by the link between `self` and `aCD`). The second purpose of LHS is to query the pre-state and to extract information that is important for the post-condition encoded by RHS. In our example, the variable `x` extracts the current value of attribute `currentTrack`. Note that the attribute `currentTrack` could have been omitted in LHS and the rule would still be applicable on exactly the same set of graphs as before (but, in this case, RHS had to be reformulated).

The RHS of `setNextTrack()` is almost identical to LHS except for the value of attribute `currentTrack`. Consequently, applying the rule on a state will change only the value of `currentTrack` on the object `self` and nothing else. The new value of this attribute is computed based on the information queried during the first step of the rule application.

3.3   Mixing Constructive and Restrictive Languages

Graph transformation rules, as they were explained so far, can capture deterministic contracts in an elegant way whereas it seems hopeless to use them for non-deterministic contracts.

Fortunately, there is a solution and the same problem has been already tackled by other constructive languages. The language B, for example, offers, besides a pseudo-programming language for computing the post-state, the construct ANY-WHERE. This construct causes a non-deterministic split in the control flow and connects the same pre-state with possibly many post-states. The non-deterministic choices are, however, restricted by a predicate, which has to be evaluated in all control flows to true. In other words, constructive and restrictive specification style is mixed. The formal semantics of ANY-WHERE is defined in [11]. For an example-driven explanation of ANY-WHERE, the reader is referred to [12].

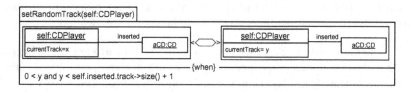

Fig. 3. Specification of `setRandomTrack` with QVT

Basically, for increasing the expressive power of graph transformations the same idea as in B can be applied. In QVT, variables can occur in RHS even if they do not occur in LHS. Consequently, the value of these fresh variables is not fixed anymore by the first step of the rule application and can be chosen non-deterministically. In order to get at least partial control over the values of these variables, QVT has added when-clauses to transformation rules. A when-clause contains constraints written in OCL. The constraint restricts the possible values not only for fresh variables used in RHS but for all elements in LHS and RHS.

The specification of `setRandomTrack()` shown in Fig. 3 takes advantage of the fresh variable y in RHS. The value of y is restricted in the when-clause what exactly captures the intended semantics.

4   Giving Graph Transformations a Loose Semantics

Although the integration of the when-clause is a necessary step to make graph transformations widely applicable and to overcome the determinism problem, this step is not sufficient. Another immanent problem of constructive languages remained unsolved. It is sometimes necessary to express in the contract that the implementations of the operation are allowed to change parts of the system state in an arbitrary way. If one puts this request to its very end, it means that in some cases the loose semantics of restrictive languages is needed.

In this section, we propose an extension of QVT that makes it possible to simulate the loose semantics of purely restrictive contracts written in OCL. These enrichments require a slight extension of QVT's notation to describe LHS and RHS.

4.1   Possible Side Effects of Restrictive Specifications

As argued in Sect. 2, the contract for `setNextTrack()` written in OCL does not exclude unintended side effects. These side effects can be classified as follows:

1. On object `self`, the values of the attributes not mentioned in the post-condition might have been changed.
2. The values of attributes of `CDPlayer`-objects different from `self` might have been changed.
3. The values of attributes of objects of other classes might have been changed.
4. An unrestricted number of objects of some classes might have been newly created.
5. An arbitrary number of existing objects except `self` might have been deleted.
6. An arbitrary number of links might have been created/deleted.

We will demonstrate in Sect. 4.3 how the contract for `setNextTrack()` shown in Fig. 2 had to be changed in order to capture each of these possible side effects. Beforehand, in the next subsection, the new constructs proposed for QVT, which are needed to simulate loose semantics, are summarized.

4.2   A Proposal for Extending QVT

Optional Creation/Deletion of Objects and Links. Graph transformation rules must be able to express that an object is optionally created or deleted. The same holds for links. So far, one can only specify that an object/link must have been created (deleted) by displaying the object/link in RHS but not LHS (in LHS but not in RHS). We propose to adorn an object/link in RHS with a question mark ('?') to mark its optional creation/deletion.

Note that it is a proven technique to adorn elements in LHS and RHS in order to modify the standard semantics of the rule. QVT and other graph transformation formalisms allow already to adorn elements with 'X' in order to express a negative application condition (NAC).

Placeholders to Denote Arbitrary Attributes/Classes. A more significant extension of graph transformations is the introduction of placeholders. Currently, QVT allows to describe the change of an attribute value only if the name of the attribute is known. One can, for example, not specify the reset of all attributes of type Integer to 0 unless all these attributes explicitly occur in the graph transformation rule.

We propose to use placeholders for attributes as a representation of arbitrary attributes. These placeholders appear in the same compartment of the object as normal attributes. In order to distinguish between normal attributes and placeholders, we start the name of the latter always with a backslash (\). This convention relies on the assumption that the name of normal attributes never starts with backslash. For example, if \att appears in the attribute compartment of an object, then it represents all attributes of this object (including attributes inherited from super-classes).

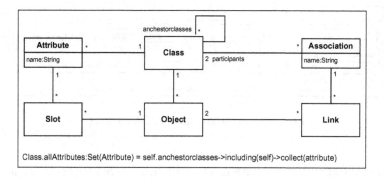

Fig. 4. Simplifed metamodel for states

Sometimes, a placeholder should not represent all possible attributes but only some of them. To achieve this, we propose to use QVT's when-clause to define using OCL constraints which attributes are represented by which placeholders. Such OCL constraints, however, refer to the metamodel of UML object diagrams. To ease the understanding, we rely here on a simplified version of the official metamodel as shown in Fig. 4.

Furthermore, in order to distinguish easily OCL constraints referring to the metamodel from ordinary ones, we decided – slightly abusing OCL's official concrete syntax – to precede within OCL expressions each navigation on the metalevel with a backslash.

Besides placeholders for attributes there are also analogously defined placeholders for classes.

4.3   Realization of Possible Side Effects

We give examples on how the side effects of OCL constraints presented in Sect. 4.1 can be simulated using our extension of QVT. In all cases, we start from the constructive specification of setNextTrack() shown in Fig. 2.

Other Attributes for Self Can Change. A naive solution could be to explicitly list all attributes of object self in both LHS and RHS and to assign in RHS a fresh variable to the attribute.

This solution is first of all tedious to write down and in addition has the limits that were already discussed: In time of writing the contract, not all subclasses of CDPlayer might be known. Be aware that the QVT rule formulated in Fig. 2 is applicable even when self matches with an object whose actual type is not CDPlayer but a subclass of it. The core of the problem is, that, when writing the contract, we cannot predict which attributes the object self actually has.

The rule shown in Fig. 5 overcomes this principal problem. Each attribute of self is represented by placeholder \attDiffCurrentTrack as long as its name is different from 'currentTrack'. This is precisely described in the when-clause by an OCL constraint: For the actual class of self (which might be a subclass

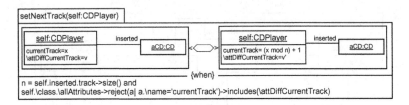

Fig. 5. Different attribute values for `self`

of `CDPlayer`) all valid declarations of attributes (including declarations from super-classes) are collected. The OCL constraint in the when-clause stipulates that the placeholder `\attDiffCurrentTrack` stands for any attribute as long as it is not named 'currentTrack' since attribute `currentTrack` cannot be changed in an arbitrary way. The value of `\attDiffCurrentTrack` in LHS is represented by variable v, which does not occur in the RHS. The new value v' in RHS shows that the value of the attribute matching with `\attDiffCurrentTrack` might have been changed during the execution of the operation.

State of Other CDPlayer-Objects Might Change. This side effect is similar to the effect of changing the state of `self` and can be captured by applying the same technique to enrich the QVT transformation. A new object `other` is added to both LHS and RHS. In RHS, the value of the placeholder `\att` is changed to a possibly new value v'.

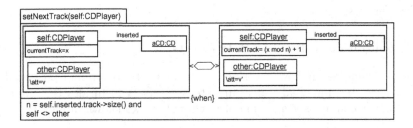

Fig. 6. Different attribute values for other objects of class `CDPlayer`

State of Objects of Other Classes Might Change. In order to simulate state changes on objects of arbitrary classes different from `CDPlayer` (and its subclasses) placeholders for classes are needed. We have introduced the placeholder `\OtherClass` whose value is restricted by an appropriate constraint in the when-clause. The technique to change the state of objects of class `\OtherClass` is the same as the one exploited above to simulate the state change of `CDPlayer`-objects.

Objects Different from Self Might Have Been Deleted. It is not enough to add the question mark to the new object `other` (that represents an arbitrary

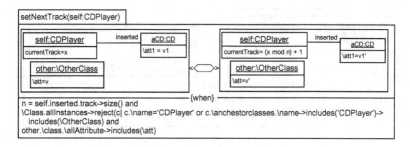

Fig. 7. Different attributes for object of other classes

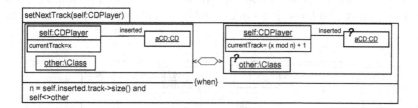

Fig. 8. Deletion of objects

object different from **self**). Unfortunately, the question mark must also be attached on all objects different from **self** that are explicitly mentioned in RHS (without such a question mark, the QVT semantics stipulates that all objects occurring in RHS are not deleted).

Objects Might Have Been Created. Optional creation of arbitrarily many objects is expressed by adding a multiobject **other** to RHS. For each class, **other** represents the set of newly created objects.

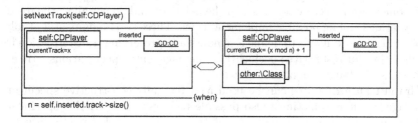

Fig. 9. Creation of objects

Links Might Have Been Created. For the optional creation of links, two arbitrary objects **o1**, **o2** are searched in LHS. The classes of **o1**, **o2** must be connected by an association with name **assoname**. RHS stipulates the optional creation of a corresponding link between both objects.

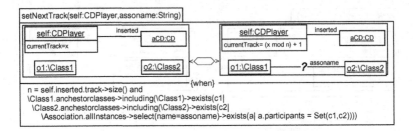

Fig. 10. Creation of links

Links Might Have Been Deleted. Analogously to the optional deletion of objects we mark also links that are deleted optionally with a question mark.

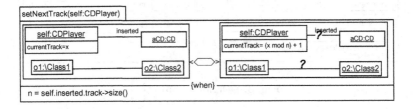

Fig. 11. Deletion of links

5   Conclusion and Future Work

In this paper, pros and cons of the two main behavior specification paradigms – constructive and restrictive style – are discussed. If restrictive languages do not provide provision for tackling the frame problem (such as OCL), then the specified contracts are comparably weak and do most often not capture the behavior intended by the user. Constructive languages suffer from the opposite problem as they sometimes prescribe too detailed the behavior and do not allow the freedom for variations among possible implementations. These two fundamental problems make it also very difficult to define a semantically preserving transformation from specifications of restrictive specification languages into specifications written in a constructive language, or vice versa.

Graph transformations can be used as a basically constructive specification language but it is sometimes also possible to pursue a restrictive specification style. Contracts given in form of a graph transformation rule have the advantage of being easily accessible by humans due to the visual format. In many cases, constructive contracts are intended and constructive contracts work well. For the case that a purely constructive semantics is not appropriate, we have given in Sect. 4 a catalog of proposals to enrich a graph transition rule so that the intended behavior is met. This approach to adapt the semantics of the rule more to the loose semantics of restrictive languages is very flexible since the user has the possibility to traverse the metamodel with OCL constraints.

A lot of work remains to be done. First of all, the proposed formalism of extended graph transformations should be implemented by a tool to resolve all the small problems that can only be recognized if a tool has to be built. In order to become confident in the formal semantics of the formalism, an evaluator needs to be implemented that can decide for any contract and any given state transition whether or not the transition conforms to the contract.

Once such a tool is available, it should be applied on bigger case studies showing or disproving the appropriateness of the proposed formalism for practical software development.

References

1. Bertrand Meyer. Applying "design by contract". *IEEE Computer*, 25(10):40–51, October 1992.
2. Bertrand Meyer. *Object-Oriented Software Construction*. Prentice-Hall, Englewood Cliffs, second edition, 1997.
3. Claudia Ermel and Roswitha Bardohl. Scenario animation for visual behavior models: A generic approach. *Software and Systems Modeling (SoSym)*, 3(2):164–177, 2004.
4. Lars Grunske, Leif Geiger, Albert Zündorf, Niels van Eetvelde, Pieter van Gorp, and Dániel Varró. *Model-driven Software Development - Volume II of Research and Practice in Software Engineering*, chapter Using Graph Transformation for Practical Model Driven Software Engineering. Springer, 2005.
5. OMG. Revised submission for MOF 2.0, Query/Views/Transformations, version 1.8. OMG Document ad/04-10-11, Dec 2004.
6. Paolo Bottoni, Manuel Koch, Francesco Parisi-Presicce, and Gabriele Taentzer. Consistency checking and visualization of OCL constraints. In *UML 2000 - The Unified Modeling Language*, volume 1939 of *LNCS*, pages 294–308. Springer, 2000.
7. Andy Schürr. Adding graph transformation concepts to UML's constraint language OCL. *Electronic Notes in Theoretical Computer Science, Proc. of UNIGRA 2001: Uniform Approaches to Graphical Process Specification Techniques*, 44(4), 2001.
8. OMG. UML 2.0 OCL Specification – OMG Final Adopted Specification. OMG Document ptc/03-10-14, Oct 2003.
9. Grzegorz Rozenberg, editor. *Handbook of Graph Grammars and Computing by Graph Transformations, Volume 1: Foundations*. World Scientific, 1997.
10. Slaviša Marković and Thomas Baar. Refactoring OCL annotated UML class diagrams. In *Proc. International Conference on Model Driven Engineering Languages and Systems (MoDELS)*, volume 3713 of *LNCS*, pages 280–294. Springer, 2005.
11. Jean-Raymond Abrial. *The B Book: Assigning Programs to Meanings*. Cambridge University Press, August 1996.
12. Thomas Baar. Non-deterministic constructs in OCL – what does any() mean. In *Proc. 12th SDL Forum*, volume 3530 of *LNCS*, pages 32–46. Springer, 2005.

Report on the 2nd Workshop on Model Development and Validation – MoDeVa

Benoit Baudry[1], Christophe Gaston[2], and Sudipto Ghosh[3]

[1] INRIA, France
benoit.baudry@irisa.fr
[2] CEA/LIST, France
christophe.gaston@cea.fr
[3] Colorado State University, USA
ghosh@cs.colostate.edu

1 Introduction

Rigorous design and validation methods appear to be more and more necessary in an industrial context. Software systems are becoming increasingly large and complex, and run the risk of serious failures from unpredictable behaviors resulting from interactions between sub-systems. Without proper standardization of modeling notations and approaches, human beings find it difficult to understand the systems.

Object-oriented and component-oriented design approaches in general, and the Model Driven Architecture (MDA) approach in particular attempt to overcome this problem. Formal methods have been intensively applied to evaluate the reliability of systems. These methods generally require adequate specification and structuring languages to describe the parts of the system under validation.

A major problem encountered when trying to combine design and validation features is that structuring languages suitable for one feature are generally not suitable for the other. For example, the object-oriented paradigm is suitable for large scale system design, since it allows anthropomorphic design based on service exchanges of basic entities. However, this paradigm is not suitable (without restriction) for validation activities, since any enrichment of a system is likely to cause loss of global properties. In the opposite way, the modular paradigm ensures properties preservation but the price to pay is a higher level of design difficulty.

The Model Design and Validation (MoDeVa) workshop aimed at being a forum for researchers and practitioners with varying backgrounds to discuss new ideas concerning links between model-based design and model-based validation. Topics of interest included design processes that support complex system modeling and formal or semi-formal refinement mechanisms. Model-based testing, languages to describe models (e.g., UML), approaches such as model-driven engineering, model driven architecture, algebraic languages, automata-based language, first order language, and propositional languages were considered. The first edition of MoDeVa took place in Rennes in France in 2004. MoDeVa was a satellite workshop of the ISSRE conference. This year MoDeVa was a satellite workshop of MoDELS. This paper is a report on this second edition.

The workshop had two parts – presentation of position papers followed by focused discussion by two separate groups. Section 2 presents summaries of the 9 papers selected for presentations. Section 3 summarizes the conclusions of the workshop.

J.-M. Bruel (Ed.): MoDELS 2005 Workshops, LNCS 3844, pp. 32–38, 2006.

2 Paper Summaries

The workshop selected 9 papers out of 17 submissions. One of the main selection criteria was that the papers clearly demonstrate a step forwards using formal approaches within a software development methodology. The use of formal approaches may incorporate the use of formal tools (proving tools, model checkers, formal testing tool) and include formal definition of semantics to deal with structuring or refinement mechanisms.

- [1] proposes a formal testing methodology dedicated to the Common Criteria ISO standard.
- [2] describes a taxonomy of faults that occur in UML design.
- [3] proposes a model based testing approach for UML specifications.
- [4] presents a rigorous and automated based approach for the behavioral validation of control software systems.
- [5] describes an approach towards increasing the robustness of the UML refinement machinery.
- [6] suggests a systematic modeling method for embedded systems.
- [7] explores the problem of ensuring correctness of model transformations.
- [8] describes a round trip engineering process that supports the specification of UML models and focuses on the analysis of specified natural language properties.
- [9] proposes an interaction-based approach for use case integration.

[1] Test Generation Methodology Based on Symbolic Execution for the Common Criteria Higher Levels – Alain Faivre, Christophe Gaston
In the field of security software, the Common Criteria (CC) constitutes an ISO standard for the evaluation of products and systems from Information Technologies. The international recognition of the Common Criteria justifies the investment undertaken by the manufacturers to obtain the certification of their products. The evaluation criteria are defined according to the Evaluation Assurance Level (EAL). There are seven EALs: EAL1 to EAL7, in an increasing order of security demand. For the upper levels of evaluation, the use of formal methods is mandatory. In that case, supplies intended to realize evaluation activities must contain components associated to modeling, proof and test. This contribution proposes a methodology and a tool (AGATHA) which allows covering the requirements associated to test generation for the upper levels of the Common Criteria. In that case, the criterion used to stop the test generation activity is defined by the standard for EAL7 as follows: the generated test case set covers all functions of the reference model. Each function must be covered "complete" way (although the term complete remains ambiguous in CC definitions). The strategy presented in the paper provides a formal meaning to this criterion and associated test generation techniques.

[2] A Taxonomy of Faults for UML Designs – Trung Dinh-Trong, Sudipto Ghosh, Robert France, Benoit Baudry, Franck Fleurey
As researchers and practitioners start adopting model-based software development techniques, the need to rigorously evaluate design models is becoming apparent. Evaluation techniques typically use design metrics or verification and validation approaches that target specific types of faults in the models. Fault models and taxonomies may be used to develop design techniques that reduce the occurrence of such faults as well as techniques that can detect these faults. Fault models can also be used to evaluate the effectiveness of verification and validation approaches. A taxonomy of faults that occur in UML designs was presented along with a set of mutation operators for UML class diagrams.

[3] Generating Test Data to test UML Design Models – Trung Dinh-Trong, Sudipto Ghosh, Robert France, Anneliese Andrews
This paper presents an approach to generating inputs that can be used to test UML design models. A symbolic execution based approach is used to derive test input constraints from a Variable Assignment Graph (VAG), which presents an integrated view of UML class and sequence diagrams. The constraints are solved using Alloy, a configuration constraint solver, to obtain the test inputs.

[4] Using Process Algebra to Validate Behavioral Aspects of Object-Oriented Models – Alban Rasse, Jean-Marc Perronne, Pierre-Alain Muller, Bernard Thirion
This paper presents a rigorous and automated based approach for the behavioral validation of control software systems. This approach relies on meta-modeling, model-transformations and process algebra and combines semiformal object-oriented models with formal validation. Validation of behavioral aspects of object-oriented models is performed by using a projection into a well-defined formal technical space (Finite State Process algebra) where model-checkers are available (e.g., LTSA; a model checker for Labeled Transition Systems). The approach also targets an implementation platform which conforms to the semantics of the formal technical space; in turn, this ensures conformance of the final application to the validated specification.

[5] On the Definition of UML Refinement Patterns – Claudia Pons
This paper describes an approach towards increasing the robustness of the UML refinement machinery. The aim of this work is not to formalize the UML notation itself, but to substantiate a number of intuitions about the nature of possible refinement relations in UML, and even to discover particular refinement structures that designers do not perceive as refinements in UML.

[6] A Modeling Method for Embedded Systems – Ed Brinksma, Angelika Mader, Jelena Marincic, Roel Wieringa
This paper suggests a systematic modeling method for embedded systems. The goal is to derive models (1) that share the relevant properties with the original system, (2) that are suitable for computer aided analysis, and (3) where the modeling process itself is transparent and efficient, which is necessary to detect modeling errors early and to produce model versions (e.g. for product families). The aim is to find

techniques to enhance the quality of the model and of the informal argument that it accurately represents the system. The approach is to use joint decomposition of the system model and the correctness property, guided by the structure of the physical environment, following, e.g., engineering blueprints. The approach combines Jackson's problem frame approach with a stepwise refinement method to arrive at provably correct designs of embedded systems.

[7] Model Transformations Should Be More Than Just Model Generators – Jon Whittle and Borislav Gajanovic

Model transformations are an increasingly important tool in model-driven development (MDD). However, model transformations are currently only viewed as a technique for generating models (and, in many cases, only code). Little is said about guaranteeing the correctness of the generated models. Transformations are software artifacts and, as such, can contain bugs that testing will not find. This paper proposes that, in fact, model transformations should do more than just generate models. In addition, they should generate evidence that the generated models are actually correct. This evidence can take the form of precise documentation, detailed test cases, invariants that should hold true of the generated models, and, in the extreme case, proofs that those invariants do actually hold. The hypothesis is that there is enough information in the definition of a transformation to provide evidence that certain properties of the generated model are true. Such information is usually left implicit. By making that information explicit and annotating the generated model, a consumer of the model increases his/her confidence that the model does what it is supposed to do.

[8] Automated Analysis of Natural Language Properties for UML Models – Sascha Konrad, Betty H.C. Cheng

It is well known that errors introduced early in the development process are commonly the most expensive to correct. The increasingly popular model-driven architecture (MDA) exacerbates this problem by propagating these errors automatically to design and code. This paper describes a round trip engineering process that supports the specification of a UML model using CASE tools, the analysis of specified natural language properties, and the subsequent model refinement to eliminate errors uncovered during the analysis. This process has been implemented in SPIDER, a tool suite that enables developers to specify and analyze a UML model with respect to behavioral properties specified in terms of natural language.

[9] Interaction-Based Scenario Integration – Rabeb Mizouni, Aziz Salah, Rachida Dssouli

This paper proposes an interaction-based approach for use case integration. It consists of composing use cases automatically with respect to interactions specified among them. A state-based pattern is defined for each of these interactions. A use case interaction graph is synthesized, which serves the detection of not only unspecified, but also implied use case invocations. Additional constraints are added to the system in order to remove such illicit interactions, called interferences.

3   Group Discussions

The audience of the workshop was completely representative of the topics of the workshop. There were people working in the research field of design and people working in the research field of formal methods. The discussion session aimed at helping to bridge the gap between those two communities. Therefore, the attendees formed two groups. One group had to discuss and provide hints to designers about the challenges in the scope of formal treatment for the UML. The second group had to isolate particular aspects of the UML language, for which a formal treatment would useful: this group chose to discuss issues related to the defining, building, using UML profiles and capturing their semantics.

3.1   Formal Treatment of UML Models

The UML is used in various ways by software developers. Some use it informally, mainly for the purpose of sketching and communicating system requirements and design. Their main requirement is flexibility to enable the representation of mental model of the system to be implemented. They generally do not intend to use these models for any form of rigorous analysis and hence, formal treatments do not apply to them.

Formal methods will be useful for development environments that focus on critical systems. Currently a number of companies use existing methodologies, languages, and tools such as B, SCADE, and SDL. They would like to use a uniform notation that would enable them to distribute models to different groups for implementation. They have considered the UML, which gives them a rich syntax for model development. However, the development of critical systems requires formal approaches for analyzing model properties. The lack of completely formal semantics in the UML prevents them from using it as it stands. For this reason, researchers have developed mappings from UML to various formal notations which are input languages for existing analysis tools. This leads to: 1) lack of uniformity in the expression of semantics; 2) use of similar models with different and hidden semantics. We need to define a formal UML semantics independent of any particular tool.

The UML is huge and deals with a lot of industrial aspects. Some of these aspects clearly go beyond software development. If we want to deal with critical system design, we should be able to restrict the UML to views that are relevant to this purpose. This restriction must be as small as possible. Indeed, the more a language introduces keywords and views, the more providing it with a formal semantics may lead to inconsistencies. Once the relevant parts of the UML are identified, an interesting approach would be to develop denotational semantics for them. We propose to follow a denotational approach because the UML is complex. We believe that providing the UML with only an operational semantics would again raise the problem of inconsistency between views. This is due to the fact that the UML allows the management of several views of the same problem. Links between those views need to be clearly stated. Thus, in order to provide a consistent semantics to the UML, we believe that a rigorous framework, such as set theory or category theory, is mandatory. Moreover the use of a denotational semantics limits the risk of interpretation errors when using formal tools to treat UML specifications. Indeed, having a denotational semantics for (a part of) the UML and a denotational semantics for the entry language of a formal tool implies to define the bridge between the two semantics by means of relation and mathematical proofs. Contrarily to such an approach, in an operational semantics approach, the bridge between two semantics is generally made by means of a translation and possibly with no hints about the correctness of the translation. Thus, a denotational approach should provide a good framework to define semantics independently of any tool.

3.2 UML Profiles

Profiles tailor the UML to specific areas - some for business modeling; others for particular technologies. For example, the Object Management Group has standard profiles for CORBA, EDOC, and patterns.

Discussions underlined the importance to have a well defined methodology to build profile in order to better understand its objective, role, use and semantics. Such methodology is already used by some users, namely for defining the OMG standard profiles, but has to be widespread in the whole community. According to the UML2 standard and the current practices, the main points are the following:

a) Profiles are based on the domain meta-model, so first:
   * Build the model of the concepts required by the domain (i.e.: the domain meta-model) with the modeling formalism you want. UML is very often used to create this domain meta-model that could facilitate the next step of mapping the domain model to UML meta-model.
   * Describe the semantics of the meta-model (either with informal text or any formalism that seems useful)
b) Profiles are implemented in UML through two steps:
   * Identify the mapping between the profile domain meta-model and the UML meta-models;. Mappings target to identify already existing concepts in the UML meta-model and the standard UML profiles that fit with the domain concepts or that could be extended, specialized to fit with the domain concepts.
   * Implement the profile by formalizing the mapping through definitions of stereotypes, tagged values, constraints, notations, semantic variation points choices, etc. Provide its UML implementation in XMI (as a UML model of the profile implementation).

A profile may contain new standard elements, such as stereotypes and tagged values, and common model elements from the UML library of predefined elements. OCL constraints define notations and can be used to understand the semantics of the new standard elements.

The semantics of a profile must be compliant with the semantics of the meta-model of UML 2.0. Additional well-form ness rules or constraints can never violate these existing in UML 2.0.

Question of which kind of formal semantics is provided by these profiles definitions has conclude that it is centered on static semantics and not covers the dynamic semantics.

The discussion group agreed that the semantics provided by these profile definitions are not sufficient from a formal point of view to capture all that is needed to allow connection to validation tools and automatic code generation.

Profiles may be combined in different manners depending on the granularity and scope. Approaches need to be developed to check the levels of abstractions of the profiles, automatically perform profile combination, and check the consistency of the combination. We need to define development processes that incorporate the use of profiles. Developers need systematic ways to determine which profile must be used on which parts of the model. Appropriate tool support can then be developed.

In addition to ongoing works on defining a profile for embedded systems (MARTE), two subjects have been identified as not sufficiently covered by the existing standard profiles:

1. Reliability: more particularly concerning dynamic behavior (e.g., transition of scenarios)
2. Traceability: general subject, partially treated by SysML for requirement traceability, but not supported for any elements, model evolutions as required in Model Driven Development.

Finally, the main open issue in the context of defining and using profiles seems to be the definition of their dynamic semantics. Several approaches can be used to define the semantics from totally informal to totally formal. They are the following:

1. Develop the semantics in natural language (this one remains mandatory, even if more formal information is given).
2. Use correspondence style rules with examples.

4 Conclusion

The content of discussions led us to draw the following conclusions. First of all, the usage of formal tools to treat UML specifications is really meaningful when dealing with critical system specifications. This is due to the fact that potential users in the field of critical system design require having a simple, totally formally grounded semantics to a subpart of the UML. Using formal tools in a different context makes less sense. Secondly, in order to be compliant with the norm, defining a subpart of the UML to be mathematically grounded could be done using a profile approach. But profile themselves should be provided with a semantics. In the next edition of MoDeVa we propose to concentrate on these issues: What subpart of the UML should be considered in the field of formal treatment? Are there several subparts (possibly overlapping) of the UML to be considered depending on the system design domains considered? How this subpart(s) should be described? How to provide and describe a formal semantics in a way which would be acceptable for the OMG?

Using Process Algebra to Validate Behavioral Aspects of Object-Oriented Models

Alban Rasse[1], Jean-Marc Perronne[1], Pierre-Alain Muller[2], and Bernard Thirion[1]

[1] MIPS, ESSAIM, Université de Haute Alsace,
12 rue des frères Lumière, 68093 Mulhouse, France
{Alban.Rasse, Jean-Marc.Perronne, Bernard.Thirion}@uha.fr
[2] IRISA / INRIA Rennes, Campus Universitaire de Beaulieu,
Avenue du Général Leclerc, 35042 Rennes, France
pierre-alain.muller@irisa.fr

Abstract. We present in this paper a rigorous and automated based approach for the behavioral validation of control software systems. This approach relies on metamodeling, model-transformations and process algebra and combines semi-formal object-oriented models with formal validation. We perform the validation of behavioral aspects of object-oriented models by using a projection into a well-defined formal technical space (Finite State Process algebra) where model-checkers are available (we use LTSA; a model checker for Labeled Transition Systems). We then target an implementation platform, which conforms to the semantics of the formal technical space; in turn, this ensure conformance of the final application to the validated specification.

1 Introduction

The increasing complexity of control software systems makes their comprehension and their construction more and more difficult [1]. The approach proposed in this paper (Fig. 1) simplifies the reliable design of these software systems through a complete software development cycle (from the specification to the code) in a coherent and automated way. It is based on existing techniques, from different fields of software engineering, and integrates:

- a specification phase based on object-oriented decomposition.
- a validation phase based on formal methods and model-checking tools, so as to provide software designers with checking techniques that improve their design quality.
- an implementation phase to ensure the coherence of the generated code according to both the validation and specification phases.
- a model-based software engineering process in accordance with Model-Driven Engineering (MDE) [2], which allows - through a metamodel architecture - the integration of the specification, the validation and the implementation phases into a coherent software development cycle. Moreover, model transformation – a key concept in MDE – helps to go from one modeling field to another, which, in turn, helps to obtain automatically, from a source model, models that are adapted to a

J.-M. Bruel (Ed.): MoDELS 2005 Workshops, LNCS 3844, pp. 39–47, 2006.

particular technical space. These transformations make the software designer's tasks easier by hiding, as far as possible, the complexity of formal tools which often require an important learning effort.

As the whole approach cannot be described in this paper, only the *specification* and *validation* phases, with the associated transformations, will be considered here (dark gray in Fig. 1).

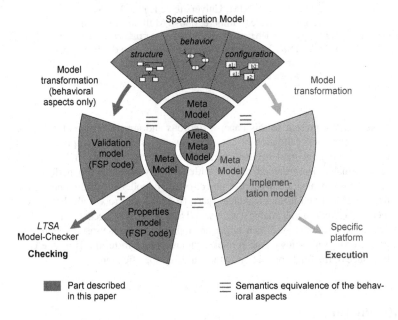

Fig. 1. Projection of the behavioral aspects into a process algebra technical space

The approach is based on a *specification model* which represents an abstraction of the control software. This model is specified using classes, objects and Finite State Machines (FSM) so as to describe the different aspects (structure, behavior, and configuration) of the system under study. FSMs have been chosen as this formalism is based on known semantics [3] which can be interpreted in terms of Labeled Transition System (LTS) [4]. The precisely defined semantics is necessary - on one hand - to allow the easier use of model transformation techniques and - on other hand - to ensure the coherence of the approach, since the behavioral aspects of the proposed models (*specification, validation* and *implementation*) are also based on semantics that can be described in term of LTS. The FSMs are translated into a process algebra [5] called Finite State Processes (FSP) [3]. This leads to a *validation model* which can be analyzed with the *Labeled Transition System Analyzer* (LTSA) model checking tool [3].

This paper is divided into four parts. The first part presents the running example which will be used to illustrate the proposed approach. The second and third sections describe an overview of the *specification model* and the *validation model* respectively. Finally, the fourth section presents the model transformation concepts necessary for the generation of the *validation model*.

2 Running Example

The system used to illustrate the present approach is a control software whose role is to manage the locomotion function of an hexapod robot [6] (Fig. 2.a). A leg moves in a cyclic way between two positions aep (anterior extreme position) and pep (posterior extreme position) (Fig. 2.b). The control architecture is based on decentralized control [7]; the walking cycle of a *leg* (L) is obtained with *local controllers* (LC) and the global behavior is obtained with six *local supervisors* (LS) which coordinate the *local controllers* (Fig. 2.c).

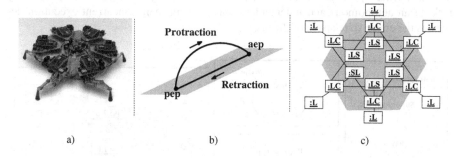

a)   b)   c)

Fig. 2. a) Mobile platform, b) Walking cycle, c) Control architecture

To ensure flexible and robust locomotion, this system must satisfy a set of liveness and safety properties. As an example, one of these liveness properties says that all the legs must always execute their walking cycle, whatever the possible execution trace of the system. And in accordance with the safety properties, one leg can only be raised if its two neighbors remain on the ground (static stability). The control software of this robot is a typical example of the software systems which must be validated to avoid severe dysfunctions at runtime.

3 Specification Model

The *specification model*, based on object-oriented models, represents an abstraction of the control software and includes three complementary aspects which represent, respectively, its structure, its behavior and its configuration.

3.1 Specification of the Structural Aspects

To describe the different types of entities present in control systems, we specify the structural aspects in the form of two conceptual levels [8]. The first level models the *passive* objects which must be controlled, while the second level corresponds to *behavioral* objects (active entities) whose role is to control *passive* objects in their state space (Fig. 3.a). This explicit representation of behaviors allows these to be considered as full objects and so, to be manipulated and organized within an object-oriented architecture. Moreover, the systematic separation of *passive* objects from *behavioral* objects helps to abstract and isolate them and thus to simplify their specification. This organization can also be generalized since a *passive/behavior* association can be considered as a new (passive) object which is, itself, supervised by another *behavior* (Fig. 3.a).

3.2 Specification of the Behavioral Aspects

We model the dynamic aspects of control systems by associating each *behavioral* class with a Finite State Machine (Fig. 3.b). Figure 3.b models the discrete behavior of a leg controlled by its *local controller*, which is itself coordinated by its *local supervisor*. Once specified in this way, the behavioral objects execute an elementary task, in an autonomous and independent manner, and their concurrent execution describes the entire state space of the six legs.

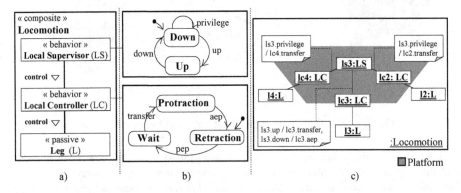

Fig. 3. *Specification model* of the *Locomotion* function: a) structural aspects, b) behavioral aspects, c) configuration aspects

To ensure reliable locomotion, some of these states - for example the state in which all the legs are raised at the same moment - must be prohibited. To restrict the entire state-space to the allowed state-space, we allow (or not) some transitions to be fired by synchronizing the actions of the LC instances with those of the LS instances. These synchronizations (or shared actions) are detailed in the configuration aspects. Moreover, we propose to combine *behavioral* and *passive* objects together in a *composite* object (Fig. 3.a), so as to explicitly represent a modeled software function (here the *Locomotion*). To make design easier and development effort profitable these *composite* can be manipulated and (re)used to model more complex software functions in a hierarchic and modular way.

3.3 Configuration Aspects

The previously described behavioral and structural aspects specify a set of possible configurations of a family of software systems in terms of classes, interactions and behaviors. Consequently, modeling a particular software system of this family requires the description of a particular configuration. This particular configuration, which is represented with an object diagram (Fig. 3.c) helps to better define the structural aspects by specifying the topology and interactions of the instances which make up the software system. Moreover, it also helps to better define the behavioral aspects by specifying - in the form of relabeling annotations [3], (*instance1.actionA /instance2.actionB*) - the actions which are shared between these instances. These shared actions allow to synchronize instances in order to obtain the desired behavior. The object diagram in figure 3.c illustrates part of the configuration of the mobile platform. This diagram shows, in accordance with the previously mentioned safety property, how the *local supervisor* ls3 allows the evolving of *local controller* lc3 according to the position of the two neighboring *legs* l2 and l4. Indeed if legs l2 and l4 are raised (lc2 and lc4 receive the privilege to do their protraction: *ls3.privilege/lc4.transfer* or *ls3.privilege/lc2.transfer*) then *leg* l3 can only be in the *Down* state (Fig. 3.b). Conversely, if the *legs* l2 and l4 remain on the ground, *leg* l3 can be allowed to rise (*ls3.up/lc3.transfer*) which will then preempt the *privilege* of its neighbors.

This last specification phase helps to complete the *specification model* whose global behavior (*Locomotion* function) must be validated so as to make sure that its specification respects the expected properties.

4 Validation Model

Simulation and model-checking techniques aim to make software reliable by ensuring designers that their models meet their requirements [9, 10]. The integration of these complementary methods into object-oriented constructions seems pertinent as they allow the efficient validation of software systems. In the proposed approach, the *validation model* is described in the form of process algebra called *Finite State Process* (FSP) [3] in order to use LTSA [3]. The advantage of LTSA is that it allows both the simulation and the checking of behavioral models.

4.1 Specification of the Validation Model Using FSP

In LTSA, a system is structured using a set of primitive processes, whose behavior is modeled in FSP in the form of expressions combining local processes and actions. The representation of the global behavior of systems is obtained with the composition of instances of these processes (*instance: Process*) and with the representation of their interactions through shared actions within a composite process. So similarly to the *specification model*, modeling a composite process allows the specification of a complex system in a modular, hierarchic way; the instances of composite processes are potentially reused in another composite. To specify the *validation model*, we collect the entities contained in the specification model (states, actions, relabeling annotations, ...) to transform these entities into FSP (i.e. section 5). Thus, as shown in Fig.4.a, for the *local controller* (LC), the behavior of a behavioral class, graphically described by its FSM (Fig. 3.b), is used to obtain the primitive process (LC) in FSP.

LC	= Retraction,		
Retraction	= (pep	-> Wait	),
Wait	= (transfert	-> Protraction	),
Protraction	= (aep	-> Retraction	).

a)

‖ Locomotion   =   (lc1 : LC ‖ lc2 : LC ‖ ...
‖ ls1 : LS ‖ ls2 : LS ‖ ...)
/ {
ls3.privilege / lc2.transfer,
ls3.up / lc3.transfer,

...

}.

b)

Fig. 4. Behavioral description in FSP, a) of the LC primitive process, b) of the *Locomotion* composite process

In a second step, the composite type instances which are presented in the configuration aspects (Fig.3.c) are used to generate the composite processes in FSP (Fig.4.b). As an example, the *Locomotion* behavior is obtained from a set of six instances (lci) of the primitive process *local controller* (LC) and six instances (lsi) of primitive processes *local supervisor* (LS). These instances are composed in a parallel way (‖), then synchronized (/) using their shared actions - thanks to the annotation (*ls3.privilege/lc2.transfer, ls3.up/lc3.transfer*, etc...) - included in the *Locomotion* composite object (Fig. 3.c). This *Locomotion* behavioral model is then checked using LTSA.

4.2 Analysis of the Validation Model

LTSA allows the interactive simulation of the different execution traces of the specified model to ensure that the latter satisfies the expected behavior. Simulation, which is a non-exhaustive validation, can be completed with a search for violation of liveness and safety properties. In the *validation model* proposed here, only the liveness properties will be presented. A liveness property asserts that « something good eventually happens » [9]. In LTSA, liveness properties are expressed with the keyword progress. The liveness property mentioned earlier (at the end of section 2) consists in checking that each *local controller* (lci) can always execute its walking cycle, which results in the recurrent detection of the *transfer* action for each *local controller* (Fig.5).

progress Leg1_Cycle = {lc1.transfer },..., progress Leg6_Cycle = {lc6.transfer }.

Fig. 5. Liveness properties in FSP

If a property is violated by the *validation model*, LTSA produces the sequence of actions leading to this violation. The designer can then modify his/her model according to the obtained results.

5 Model Transformation

Model-Driven Engineering [2] aims to unify software activities from the specification down to the executable code production, through the integration of heterogeneous models into coherent software developments. This coherent integration is only possible - according to MDE - through a formally defined metamodeling architecture which allows - through different levels of abstraction (models, metamodels, metametamodel) - the precise definition of the concepts used to characterize a particular type of (meta)model. In this architecture, metamodels describe all the concepts necessary for the definition of a specific type of models, while the metametamodel specifies the concepts that are common to the metamodels used. So, from these common concepts, a set of relations between the entities of the metamodels can be deduced. Table 1 describes the correspondence of the concepts of the *specification metamodel* and those of the *validation metamodel*.

Table 1. Correspondence between the *specification* and *validation metamodel*

Specification metamodel	Validation metamodel
Behavior classes	Primitive processes (Pp)
Instances	Instance of Pp
FSM states	Local processes
FSM action	Action prefix
Guard	Guard
Composite classes	Composite processes
Shared action	Relabeling
…	…

The transformation rules which can be deduced from these relations are applied to the entities of a source model (here, the *specification model*) in order to obtain the entities of the target model (here, the *validation model*) in a systematic way. Moreover, the explicit representation of the metamodels and transformation rules allows the use of model transformation tools for the automated generation of specific target models (Fig. 6). In accordance with MDE, the present approach is based on the concepts of models, metamodels and model transformations and has been prototyped with a metamodeling environment – MetaEdit [11] - in order to transform the *specification model* into a *validation model* (FSP code). The FSP code obtained in this way can directly be analyzed with the LTSA tool. As the proposed models respect the LTS semantics, the semantic gap between these models is reduced, which makes the transformation between models easier. Moreover, the use of model transformation tools makes the proposed approach even more reliable by avoiding the errors that would be caused by manual transcriptions.

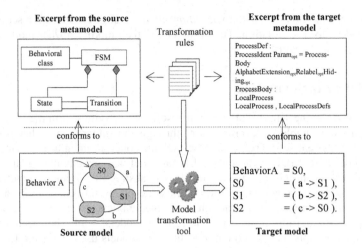

Fig. 6. Conceptual representation of metamodeling

As said in the introduction, the aim of the present approach is to produce an execu-table code for the implementation of validated control software. However, even if the joint use of object-oriented techniques, checking tools and model transformation techniques makes software development easier and more reliable, it does not guaran-tee that the implementation conforms with the validation. That is why, the approach presented in this paper is part of a global software development (Fig. 1) in which the use of a framework and a runtime platform – also in conformity with LTS semantics – helps to reduce the semantic gap between the models and thus allows the easier gen-eration of a code in accordance with the *specification* and *validation models* [12]. So, this approach allows the creation of a coherent software development cycle that inte-grates specification, validation and implementation phases.

6   Conclusion and Perspective

This paper has presented an approach combining object-oriented techniques with formal validation and MDE, to ensure the validated specification of control software. In a first step, it proposes an object-oriented specification completed with FSM for the modeling of software systems. The *specification model* thus obtained is sufficiently precise to be used as a source model for automated software generation. It can be transformed into a process algebra so as to be validated with a model-checking tool. This approach which has been applied on a locomotion software system has the ad-vantage of making the conception of software systems easier while increasing their reliability and also of being integrated in a coherent global development ranging from the specification to the implementation. We will continue this work, in a first step, by the checking of other liveness and safety properties to validate more effectively the *Locomotion* function of the robot. In a second step, we plan to implement the ap-proach on a number of various applications to test its robustness.

References

1. Sanz, R., Pfister, C., Schaufelberger, W. and De Atonio, A., Software for Complex Controllers In: Control Of Complex Systems (Karl Astrom, P. Albertos, M. Blanke, A. Isidori, W. Schaufelberger, R. Sanz, Ed.). Springer-Verlag, London (2001) 143-164.
2. Bézivin. In search of a Basic Principle for Model-Driven Engineering, Novatica Journal, Special Issue (2004).
3. Magee, J. and Kramer, J., Concurrency. State Models & Java Programs. John Wiley & Sons, Chichester, UK (1999).
4. Arnold, A., Finite Transition System, Prentice Hall, Prentice Hall (1994).
5. Bergstra, J.A., Ponse, A. and Smolka, S.A. editors, Handbook of Process Algebra. Elsevier Science, Amsterdam (2001).
6. Thirion, B. and Thiry, L., Concurrent programming for the Control of Hexapode Walking, ACM Ada letters, n°21 (2002) 12-36.
7. Lin, F., and Wonham W.M., Decentralized Control and Coordination of Discrete-Event Systems with Partial Observation. IEEE Transactions on Automatic Control, vol.35, n°12 (1990) 1330-1337.
8. Perronne, J.M., Rasse, A., Thiry, L., Thirion, B., A Modeling Framework for Complex Behavior Modeling and Integration, Proceedings of IADIS'05, Algrave, Portugal (2005).
9. Bérard, B. et al. Systems and Software verification. Model-Checking Techniques and Tools, Springer (2001).
10. Clarke, E.M., Grumberg, O. and Peled, D. Model checking, The MIT Press, Cambridge, Mass. (1999).
11. Domain Specific Modeling with MetaEdit+, January 2005, http://www.metacase.com/
12. Rasse, A., Perronne JM., Thirion, B. Toward a Validated Object-Oriented Design Approach to Control Software. Proceedings of 16th IFAC World Congress, Prague, Czech Republic (2005).

Automated Analysis of Natural Language Properties
for UML Models*

Sascha Konrad and Betty H.C. Cheng**

Software Engineering and Network Systems Laboratory,
Department of Computer Science and Engineering,
Michigan State University, 3115 Engineering Building,
East Lansing, Michigan 48824 USA
{konradsa, chengb}@cse.msu.edu

Abstract. It is well known that errors introduced early in the development process are commonly the most expensive to correct. The increasingly popular model-driven architecture (MDA) exacerbates this problem by propagating these errors automatically to design and code. This paper describes a round trip engineering process that supports the specification of a UML model using CASE tools, the analysis of specified natural language properties, and the subsequent model refinement to eliminate errors uncovered during the analysis. This process has been implemented in SPIDER, a tool suite that enables developers to specify and analyze a UML model with respect to behavioral properties specified in terms of natural language.

1   Introduction

Errors introduced early in the development process are known to have significantly higher correction costs [1]. To worsen this problem, in the increasingly popular model-driven architecture (MDA) [2], platform-independent models are transformed to platform-specific models via transformation techniques. As such, these errors are directly propagated to the platform-specific models and may also be propagated to code, thereby motivating their detection in the platform-independent models. Validating UML models according to metrics and design guidelines can be an effective means to catch structural errors [3, 4], but generally not behavioral modeling errors. Several tools for the behavioral analysis of UML models have been developed, where a user typically specifies properties in terms of formal specification languages. However, these formal specification languages often have a complex syntax and semantics and are, therefore, rarely used in practice. To ease the use of formal specification languages, we have developed a customizable process for specifying properties of formal system models in terms of natural language and formally analyzing these properties using various formal analysis tools [5].

---

* This work has been supported in part by NSF grants EIA-0000433, EIA-0130724, CDA-9700732, CCR-9901017, Department of the Navy, Office of Naval Research under Grant No. N00014-01-1-0744, Eaton Corporation, Siemens Corporate Research, and in cooperation with Siemens Automotive, Detroit Diesel Corporation, and General Dynamics Land Systems.
** Corresponding author.

J.-M. Bruel (Ed.): MoDELS 2005 Workshops, LNCS 3844, pp. 48–57, 2006.

Several other tools exists to support the design and validation of system models. Commercial tools commonly offer validation and/or animation capabilities, such as Rhapsody [6] and Rational XDE [7]. In general, these tools aid in uncovering structural errors, but are not designed for the analysis of behavioral properties of a system model. Other tools have been developed for the formal analysis of system models specified in terms of UML, such as vUML [8], Hugo [9], and Fujaba [10]. However, these tools have still not gained a widespread use in industry. One main reason is the need to use complex specification logics and/or formal analysis tools. Consequently, only users with an advanced knowledge in formal methods are inclined to use these tools for the specification and analysis of their system models.

In this paper, we present three main contributions: First, we developed a process for specifying and analyzing formal properties, where the objective is to make the formal nature of the specification and analysis process transparent to the user. As such, property templates based on specification patterns developed by Dwyer *et al.* [11] can be specified in natural language and used to analyze the system model. We implemented this process in SPIDER (Specification Pattern Instantiation and Derivation EnviRonment), and we show how SPIDER can be used in combination with a previously developed UML formalization framework, termed Hydra [12], for the analysis of UML models. Second, to facilitate the specification process, we provide support for instantiating the natural language property templates with information that is automatically extracted from the formal system model under consideration. Third, the process is customizable for different domain-specific natural language vocabularies and specification styles, specification pattern systems, and analysis tools.

In this work, we show how our process can be used to specify and analyze natural language properties of UML models. More specifically, our round trip engineering process is configured to read UML 1.4 [13] models[1] specified in terms of XMI 1.1 [15] and generate the formal specification language Promela for the model checker Spin [16]. Natural language properties are derived using a grammar [17] that supports the specification patterns by Dwyer *et al.* [11]. Our grammar supports the natural language representation of these specification patterns. In this paper, the grammar is used to specify linear-time temporal logic (LTL) properties [18], the property description language of the Spin model checker. The grammar can be customized according to vocabulary and specification style of a domain. For example, the vocabulary and natural language specification style to capture a cause-effect property for the embedded systems domain may be different from that used for a web service application. As such, the mappings from the structured natural language grammar to the specification patterns should reflect the appropriate intent. In addition, the semantic UML mapping rules of Hydra can be customized and adapted to other domains [12]. In this paper, we use a semantic interpretation considered to be suitable for the embedded systems domain. Our approach does not require the user to know the specific syntax and semantics of the formal specification language used or the details of the analysis procedures of the targeted formal analysis tool. An analysis process can be automatically executed and the analysis results are displayed to the user in a form easy to comprehend.

---

[1] CASE tool support for the recently finalized UML 2.0 [14] is still limited.

Overall, we introduce a customizable process that combines the completeness of a pattern system for specifying properties of UML models with the accessibility of a natural language representation, and present a prototype implementation termed SPIDER. To validate our approach, we have applied the process and tools to several examples from industry, including an electronically controlled steering system and an adaptive light control system. The remainder of the paper is organized as follows. Section 2 describes our process and the main components of SPIDER in more detail. Section 3 examines related work. Finally, Section 4 gives concluding remarks and discusses future work.

2   Specification and Analysis

This section introduces our specification and analysis process and also overviews major SPIDER elements. Figure 1 contains a UML activity diagram overviewing the process, where the first two steps of the process are initialization steps and can be performed in any order. The shaded swimlane indicates this portion of the process performed by an administrator for domain customization purposes. The process is illustrated with a running example, the formal specification of the natural language property:

> Whenever *process()* of the Processor has been called, then eventually the Processor returns to the Idle state.

(1) Configuring the Process and Deriving a Property

In the first initialization step, a specification pattern system has to be created. A specification pattern system is a collection of properties, specified in terms of one or more formal specification languages. Each property is also specified in terms of natural language with an accompanying natural language grammar. In SPIDER, the *Pattern System Manager* (shaded portion of Figure 1) is used to create and associate formal properties to their natural language representations, or a previously created pattern system can be loaded. For this paper, the specification pattern system consists of formal properties from the specification patterns by Dwyer *et al.* [11] and a corresponding natural language grammar [17]. The specification pattern system contains several patterns applicable to software properties specified in different formalisms, such as LTL [18], computational tree logic (CTL) [19], graphical interval logic (GIL) [20], and quantified regular expressions (QRE) [21]. Specification patterns are categorized into two major groups: *occurrence patterns* and *order patterns*. Occurrence patterns are concerned with the occurrence of single states/events during the execution of a program, such as *existence* and *absence* of certain states/events. Order patterns, on the other hand, are concerned with the relative order of multiple occurrences of states/events during the execution of a program, such as *precedence* or *response* relations between states/events. The specification patterns have been found sufficient to specify most commonly occurring properties [11]. However, while the pattern system is largely reusable, the structured natural language grammar may have to be adapted to accommodate the specification style of a specific domain.

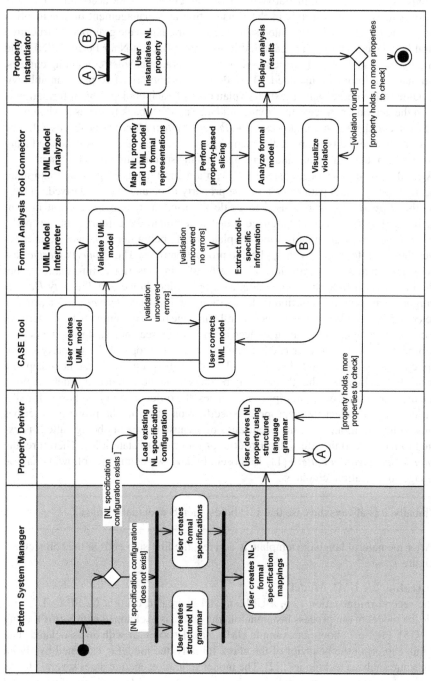

Fig. 1. UML activity diagram overviewing our specification and analysis process

The *Pattern System Manager* is intended to be used by domain experts and formal methods experts as an administrative tool that configures SPIDER according to a specification pattern system. It aids in the construction and management of specification pattern systems with their associated structured natural language grammars. Structured natural language grammars are captured in Extended Backus-Naur Form (EBNF) and internally translated into a BNF representation. For grammar rules containing choices, additional descriptors are included. These descriptors comprise two parts: an abbreviated name of the choice and a textual explanation of each choice. This information is used in the derivation process to provide guidance and feedback to the user when making a choice in the derivation process. The *Pattern System Manager* is also used by the formal methods experts to create the mappings between the sentences generated from the natural language grammar and elements from the specification pattern system.

After the process has been instantiated with a natural language grammar and mappings to a specification pattern system, the property to be analyzed is derived. In SPIDER, the *Property Deriver* is used to guide the user in a stepwise fashion in constructing a structured natural language property template for capturing the property. Non-terminals are highlighted in the template that is being derived, and the user resolves these non-terminals with applicable production rules. The *Property Deriver* assists the user in making specification choices by offering descriptive information about each choice. Each time the user highlights a particular choice, the *Property Deriver* highlights corresponding descriptors. In addition, the *Property Deriver* gives a preview of selecting a particular choice for the natural language property template being derived.

For our running example, the user needs to perform three choices during the derivation process. At first, the user needs to decide what the scope of the property is. For simplicity, we assume a global scope is selected for the property. In the next step, the user needs to choose whether the property belongs to the occurrence or order category. Since the property involves multiple occurrences, the order category is chosen. Finally, the user needs to select the appropriate specification pattern. The property describes a cause-effect relation, since the occurrence of a cause (*process()* being called) is expected to have a certain effect (the Processor returning to state Idle). Therefore, the *Response Specification Pattern* [11] is chosen. Finally, we obtain the following natural language specification template:

> Globally, it is always the case that if P holds, then S eventually holds.

After the natural language template is derived, the first step ends at the connector A in Figure 1.

(2) Creating the UML Model

In the second initialization step, a UML model is created using a CASE tool. To include the model in our process instantiation, the model is exchanged with SPIDER using XMI [15]. Figure 2 shows an example UML class Processor with an associated state diagram capturing the behavior of the class. Initially, the model is validated by Hydra using static analysis techniques [22]. The model validation encompasses several checks for intra- and inter-diagram validity, such as checks for well-formedness of names and expressions, missing initial states, states without incoming or outgoing transitions, and

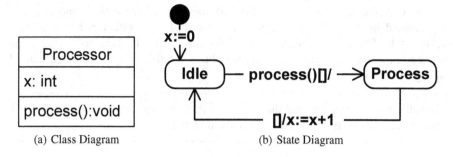

(a) Class Diagram   (b) State Diagram

Fig. 2. Example UML model

undeclared variables, signals, or types. If errors are found during the validation that prevent a formally specified model from being generated from the UML diagrams, then the user is prompted to correct these errors before proceeding. After the model passes the validation checks, the *UML Model Interpreter* automatically extracts information about model elements from the UML model, such as the names of classes, variables, signals, and states. For example, for the UML diagram in Figure 2, the *UML Model Interpreter* extracts the following information for class Processor:

Variable name(s): x
Signal name(s): *process*
State name(s): Idle, Process

The *UML Model Interpreter* is part of the *Formal Analysis Tool Connector* that is used to connect SPIDER with UML tools and the Spin model checker. In general, the tool connector enables SPIDER to extract information from a system model, create formal specifications of properties in a form suitable for a particular formal analysis tool, execute the verification of a property, and analyze the output generated by a verification run of the formal analysis tool. SPIDER allows additional *Formal Analysis Tool Connector* components to be plugged in. Therefore, making it extensible to numerous analysis tools beyond the ones explicitly mentioned in this paper. After the information has been extracted from the UML system model, the second step ends at the connector B in Figure 1.

(3) Instantiating the Property
After the previous two steps have reached connectors A and B, the information extracted by the *UML Model Interpreter* is then used by the *Property Instantiator* to instantiate the structured natural language template with boolean propositions containing model-specific elements. In addition to specifying boolean expressions on variable values of UML classes, two other predicates are supported in the boolean propositions: (1) A call(...) predicate to specify that an signal of a class is called and (2) an enter(...) predicate to specify that a class enters a specific state.

In order to instantiate the property template for our running example, we need to replace P and S with appropriate boolean propositions generated from the information extracted from the system model in the previous step. The cause P

needs to describe that *"process()* of the **Processor** has been called" and is therefore replaced by `call(Processor.process())`. The effect S needs to capture that "the **Processor** returns to the **Idle** state", and is therefore replaced by
`enter(Processor:Idle)`. Finally, we obtain the following instantiated natural
language property:

> Globally, it is always the case that if `call(Processor.process())` holds,
> then `enter(Processor:Idle)` eventually holds.

(4) Analyzing the Property

After the instantiation step is completed, the model can be analyzed for adherence to
the specified property. In SPIDER, the *UML Model Analyzer*, which is also part of the
Formal Analysis Tool Connector, maps the instantiated natural language template to
the corresponding specification pattern instances, namely LTL formulae [18] for the
Spin model checker [16]. In order to enable the analysis of the property in our running
example, the above instantiated natural language property is mapped to the following
LTL formula:

$$\Box(\text{call}(\text{Processor.process}()) \rightarrow \Diamond(\text{enter}(\text{Processor:Idle})))$$

In order to reduce the cost of model checking, we perform an automated abstraction
of the formal model before executing the analysis. The *UML Model Analyzer* performs
a property-based slicing on the formal system model, where it invokes the slicing algorithm provided by Spin[2] and removes constructs identified as redundant. After the
slicing is complete, SPIDER invokes the Spin model checker and performs the analysis.

(5) Displaying Analysis Results

After the model checking has completed, the *UML Model Analyzer* provides analysis
results back to the *Property Instantiator*, which are then visually presented to the user
using a traffic light icon. Red indicates that the property was violated and a counter
example is returned; Green indicates that the property holds for the selected model; and
Yellow indicates that problems occurred during the analysis process that prohibited the
successful verification of the property. Example problems include exceeding the available system memory for storing the states of the model during an exhaustive state space
exploration. If a violation of a property is found, then the user can visualize the execution that lead to the violation, correct the model, and repeat the analysis. Finally, when
the property holds on the selected model, the user can analyze additional properties or
exit from the tool and the analysis process.

3   Related Work

Several tools have been developed for the formal analysis of system models specified
in terms of UML, such as vUML [8], HUGO[/RT] [23], and Fujaba [10]. In addition,

---

[2] The slicing algorithm of Spin is sound and complete with respect to any property specifiable
in terms of LTL [16].

some commercial tools commonly offer validation and/or animation capabilities, such as Rhapsody [6] and Rational XDE [7]. While these tools also have similar purposes when compared to SPIDER configured with Hydra, they do not offer support for the specification of properties in terms of natural language. On the other hand, numerous approaches [5] construct formal specifications in different forms (such as temporal logics, OO-based representations, Prolog specifications), from natural language to support a variety of tasks, ranging from completeness and consistency checking to formal validation and verification. While these approaches allow the use of moderately restricted natural language (a completely unrestricted language is considered undesirable for practical and technical reasons [24]), this type of extraction is a more ambitious goal than our approach using syntax-guided derivation and model-based instantiation, since it requires advanced natural language processing approaches and techniques to deal with imprecision and ambiguities inherent to natural language specifications. In summary, none of these approaches combines the completeness of a pattern system, the support for real-time properties, amenability for formal validation and verification with a wide variety of formal validation and verification tools, and the accessibility of a natural language representation in any natural language subset for which a context-free, non-circular grammar can be constructed.

Several other projects have investigated how to make specification patterns more accessible via more informal representations. Smith *et al.* developed Propel [25], where they extended the specification patterns by Dwyer *et al.* [11] to address important and subtle aspects about a property, such as what happens in a cause-effect relation if the cause recurs before the effect has occurred. These extended specification patterns are specified in terms of finite-state automata instead of temporal logic formulae, and natural language templates help a specifier to precisely capture a property in natural language. In contrast to our approach, they focus on capturing subtle properties of individual specification patterns, rather than applying the specification patterns to the analysis of UML models. Mondragon *et al.* developed a tool called Prospec [26] for the specification of properties based on Dwyer *et al.*'s specification patterns. The tool offers assistance in the specification process and extends the specification pattern system by Dwyer *et al.* with compositional patterns. Differing from our tool suite, they do not include support for natural language representations.

4   Conclusions

We have presented a configurable process for UML model analysis implemented in the SPIDER toolkit. We expect several benefits to be gained from using SPIDER. First, users less experienced in the specification of formal properties are able to create formally-analyzable natural language representations of properties for their UML models. Feedback from industrial collaborators has indicated that this specification style is preferred over formal specification languages. Second, SPIDER is extensible to the use of several formal analysis tools by offering the ability to plug in additional *Formal Analysis Tool Connector* components. Therefore, a wide variety of formal analysis tools can be used to analyze the behavioral properties. Currently, SPIDER supports the Spin model checker [16] for UML models and support for additional formal analysis tools is being developed.

Third, SPIDER provides a single environment for specification construction and analysis. The tool suite enables a user to automatically analyze a system model and visualize the analysis results. Currently, our tool is targeted at the novice specifier, as evidenced by the step-by-step guidance during the derivation process and making the formal specification language transparent to the user. We acknowledge that the stepwise, specification-facilitating features, while helpful for the novice user, might be too constraining for users with advanced knowledge in formal specification and analysis. This problem is commonly encountered in syntax-directed editing approaches [27] and we are investigating techniques to mitigate these problems, such as the use of multiple views and different levels of assistance for the derivation and instantiation tasks.

Future work will investigate how to incorporate previously developed real-time extensions to our formalization framework [28] and specification patterns [17]. This work will also examine how to best visualize the analysis results. Finally, we are continuing to work with industrial collaborators to obtain feedback on the usability of SPIDER.

References

1. Lutz, R.R.: Targeting safety-related errors during software requirements analysis. In: SIGSOFT'93 Symposium on the Foundations of Software Engineering. (1993)
2. Object Management Group: Model driven architecture. http://www.omg.org/mda/ (2005)
3. Berenbach, B.: The evaluation of large, complex UML analysis and design models. In: Proceedings of the 26th International Conference on Software Engineering (ICSE'04), IEEE Computer Society (2004) 232–241
4. Cheng, B.H.C., Stephenson, R., Berenbach, B.: Lessons learned from metrics-based automated analysis of industrial UML models (an experience report). In: Proceedings of the ACM/IEEE 8th International Conference on Model Driven Engineering Languages and Systems, Montego Bay, Jamaica (2005) 324–338
5. Konrad, S., Cheng, B.H.C.: Facilitating the construction of specification pattern-based properties. In: Proceedings of the IEEE International Requirements Engineering Conference (RE05), Paris, France (2005)
6. I-logix: Rhapsody (2005) http://www.ilogix.com/rhapsody/rhapsody.cfm
7. IBM: Rational Rose XDE Developer (2005) http://www-306.ibm.com/software/awdtools/developer/rosexde/.
8. Lilius, J., Paltor, I.P.: vUML: A tool for verifying UML models. In: Proceedings of the 14th IEEE International Conference on Automated Software Engineering (ASE99), Washington, DC, USA, IEEE Computer Society (1999)
9. Schäfer, T., Knapp, A., Merz, S.: Model checking UML state machines and collaborations. Electronic Notes in Theoretical Computer Science 55(3) (2001)
10. Nickel, U., Niere, J., Zündorf, A.: The FUJABA environment. In: Proceedings of the 22nd International Conference on Software Engineering, New York, NY, USA, ACM Press (2000) 742–745
11. Dwyer, M.B., Avrunin, G.S., Corbett, J.C.: Patterns in property specifications for finite-state verification. In: Proceedings of the 21st International Conference on Software Engineering, IEEE Computer Society Press (1999) 411–420
12. McUmber, W.E., Cheng, B.H.C.: A general framework for formalizing UML with formal languages. In: Proceedings of the IEEE International Conference on Software Engineering (ICSE01), Toronto, Canada (2001)

13. Object Management Group: UML Specifications, Version 1.4 (2002) `http://www.omg.org/cgi-bin/doc?formal/04-07-02`.
14. Object Management Group: UML 2.0 Superstructure Specification (2004) `http://www.omg.org/cgi-bin/doc?ptc/2004-10-02`.
15. Object Management Group: OMG-XML metadata interchange (XMI) specification, v1.1 (2000) `http://www.omg.org/cgi-bin/doc?formal/00-11-02`.
16. Holzmann, G.: The Spin Model Checker, Primer and Reference Manual. Addison-Wesley, Reading, Massachusetts (2004)
17. Konrad, S., Cheng, B.H.C.: Real-time specification patterns. In: Proceedings of the International Conference on Software Engineering (ICSE05), St Louis, MO, USA (2005)
18. Manna, Z., Pnueli, A.: The temporal logic of reactive and concurrent systems. Springer-Verlag New York, Inc. (1992)
19. Clarke, E.M., Emerson, E.A., Sistla, A.P.: Automatic verification of finite-state concurrent systems using temporal logic specifications. ACM Transactions on Programming Languages and Systems (2) (1986) 244–263
20. Ramakrishna, Y.S., Melliar-Smith, P.M., Moser, L.E., Dillon, L.K., Kutty, G.: Interval logics and their decision procedures: Part I + II. Theoretical Computer Science **166;170**(1-2) (1996) 1–47;1–46
21. Olender, K.M., Osterweil, L.J.: Cecil: A sequencing constraint language for automatic static analysis generation. IEEE Transactions on Software Engineering **16**(3) (1990) 268–280
22. Campbell, L.A., Cheng, B.H.C., McUmber, W.E., Stirewalt, R.E.K.: Automatically detecting and visualizing errors in UML diagrams. Requirements Engineering Journal **7**(4) (2002) 246–287
23. Knapp, A., Merz, S., Rauh, C.: Model checking timed UML state machines and collaborations. In Damm, W., Olderog, E.R., eds.: 7th International Symposium on Formal Techniques in Real-Time and Fault Tolerant Systems (FTRTFT 2002). Volume 2469 of Lecture Notes in Computer Science., Oldenburg, Germany, Springer-Verlag (2002) 395–414
24. R. Nelken, N. Francez: Automatic translation of natural-language system specifications into temporal logic. In Rajeev Alur, Thomas A. Henzinger, eds.: Proceedings of the Eighth International Conference on Computer Aided Verification CAV. Volume 1102., New Brunswick, NJ, USA, Springer Verlag (1996) 360–371
25. Smith, R.L., Avrunin, G.S., Clarke, L.A., Osterweil, L.J.: Propel: An approach supporting property elucidation. In: Proceedings of the 24th International Conference on Software Engineering, ACM Press (2002) 11–21
26. Mondragon, O., Gates, A.Q.: Supporting elicitation and specification of software properties through patterns and composite propositions. International Journal on Software Engineering and Knowledge Engineering **14**(1) (2004) 21–41
27. Khwaja, A.A., Urban, J.E.: Syntax-directed editing environments: Issues and features. In: SAC '93: Proceedings of the 1993 ACM/SIGAPP Symposium on Applied Computing, ACM Press (1993) 230–237
28. Konrad, S., Campbell, L.A., Cheng, B.H.C.: Automated analysis of timing information in UML diagrams. In: Proceedings of the Nineteenth IEEE International Conference on Automated Software Engineering (ASE04), Linz, Austria (2004) 350–353 (Poster summary).

Modeling and Analysis of Real-Time and Embedded Systems

Susanne Graf[1], Sébastien Gérard[2], Øystein Haugen[3], Iulian Ober[1], and Bran Selic[4]

[1] VERIMAG, Grenoble, France
{Susanne.Graf, Iulian.Ober}@imag.fr
[2] CEA-List, Sacley, France
Sebastien.Gerard@cea.fr
[3] University of Oslo, Norway
Oystein.Haugen@ifi.uio.no
[4] IBM, Canada
bselic@ca.ibm.com

Abstract. This paper presents an overview of the workshop MARTES on Modeling and Analysis of Real-time and Embedded Systems that has taken place for the first time in association with the MODELS/UML 2005 conference. The main themes discussed at this workshop concerned (1) methodologies and tools for quantitative analysis and (2) methodologies and languages for modeling quantitative aspects of real-time and embedded systems in the context of model driven development.

1 Introduction

The idea of model-based development, in which models representing specifications of functional aspects are compiled into code for particular platforms, is a very attractive idea. In particular application domains, tools supporting such an approach have been developed already in the past. A good example is the SCADE tool for the development of real-time controllers with guaranteed properties for very simple non-distributed platforms or for platforms like TTA maintaining for the application the illusion of a non distributed platform [CR01, CM05].

The more recent OMG Model Driven Architecture (MDA) initiative puts forward the similar idea that in general future process development will focus on models, thus keeping application development and underlying platform technology as separate as possible, where the aspects influenced by the underlying platform technology concern mainly non-functional aspects and communication primitives.

A significant consequence of the MDA paradigm is the possibility to build application models that can be conveniently ported to new technologies – like new implementation languages or middleware – with minimal effort and risk, and that can be analyzed – directly or through model transformation – in order to validate or/and verify real-time properties and schedulability.

As already mentioned, in the area of DRES (Distributed, Real-time and Embedded Systems), this model-oriented trend is also extremely promising, and it should be extended to more general frameworks than the before-mentioned ones. DRES however, have particular demands concerning the useful modeling concepts, semantic interoperability of models and tools or the use of verification methods.

J.-M. Bruel (Ed.): MoDELS 2005 Workshops, LNCS 3844, pp. 58–66, 2006.

The Unified Modeling Language UML aims at providing an integrated modeling framework encompassing architecture descriptions and behavior descriptions. Even though UML 2.0 includes a simple time model, real-time aspects are not yet handled in a completely satisfactory fashion and are also not well integrated today in existing tools. A first step to the inclusion of extra-functional characteristics into the modeling framework has been achieved by the "UML profile for Schedulability, Performance and Time" [OMG03]. More recently, several efforts have been and are being undertaken to improve this initial proposal in several aspects, e.g. to integrate the profile with UML 2.0 rather than UML 1.4.

- A "UML Profile for Modeling Quality of Service and Fault Tolerance Characteristics and Mechanisms (QoS)" [OMG04].
- The IST project Omega [Omega] aimed precisely at the definition of a UML profile for real-time and embedded systems with a semantic foundation [GOO05] and with tool support for validation [OGO05]. Notice that this real-time framework defines a set of modeling elements, expressive enough to define a precise semantics for all the time constraints introduced in SPT as tag values or stereotypes by means of constraints between well defined occurrences of *events*. Events represent time points, and we have defined naming conventions for events associated with the execution of any syntactic construct[1].

The objectives of the MARTES workshop were to discuss the possible uses and deficiencies of the existing profiles, as well as the usefulness of new features, in particular in the context of ongoing efforts in model driven development, such as the current call for proposal MARTE "Modeling and Analysis of Real Time and Embedded systems". A motivation for this call was to express modeling paradigms, such as the synchronous approach, that are used in the context of real-time and embedded systems, but have not been addressed so far by UML. Another issue addressed by this call is the expression of real-time properties and requirements and their analysis. Another ongoing development important for real-time and embedded systems which has been discussed already in previous workshops is related to the development of a notation for semantics.

Finally, a goal of this workshop was to bring together researchers from academia and industry to discuss and progress on these issues, as well as other issues in the context of time, scheduling and architecture in UML and UML-related notations, such as notations for expressing time and architecture related requirements, semantic issues, analysis tools and modeling paradigms.

2 The Contributions

Eight quality contributions were presented at the workshop, backed by a full paper or by a shorter position paper. All the papers together are available on the workshop

---

[1] This is a similarity to UML 2.0 where with every behavior execution is associated a start and a finish event, but we have introduced a concrete syntax for these events, and we have defined a set of concrete attributes these events may have.

webpage[2]. Here, we provide a short summary of the individual papers. They looked at the workshop's themes from very different angles. Two of them appear in these proceedings; they have been chosen for their intrinsic quality and particular interest for the subjects of this workshop.

2.1 A Unified Approach for Predictability Analysis of Real-Time Systems Using UML-Based Control Flow Information [GBL05]

The aim of this position paper is an approach to *predictability analysis* for (distributed) Real-Time Systems (RTS) based on UML. The models are mainly standard UML 2.0 Sequence Diagrams (SD), and the analysis is based on a control flow analysis method for SD, augmented with analysis of timing and distribution information.

The approach targets resource usage analysis, load forecasting, and dynamic dependency analysis in time-dependent systems, in particular in early phases of the software lifecycle. Standard UML models and extensions are used as input. The use of the profiles is demonstrated on hand of a case study, in which the resource usage of network traffic is analyzed in a distributed RTS.

There is a common core for the different predictability analyses proposed, namely the control flow analysis of SD. The hope is that this does increase reusability of analysis information and will simplify the implementation of other predictability analysis algorithms.

2.2 Modular Verification of Safe Online-Reconfiguration for Proactive Components in Mechatronic UML [GH05]

While traditionally the environment considered by an autonomous mechatronic system consisted only of the measurable surrounding physical world, today's advanced mechatronic systems are complex distributed systems acquiring sensor values and sending commands through buses or even wireless networks. In this context, mechatronic systems consist of cooperating agents optimizing the system behavior by adjusting their local behavior and cooperation structure to better serve their current goals depending on the experienced mechanical and information environment. The *Mechatronic UML approach* defines a profile and a methodology for the component-wise development of such self-optimizing mechatronic systems by providing a notion for *hybrid components* represented by state machines: states correspond to modes in which particular control laws are used (laws which might be developed using tools like Simulink), and mode changes are used to adapt the control laws due to particular observations in the system.

At last year's workshop, an environment for modular analysis integrated in the Fujaba tool [BGN+04] has been presented for the verification of purely reactive behavior with only restricted time constraints, where modularity is obtained through particular required and provided interfaces represented by state charts. This environment has been adapted for applying model checking to verify safe modular reconfiguration for systems which include components with complex time constraints and proactive behavior. The tool is demonstrated on a case study, an automatic shuttle

---

[2] See http://www.martes.org/

system in which shuttles may build convoys to save energy. The tool also includes automatic code generation for the particular platform used in the case study, which makes it of particular practical interest.

We considered that this approach was a particularly interesting demonstration of the usefulness of UML for model based development in a particular application domain.

2.3   Timing Analysis and Validation of the Embedded MARS Bus Manager [OGY05]

This paper presented the profile for modeling real-time systems and their requirements defined in the Omega project [GOO05] by using it in a case study done by an industrial user with the IF/IFx tool developed for this profile [OGO05].

The aim of the profile is, contrary to the one presented [GH05], not to be bound to a particular methodology for a particular set of application, but to be adaptable to a larger set of applications. The Omega real time profile provides means for specifying the timing of design models – at different levels of abstraction – by using timers and clocks in system objects for handling time-dependent design or in environment objects for describing an environment with particular timing properties. Platform dependent execution times needed for the analysis are annotated back into the models. Requirements are represented by "observers", state machines triggered by semantic level events and representing acceptors of timed languages of such events. Observers can express arbitrary properties and in particular all those "standard property patterns" identified in SPT or in [EDG+05] below. Observers are also related to protocol machines, as they represent externally visible properties of some context; the difference is that they can refer to more semantic level events and have acceptance and ignore states allowing the expression of richer properties.

The aim of the paper was to show the usability of the Omega profile and its tools for designers of real-time systems on hand of a case study in which functional decomposition has been used for modular verification of a small system with complex timing properties.

2.4   Validating Temporal Properties of a Deployed Application with an MDD Approach [HCB+05]

This paper shows another usage of the Omega profile, but in the context of telecommunication systems where the description of the deployment of functional service components on a distributed platform and timing properties are important issues. The paper proposes a particular methodology for representing (static) software and platform architectures by component diagrams annotated with properties expressing the relevant typing information for different kinds of resources. Also some dynamic aspects related to resources, such as processor usage policies, are represented by a small number of keywords. The dynamic aspects of the developed services by composition of service components are described by means of Live Sequence Charts [DH99, HKP04], a non-standard notation, similar to Sequence diagrams but appropriate for the expression of properties of systems rather than of particular runs. Notice that they are of similar expressiveness as the above mentioned observers but propose a different style, well adapted for service level requirement specifications. Using the available LSC tools, requirements are first analyzed as such and then translated into state machine models. These state machine models are then composed with the platform model and analyzed with the IF/IFx tool.

The paper suggests also the use of symmetry reduction techniques as an alternative to the use of modular abstractions proposed in [OGY05] as it is potentially easier to automate, and is useful for analyzing systems with reasonably small multiplicities.

Using another model transformation to appropriate tools, still under development, these specifications will also be used for the validation of QoS properties of statistical nature.

2.5   Modeling and Analysis of Concurrent and Real-Time Object-Oriented Designs [PG05]

This position paper proposes a method for early design analysis, in which hierarchical colored Petri nets (CPN) are used for capturing the dynamic aspects of an object oriented architecture provided by an UML based model. The UML model is transformed in a structural way based on appropriate stereotypes and templates, into a CPN and partially completed at the CPN level. The proposed approach is essentially top-down, making intensive use of hierarchical construction. On the resulting model existing analysis tools can be used. For Petri nets there exist syntax level analysis methods for validating control invariants and deadlock freedom, but here the main interest was the use of the powerful (simulation based) state space and performance analysis provided by the tool DesignCPN [Jen99].

Like in the previous paper, an important aspect is the use of the same model for requirements and performance oriented analysis. Currently, the flow of the method is addressing designers familiar with both notations, UML and Petri nets. A tool-supported method for translating back the resulting CPN models into UML is future work.

2.6   Introducing Control in the Gaspard2 Data-Parallel Metamodel: Synchronous Approach [LDB+05]

This paper is about the introduction of explicit control into the array oriented language Gaspard2, used for programming of computation intensive reactive systems. The aim is to exploit the explicit representation of data parallelism for deriving efficient code or hardware for a given platform. The derivation of code for complex and distributed platforms requires taking into account specific timing information and some kind of architecture exploration. In order to reuse existing code generation algorithms based on the synchrony hypothesis, it is needed to explicitly introduce both timing information and control. At user level, this is done by means of a particular UML profile which introduces explicit control by state machines used as mode automata [MR98]. In order to reuse existing code generation tools, the functional specification and the extensions with explicit control and times are mixed into a unique array specification, in which time and control correspond to particular dimensions. The obtained specification is used for validation and code generation.

This is interesting work, very much related to the approach proposed earlier in [GH05] or to recent proposals for extending SCADE for distributed platforms, or also to the work on compilation for the synchronous language Signal. Presently, the verification is done separately for the functional model and for timing and control. To evaluate to what extent this is realistic and to provide useful results, are the objectives of future work.

2.7 Some Requirements for Quantitative Annotations of Software Designs [PW05]

The main aim of this paper is to provide general mechanisms for the definition of QoS annotations and a comparison of the expressiveness of existing profiles.

This effort is made in the context of work for the MARTE profile. In MARTE, the general mechanisms introduced will be used to indicate timing and memory-usage properties of the software and of its behavior, as well as timing, capacity and utilization properties of resources. Other kinds of non-functional requirement analysis need different types of characteristics; for instance reliability analysis calls for failure rates and probabilities.

The authors define a meta-model of quantitative annotations that identifies which quantities are relevant to the analysis domain; this meta-model will then help to define the issues that need to be resolved for each analysis domain: (1) which is the quantitative domain the analysis is working on, (2) how quantitative characteristics are attached to model elements, (3) how different quantitative characteristics are related to each other and finally (4) the actual expression of constraints on and between quantitative characteristics which may represent hypotheses or requirements on the system. Especially for performance analysis, it is important to distinguish "realizations" that are values for characteristics that actually occur during execution runs and "measures" defining statistical properties over all realizations in any run.

The paper considers how two previous profiles, SPT [OMG03] and QOS [OMG04], address these requirements and raises issues and questions related to defining a UML profile for MARTE.

2.8 A General Structure for the Analysis Framework of the UML MARTE Profile [EDG+05]

This paper focuses like [PW05] on the expression of non functional properties in the context of MARTE, under a slightly different angle. It aims to provide a robust basis to the MARTE profile for Modeling and Analysis of Real-Time and Embedded systems. It analyzes in particular the existing annotating mechanisms of extra-functional properties and some specific requirements of the concerned RFP to consistently derive a preliminary framework for the subprofile concerning analysis and expression of requirements.

It mainly focuses on providing a Quantitative Analysis domain model which gives a good account of the relevant attributes and measures and their relations in the form of catalogs. It includes a flexible mechanism to easily add and suppress QoS attributes without changing the associated Domain Model and Profile, which covers inclusion of modeling capability for new analysis techniques.

The analysis domains covered include both performance and scheduling analysis. Its final aim is indeed to allow the unification of the existing Schedulability and Performance modeling sub-profiles in the pertinent aspects, whereas letting them separated in the specialized ones. For this purpose, it is structured into four modeling views which influence the relevant analysis techniques and which are the workload, behavior, allocation and the platform view.

3 Workshop Discussions and Results

Most presentations directly addressed modeling or validation of systems with real-time properties, and most of them are more or less related to UML. Some approaches proposed the use of UML and provided therefore some extensions, whereas some proposed completion of UML modeling by external formalisms, such as Petri nets [PG05] or array languages [LDB+05]. All validation approaches include naturally mappings into analysis specific formalism. Two papers were directly related to the ongoing effort for the MARTE RFP. Contrary to last year, no paper provided in-depth discussion of semantic issues.

The approaches presented in [GH05, LDB+05] are complete, in the sense that they provide tools for both validation and code generation, the other ones propose rather a high-level design and refinement approach, including platform related characteristics as far as they are needed for validation, but no actual code generation. They are meant for complementing some code generation process which does not exist or at least is not made precise.

The approaches presented in [GBL05, HCB+05, PG05] propose analysis for service oriented requirement specifications; in [HCB+05] it is also proposed to later on check these requirements against the design level specifications of software components defining the actual system, where in the future tools based on synthesis methods may be used for generating such design specifications.

The approaches in [GH05, OGY05, LDB+05] work on design specifications. In [LDB+05], they main accent is on code generation by guaranteeing the specified design. Emerging global properties of runs (temporal properties) are not really addressed. In [GH05] verification of temporal safety properties is done locally on individual components, where a methodology based on refinement is used for addressing global properties. [OGY05] does allow specification of global temporal properties, where the "observers" used for that purpose represent properties of all interactions, rather than under specifications as it is the case for sequence diagrams. Both [GH05] and [OGY05] do verification compositionally, where decomposition of properties and designs is used to make verification tractable. In [GH05] decompositions are always checked for refinement, whereas in [OGY05] abstraction is used to show that a decomposed system still satisfies the same global properties.

We may notice that most approaches go along with some methodology bound to some application domain. In the discussion arose the question which method could also be useful for the problem (often some particular case study) solved by the other approaches. Indeed, the approaches are quite complementary, but not all the approaches match the need of all addressed domains.

In particular, the application domain of real-time controllers, addressed in [GH05, LDB+05] and to some context also in [OGY05] which have to satisfy hard real-time constraints, scenario-based performance analysis seems to play a less important role, whereas in the strongly service oriented systems, as for example those presented in [HCB+05], beyond statistical properties, mainly untimed safety properties are relevant which depend however on a timed model.

4 Conclusions

Compared with last year, where we have noted in the context of real-time analysis a clear trend towards either small profiles, including just what is available for the targeted validation tools or profiles providing rich but rigid catalogs of properties, the situation has slightly evolved.

With respect to the analysis of real-time properties, the MARTE profile includes some catalog representative for the domain of real-time properties, but it aims also at providing means for the expression of general, user defined properties and moreover, it is less biased to annotations of interactions. However, it still provides syntax and means to extend syntax, without providing also appropriate means for defining the semantics of the proposed annotations. An important result of the workshop is the merging of the proposals made in [PW05] and in [EDG+05]; the result is [EGP+05] which has been chosen for inclusion in the conference proceedings.

Concerning validation of real-time constraints, we consider that the most important issue is to provide methodologies making this kind of "intrinsically global properties" compositional. We found that [GH05] represents the most complete approach with this respect, and we have therefore chosen this paper to appear in the proceedings.

References

[BGHS04] S. Burmester, H. Giese, M. Hirsch, and D. Schilling. Incremental Design and Formal Verification with UML/RT in the FUJABA Real-Time Tool Suite, in Wshp on Specification and Verification of Real Time Embedded systems, SVERTS 2004.

[CM05] P. Caspi and O. Maler. From Control loops to real-time programs. In Handbook of Networked and Embedded Control Systems. CRC Press, 2005.

[CR01] P. Caspi and P. Raymond. From Control system design to embedded code: the synchronous data-flow approach. In 40th IEEE Conference on Decision and Control (CDC'01), Florida, December 2001.

[DH99] W. Damm and D. Harel. LSCs: Breathing life into Message Sequence Charts. In FMOODS'99 IFIP Int. Conf. on Formal Methods for Open Object-Based Distributed Systems. Kluwer, 1999. Also to appear in Journal on Formal Methods in System Design.

[EDG+05] Huascar Espinoza, Hubert Dubois, Sébastien Gérard, and Julio Medina. A General Structure for the Analysis Framework of the UML MARTE Profile. In [GGHS05].

[EGP+05] Huáscar Espinoza, Hubert Dubois, Sébastien Gérard, Julio Medina, Dorina C. Petriu, Murray Woodside. Annotating UML Models with Non-Functional Properties for Quantitative Analysis. In these proceedings.

[GBL05]   Vahid Garousi, Lionel Briand and Yvan Labiche. A Unified Approach for Predictability Analysis of Real-Time Systems using UML-based Control Flow Information. In [GGHS05].

[GGHS05]   S. Gérard, S. Graf, O. Haugen, and B. Selic, editors. MARTES 2005, Workshop on Modelling and Analysis of Real Time and Embedded Systems, with MODELS 2005.

[GH05]   Holger Giese and Martin Hirsch. Modular Verification of Safe Online-Reconfiguration for Proactive Components in Mechatronic UML. In [GGHS05] and these proceedings.

[GOO05]   S. Graf, I. Ober, and I. Ober. Timed annotations in UML. STTT, Int. Journal on Software Tools for Technology Transfer, 2005. under press.

[HCB+05]   Jean-Louis Houberdon, Pierre Combes, Jean-Philippe Babau, and Isabelle Auge-Blum. Validating temporal properties of a deployed application with an MDD approach. In [GGHS05].

[HKP04]   D. Harel, H. Kugler, and A. Pnueli. Smart Play-Out Extended: Time and Forbidden Elements . In Int. Conf. on Quality Software (QSIC04). IEEE Press, 2004.

[Jen99]   K. Jensen, "DesignCPN," 4.0 ed. Aarhus, Denmark: University of Aarhus, 1999

[LDB+05]   Ouassila Labbani, Jean-Luc Dekeyser, Pierre Boulet, and Eric Rutten. Introducing Control in the Gaspard2 Data-Parallel Metamodel: Synchronous Approach. [GGHS05].

[MR98]   F. Maraninchi and Y. Rémond, *Mode-automata: About modes and states for reactive systems*, European Symp. On Programming ESOP, LNCS 1381, Lisbon, Portugal, 1998

[OGO05]   I. Ober, S. Graf, and I. Ober. Validating timed UML models by simulation and verification. Int. Journal on Software Tools for Technology Transfer, 2005. Under press.

[OGY05]   Iulian Ober, Susanne Graf, and Yuri Yushtein. Timing analysis and validation of the embedded MARS bus manager. In [GGHS05].

[Omega]   The homepage of the Omega project http://www-omega.imag.fr/

[OMG03]   OMG. UML Profile for Schedulability, Performance, and Time, formal/03-09-01, 09/2003.

[OMG03b]   OMG. Object Constraint Language, version 2.0. Final adopted specification, document ptc/2003-10-14, 10/2003.

[OMG04]   OMG. UML Profile for Modelling Quality of Service and Fault Tolerance Characteristics and Mechanisms. Specification, ptc/2004-06-01, 06/2004.

[PG05]   Robert Pettit and Hassan Gomaa. Modeling and Analysis of Concurrent and Real-Time Object-Oriented Designs. In [GGHS05].

[PW05]   Dorina Petriu and Murray Woodside. Some Requirements for Quantitative Annotations of Software Designs. In [GGHS05].

Modular Verification of Safe Online-Reconfiguration for Proactive Components in Mechatronic UML*

Holger Giese and Martin Hirsch**

Software Engineering Group, University of Paderborn,
Warburger Str. 100, D-33098 Paderborn, Germany
{hg, mahirsch}@uni-paderborn.de

Abstract. While traditionally the environment considered by an autonomous mechatronic systems only consists of the measurable, surrounding physical world, today advanced mechatronic systems also include the context established by the information technology. This trend makes mechatronic systems possible which consist of cooperating agents which optimize and reconfigure the system behavior by adjusting their local behavior and cooperation structure to better serve their current goals depending on the experienced mechanical and information environment. The MECHATRONIC UML approach enables the component-wise development of such self-optimizing mechatronic systems by providing a notion for hybrid components and support for modular verification of the safe online-reconfiguration. In this paper, we present an extension to the formerly presented solution which overcomes the restriction that only purely reactive behavior with restricted time constraints can be verified. We present how model checking can be employed to also verify the safe modular reconfiguration for systems which include components with complex time constraints and proactive behavior.

1 Introduction

To realize advanced mechatronic systems such as intelligent cooperating vehicles, the engineers from the different disciplines mechanical engineering, electrical engineering, and software engineering have to cooperate successfully. The development of such systems becomes even more challenging, if the mechatronic systems should be able to adjust their behavior and structure at run-time (cf. self-adaptation and self-optimization [1]).

The environment of autonomous mechatronic subsystems today no longer consists only of the physical world. In addition, the context built by the interconnection of the system via information technology such as local bus systems or wireless networking technology has to be taken into account. Therefore, today more flexible mechatronic systems are developed which require complex online reconfiguration schemes for the control algorithms which can effect not only a single component but whole hierarchies of connected components.

---

* This work was developed in the course of the Special Research Initiative 614 - Self-optimizing Concepts and Structures in Mechanical Engineering - University of Paderborn, and was published on its behalf and funded by the Deutsche Forschungsgemeinschaft.
** Supported by the University of Paderborn.

J.-M. Bruel (Ed.): MoDELS 2005 Workshops, LNCS 3844, pp. 67–78, 2006.

The MECHATRONIC UML approach provides an approach for the component-wise development of such complex self-optimizing mechatronic systems. It supports a component notion and the specification of required online reconfiguration activities which go across multiple levels of a component hierarchy [2]. Therefore, online-reconfiguration can be employed also on the higher levels of the system control but also across the boundaries traditionally given by the involved disciplines. The MECHATRONIC UML approach also supports model checking techniques for real-time processing at the higher levels. It addresses the scalability problem of these techniques by supporting a compositional proceeding for modeling and compositional verification of the real-time software when using the UML 2.0 component model and the corresponding definition of ports and connectors as well as patterns [3].

In [2], an approach to combine such a compositional approach with techniques to ensure the proper modular reconfiguration has been presented which require a rather restricted purely reactive behavior and rather restricted local timing constraints for the subordinated components. More complex timing constraints including clock invariants which enforce certain reconfiguration sequences or proactive behavior in the sense that the subordinated component autonomously decides that a reconfiguration is required is currently not supported. In this paper, we present how the verification of the safe reconfiguration can be accomplished with model checking to also cover these two cases.

The paper proceeds with an informal introduction on modeling with the MECHATRONIC UML approach by means of an example given in Section 2 and some remarks on the current tool support. To point to the limitations of the existing approach the example is extended with proactive behavior and non complex timing constraints which effect the reconfiguration. The concepts and first evaluation results for verifying the safe reconfiguration follow in Section 4. We close the paper with a discussion of related work (Section 5) and a final conclusion including an outlook on planned future work in Section 6.

2   Modeling and Current Tool Support

In this section, we introduce our MECHATRONIC UML approach focusing on modeling with hybrid components (cf. [2]). Furthermore, we present our current tool support for modeling and verification of hybrid systems.

To outline our approach, we employ an example which stems from the RailCab[1] research project at the University of Paderborn. Autonomous shuttles are developed which operate individually and make independent and decentralized operational decisions.

The shuttle's active suspension system and its optimization is one example for a complex mechatronic system whose control software we design in the following. The schema of the relevant physical model of our example is shown in Figure 1(a).

The suspension module is based on air springs which are damped actively by the displacement of their bases and three vertical hydraulic cylinders which move the bases of the air springs via an intermediate frame – the suspension frame. The vital task of the system is to provide the passengers a high comfort and to guarantee safety when

---

[1] http://www-nbp.upb.de/en/index.html

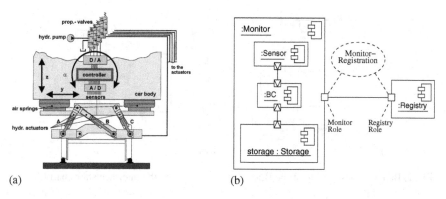

(a)   (b)

Fig. 1. 1(a) Scheme of the suspension module / 1(b) Monitor and its environment

controlling the shuttle's car body. In order to achieve this goal, multiple feedback controllers are used with different capabilities in matters of safety and comfort [4].

We focus on 3 controllers which provide the shuttle different comfort: The Reference controller provides sophisticated comfort by referring to a trajectory describing the required motion of the coach body in order to compensate the current track's unevenness, slopes, etc. To guarantee stability, all sensors have to deliver correct values. In case of e.g. incorrect values the less comfortable Absolute controller has to be applied, which requires only the vertical acceleration as input. If this sensor fails, our Robust controller, which provides the lowest comfort, but requires just standard inputs to guarantee stability, has to be applied. We have to distinguish between two different cases: *atomic switching* and *cross fading*. In the case of atomic switching, the change takes place between two computation steps. If the operating points of the controllers are not identical, it will be necessary to cross-fade between the two controllers.

The architecture of the suspension module is depicted in Figure 1(b). The Monitor component coordinates its embedded components BC, Sensor, and Storage. Further, it communicates via the MonitorRegistration pattern with the Registry. If Registry sends the information about the upcoming track section to Monitor, the Monitor stores it in the Storage component. Sensor provides the signals. To model the hierarchical embedding of the BC component into the Monitor component, aggregation for UML 2.0 components is used. The non-hierarchical link of the Monitor component to the Registry component is described by two ports (as defined in the UML 2.0 as unfilled boxes) and a connector.

To additionally model the quasi-continuous aspects of the model in form of communication via continuous signals, we extend the UML by *continuous ports*, depicted by framed triangles whose orientation indicates the direction of the signal flow. The behavior of the hybrid component is specified by means of an extension of UML State Machines called *hybrid reconfiguration charts*. We employ Real-Time Statecharts [5] to describe required real-time behavior and we describe the continuous behavior by embedding appropriate basic quasi-continuous block configurations (cf. the BC component behavior in Figure 2(a)).

While a common hybrid automaton specification requires always the same input and output signals for every location, the required controller logic with its specific required input and provided output signals is specified within each state of a hybrid reconfig-

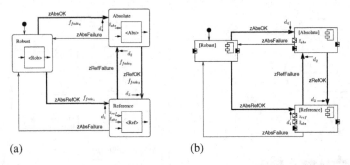

(a)   (b)

Fig. 2. Behavior description of the BodyControl (2(a)) and the interface state chart (2(b))

uration chart (cf. Figure 2(a)). The continuous ports that are required in each of the three interfaces are filled black, the ones that are only used in a subset of the states are filled white. In our notion of hybrid reconfiguration charts, we introduce additional *fading-transitions*, which are visualized by thick arrows, while atomic switches have the shape of regular arrows. Parameters of a transition are: A source- and a target-location, a guard and an event trigger, information on whether or not it is an atomic switch, and, in the latter case, a fading strategy (f_{fade}) and the required fading duration interval $d = [d_{low}, d_{up}]$ specifying the minimum and maximum duration of fading.

For embedding or connecting a hybrid component, we do not need all details of the component realization, but only enough information about its externally observable behavior such that compatibility can be analyzed. In Figure 2(b) the related *interface state chart* of the BC component is displayed. The interface state chart abstracts from the continuous behavior, it still contains the information about the input-output dependencies and permits us to abstract from all internal variables and internal signals.

Therefor, we present in the following a concept for the behavioral embedding of the subcomponents within the hybrid reconfiguration charts of a component, which permits to check consistency w.r.t. reconfiguration at a purely syntactical level.

The behavioral embedding of subcomponents is realized by assigning a configuration of aggregated subcomponents (not only quasi-continuous blocks) to each state of a hybrid reconfiguration chart by means of UML instance diagrams (see Figure 3). A switch between the states of the monitor chart then *implies* a switch between states of the interface state charts of the embedded components.

The behavior of the Monitor component is specified by a hybrid reconfiguration chart (cf. Figure 3). We have assigned the BC component in the appropriate state to each state of the upper orthogonal state of the chart. E.g., the BC component instance in state Reference has been (via a visual embedding) assigned to the location AllAvailable of the monitor where sensors z_{ref} as well as $\ddot{z}_{abs}$ are available. The communication with the Registry is described in the lower orthogonal state of Figure 3 (cf. [2]). The upper orthogonal state consists of the states RefAvailable and AllAvailable which represents whether the required reference curve is available for the *current* track. The upper state is synchronized by the lower one.

For the outlined MECHATRONIC UML approach there exists tool support. Especially two specific verification tasks for the resulting systems are supported. At first the real-time coordination of the distributed software, which is modeled with UML 2.0

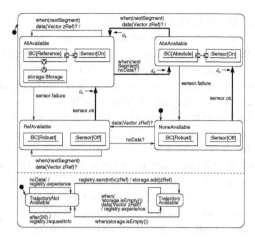

Fig. 3. Behavioral embedding in the Monitor realization

components and connectors is verified using a compositional model checking approach based on verified coordination patterns [3]. Secondly, a restricted subset of the outlined hierarchical component structures for modeling of discrete and continuous control behavior is checked for the consistent reconfiguration and proper real-time synchronization w.r.t reconfiguration [2]. In addition, the second approach can be embedded into the first one.

The current results enable the systematic development of complex mechatronic systems with safe online-reconfiguration, as in the current practice of mechatronic systems the strict hierarchical approach with strict top-down command order is standard. However, a number of limitations result which seem to unduly restrict the design space for more advanced modular designs of mechatronic systems in the future.

3   Complex and Proactive Behavior

One severe restriction is that in interface state charts only the duration of transitions can be specified but not their time-triggered execution. Examples where an extension to more general time constraints in the interface state chart seem beneficial are, for example, restrictions on the frequency of mode switches. In our example, the engineer could more easily ensure the stability of the underlying system if the interface state chart restricted that after a switch from state Reference to state Absolute a certain time threshold should elapse before the BC component permits to switch back to the more comfortable Reference state.

Another limitation is the strict top-down command order. While the processing of the sensor error already indicates that we have to consider errors of the subcomponents, the current form of interface state charts does not permit to encode a required reaction time or switching of the mode within the interface. Thus, whether a required reaction of the embedding component results or not is currently not included in the interface. Therefore, besides only emitting warnings, error reports, or wishes to the embedding component, true *proactive* behavior in the interface state charts seems favorable such that when sending an error report the interface state chart can also initiate that within a given time frame the current state has to be left. As example for proactive behavior, consider the case that BC component detects that the operation with the reference data results in unexpected problems and wants to report this to the embedding Monitor component, the BC component may in addition specify in the interface state chart that therefore the reference mode has to be left within a given deadline to ensure that the observed behavior is not critical.

We can characterize these cases where more expressive notion of interface automaton are required as follows: An interface automaton M is *complex* if it is not simple but still deterministic. An interface automaton M is *proactive* if it autonomously decides that a reconfiguration is required which results in a non-deterministic behavior.

In Section 2, the suspension module was introduced and thereon the control software was modeled. One characteristic of the control software was the top-down command order. It was not possible for the BC component to influence the Monitor component via direct events. E.g. if any error occurs when the BC component is in the Reference state, the BC component has to switch to the Robust state and has to inform the superordinate Monitor component to react in an adequate way. Furthermore, we want to avoid perpetual uncontrolled switching between Absolute and Reference.

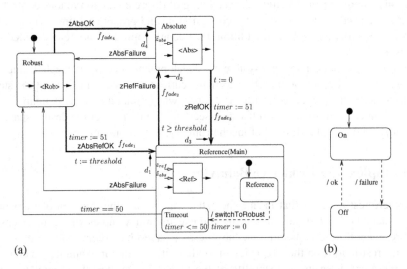

(a)   (b)

Fig. 4. Behavior description of the BC component (4(a)) and Sensor component (4(b))

In Figure 4(a), the redesigned BC component is depicted. The behavior of the former BC component is extended by proactive behavior. When the BC component is in the Reference state, the component is now able to decide autonomously to switch to the Robust state. Due to non-urgent transitions (dashed line), non-determinism is introduced. This is modeled as follows: While staying in the Reference state, the body control sends a message switchToRobust to the superordinate Monitor component. This done, the BC component pauses in a Timeout state. If the timeout is reached, the BC component switches to Robust. To control the switching between Absolute and Reference, a timer t is introduced. Everytime the Reference state is entered from the Absolute state, a clock t is set to zero. To avoid an immediate return back to Absolute, a guard, representing a threshold, t>=threshold, is added to the transition. All other incoming transitions to the Reference state get an additional assignment t:=threshold, thus the threshold is "omitted". In Figure 4(b) the interface state chart of the sensor component, consisting of two states, on and off, is depicted.

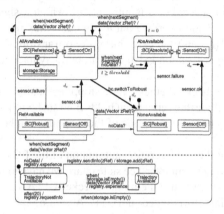

Fig. 5. Behavioral embedding in the Monitor realization

Similar to Figure 3, the behavior of the Monitor component is depicted in Figure 5. In addition to the old Monitor component, we have to take into account the proactive and timing behavior of the subordinated components. Since the body control now sends the switchToRobust message, the monitor component has to consume this message.

4   Checking Complex and Proactive Subcomponents

To adjust our modular reasoning approach to the extensions outlined in the last section, we have to provide checks for refinement and correct embedding which support the introduced more expressive interface automata.

4.1   Checking Refinement

Complex and proactive components do not result in a *simple* interface state chart and thus the checking procedure for ensuring that the interface state chart corresponds to the component behavior is not applicable.

In [6], an approach for checking the employed notion of refinement ($M \sqsubseteq_{RT} M^I$) has been presented which requires that M^I is deterministic. If the interface state chart M^I is complex but not proactive, we can thus employ this approach. For a deterministic M^I we have to derive a corresponding test automaton M_t^I as described in [6] and then check $M \| M_t^I$ for time stopping deadlocks.

If, however, the interface state chart M^I is proactive and thus not deterministic, we have to look for alternatives, as we cannot derive a deterministic timed automaton for each non-deterministic one (cf. [7]). Analyzing the limitation of the approach outlined in [6], we can conclude that the branching within the on-the-fly traversed cross-product simply requires that a unique mapping to a state in the refined model exists which is guaranteed in [6] by the deterministic character of M^I.

We propose to exploit the mapping $map : L_p^I \rightarrow L$ between the passive states of the interface automaton and related states in the underlying realization to achieve a feasible solution for this case. For a mapping map which assigns to each realization state exactly one state of the interface automaton and thus map^{-1} is a function and we write $l' = map^{-1}(l)$) and the case that no two transitions with the same source location, label, and target location exist, we can build syntactically the cross-product $M' = M^I \times_{map} M$.

We can then simply check whether a time stopping deadlock or a *bad state* can be reached in M' and conclude that refinement holds if no such violation has been detected. A more detailed and technical description of the mapping can be found in [8] and will be omitted here.

To verify if the hybrid reconfiguration automaton of the BC component is a correct refinement of the BC component interface state chart, we have to built a timed automata model as explained above. We use the model checker UPPAAL [9] for the verification and check the constraints, formulated in TCTL, A[] not deadlock and E<> BodyControl.Error ensuring the correct refinement. The verification took about 1.21 seconds and at maximum about 8032 KB were allocated by the verifier[2].

4.2   Checking the Embedding

To realize the dynamic checking for the prove of correct reconfiguration behavior, the hybrid reconfiguration chart and the interface state chart have to be transformed to an appropriate model which can be handled by a model checker. In [10], transformation rules from Real-Time Statecharts to timed automata were introduced. In the following, we reuse and extend theses transformation rules.

In hybrid reconfiguration charts, component instances are embedded in locations. During the transformation, the instances are omitted because the associated interface state charts are also transformed. Due to this fact, for the transformation of locations, we can apply the same ones as for Real-Time Statecharts.

In addition to the locations, the transitions have to be transformed. In contrast to Real-Time Statecharts, a transition is associated with a fading function. Since the fading function does not affect the real-time behavior, it is omitted, too. Hence the same transformation as for Real-Time Statecharts is used. As mentioned before, the interface state charts of the embedded component instances have to be transformed. It has to be guaranteed that the embedded component instance leaves an internal location iff the superordinate component leaves a location. For example, when the monitor component leaves the location NoneAvailable, the embedded component instance BC has to leave the internal location Robust. To achieve this behavior, we use the synchronization semantics from the timed automata model. The superordinate component has the

---

[2] The verification was done on a Pentium 4, 2.4 GHz, 1 GB memory, OS Linux Redhat.

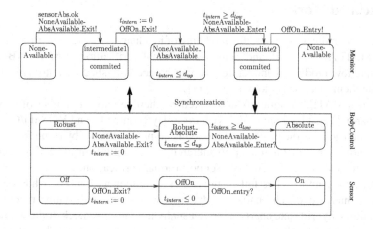

Fig. 6. Synchronization between **Monitor**, **Sensor**, and **BodyControl**

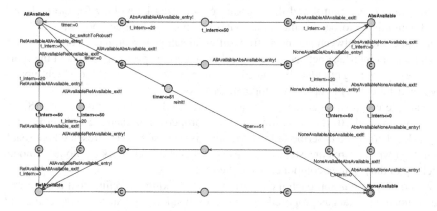

Fig. 7. Timed Automaton of the Monitor state chart

meaning of a sender (!), whereas the embedded component instances have the meaning of a receiver (?). In the case of more than one embedded component instance, we use a chain of committed locations (cf. [9]) for synchronization. In Figure 6, an example is depicted.

For the evaluation, we use the real-time model checker UPPAAL [9]. As an example the transformed timed automata of the interface state chart of the of the Monitor component is depicted in Figure 7. For clarity, we do not depict the timed automaton of the Sensor (the transformation is rather trivial). For the verification the automata are executed in parallel. We check the property A[] not deadlock. As result of the verification, we get that the system is deadlock free. In particular, this means we have a correct embedding of all components. The verification took about 0.31 seconds and at maximum about 2092 KB were allocated by the verifier.

5   Related Work

The *de facto* industry standard for modeling of mechatronic systems with hybrid behavior is MATLAB/Simulink and Stateflow[3]. Formal verification of MATLAB/Simulink and Stateflow models of moderate size can be accomplished by automatically transforming them to hybrid automata (cf. [11]).

Besides MATLAB/Simulink and Stateflow, there are also a number of approaches, like Charon [12], Masaccio [13], HyCharts & HyRoom [14], and Hybrid I/O Automata [15], which address the problem of modeling complex systems by some form of hybrid state charts. Some of them support hierarchy and parallelism as well as a notion of component and some of them even support formal verification.

All existing approaches fail in providing a component concept which supports a dynamic interface which enables to decompose systems with online reconfiguration into multiple hybrid state charts. Thus, a usually not feasible check of the whole system is required to ensure that a system with complex reconfiguration such as the presented example is correct w.r.t. the reconfiguration and real-time behavior.

Another consequence is that in these approaches the control engineering know-how for the continuous control and the software engineering know-how for the real-time coordination have to be specified both within a single hybrid component and thus a tight cooperation between engineers from different camps is required. In our approach, in contrast, an interface between the control engineering specific details and the more software engineering oriented distributed real-time processing is possible which support more realistic loosely coupled development processes.

Available compositional reasoning approaches for hybrid systems [16, 17, 18] require high manual effort of inventing auxiliary properties to enable a full verification to decide whether the described reconfiguration is consistent. The presented approach in contrast will ensure consistency by means of a syntactical check or modular model checking of the separate components and their interfaces.

We employ in our approach the algorithm for checking the refinement relation between timed automata as proposed in [6]. As outlined in the paper, for proactive and thus non-deterministic interface automata this approach is not applicable.

In [19], an algorithm for checking the existence of a simulation relation to investigate the opportunities of refinement checking for Cottbus Timed Automata is developed. The approach is restricted to simulation and closed timed automata with integer semantics, while we require a stronger form of refinement (ready simulation).

6   Conclusion and Future Work

Within this paper, we presented an incremental improvement of our modular verification approach for checking that the online-reconfiguration of MECHATRONIC UML models is safe. In our earlier proposal [2], severe restrictions to the expressiveness of the supported component interface are employed to ensure that efficient checks can be used which do not have to consider the whole state space. In this paper, we present support for more expressive interfaces which include complex timing constraints and

---

[3] http://www.mathworks.com

proactive behavior employing model checking. The underlying concepts are outlined and formally defined. In addition, first experimental results are reported.

While modeling of hybrid systems with the MECHATRONIC UML approach is already supported by the FUJABA Real-Time Tool Suite[4], the described refinement checks and the check for the correct embedding are currently under development.

In future work, we plan to further improve and extend our approach w.r.t. modeling and verification such that the full hybrid behavior of the components is covered. On particular next step is to apply the general checking procedure for simulation as presented in [19] for checking our notion of refinement by generalizing our extension of the automata presented in Section 4.1 (cf. [8]).

References

1. Janos Sztipanovits, Gabor Karsai, and Ted Bapty. Self-adaptive software for signal processing. *Commun. ACM*, 41(5):66–73, 1998.
2. Holger Giese, Sven Burmester, Wilhelm Schäfer, and Oliver Oberschelp. Modular Design and Verification of Component-Based Mechatronic Systems with Online-Reconfiguration. In *Proc. of 12th ACM SIGSOFT Foundations of Software Engineering 2004 (FSE 2004), Newport Beach, USA*, pages 179–188. ACM Press, November 2004.
3. Holger Giese, Matthias Tichy, Sven Burmester, Wilhelm Schäfer, and Stephan Flake. Towards the Compositional Verification of Real-Time UML Designs. In *Proc. of the European Software Engineering Conference (ESEC), Helsinki, Finland*, pages 38–47. ACM Press, September 2003.
4. T. Hestermeyer, P. Schlautmann, and C. Ettingshausen. Active suspension system for railway vehicles-system design and kinematics. In *Proc. of the 2nd IFAC - Confecence on mechatronic systems*, Berkeley, California, USA, 9-11December 2002.
5. Sven Burmester, Holger Giese, and Wilhelm Schäfer. Model-driven architecture for hard real-time systems: From platform independent models to code. In *Proc. of the European Conference on Model Driven Architecture - Foundations and Applications (ECMDA-FA'05), Nürnberg, Germany*, LNCS, pages 1–15. Springer Verlag, November 2005.
6. Henrik Ejersbo Jensen, Kim Guldstr, Kim Guldstr, and Arne Skou. Scaling up Uppaal Automatic Verification of Real-Time Systems using Compositionality and Abstraction. In *Proceedings of the 6th International Symposium on Formal Techniques in Real-Time and Fault-Tolerant Systems (FTRTFT 2000)*, volume 1926 of *LNCS*, Pune, India, September 2000. Springer Verlag.
7. Stavros Tripakis. Folk theorems on the determinization and minimization of timed automata. In *Formal Modeling and Analysis of Timed Systems: First International Workshop, FORMATS 2003, Marseille, France, September 6-7, 2003. Revised Papers*, volume 2791, pages 182 – 188, 2004.
8. Holger Giese and Martin Hirsch. Timed and Hybrid Refinement in Mechtronic UML. Technical Report tr-ri-03-266, University of Paderborn, Paderborn, Germany, December 2005.
9. Gerd Behrmann, Alexandre David, and Kim G. Larsen. A tutorial on UPPAAL. In Marco Bernardo and Flavio Corradini, editors, *Formal Methods for the Design of Real-Time Systems: 4th International School on Formal Methods for the Design of Computer, Communication, and Software Systems, SFM-RT 2004*, volume 3185 of *LNCS*, pages 200–236. Springer Verlag, September 2004.

---

[4] http://www.fujaba.de

10. Sven Burmester, Holger Giese, Martin Hirsch, and Daniela Schilling. Incremental design and formal verification with UML/RT in the FUJABA real-time tool suite. In *Proceedings of the International Workshop on Specification and vaildation of UML models for Real Time and embedded Systems, SVERTS2004, Satellite Event of the 7th International Conference on the Unified Modeling Language, UML2004*, October 2004.

11. Aditya Agrawal, Gyula Simon, and Gabor Karsai. Semantic Translation of Simulink/Stateflow models to Hybrid Automata using Graph Transformations. In *International Workshop on Graph Transformation and Visual Modeling Techniques, Barcelona, Spain*, 2004.

12. R. Alur, T. Dang, J. Esposito, R. Fierro, Y. Hur, F. Ivancic, V. Kumar, I. Lee, P. Mishra, G. Pappas, and O. Sokolsky. Hierarchical Hybrid Modeling of Embedded Systems. In *First Workshop on Embedded Software*, 2001.

13. Thomas A. Henzinger. Masaccio: A Formal Model for Embedded Components. In *Proceedings of the First IFIP International Conference on Theoretical Computer Science (TCS)*, volume 1872 of *LNCS*, pages 549–563, 2000.

14. R. Grosu, T. Stauner, and M. Broy. A modular visual model for hybrid systems. In *Proc. of Formal Techniques in Real-Time and Fault-Tolerant Systems (FTRTFT'98)*, volume 1486 of *LNCS*. Springer Verlag, 1998.

15. Nancy Lynch, Roberto Segala, and Frits Vaandrager. Hybrid I/O Automata Revisited. In *Proceedings of the 4th International Workshop on Hybrid Systems: Computation and Control (HSCC 2001), Rome, Italy, March 28-30, 2001*, volume 2034 of *LNCS*, pages 403–417. Springer Verlag, 2001.

16. Leslie Lamport. Hybrid systems in tla+. In *Hybrid Systems*, pages 77–102, London, UK, 1993. Springer Verlag.

17. Thomas A. Henzinger, Marius Minea, and Vinayak Prabhu. Assume-Guarantee Reasoning for Hierarchical Hybrid Systems. In *Proceedings of the 4th International Workshop on Hybrid Systems: Computation and Control (HSCC 2001), Rome, Italy, March 28-30, 2001*, volume 2034 of *LNCS*, pages 275–290. Springer Verlag, 2001.

18. Thomas A. Henzinger, Christoph M. Kirsch, Marco A.A. Sanvido, and Wolfgang Pree. From Control Models to Real-Time Code Using Giotto. In *IEEE Control Systems Magazine 23(1):50-64, 2003. A preliminary report on this work appeared in C.M. Kirsch, M.A.A. Sanvido, T.A. Henzinger, and W. Pree, A Giotto-based helicopter control system, Proceedings of the Second International Workshop on Embedded Software (EMSOFT)*, volume 2491 of *LNCS*, pages 46–60. Springer Verlag, 2002.

19. Dirk Beyer. Efficient reachability analysis and refinement checking of timed automata using BDDs. In T. Margaria and T. F. Melham, editors, *Proceedings of the 11th IFIP WG 10.5 Advanced Research Working Conference on Correct Hardware Design and Verification Methods (CHARME 2001)*, volume 2144 of *LNCS*, pages 86–91. Springer Verlag, 2001.

Annotating UML Models with Non-functional Properties for Quantitative Analysis

Huáscar Espinoza[1], Hubert Dubois[1], Sébastien Gérard[1], Julio Medina[2],
Dorina C. Petriu[3], and Murray Woodside[3]

[1] CEA Saclay, DRT/LIST/DTSI/SOL/L-LSP,
F-91191, Gif sur Yvette Cedex, France
{huascar.espinoza, hubert.dubois, sebastien.gerard}@cea.fr
[2] Universidad de Cantabria, Departamento de Electrónica y Computadores,
Av. Los Castros s/n, 39005 Santander, Spain
medinajl@unican.es
[3] Carleton University, Department of Systems and Computer Engineering,
1125 Colonel By Drive, Ottawa, ON, Canada, K1S 5B6
{petriu, cmw}@sce.carleton.ca

Abstract. This work is motivated by the recent Request For Proposals issued by OMG for a new UML Profile named "Modeling and Analysis of Real-Time and Embedded systems". The paper describes first some domain concepts for annotating Non-Functional Properties (NFPs), whose focus is on supporting temporal verification of UML-based models. Particular emphasis is given to schedulability and performance analysis for real-time systems. We discuss next some general requirements for NFP annotations and evaluate how the UML profiles for "Schedulability, Performance, and Time Specification" and for "Modeling Quality of Service and Fault Tolerance Characteristics and Mechanisms", address these requirements. Last but not least, the paper proposes a preliminary framework for describing NFPs by considering the major requirements previously stated and by analyzing some UML mechanisms to attach NFPs to model elements.

1 Introduction

The change of focus from code to models promoted by OMG's Model Driven Architecture (MDA) raises the need to integrate the analysis of non-functional requirements of UML models (such as performance, schedulability, reliability, scalability, etc.) in the development process of Real-Time and Embedded Systems (RTES). Different kinds of analysis techniques require different annotations in the UML models to express quantitative and qualitative non-functional requirements and properties.

The focus of this paper is on annotations for quantitative analysis techniques used for the verification and validation of temporal characteristics of RTES. Such annotations are required to bridge the gap between the domains of software development and analysis, because they should be usable by software designers but, at the same time, they also must support the analysis model concepts. This paper discusses the problem of adding non-functional properties to an UML model, but does not address other related problems, such as transforming an annotated UML model into an analysis one, evaluating the analysis model, or reporting the results back to UML models [8].

J.-M. Bruel (Ed.): MoDELS 2005 Workshops, LNCS 3844, pp. 79–90, 2006.

The solution proposed by OMG to the problem of extending the power of expression of UML for different application domains is to define standard UML profiles. Two examples of profiles able to add annotations for non-functional characteristics are the "UML Profile for Schedulability, Performance, and Time Specification" (SPT) [11] and the "UML Profile for Modeling Quality of Service and Fault Tolerance Characteristics and Mechanisms" (QoS&FT) [13]. In order to upgrade SPT to UML 2.0 and extend its scope with RTES modeling capabilities, a Request For Proposals (RFP) was issued for a new UML Profile named MARTE ("Modeling and Analysis of Real-Time and Embedded systems") [12]. The goals of this paper are to give a first reflection on the analysis concerns for the upcoming UML MARTE profile and to promote its standardization at the OMG.

Some of this underlying work is supported by the Accord|$_{UML}$ project [3, 7] and by the MAST (Modeling and Analysis Suite for real-Time applications) project [10] to connect UML models of real-time embedded systems with schedulability analysis tools. A first experimental approach was defined in [15], where the authors have presented a schedulability analysis model which is semi-automatically derived from a conception model, and is then analyzed [9]. MAST defines and builds UML conceptual models, which align quite well with the SPT profile concepts, for the consideration of timing properties in object-oriented distributed systems.

A rich body of work on performance analysis from UML models has been surveyed in [1]. Examples of UML model transformations to different performance modeling formalisms are: from UML to Layered Queueing Networks in [8, 16], to Stochastic Petri Nets in [2], and to multiple performance models in [19].

Other UML profiles for different quantitative analyses have already been proposed in the literature, such as a reliability profile in [4], a profile with formal semantics dedicated to real-time modeling named OMEGA in [6], and a profile for real-time constraints with OCL in [5].

The paper is organized as follows. Section 2 describes the domain model for non-functional property annotations for quantitative analyses. Section 3 presents a list of requirements for NFP annotations. Section 4 compares briefly the advantages and disadvantages of the SPT and QoS&FT Profiles. Section 5 presents our proposal for a framework for NFP annotations for MARTE, which realizes the domain model introduced in Section 2. Finally, the conclusions are presented in Section 6.

2   Domain Model for Non-functional Properties Annotations

2.1   Domain Model

The *model* of a computing *system* describes its architecture and behavior by means of *model elements* (e.g., resources, resources services, behavior features, logical operations, configurations modes, modeling views), and the externally visible properties of those model elements. When we refer to *properties*, this includes the *functional* and also the *non-functional properties*. Functional properties describe what a system model does, and non-functional properties how it does it.

In the context of model-driven development approaches for real-time and embedded systems, modeling of Non-Functional Properties (*NFPs*) is essential for the quantitative analysis of the system (see Figure 1). NFPs provides information about different characteristics, as for example throughput, delays, overheads, scheduling policies, correctness.

Quantitative analysis techniques are used to verify early NFPs of interest (e.g., response times, utilization, queue sizes) based on other available NFPs (e.g., worst case execution times -WCET-, deadlines). The analysis techniques considered in this paper belong to the two following analysis domains: *Schedulability* and *Performance*. Further work will also cover *WCET Analysis*. Schedulability analysis uses mathematical means (e.g., RMA-based techniques) to predict whether a set of software tasks meets its timing constraints and to verify its temporal correctness. Performance analysis uses statistical techniques (e.g., queuing theory, Petri Nets, etc.) to determine whether a system will meet its performance requirements (such as response time or throughput).

Due to the abstraction involved in the construction of a model, only some NFPs are relevant to a certain Quantitative Analysis. In other words, a given Quantitative Analysis uses a set of NFPs which establish the ontology of the analysis domain.

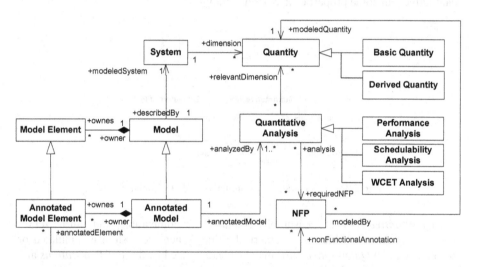

Fig. 1. Domain model for Non-Functional Property annotations

According to measurement theory, physical *Systems* (see Figure 1) are characterized along different dimensions that correspond to a set of measurement *Quantities*, which can be *Basic* or *Derived*. The most used Basic Quantities are length, mass, time, current, temperature and luminous intensity. The units of measure for the basic quantities are organized in systems of measures, such as the universally accepted *Système International* (SI) or International System of Units. Values are expressed in the same unit and can be compared. Derived Quantities (e.g., area, volume, force, frequency, etc.) are obtained from the Basic Quantities by known formulas.

A *Model* of a System (which is considered here to be expressed in UML) can be extended by standard UML mechanisms with additional semantic expressing concepts from a given analysis domain. An *Annotated Model* contains *Annotated Model Elements*, which are UML model elements extended by standard UML mechanisms. For example, some typical performance-related *Annotated Model Elements* are: *Step* (a unit of execution as defined in the SPT profile), *Scenario* (a sequence of Steps), *Resource* (as defined in the General Resource Model of SPT), *Service* (an operation offered by a *Resource* or by a component of some kind, which may be further defined by a *Scenario*).

An *Annotated Model Element* has certain non-functional characteristics represented by NFPs. The annotations are specified by the designer in the UML model and attached to different model elements. Examples are: the total delay of a *Step* when executed (including queueing delays), the utilization of a *Resource*, the response time and throughput of a *Service*, etc.

2.2 Quantitative and Qualitative NFPs

In general, a NFP can be either *qualitative* or *quantitative*, as shown in Figure 2. Most of the NFPs used for quantitative analysis (such as performance or schedulability) are quantitative, but some properties may be qualitative.

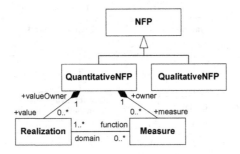

Fig. 2. Domain model for Quantitative and Qualitative NFPs

A *Quantitative NFP* is measurable, countable, or comparable, and can be represented by an amount which is a numerical value. When the system is simulated or executed, a given *Quantitative NFP* may be characterized by a set of *Realizations* and *Measures* (see Figure 2). *Realizations* (also called *Sample Functions*) represent a set of values that occur for the *Quantitative NFP* under consideration at run-time (for instance, measurements collected from a real system or a simulation experiment). A *Quantitative NFP* may be realized once or repeated times over an extended run. In a cyclic deterministic system, in which each cycle has the same values, a single Realization is sufficient to characterize completely the *Quantitative NFP*. In performance analysis with random traffic, a long run producing long sequences of values may be necessary in order to obtain accurate evaluation results.

A *Measure* is a (statistical) function (e.g, mean, max, min, median, variance, standard deviation, histogram, etc.) characterizing the set of Realizations. Measures may be computed either directly by applying the desired function to the set of Realizations values, or by using theoretical functions of the probability distribution given for the respective *Quantitative NFP*.

In any case, even Realization sets are not annotated directly on the UML model (too much information!) They are represented instead in an abstract way through the corresponding Measures, which should be annotated on the UML model.

On the other hand, a ***Qualitative NFP*** refers to inherent or distinctive characteristics that are not easy to measure directly. In general, a *Qualitative NFP* is denoted by a label (e.g., "bronze", "silver" and "gold" level of service) representing a high-level of abstraction characterization that is meaningful to the analyst and the analysis tools. More specifically, a *Qualitative NFP* takes a value from a list of allowed values (e.g., an enumeration data type), where each value identifies a possible alternative. When looking in more detail at a *Qualitative NFP*, it may be possible to define it in function of a set of criteria, which may be in turn qualitative or quantitative. Some *Qualitative NFPs* have precisely-known meanings that can be interpreted by the analysis domain, for example the choice of a scheduler type for a processor, or the choice of a statistical distribution for the latency of a network. In both of these examples, the full specification of the property requires not only a qualitative value, but also some quantitative parameters, as for instance:

```
Scheduler-type = roundRobin(quantumSize)
Latency-value = gamma(mean, variance)
```

3   Requirements for NFP Annotations

In our context, "annotation" is a process of attaching information to selected UML model elements. We must be able to annotate NFPs to structural elements such as objects and nodes, as well as behavioral elements such as lifelines, execution-occurrences, messages, activities and transitions. We identified different requirements for attaching NFPs to model elements which are described in the rest of the section.

3.1   Variables and Expressions

In most quantitative evaluations, some of the expressed quantities are derived from other quantities. This particularity is so fundamental to quantitative studies that it must be provided in the annotations discussed in this paper. As a motivating example, let us suppose that there is a characteristic size (call it *$dataSize*, in bytes) of a data structure that is stored, retrieved, processed and passed in messages. The CPU cost of operations, the delay for transmitting messages, the memory space required for storage, are all functions of *$dataSize*. It is much easier as well as more informative, to define these quantitative properties by expressions; also, the evaluation is more robust to changes in the design or the usage of the system, that could change the value of *$dataSize*. We can call *$dataSize* an independent parameter of the evaluation.

From this example, it is easy to see that an important requirement is to be able to annotate NFPs not only with concrete values, but also with variable names and expressions. However, defining variable names in the annotation space raises the question of scope. For instance, it should be possible to combine views and diagrams created separately into a single analysis, where the same name may have been used more than once. Some way to disambiguate these names is necessary. The scoping mechanisms should also handle the problem of UML models that are simultaneously annotated for multiple kinds of analysis.

Another requirement drawn from the above example is that there is a need for *independent evaluation parameters* that may affect many other NFPs through dependencies, which in turn can be expressed through functional relationships. These evaluation parameters need to be attached to the analysis as a whole, either at the level of a UML diagram or at the level of a collection of diagrams.

3.2 Sources of NFPs

It is a peculiarity of the NFPs that the same property may be defined separately from different sources. An obvious example is *required* values, versus *achieved* values, but additional subdivisions may arise. For example, the achieved value may be measured in a certain test (there may be more than one of these for the same NFP), or be estimated by an analytic model. Values may be stated for different execution environments. Input attributes may take *assumed* values based on the expertise of the designer/analyst, and there may be more than one of these (e.g., for worst-case and best-case, or representing the expertise of different parties). The ability to designate different sources and to compare the values given by different sources is fundamental to the full exploitation of the evaluation methodology.

It would be desirable to support user-definable sources, apart from the strings described to convey details. However, for tool support it seems desirable to define a list of standard codes for required and achieved values. It should clearly be possible to define as many versions of a single NFP, from different sources, as necessary. The capability for defining details could be used to list the results of a series of tests or model analyses representing different platforms, or different imposed load levels.

The purpose of expressing different sources is to gather the maximum information from the designer side. Automated analysis tools will have to filter the values according to the kind of data needed for the current analysis.

3.3 Usability of NFPs

Other requirement for NFP annotations is a tradeoff between usability and flexibility. Usability suggests the merit of defining a set of standard NFPs for a given analysis domain, so they can be easily referred to and, consequently, every user of the annotations means the same thing. For NFPs with well-known variants, a set of definitions can be standardized, which cover the important cases with differently-named measures; these can be translated if necessary by domain specialists for the use of an analysis tool with different names. However there are some NFPs whose meaning is model-dependent. This requires a capability for users to define their own NFPs. Thus flexibility and expressive power requires that the users have the capability to define their own quantitative measures, but usability requires a set of standard measures that can be used in straightforward way.

4 Comparing the SPT and QoS&FT Profiles

As mentioned, the background for MARTE comes from two existing profiles: SPT and QoS&FT. While SPT is specifically customized for the real-time systems domain, QoS&FT profile has a broader scope that includes all kinds of QoS properties. The MARTE RFP asks for a full compliance with the UML profile for QoS&FT. It is true that the QoS&FT profile already defines a framework to express NFPs. However, it exist some strong reasons to define a different framework in the context of MARTE:

- In general, the term "QoS" is associated to the aptitude of a service for providing a suitable quality level to the different demands of its clients. The NFPs considered here have a larger extent, and may describe the internals and externals of the system, some of them directly related to the users of resource services and their QoS perception and others not.
- The QoS&FT profile supports modeling of NFPs, with statistical qualifiers and measurement units. However, it ignores some necessary attributes such as measurement sources, property versions, variables, and values defined by mathematical expressions.
- The QoS&FT profile provides a flexible mechanism to store pre-defined QoS Characteristics. However, it requires too much effort for the users due to its three-step annotation process: a) define a *QoS Catalog* with the most common *QoS Characteristics* for each analysis domain, b) derive a *Quality Model* for each application by instantiating template classes from the catalog and c) annotate UML models with *QoS Constraints* and *QoSValues* (which imply the creation of extra objects required just for annotation purposes).

On the other hand, the SPT profile provides a straightforward annotation mechanism through predefined stereotypes end tagged values, and supports already some of the requirements for NFP annotations, such as symbolic variables and expressions through its specialized *Tag Value Language* (TVL). Table 1 compares different features of the two profiles.

Table 1. Comparison of SPT and QoS&FT profiles

Requirement	SPT Profile	QoS&FT Profile
Annotation process	Light-weight	Heavy-weight
Allows for user-defined measures	No (measures are predefined)	Yes (targeted for user-defined measures)
Type for time values	RTtimeValue	No
User-defined delay measure between an arbitrary pair of events	No	No
Expressions for defining quantitative NFPs	Yes Part of the TVL language	No
Quantitative variables and independent evaluation parameters	Yes Part of the TVL language	No
Expressions for defining constraints	Limited	Yes Full power of OCL

In summary, we can say that SPT's modeling method and annotation style are really simple for users (namely light-weight), but its structure is not flexible enough to allow for new user-defined QoS properties or for different analysis techniques. Conversely, the QoS&FT profile's annotation style is more complicated for users (namely heavy-weight), but its structure is more flexible because of the library style for defining QoS properties, OCL constraints to describe complex QoS functions, and useful qualifiers for QoS properties. In our work, we intend to provide a flexible and straightforward framework for MARTE while adopting the best modeling practices from both profiles.

5 Proposed Framework for MARTE NFP Annotations

In this section, we describe our proposal of a NFP modeling framework intended to meet the major requirements stated in Sections 2-4. Figure 3 shows the core UML metamodel to support major NFPs descriptions.

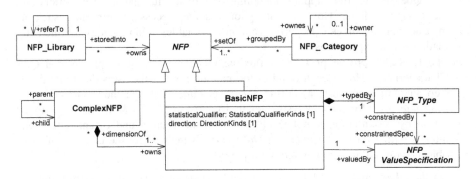

Fig. 3. Core NFP: Abstract Syntax

A given Quantitative Analysis domain uses a set of NFPs which are organized in a *NFP Library*. For instance, in the case of software performance analysis, the NFPs are throughput, response time, utilization, CPU execution demand, etc. Likewise, NFPs can be grouped into *NFP Categories*, similarly to the way in which the *QoS Characteristics* are grouped into *QoS Categories* in the QoS&FT profile.

The Core NFP package provides the capability of annotating model elements by *Complex NFP* or directly by *Basic NFP*. The first one is just a constructor, and the second one the concrete holder of NFPs. For instance, we could represent the *Arrival Pattern* property as a data structure (i.e., Complex NFP) that has a number of attributes: *Pattern, Period, Minimum Arrival Time*, etc. (i.e., Basic NFPs) which will be associated to a concrete value. A Basic NFP can represent either a quantitative property (ultimately a *value* and a *unit*) or a qualitative property (e.g, enumeration type or string). Also, a Basic NFP can be a realization (e.g., a set of values) or a statistical function (mean, variance, etc.).

Thus, Complex NFPs (e.g., response latency, processor throughput, correctness) are a generalization of QoS Characteristics described in the QoS&FT Profile. Basic NFPs (e.g. event period, minimum arrival time, WCET, deadline, scheduling optimally criterion) corresponds to the QoS Dimensions of the QoS Profile. We adopt the attributes *Statistical Qualifier* (e.g., max, min, mean, variance) and *Direction* (e.g. increasing, decreasing) from the QoS profile, but we remove the *Unit* attribute because we are interested on defining the units at the *user model* level.

Each Basic NFP has a *NFP Type* that constrains the specification of their values. At level of user models, we can apply different versions of *NFP Value Specifications* for each Basic NFP.

In Figure 4, we show the domain model for different Basic NFP types. *NFP_type* includes the general attributes *source* (e.g., required, estimated, calculated) and *Language* used for specifying the textual notations of the *Value Specification*. In the same way, specific NFP types use a set of pre-defined *units* (e.g., ms, s, kB/s). *Units* are at-tributes of most Quantitative NFP and it is important that standard forms are used. For space reasons, we do not show here the predefined units (e.g., duration units, size units). In order to complete the description of different types, the *values* of each par-ticular Basic NFP will be specified according to its NFP Type.

The NFP Type concept proposed here allows for the definition of types for anno-tating NFP values similar to the *RTtimeValue* type in SPT. However, we propose to use a different taxonomy (Figure 4).

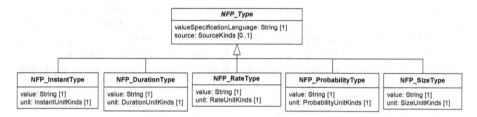

Fig. 4. NFP Types: Abstract Syntax

In order to define the legal lexical atoms to specify NFP values, we use the model presented in Figure 5. A *value* can be specified as a constant value (*NFP Constant*), as a variable (*NFP Variable*) or as an expression (*NFP Expression*).

NFP Constant is a literal expression that represents a constant. In addition to the Literal constants supported by UML, we include *List* and *Real* constants. List con-stants are literals of heterogeneous types that can be combined into a list of items be-tween a set of parentheses, with individual items separated by commas. Notice that, here, we do not define the grammar for the syntax of textual annotations.

NFP Variable can be used as placeholders for results from analysis tools in the UML annotations, or to support relationships between different NFPs. We adopt the SPT's syntax "*$string*" for variable names in the annotation domain, to distinguish them from names used in the UML model itself.

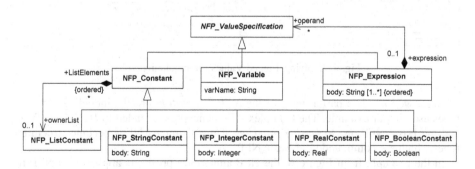

Fig. 5. NFP Value Specification Abstract Syntax

NFP Expressions are used to derive NFPs from other NFPs. An expression can be a simple constant or variable, or it can be a compound expression formed by combining expressions through operators. From an analysis point of view, allowing for NFP Expressions makes the analysis more flexible and more robust to change.

Next, we have to define the mechanism for attaching the MARTE annotations to UML model elements while providing flexibility and usability as discussed in Section 3.3. We consider two potential mechanisms: *Tagged Values* and *Constraints*. Tagged values are value slots associated to attributes of specific UML stereotypes, hence, one tagged value characterizes just one model element. On the other hand, a constraint is a condition expressed in natural language text or in a machine readable language (e.g., OCL) for declaring some semantics of one or various model elements. This is useful if we define NFPs that involve more than one element (for instance, a delay between two different events). Thus, we are interested in supporting both mechanisms.

Figure 6 illustrates the alternative in which tagged values are used for annotating NFPs (only a simplified version is shown).

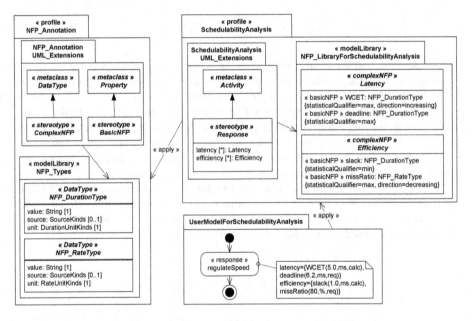

Fig. 6. Applying Tagged Values for annotating NFPs

Here, we include a partial view of the *NFP Annotation* profile, including the NFP types used in our example. The Complex NFP concept is extended to *UML DataType*, and the Basic NFP one to *UML Properties*. Thus, Complex NFPs become structured types which are compounded of Basic NFP.

In the example from Figure 6, the NFP annotation profile is applied to a NFP library for Schedulability Analysis. Most features of Basic NFPs are declared in this library, as well as their assigned NFP types. Furthermore, the Complex NFPs defined here are used, in turn, as *types* of generic attributes associated to stereotypes for

Schedulability Analysis. For instance, the *response* stereotype has the generic attributes *efficiency* and *latency,* which are typed with the corresponding Complex NFPs.

Finally, we are able to apply the Schedulability Analysis profile, and consequently the underlying NFP library to user models. This structure allows users to attach complex structures of NFPs to UML model elements in a standardized way. Moreover, user-defined NFPs can be added by modifying the existing libraries.

6 Conclusions

This paper defines a framework for annotating NFPs that are necessary for different kinds of quantitative analyses. The relationships between NFPs annotations and UML model elements are discussed. Based on the domain concepts, a list of requirements for attaching NFPs annotations to UML model elements is established. A summary of how the existing SPT and QoS&FT profiles meet these requirements is also presented. The goal is to understand and clarify the premises for some of the requirements in the MARTE RFP, in order to refine them and to make sure that they are consistent, complete and capture all the expressive power needed for a future MARTE solution.

The proposed approach for NFPs annotations involves the adoption of some useful structural concepts (e.g., libraries, categories) and qualifiers (e.g., statistical qualifiers, units) from the UML profile for QoS&FT, as well as its library style (i.e., catalogs) for defining domain-specific NFPs. However, some considerations to reduce its inherent complexity and to facilitate the modeling process are taken. Additionally, some key features provided by the SPT profile are adopted. For instance, we formalize, by means of MOF metamodels, some concepts supported by the TVL syntax to annotate constant, variable and expression values. In this manner, we intended to provide a flexible and straightforward framework for supporting a wide variety of NFPs annotations while adopting best modeling practices of both UML profiles.

Acknowledgements

The research of the Carleton team is supported by the Natural Sciences and Engineering Research Council of Canada (NSERC). The CEA team is partially supported by the PROTES project of the CARROLL French Research program. Huascar Espinoza is supported by the Programme AlBan of the European Union, scholarship No. E04D028544BO.

References

1. Balsamo, S., Di Marco, A., Inverardi, P., Simeoni, M., "Model-based performance prediction in software development: a survey" IEEE Transactions on Software Engineering, Vol 30, N.5, pp.295-310, May 2004.
2. S. Bernardi, S. Donatelli, and J. Merseguer, "From UML sequence diagrams and statecharts to analysable Petri net models" in Proc. of 3rd Int. Workshop on Software and Performance (WOSP02), pp. 35-45, Rome, July 2002.

3. CEA, I-Logix, Uppsala, OFFIS, PSA, MECEL, ICOM, "UML based methodology for real time embedded systems," version 1.0, April 2003, Project IST 10069 AIT-WOODDES.

4. V. Cortellessa, A. Pompei, "Towards a UML profile for QoS: a contribution in the reliability domain", In Proc. 4th Int. Workshop on Software and Performance WOSP'2004, pp.197 - 206, Redwood Shores, California, 2004.

5. S. Flake, W. Mueller, "A UML Profile for Real-Time Constraints with the OCL" In J. M. Jezequel, H. Hussmann, S. Cook (Eds.) UML'2002, Dresden, Germany LNCS (2460), pp. 179 – 195, Springer Verlag 2002.

6. S. Graf, Ileana Ober, Iulian Ober "Timed annotations in UML", accepted to STTT, Int. Journal on Software Tools for Technology Transfer, Springer Verlag, 2004

7. A. Lanusse, S. Gérard, F. Terrier, "Real-time Modelling with UML: The ACCORD Approach", In Proceedings of the UML'98, Springer Verlag LNCS 1618.

8. L. Lavagno, G. Martin, and B. Selic, "UML for Real. Design of Embedded Real-Time Systems," Kluwer Academic Publishers, 2003.

9. D. Lugato, C. Bigot, Y. Valot "Validation and automatic test generation on UML models: the AGATHA approach", In Proceedings of the Workshop FMICS, ENTCS 66 n°2, 2002.

10. J.L. Medina, M. González Harbour, and J.M. Drake, "MAST Real-Time View: A Graphic UML Tool for Modeling Object-Oriented Real-Time Systems" Proceedings of the 22nd IEEE Real-Time Systems Symposium (RTSS 2001), London, UK, IEEE Computer Society Press, pp. 245-256, December 2001.

11. Object Management Group, "UML Profile for Schedulability, Performance, and Time", Version 1.1. 2005. OMG document: formal/05-01-02.

12. Object Management Group, "UML Profile for Modeling and Analysis of Real-Time and Embedded systems (MARTE)", RFP. 2005. OMG document: realtime/05-02-06.

13. Object Management Group, "UML Profile for Modeling Quality of Service and Fault Tolerance Characteristics and Mechanisms", 2004. OMG document ptc/04-09-01.

14. J. C. Palencia and M. G. Harbour, "Exploiting Precedence Relations in the Schedulability Analysis of Distributed Real-Time Systems", Proceedings of the 20th Real-Time Systems Symposium, IEEE Computer Society Press, pp 328-339, December 1999.

15. T.H. Phan, S. Gérard and D. Lugato. "Schedulability Validation for UML-modeled real-time systems with symbolic execution and jitter compensation". ERCT Workshop, 2003.

16. D.C. Petriu, "Performance Analysis with the SPT Profile", in Model-Driven Engineering for Distributed and Embedded Systems, (S. Gerard, J.P. Babeau, J. Champeau, Eds), pp. 205-224, Hermes Science Publishing Ltd., London, England, 2005.

17. B. Selic, "A Generic Framework for Modeling Resources with UML", IEEE Computer, Vol.33, N. 6, pp. 64-69. June, 2000.

18. Sha, L., Abdelzaher, T., Arzen, K., E., Cervin, A., Baker, T., Burns, A., Buttazzo, G., Caccamo, M., Lehoczky, J., Mok, A., K., "Real Time Scheduling Theory: A Historical Perspective", Real-Time Systems Journal, Vol. 28, No, 2-3, pp. 101-155, 2004.

19. C.M. Woodside, D.C. Petriu, D.B. Petriu, H. Shen, T. Israr, J. Merseguer, "Performance by Unified Model Analysis (PUMA)", In Proc. of 5th Int. Workshop on Software and Performance WOSP'2005, pp.1-12, Palma, Spain, July 2005.

Report of the 7th International Workshop on Aspect-Oriented Modeling

Jörg Kienzle[1], Jeff Gray[2], and Dominik Stein[3]

[1] School of Computer Science, McGill University, Montreal, QC, Canada
[2] Department of Computer and Information Sciences,
University of Alabama at Birmingham, Birmingham, AL, USA
[3] Institute for Computer Science and Business Information Systems,
University of Duisburg-Essen, Essen, Germany
Joerg.Kienzle@mcgill.ca, gray@cis.uab.edu, dominik.stein@icb.uni-due.de

Abstract. This report summarizes the outcome of the 7th Workshop on Aspect-Oriented Modeling (AOM) held in conjunction with the 8th International Conference on Model Driven Engineering Languages and Systems – MoDELS 2005 – in Montego Bay, Jamaica, on the 2nd of October 2005. The workshop brought together researchers and practitioners from two communities: aspect-oriented software development (AOSD) and software model engineering. It provided a forum for discussing the state of the art in modeling crosscutting concerns at different stages of the software development process: requirements elicitation and analysis, software architecture, detailed design, and mapping to aspect-oriented programming constructs. This paper gives an overview of the accepted submissions, and summarizes the results of the different discussion groups.

1   Introduction

This paper summarizes the outcome of the 7th edition of the successful Aspect-Oriented Modeling Workshop series. An overview of what happened at previous editions of the workshop can be found at http://dawis.informatik.uni-essen.de/events/AOM_MODELS2005/preveds.shtml. The workshop took place at the Half Moon Resort in Montego Bay, Jamaica, on Sunday, October 2nd 2005, as part of the 8th International Conference on Model Driven Engineering Languages and Systems – MoDELS 2005[1], formerly known as the series of conferences on the Unified Modeling Language. Participation to the workshop was open to anyone attending the conference, and as a result there were approximately 40 participants. A total of 14 position papers were submitted and reviewed by the program committee, 12 of which were accepted to the workshop. In order to leave enough time for discussion, only the morning sessions were dedicated to presentations. Based on the reviews of the papers, six of the papers were allocated 10-minute presentation slots, five papers were chosen for 20-minute presentation slots with the intention to stimulate and provide provocative input to the afternoon discussions. Before the lunch break, the attendees were asked to submit a list of

J.-M. Bruel (Ed.): MoDELS 2005 Workshops, LNCS 3844, pp. 91–99, 2006.
© Springer-Verlag Berlin Heidelberg 2006

questions for the afternoon discussion session. Based on these questions, the attendees split into two groups: a "model-transformation and aspect-oriented modeling" group, and a "core aspect-oriented modeling concepts and aspect-oriented software processes" group. The results of the discussion groups were collected at the end of the workshop, and presented and re-discussed with the entirety of the workshop participants.

The rest of this report is structured as follows: Section 2 gives an overview to the accepted papers. Section 3 summarizes the results of the discussion groups. Section 4 concludes the report and presents identified future research directions.

2   Overview of Accepted Position Papers

Robert France from Colorado State University presented a position paper in which the authors explore the relationship between (aspect-oriented) model composition and model transformation[2]. They compare two high-level architectures of model transformation engines that could achieve aspect-oriented composition of models. One architecture describes a very specialized/dedicated transformation engine that takes a primary model, an aspect model, composition directives, and signature definitions as input to finally produce the composed model. The second architecture is very generic and symmetric. It takes a primary model and an aspect model and bindings as an input to produce the composed model.

Wolfgang Grieskamp from Microsoft Research presented a framework for composing behavioral models [3]. In the framework, different aspects of the system behavior are described using action machines (state machines or scenarios). These models can then be symmetrically composed and transformed to yield integrated models that can be used for model checking, refinement checking, and testing purpose. The techniques described in the paper rely on symbolic representation of values and state.

Mark Mahoney from Carthage College described a technique that enables weaving crosscutting concerns expressed in Live Sequence Charts (LSC) [4]. He presented how one can use pattern matching techniques in the pre-charts of an LSC to define "cross-cutting triggers" (similar to pointcuts in standard AOP languages), that activate the behavior described in an associated main chart (comparable to an AOP advice).

Jaime Pavlich-Mariscal from the University of Connecticut presented how they modeled access control schemas using role slices, and how they used aspect-oriented programming techniques to implement their system [5]. They outlined their goals to extend role slices with dynamic facilities. Thereo, their future research directions include adding support for access control based on run-time elements, as well as relating role-slice hierarchies with class hierarchies. These changes at the modeling level might require new AOP language features to implement them.

Jean-Paul Bodeveix from the Paul Sabatier University in Toulouse showed how one can specify real-time constraints in EMITL (Event Metric Interval Temporal Logic), and then transform this description into timed automata, and finally into a B specification [6]. This timing information can then be combined with a B specification of the functional behavior of a system to result in a composed B specification that specifies the functional and the timing behavior.

Tihamér Levendovszky from Budapest University of Technology and Economics presented how they used aspect-oriented techniques for applying OCL constraints [7]. He presented the Visual Modeling and Transformation System (VMTS), a meta-modeling environment, together with its Visual Control Flow Language (VCFL), a language allowing to express model transformations using graph rewriting techniques. VCFL uses OCL constraints to define constraints on the nodes of the transformation steps and to choose between different control flow branches. Often, the same constraint has to be repetitively applied to many different places in a transformation. Aspect-orientation can help to modularize such crosscutting constraints.

Aswin Van Den Berg from Motorolla Labs presented a framework for modularizing crosscutting concerns in embedded software, and how this framework can automate the composition of concerns at different phases of the code generation process [8]. He presented AspectSDL, an aspect-oriented framework that makes it possible to compose SDL statecharts. The aspect weaver composes core models and aspect bean models according to a binding definition (connector) and weaving strategy definitions. The ultimate goal is to perform consistency checks on the composed model, as well as to use it for simulation purpose.

Ana Moreira from the University of Lisbon presented how to build a metadata repository that describes the content, quality, structure, and other important data of concerns during the early stages of software development [9]. Such a repository allows a developer to navigate over all stored information to facilitate reuse, version control, and traceability.

In his second presentation, Robert France showed how they extended their aspect-oriented modeling approach to use signatures when composing models [10]. In their approach, crosscutting functionality is described by aspect-models and the core application functionality is described by a primary model. When composing models, model elements are merged with one another if their signatures match. A signature in this case consists of some or all properties of a model element as defined in the UML metamodel.

Andrew Jackson from Trinity College in Dublin presented the high-level view of a generic aspect-oriented design process [11]. The paper defines the core requirements of an aspect-oriented process to include support for modularization, composition, conflict resolution, and internal and external traceability. In addition, a good process must be an open, customizable, platform independent process that integrates with existing software development methodologies. It should support quality assurance metrics, staged adoption, and product families. Based on these requirements, the paper defines a process architecture with the following phases: concern identification and classification, design tests, reuse design, concern module design, composition specification design, verification, and refinement.

Andrew also agreed to present [12], a paper that describes how model-driven software development and an aspect-oriented modeling technique called "Aspectual Collaborations" can be brought together by providing a graphical composition mechanism.

3   Summary of the Discussion Groups

The following section summarizes the results of the afternoon working group sessions. The participants split into two groups – a "Model Transformation" and a "Core Aspect-Oriented Concepts" group – to discuss the questions submitted by the attendees before the lunch break.

3.1   Model Transformation Group

The model transformation working group was charged with the task of discussing various issues related to the transformation mechanisms of model weaving. The questions discussed are highlighted below along with summary comments.

What Is Model Transformation? Before getting into the details of aspect weaving at the modeling level, the working group began with a discussion of the meaning of model transformation in general. A distinction was made between a source model and the target model. In some cases, there may be multiple sources and targets. The participants agreed that model transformation can be summarized as graph transformation, where a model is a set of typed nodes in a hypergraph that are manipulated according to the goals of a transformation rule. The process of model transformation eventually reaches a fixed point after multiple iterations among a set of transformation rules.

What Is Model Weaving? There are two essential characteristics that seem to be common among most model weavers: 1) a pattern matching engine, like a pointcut language that provides quantification among modeling elements, and 2) a composition mechanism that transforms source models according to a new concern. In general, there were three types of weaving that were discussed:

- Static weaving on static structure, such as weaving into class diagrams where the semantics are pre-existing
- Static weaving on dynamic behavior, such as weaving into state-charts
- Dynamic weaving on dynamic behavior, which is the current focus of dynamic AOP languages. The working group could not identify a typical usage scenario for this type of weaving at the modeling level. Furthermore, the issue of dynamic weaving on static structure was not very clear within the modeling context.

Is Model Transformation Equivalent to Weaving? The working group discussed the relationship between model transformation and model weaving. It was determined that all weaving is a model transformation, but not all model transformation is weaving (e.g., model refactoring can be a model transformation that is not crosscutting). This is similar to the relation of program transformation to aspect code weavers, where an aspect is a special type of program transformation that captures crosscutting concerns.

Are There Generic Patterns for Model Transformation and Weaving?
An interesting thread arose from the discussion that examined whether common patterns of transformation have emerged from the experience of model transformation experts. Two patterns that were mentioned are *Find a Leaf*, which can be used to flatten hierarchical structures, and *Transitive Closure*, which can be used to collect modeling attributes during stages of a model transformation. It was also observed that the UMLAUT tool uses visitors, abstract factory, and other well-known design patterns for transformations in an OO style, and can be made specific for different models of computation (e.g., stateflow).

Is Model Weaving Fundamentally the Same as Applying Rules in a Rule-Based Engine? One of the working group participants asked if a rule-based engine could be used for model weaving. The consensus of the group was that a rule language could theoretically capture some categories of crosscutting in a model, but the pragmatic application was less clear. It was suggested by one member that a model engineer often desires a higher level of abstraction. Several comparisons were presented as analogies to using rules for aspect weaving, and why a more focused language would be more desirable. Some of those counterexamples include:

- C++ abstractions to support objects can be simulated as C function pointers, but a pointer approach lacks the level of abstraction provided by pure OO constructs.
- Database triggers can capture limited crosscutting concerns in stored procedures, but the same language cannot be used for general AOP.
- Metaobject protocols and reflection can also be used to address crosscutting concerns, but are not as easy to use as a pure aspect language.

The summary from this discussion is that there exists a tradeoff between naturalness of expression and power of language. A rule-based language could be used in some cases to describe modeling aspects, but the naturalness and applicability are not as evident when compared to a pure aspect modeling language.

How Can Properties of Model Weaving Be Proven? There was concern among the participants regarding the manner in which the resulting properties of the model weaving could be proven. This question was re-stated in terms of traditional verification (i.e., is the weaving itself performed correctly?) and validation (i.e., is the result that which was in the mind of the designer?). This was cited as a strong need for future work, with little being done on the topic so far. The composition of modeling aspects and the resulting behavior is trivial if the concerns are orthogonal (i.e., no interference), but more challenging if non-orthogonal (e.g., composing two separate access control aspects, such as RBAC and mandatory access control).

What Are the Performance Issues Associated with Aspect Modeling?
The notion of performance as it relates to aspect modeling can be broken down into three separate questions. The first issue relates to the actual performance of the model weaver itself (i.e., how long does it take to weave the models?). Of course, this will depend on the size of the source model and the speed of the model weaving tool. A second type of performance issue concerns the resulting size of the target model. An explosion of the size of the model after weaving may inhibit further analysis and generation. A third version of this question may apply to the performance of the actual modeled system. The desire to model performance using aspects may be motivated by different domain requirements, such as a model for real-time embedded systems. The ability to modularize crosscutting modeling concerns related to performance may enable a model engineer to change properties of a model in a rapid manner as compared to a tedious and error prone manual approach.

3.2   Core Aspect-Oriented Concepts Group

The core aspect-oriented concepts group looked at the issues that arise when applying aspect-oriented modeling techniques to real-world models.

How Do Existing Aspect-Oriented Modeling Techniques Scale? Several participants with industrial background expressed their concerns about how existing aspect-oriented modeling techniques would scale to systems with hundreds of classes and aspects. Participants from Motorola mentioned that aspect-oriented techniques actually do work well in industrial settings, even in large scale systems, provided that the number of aspects is small. Orthogonal aspects such as logging work particularily well. The discussion group identified the lack of availability of real-world UML models, i.e. models with hundreds of classes, as one of the reasons why current AOM approaches have been applied to toy examples only. Also, functional crosscutting concerns are not trivial to identify and modularize. The problem of aspect dependencies and conflict detection was determined as one of the main scalability challenges.

Some argued that in order to achieve scalability we need a common core meta-model. The UML meta-model was deemed to be missing the power to express relationships among different models. Some suggested the definition of an AML – an Aspect Meta Language – that provides a unified type space linking UML and aspects together.

Does Aspect-Oriented Modeling Improve Reuse? There has not been a lot of evidence that aspect-orientation improves reuse. The attendees of the workshop figured that the reason for this is the lack of a good aspect-oriented design process, and the fact that students and programmers in general are not educated to write reusable code, even for object-oriented systems. Different aspect-oriented approaches are also not compatible, which makes reuse very difficult. Again, the use of a common meta-model could improve this situation.

How Good Are Aspect-Oriented Modeling Tools? In aspect-oriented modeling, there is a big need for flexible tools. Unfortunately, tool vendors like to provide their home-grown extensions to UML, but do not allow (or make it very complicated for) users to extend the tool on their own. The only solution nowadays is to export models and then write "filter-like" mini-tools that parse the exported file and apply the desired transformations on it. Tools are also inflexible because they often present only one view of the system to the developer at a given time. For some approaches it would be nice to simultaneously display multiple models, e.g. the primary model and an aspect model. Since this is currently not supported, a lot of mental work has to be performed by the developer during design.

What Decisions Are Human Decisions and What Choices Can Be Automated? Many model transformations need additional human input in order to be applied to a given model. Sometimes the choice of the model transformation to be applied is done by a human. It is important to record these human decisions, and why these decisions have been made, in order to provide traceability and accountability during software development. It is not yet clear from which point on the generation of code can be completely automated.

Should it Be Allowed to "Restrain" Aspects, e.g. Hide Join Points from Other Aspects in the System? The discussion started out from the question of why aspects are better than components. Components in the past have promised out-of-the-box reuse in the sense of "buy your component to take care of concern X". However, reuse of components only seems to work for very specific concerns. Some participants argued that aspects will deliver, because they are so flexible. Others argued that aspects are so flexible as to be useless.

This raised the question of whether it should be possible to restrict aspect configurations to not expose their join points to other parts of the system. The arguments in favor of restriction were the conservation of important software engineering properties such as encapsulation and information hiding. Controlling the scope of aspects can also help to distribute development of large systems among different teams without the danger of having one aspect in one part of the system unintentionally affecting other parts of a system. Finally, restriction would allow to ensure non-functional and run-time properties such as execution time, etc. On the other hand, the major argument against restriction is the fact that unrestricted aspects make it possible to add functionality anywhere. This allows for rapid development and prototyping because developers can focus on a smaller part of the project without having to worry about designing for future extension. Also, unrestricted aspects can help tremendously in a world where requirements are likely to change.

What Benefits Does Aspect-Oriented Modeling Bring to Industry? Aspect-orientation was identified as an elegant way to perform "functional decomposition" for large industrial projects. It provides a flexible framework in which concerns can be identified and resolved at different levels of refinement.

It allows developers to postpone decisions and focus on important concerns first, maybe even implement a prototype, without having to worry about other concerns. Thanks to aspect-orientation, secondary concerns can be added to the system at a later phase.

4   Concluding Remarks

The workshop continued the tradition of having a very diverse representation of participants. The authors came from seven different countries (Argentina, France, Germany, Hungary, Ireland, Portugal, and USA), the organizing and programming committees represented nine countries (Canada, China, France, Germany, Ireland, Israel, Netherlands, Switzerland, and USA). In addition to the geographical diversity, the AOM workshop also attracted participants with wide research interests in aspects across the entire spectrum of the development lifecycle. As a result, this provided opportunities for a variety of opinions that were well-informed from the accumulated experience of the participants.

The growth of the workshop continued to increase, which indicates a strong interest in the area among researchers in aspect-oriented modeling. Many of the participants felt a new sense of maturity at the workshop that has not been evident in past editions. For example, the previous debates over definition of terms and mechanisms were replaced with deeper discussions focused on the core issues that need to be addressed to move the area into a common modeling practice. With this workshop report, we'd like to give researches who couldn't attend the workshop the opportunity to gain insights to these issues, and to point out a future research agenda in the field of aspect-oriented modeling.

Acknowledgements

The organizers spent a lot of time ensuring that the workshop was a success. The organizers for this edition of the workshop were Omar Aldawud, Tzilla Elrad, Jeff Gray, Mohamed Kandé, Jörg Kienzle, and Dominik Stein. An expert program committee provided assistance in reviewing the submitted papers. The members of the program committee were Mehmet Aksit, Elisa Baniassad, Jean Bézivin, Siobhán Clarke, Robert France, Sudipto Ghosh, Stefan Hanenberg, Shmuel Katz, Raghu Reddy, Martin Robillard, and Christa Schwanninger. Last but not least, we'd like to thank all submitters and participants of the workshop who contributed with their papers and positions.

References

1. Briand, L., Williams, C., eds.: 8th International Conference on Model Driven Engineering Languages and Systems, Montego Bay, Jamaica, Oct. 2-7, 2005. Number 3713 in Lecture Notes in Computer Science, Springer Verlag (2005)
2. Baudry, B., Fleury, F., France, R., Reddy, R.: Exploring the relationship between model composition and model transformation. In: 7th International Workshop on Aspect-Oriented Modeling, Montego Bay, Jamaica, Oct. 2nd, 2005. (2005)

3. Grieskamp, W., Kicillof, N., Campbell, C.: Behavioral composition in symbolic domains. In: 7th International Workshop on Aspect-Oriented Modeling, Montego Bay, Jamaica, Oct. 2nd, 2005. (2005)

4. Mahoney, M., Elrad, T.: Weaving crosscutting concerns into live sequence charts using the play engine. In: 7th International Workshop on Aspect-Oriented Modeling, Montego Bay, Jamaica, Oct. 2nd, 2005. (2005)

5. Pavlich-Mariscal, J., Michel, L., Demurjian, S.A.: Role slices and runtime permissions: Improving an AOP-based access control schema. In: 7th International Workshop on Aspect-Oriented Modeling, Montego Bay, Jamaica, Oct. 2nd, 2005. (2005)

6. Rached, M., Bodeveix, J.P., Filali, M., Nasr, O.: Real-time aspects: Specification and composition in b. In: 7th International Workshop on Aspect-Oriented Modeling, Montego Bay, Jamaica, Oct. 2nd, 2005. (2005)

7. Lengyel, L., Levendovszky, T., Charaf, H.: Real-time aspects: Specification and composition in b. In: 7th International Workshop on Aspect-Oriented Modeling, Montego Bay, Jamaica, Oct. 2nd, 2005. (2005)

8. Cottenier, T., Van Den Berg, A., Elrad, T.: Modeling aspect-oriented compositions. In: 7th International Workshop on Aspect-Oriented Modeling, Montego Bay, Jamaica, Oct. 2nd, 2005. (2005)

9. Ferreira, R., Raminhos, R., Moreira, A.: Metadata driven aspect specification. In: 7th International Workshop on Aspect-Oriented Modeling, Montego Bay, Jamaica, Oct. 2nd, 2005. (2005)

10. Reddy, R., France, R., Gosh, S., Fleury, F., Baudry, B.: Model composition - a signature based approach. In: 7th International Workshop on Aspect-Oriented Modeling, Montego Bay, Jamaica, Oct. 2nd, 2005. (2005)

11. Jackson, A., Clarke, S.: Towards a generic aspect-oriented design process. In: 7th International Workshop on Aspect-Oriented Modeling, Montego Bay, Jamaica, Oct. 2nd, 2005. (2005)

12. Groher, I., Bleicher, S., Schwanninger, C.: Model-driven development for pluggable collaborations. In: 7th International Workshop on Aspect-Oriented Modeling, Montego Bay, Jamaica, Oct. 2nd, 2005. (2005)

Modeling Aspect-Oriented Compositions

Thomas Cottenier[1,2], Aswin van den Berg[1], and Tzilla Elrad[2]

[1] Software and Systems Engineering Research, Motorola Labs,
1300 E Algonquin Road, 60173 Schaumburg, IL, USA
{thomas.cottenier, aswin.vandenberg}@motorola.com
[2] Concurrent Programming Research Group, Illinois Institute of Technology,
3300 S Federal Street, 60616 Chicago, IL, USA
{cotttho, elrad}@iit.edu

Abstract. Crosscutting concerns are pervasive in embedded software, because of the various constraints imposed by the environment and the stringent QoS requirements on the system. This paper presents a framework for modularizing crosscutting concerns in embedded and distributed software, and automating their composition at the modeling level, for simulation and validation purposes. The proposed approach does not extend the semantics of the UML in order to represent aspects. Rather, it dedicates a metamodel to the representation of the composition semantics between aspects and core models. The paper illustrates this approach by presenting a model weaver for SDL statecharts developed at Motorola Labs. Crosscutting behavior is designed with plain SDL statecharts and encapsulated into modules called aspect beans. The weaver looks at the aspect beans and the core SDL statecharts from a perspective that is defined by lightweight extensions to the SDL and UML metamodels. A connector metamodel defines the structure of the aspect-to-core binding definition. Finally, a weaver behavioral metamodel defines composition primitives for specifying weaving strategies.

1 Introduction

Model-Driven Development (MDD) is a software development methodology that emphasizes precise modeling for automated generation of optimized code. MDD techniques also target automated simulation, verification, use-case validation and test case generation. MDD approaches have been widely adopted in the industry, especially for the development of applications that have stringent performance requirements, such as embedded control software for telecommunication devices.

Embedded Software applications are especially difficult to design and build because of the constraints placed on them and because of the problem domain. The telecommunication industry has therefore driven a research effort towards a standard specification language for real-time, stimulus response systems, the Specification and Description Language (SDL) [1]. SDL is standardized as an ITU recommendation, and has continually evolved since its first version in 1980 to now include Object-Oriented features. In SDL, the basis for description of behavior is communicating Extended State Machines that are represented by processes. Communication is represented by signals that can take place between processes or between processes and the

J.-M. Bruel (Ed.): MoDELS 2005 Workshops, LNCS 3844, pp. 100–109, 2006.

environment of the system. Under pressure of the industry, the UML 2.0 has adopted some core features that are inspired by the SDL, such as a framework for dealing with Actions. The UML profile for Communicating Systems (UML-CS) [2] complements these extensions, to provide full support for SDL modeling, within the UML. For example, the UML-CS provides support for the definition of timers. Over the years, the industry has developed powerful code generators that take SDL models as input, map the models to some internal code representation and perform aggressive code optimizations. The generated code is mostly C code.

Typically, the process from requirement analysis to implementation and testing involves the following steps. The initial requirements are collected in a text document. System analysis results in UML models and Message Sequence Charts (MSC) [3] that capture the typical scenarios. The classes are mapped to SDL semi-automatically, and the SDL diagrams are completed manually to a level where they can be checked for consistency, simulated and validated. A test suite is generated from the SDL specification and finally, executable code is generated fully automatically.

Yet, the modeling process is time-consuming and error prone. All implementation details need to be reflected at the modeling level, before the application models can be simulated, and code can be generated. Many of these implementation details relate to the non-functional requirements of these applications, such as fault-tolerance, logging or security. In many cases, the hierarchical decomposition paradigm of SDL does not enable those concerns to be well modularized into separate SDL modules.

The Aspect-Oriented Software Development (AOSD) [4] community identifies those concerns as being crosscutting concerns. Their implementation cannot be well encapsulated within the modularity units of the language, because they follow different composition rules. Crosscutting concerns are pervasive in embedded software, because of the various constraints imposed by the environment and the stringent QoS requirements on the system. During the initial design phases, these concerns cannot be mapped from requirement to design in isolation, and end up tangled with model elements that implement other requirements.

This work proposes a framework for modularizing crosscutting concerns in embedded software, and automating their composition at different phases of the code generation process, including the modeling level, the different intermediary code representation levels and at the level of the final generated code. This paper discusses aspect modeling within the framework.

2 Approaches to AO Modeling

2.1 Lightweight UML Extension

The lightweight extension to the UML approaches take advantage of the UML extension mechanisms (stereotypes, tagged values and constraints) to refine the UML metamodel as to support AOP language constructs. The works of Pawlak [6], Aldawud [7] and Stein [8] fall into this category. These approaches provide graphical notations for aspects, for example, by defining pointcut associations, which link advices to joinpoints. The aspects tend to be tightly coupled to the core model. For large projects, the relations might involve many classes of the application, and the visual representation of crosscutting does not scale well. The result of composition is complex and difficult to read and comprehend. The design model looks like a woven model.

The authors' position is that joinpoints are a validation and verification issue. This implies that during the design phase, we do not want to know where the joinpoints are, and hence, we do not need an explicit modeling construct for them.

2.2 Heavyweight UML Extension

The proponents of heavyweight extensions to the UML argue that aspects need to be first-class elements in the UML, because lightweight extension mechanisms are not expressive enough to capture weaving semantics by themselves, The heavyweight UML extension approaches define a self-contained metamodel that fits AOSD. The metamodel is obtained by tailoring the UML kernel metamodel. Heavyweight extensions provide graphical notations for aspects, but do not define the weaving concept explicitly. The works of Kandé [9], Han [10] and Lions [11] fall into this category.

Heavyweight approaches are complex to implement. Furthermore, when extending the UML metamodel, all the tools that realize test case generation, model validation and code generation need to be refactored to support the new AO metamodel.

2.3 Model Transformation Approaches

Model transformation approaches recognize the weaving process as a concept in the expanded metamodel of the UML. Model weaving approaches realize the coordination of crosscutting concerns with a base model through model transformation. Model weaving provides the capability to describe the essence of a concern into a separate model and transform other models accordingly. These approaches have the disadvantage that the AOP language constructs have no clear counterpart at the modeling level. The work of Gray [12] falls into this category.

2.4 Hybrid Approaches

Hybrid approaches to AOM recognize weaving as a concept in the modeling process, but leverage the weaving process by extending the UML metamodel. Typically, the metamodel for modeling core program elements is extended to support a join point model. The metamodel for modeling aspects is extended to support the notion of aspect, advice, pointcut and intertype declaration. A model weaver composes the aspect models with the core models by associating advice bodies to joinpoints, and intertype declaration to core model elements.

Tkatchenko [13] proposes a simple joinpoint model that is implemented through a heavyweight UML extension. The weaving process can partly be made implicit, because the extended metamodel extension captures part of the weaving semantics.

The work of Clarke and Baniassad [14] proposes a UML design model that encompasses different separation-of-concern techniques, including aspect-oriented decompositions. A Theme represents a modularized view of a requirement or concern in the system. The behavior of aspects is modeled using diagram templates. Themes are coordinated semi-automatically by an engine that applies merge and replace rules, and parameterizes the diagram templates, by binding adviced methods to concrete joinpoints.

The work of Reddy [15] also takes advantage of UML templates for designing generic crosscutting features. Before composing the models the weaver instantiates the aspect models by binding application-specific elements to the template parameters.

2.5 AOM and MDA

The hybrid approach has interesting connections with the OMG Model Driven Architecture (MDA) [6]. The MDA separates platform independent details from the platform specific details of the system in a series of models. The approach is for each concern, to automatically expand more abstract diagrams by substituting the more concrete sub-diagrams into the abstract one. MDA proceeds by defining model transformation specifications that will automatically introduce, for example, platform specific behavior into a platform independent model. The transformation maps model elements of one domain metamodel to model elements of a target metamodel. The transformation is defined according to a transformation metamodel that defines the primitives of the transformation.

The hybrid approach defines a domain metamodel (a metamodel for modeling aspects), a target metamodel (a metamodel to visualize crosscutting behavior) and model transformation rules that conform to an AOSD metamodel. Aspects inject some more specific concern implementations into a more abstract model.

The relationship between MDA model transformations and model weaving is analogous to the relationship between AOP languages and Meta Object Protocol (MOP) languages. MOP's enable more powerful transformations, but are hard to write. AOP restricts the transformation space to a limited set of transformations, on a limited set of language elements. Aspects are less powerful, but provide better modularization units, and cover much of the MOP transformation space.

3 Aspect-Oriented Composition for Communicating Systems

3.1 Requirements

In an MDD setting, the SDL statechart weaver needs to accommodate the following constraints:

- The semantics of the SDL metamodel elements used to model the core application can not be modified to accommodate aspect weaving. It should be possible to simulate, validate and generated code from those models with the existing MDD tool suite.
- The aspect behavior needs to be specified in standard SDL, so that crosscutting behavior can be simulated and validated independently, and that code can be generated with the existing MDD tool suite. The metamodel used to model aspect behavior can therefore not break the semantics of SDL.
- It should be possible to validate and simulate the result of the composition between core models and aspect models using the existing MDD tool suite. The statechart weaver should therefore produce models that conform to the SDL metamodel.

Within an industrial setting and a specific domain, many crosscutting concerns tend to have common implementations from an application to another. The models that implement crosscutting concerns are themselves reusable from one application to another. What differs from one application to another are the bindings between aspect and core model. Therefore, we adopt an Aspect-Oriented architecture that involves a connector – a component that binds generic (within the domain) advices to application specific joinpoints. It encapsulates pointcut expressions and context binding definitions between joinpoints and named advices. The aspect advices are therefore made more reusable, as they do not depend on application-specific pointcut expressions.

This approach differs from the previous ones in that neither the core models, neither the aspect models require specific support for aspect-orientation. The author's position is that much of the complexity of aspect-oriented modeling is due to the difficulty of representing the aspect/core semantic interactions. This complexity can be overcome by defining separate diagrams that model the composition between the aspect behavioral diagrams and the core models.

3.2 AspectSDL: An SDL Statechart Weaver

The crosscutting behavior is modeled using regular SDL statecharts. Those models are referred to as SDL Aspect Beans. A connector defines the bindings between aspect bean statecharts and the core model statecharts. Figure 1 illustrates the architecture of the AspectSDL weaving engine. The SDL statechart weaver operates according to four distinct metamodels:

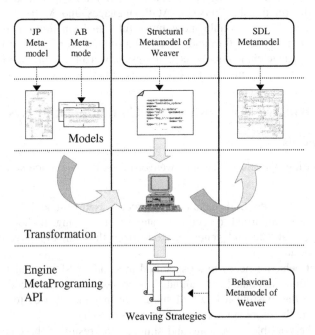

Fig. 1. Architecture of the AspectSDL weaving engine. The SDL statechart weaver operates according to four distinct metamodels: a joinpoint metamodel, an aspect bean metamodel, a connector metamodel and a behavioral metamodel of the weaver.

- A lightweight extension to the SDL profile that defines the joinpoint concept for SDL statecharts
- A lightweight extension to the UML metamodel that defines the concepts of aspect bean, advice, and intertype declaration.
- A connector metamodel that specifies how the bindings between aspect beans and model elements are defined. The connector metamodel is a structural weaving metamodel. It defines the static concepts the model weaver uses to identify crosscutting, such as pointcut and advice declaration.
- A behavioral weaving metamodel that specifies how weaving strategies are defined. A weaving strategy defines the operations to be performed to bind an aspect bean element to the core model. Weaving strategies define the weaving semantics. The behavioral weaving metamodel defines a metaprogramming API for the weaving engine.

4 AspectSDL Metamodels

4.1 Aspect Bean Profile

The Aspect Bean profile defines how the AspectSDL weaver looks at the Aspect Bean SDL statecharts. Aspect Beans are defined as Class stereotypes. We adopt an aspect model where advices have an explicit name. This allows advices to be defined independently of pointcut expressions. Advices are defined as Operation stereotypes. This is consistent with Stein's UML notation for Aspect-Oriented Design [8]. An advice is a special kind of operation that may not be called explicitly. InterType attributes are defined as Attribute stereotypes and InterType operations are defined as Operation stereotypes.

4.2 Joinpoint Profile

The extensions to the SDL metamodel described in this section are defined with respect to the UML profile for SDL [2], as represented in Telelogic TAU G2 [16].

The Joinpoint profile defines which elements in the SDL statecharts can be considered as joinpoints. The joinpoint metamodel should be as simple as possible. A simple joinpoint metamodel is one that allows various types of joinpoints to be treated uniformly. The Action concept of UML 2.0 matches the concept of a joinpoint well. An action is the finest level of granularity for the specification of a method. All methods directly or indirectly contain actions. When a method is executed, all or some of these actions are executed. The action concept captures all the caller side types of joinpoints in an Aspect language.

The Joinpoint profile defines a call joinpoint as an Action stereotype. The "CallJoinpoint" stereotype applies to all Actions that have an "Action Expression". During the weaving process, all actions whose action expression matches a call pointcut expression are selected as active joinpoints.

Method execution joinpoints are not captured by the Action concept. A method execution joinpoint can be seen as a UML 2.0 Method. A Method is the implementation of an operation, describing how it is executed at runtime. A method is associated to an expression that identifies the operation it implements.

The Joinpoint profile defines an execution joinpoint as a Method stereotype. During the weaving process, all methods whose expression matches an execution pointcut expression are selected as active joinpoints.

As shown in Figure 2, there is a nice symmetry between caller side and execution joinpoints. While execution joinpoints own an entry and an exit operation, caller side joinpoints are owned by an entry State and an exit State. The entry and exit relationships correspond to the location where before, after and around advice elements are woven. Most types of joinpoints are covered by the metamodel, while it does not capture elements that are irrelevant to aspect weaving. In [13], Tkatchenko proposes a Joinpoint metamodel, where all elements that include a declaration signature are considered joinpoints. Yet, this metamodel captures elements that are irrelevant to aspect weaving, while it does not cover method return or method execution joinpoints.

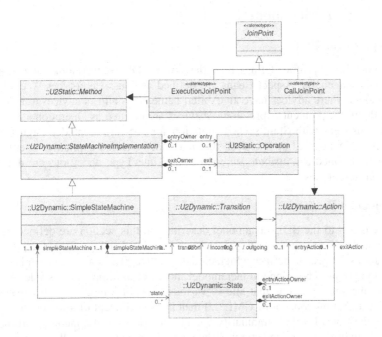

Fig. 2. The Joinpoint Profile

Figure 3 depicts some of the joinpoints that are captured by the caller side joinpoint stereotype. Aside from the usual types of joinpoints such as method call (ExpressionAction), exception throwing (ThrowAction), and the return joinpoint (ReturnAction) it also supports new types of joinpoints that are useful for embedded and distributed software development, such as Set Timer, Reset Timer, Send Signal and Receive Signal.

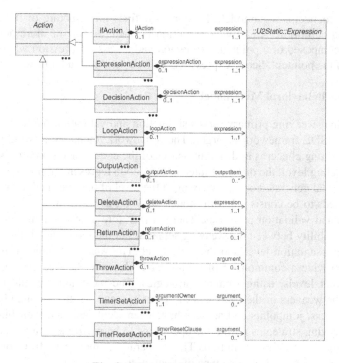

Fig. 3. Caller side joinpoint types

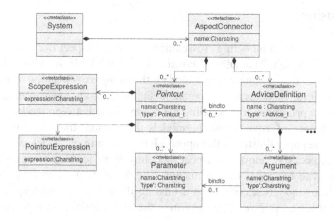

Fig. 4. The Connector Metamodel

4.3 Connector Metamodel

The connector is used in the first phase of the weaving process, to identify all active joinpoints in the core model, and the advices of the aspect bean. The connector also defines the binding between advice arguments and pointcut parameters. It captures context passing between the core model elements and the aspect bean model elements. The connector metamodel of Figure 4 defines the structure of the aspect-to-core binding definition. An Advice definition is bound to one or more pointcuts. A pointcut is composed of a pointcut expression and a scope expression which narrows the scope of the pointcut. Scope expressions include 'within' and 'cflow' expressions.

4.3 Weaver Behavioral Metamodel

SDL statechart weaving primary serves simulation and validation purposes. The goal of the AspectSDL framework is larger. The framework intends to provide pluggability of crosscutting concerns at different phases of the code generation process, including the modeling level, the different intermediary code representation levels and at the level of the final generated code. Weaving at the level of the intermediary code representation needs to be consistent with model weaving, as to not affect the simulation, verification and validation processes. There is therefore a need for mechanisms that provide traceability between the weaving semantics at the model level, the intermediary code representation level and the code level. The weaver behavioral metamodel intends to provide a common set of primitives to describe the weaving semantics at those different levels, using weaving strategies. The metamodel would enable the actions of the weavers of the framework to be consistent. At the second phase of the weaving process, joinpoints and advices have been identified, and their bindings are defined. Weaving strategies define the operations to be performed on the core model to implement the binding definition. These operations may vary from one type of joinpoint to another and from one type of diagram to another.

5 Conclusions

We distinguish between modeling crosscutting behavior (Aspect Beans) and modeling the aspect composition. The authors' position is that the UML is suited for modeling aspect beans, but that it cannot accommodate the complex semantics of the weaving process. Therefore, we dedicate a separate metamodel for an aspect connector, whose role is to define primitives for modeling the composition between models that encapsulate the behavior of aspects and the models that capture the core concerns of the application. The paper illustrates this approach by presenting a model weaver for SDL statecharts. AspectSDL adopts an aspect modeling approach that recognizes weaving as a specific type of model transformation. The AspectSDL composes core models and aspect bean models according to a binding definition (connector) and weaving strategy definitions. Lightweight extension to the SDL profile are proposed, a connector metamodel is presented and a weaver behavioral metamodel is discussed.

Acknowledgements

This work is partially supported by CISE NSF grant No. 0137743, and performed at Motorola Labs.

References

1. ITU, Z. 100: Specification and Description Language (SDL), ITU-T, Geneva (2000)
2. ETSI: UML Profile for Communicating Systems, DTR/MTS-00085 (2004)
3. ITU, Z.120: Message Sequence Charts (MSC), ITU-T, Geneva (2000)
4. Kiczales, G., *et Al.*: Aspect-Oriented Programming. Proceedings of the European Conference on Object-Oriented Programming, Springer-Verlag (1997)
5. OMG: Model-Driven Architecture homepage http://www.omg.org/mda/ (2000)
6. Pawlak, R., *et Al.*: A UML Notation for Aspect-Oriented Software Design. 1st International Workshop on Aspect Oriented Modeling at the 1st International Conference on Aspect-Oriented Software Development, Enschede, The Netherlands (2002)
7. Aldawud, O., Elrad, T., Bader, A.: A UML Profile for Aspect- Oriented Software Design. 3rd International Workshop on Aspect Oriented Modeling at the 2nd International Conference on Aspect- Oriented Software Development, Boston, USA (2003)
8. Stein, D., Hanenberg, S., Unland, R.: A UML-Based Aspect-Oriented Design Notation for AspectJ. Proceedings of the 1st international conference on Aspect-Oriented Software Development, Enschede, The Netherlands (2002)
9. Kandé, M..M., Kienzle, J.,Strohmeier, A.: From AOP to UML , A Bottom-Up Approach, Aspect-Oriented Modeling with UML workshop at the 1st International Conference on Aspect-Oriented Software Development, Enschede, The Netherlands (2002)
10. Han, Y., Kniesel G., Cremers A.: Towards Visual AspectJ by a Meta Model and Modeling Notation, 6th International Workshop on Aspect-Oriented Modeling at the 4th International Conference on Aspect-Oriented Software Development, Chicago, USA (2004)
11. Lions, J.M., Simoneau, D., Pilette, G., Moussa, I.: Extending OpenTool/UML Using Metamodeling : An aspect-oriented programming case study, 2nd International Workshop on Aspect Oriented Modeling, UML 2002, Dresden, Germany (2002)
12. Gray, J.: Aspect-Oriented Domain-Specific Modeling: A Generative Approach Using a Meta-weaver Framework, Ph.D. Dissertation, Department of Electrical Engineering and Computer Science, Vanderbilt University, Nashville (2002)
13. Tkatchenko, M., Kiczales, G.: Uniform Support for Modeling Crosscutting Structure, 6th International Workshop on Aspect-Oriented Modeling at the 4th International Conference on Aspect-Oriented Software Development, Chicago, USA (2004)
14. Clarke, S., Baniassad, E.: Aspect-Oriented Analysis and Design. The Theme Approach Addison-Wesley, Object Technology Series, ISBN: 0-321-24674-8 (2005)
15. Reddy, R., France, R., Georg, G.: An Aspect-Oriented Modeling Approach to Analyzing Dependability Features, 6th Workshop on Aspect-Oriented Modeling at the 4th International Conference on Aspect-Oriented Software Development, Chicago, USA (2002)
16. Telelogic: TAU G2 homepage, http://www.telelogic.com/products/tau/index.cfm (2005)

Towards a Generic Aspect Oriented Design Process

Andrew Jackson and Siobhán Clarke

Distributed Systems Group, Trinity College Dublin, Dublin 2, Ireland
{Andrew.Jackson, Siobhán.Clarke}@cs.tcd.ie

Abstract. Aspect oriented design (AOD) research is fragmented. Barriers to AOD adoption are, in part, due to this fragmentation. Individually, many approaches provide elegant solutions to subsets of particular key issues related to AOD. Collectively, a significant set of these issues are addressed. We propose integrating existing AOD approaches through a generic AOD process. It is our intuition that such integration will consistently address the issues relevant to AOD.

1 Introduction

There have been many approaches to Aspect Oriented Design (AOD). Each approach attempts to capture and address significant issues relating to crosscutting in design. We have surveyed twenty-two AOD approaches [9] and have found that many approaches to AOD are language focused - either ignoring or assuming an implicit complementary AOD process. We have identified several key issues a designer may face during the AO design process. These include: How to identity and classify concerns for design, How to test concern designs, how to reuse concern designs, how to design concern modules, how to design composition specifications, and how to refine AO designs. The Theme [1] process and the Use Case driven (AOSDUC) [10] process provide the most complete and explicit treatments of the AOD issues. As such, these approaches have heavily influenced our approach. Other approaches that have significantly impacted our approach include: State charts and UML Profiles (SUP) [3], Aspect-Oriented Design Modeling (AODM) [13], Aspect-Oriented Architecture Modeling (AAM) [4], UML for Aspects (UFA) [8], Architectural Views of Aspects (AVA) [11], Aspect Modeling Language (AML) [6], Aspect Oriented Component Engineering (AOCE) [7] and CAM/DAOP [5]. Many of these approaches are focused on AOD language support but implicitly describe processes to deal with specific subsets of AOD issues. Individually, these approaches provide elegant solutions to subsets of particular key issues which relate to AOD. Collectively, a significant set of these issues are addressed by these approaches. To address all of these issues, we propose an integration of existing AOD approaches through a generic AOD process. It is our intuition that such integration will address the issues relevant to AOD. In Section 2, we present a generic AOD process model and possible configurations of process instantiations. In Section 3, we provide a detailed description of the AOD process activities. For each activity, we also describe related AOD approaches that are candidates for integration. In Section 4, we present a summary and our future work.

J.-M. Bruel (Ed.): MoDELS 2005 Workshops, LNCS 3844, pp. 110–119, 2006.

2 AOD Process

As acceptance of the AO paradigm is grows, there seems to be a growing consensus that existing research should now be integrated. Our goal is to remove the barriers to AOD adoption through provision of a generic AOD process. We anticipate that doing so will make the adoption of AOD a significantly easier task. Our initial generic AOD process model is presented in Figure 1. The process model contains seven distinct design activities, which can be engaged in flexible a sequence. Each of the activities in the AOD process deals with particular AOD related issues. Each activity is described in detail in Section 3.

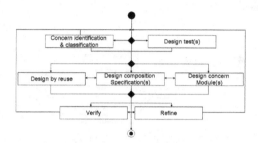

Fig. 1. Generic AOD Process

2.1 Process Configurations

Here we describe the configurable properties of the generic AOD process.

2.1.1 Configuring Activities Sequences
Activity sequences are highly configurable in this process. A significant example of this flexibility is at the start of the process. The process can begin by engaging the concern identification and classification, design test(s), design by reuse, design composition specification(s) or design concern module(s) activities. The designer can choose the activities and the sequence in which they need to be engaged to meet the designer's needs. The designer can select and configure the sequence of activities that they deem appropriate for specific contexts. Although the process is flexible, it does have some constraints. A significant constraint in any instantiation of the process is that one of the core activities (reuse by design, design composition specification and design concern module) must be executed.

2.1.2 Degrees of Refinement
The AOD process can be executed once or recursively. The refinement activity of the design process indicates that the process may be executed recursively. Employing a horizontal layered design process is a concept that has recently been popularized through MDA[1]. This recursive approach to AO design has been investigated in the CAM/DAOP design process [5]. Other approaches, when integrated, support staged

---

[1] MDA http://www.omg.org/mda/

design. UFA [8] and AML [6], the AspectJ refinement of UFA, is a good example of a staged design process model created from approach integration. Figure 2 depicts a model of refinement. This model can be extended or constrained as appropriate. It begins with an initial design process that creates a high level design or analysis model. This is then refined into a middle level design. This is a complete design but it remains platform independent. Low level design is a platform specific refinement of the middle level design. Following such a model of refinement allows design decisions to be encapsulated. At the analysis level, decisions relating to concern identification, concern relationship classification and assigning responsibilities to concerns can be defined. At the middle level, the decisions relating to platform independent designs can be taken. At the low level, decisions relating to the realisation of specific platforms can be made.

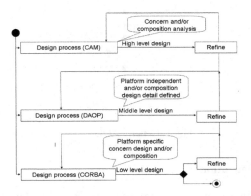

Fig. 2. Degrees of Refinement

By encapsulating the specific decisions in a refinement model, the designer can focus on the decisions are appropriate to their context. For example, and as illustrated in Figure 2, the CAM/DAOP [5] approach separates the design decisions into three stages. At a high level, there are decisions made to define "the basic entities and the structure of the system from an architectural point of view". These decisions are based on a computational model, which "focuses on the functional decomposition of the system into objects which interact at interfaces, exchanging messages and signals that invoke operations and deliver service responses, but without detailing the system precise architecture, or any of its implementation details". The product of this is a component aspect model (CAM). This model is a description of the components and aspects of an application. At the middle level, decisions are made to define how "components and aspects are weaved, and how the abstract entities of the CAM model can be represented from the computational and engineering viewpoints". The result of these decisions is a DAOP model, which is a specialisation of the CAM model. At the low level, decisions are taken to describe the DAOP model "from a technology viewpoint". In this model decisions on how "to implement the DAOP platform using Java/RMI, CORBA, EJB, or .NET, using their corresponding services and mechanisms" are taken.

2.1.3 Iteration Strategies

Refinement reduces complexity through partitioning the design process along a horizontal dimension. The generic AO design process can also be partitioned vertically through applying iterative design. There are two high level elements to be designed in a generic AO design process – a concern and a composition specification. It is our initial intuition that it makes sense for these elements to be addressed through separate iterations of the design process.

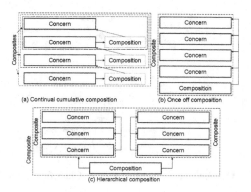

Fig. 3. Iterative strategies

Figure 3 depicts three possible strategies for applying the generic AO process in an iterative process. The boxes with solid lines represent iterations and boxes with broken lines represent composite concerns (the product of composition). Diagram (a) - *Continual cumulative composition*, depicts the process when applied in a more traditional manner. Composition specifications are designed at the end of iterations. In this strategy there is a cumulatively growing composite concern to which concerns developed per-iteration are applied. Diagram (b) - *Once off composition*, shows that concerns and the composition specification can be developed in separate iterations. In this strategy concerns can be designed first, a composition specification may then be devised to specify how the concerns are to be integrated into a composite concern. The alternative is to firstly design composition specification. This would describe the concerns that need to be integrated. Diagram (c) - *Hierarchical composition*, follows a hierarchical iteration pattern. In this strategy composites are created through iterative design, the composition specifications for the integration of composites are then designed in a separated iteration.

3 AOD Activities and Related Work

The generic AOD process represents an integration of several related works. In this section we discuss the related work in relation to the activities of the AOD process. The verification activity is not addressed here. The primary purpose of this activity is to facilitate the integration of formal methods in design.

3.1 Concern Identification and Classification

Identifying and classifying concerns is supported by and several AOD approaches. Theme [1] and AOCE [7] are examples of approaches that provide support for concern identification and classification. The SUP [3] approach identifies crosscutting concerns building an Object Oriented (OO) model and extracting crosscutting concerns from that model.

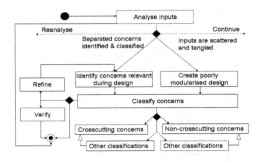

Fig. 4. Concern Identification & Classification

Our process integrates these approaches. In Figure 4, the process begins with input analysis. After analysis, the process may be ignored if concerns are fully identified and classified. The input can be rejected and returned for analysis (in complementary AO requirements engineering and AO architecture design processes [9]). Imperfect input (such as OO input in SUP) can be handled by creating models of imperfect input and identifying crosscutting concerns therein. Also concern relevant to the design process can be identified, some concerns emerge during design that are not present in requirements. Once concerns are identified, they must be classified. Classification defines the concern type through describing the relationships between the identified concerns. We define two types of concern classification – crosscutting and non-crosscutting. We recognise that these may be extended.

3.2 Design Tests

There are number of possibilities emerging to provide AO testing support [14]. It is our belief that the ability to test designs will significantly reduce defects in design and resulting implementation. Work is underway to introduce executable design tests [2]. Currently there are very few means of testing AO design. The application of use case specifications to test concern designs is described in [10]. The comparison of composite (basic, sub, alternative and/or extensional) flows against concern design is the basis for the test. These composite flows can be specified as concern test design modules.

The process of testing AO designs is presented in Figure 5. Designing AO tests can include reusing existing tests (concern modules and composition specifications), creating tests for concern modules and designing tests for composition specifications or composing concern module tests to test composition specifications. The process allows the designer to choose the order in which deign testing activities are engaged. Tests can also be verified and refined where appropriate.

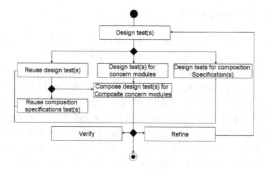

Fig. 5. Design Tests

3.3 Design by Reuse

Particular approaches to AOD support design reuse. AAM [4], for example, supports reuse of crosscutting design modules. AAM describes reusable crosscutting design modules as "context-free aspects". These are reused by applying system design elements or context to the context-free aspect. UFA [8] follows a similar pattern, supporting reuse of crosscutting design modules or "abstract aspects" through a "connector" or a set of design elements from the concern or composite concerns to which the "abstract aspect" should be applied. Design by reuse is illustrated in Figure 6. This process involves searching a design repository for an appropriate design, deciding if the design can be reused, and then applying the reused element in a system design context. When design elements cannot be reused, they need to be designed from scratch. This process also allows concern and composition specification designs that are candidates for reuse to be "de-contextualized" or abstracted and added to a design repository.

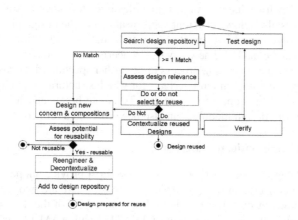

Fig. 6. Design by Reuse

3.4 Concern Module Design

Twenty-one of the twenty-two AOD approaches that we have surveyed [9] provide support for designing crosscutting concerns separately in UML AOD languages. Some approaches also support the modularization of non-crosscutting concerns. Significant examples of this include - AOSDUC [10], AVA [11] and Theme [1]. Approaches such as AODM [13] and AAM [4] provide means for representing crosscutting concerns within separate design modules. We have not restricted the process to provide support for the separate design of crosscutting concerns. This process facilitates the design of both crosscutting and non-crosscutting concerns as first-class entities. Because of the overwhelming support for UML in the AOD community [9], we are basing our concern module design on a UML design process.

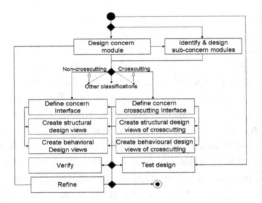

Fig. 7. Concern Module Design

Figure 7 illustrates the process of designing a concern module. The design process includes the ability to refine the concern modules into sub-concerns (taken from AVA [11]). The process also allows different specialisations of the design process. There are three choices non-crosscutting, crosscutting and other classifications. Other process specialisations can be made for new types of concern that may emerge. This allows the non-crosscutting and crosscutting process to be further specialised. In cases the process mandates the creation of an initial interface, for which structural and behavioural views (UML diagrams) of the concern are created. Tests can be created before or after the design. The concern design modules can also be verified and refined.

3.5 Composition Specification Design

All of the AOD approaches that we have surveyed [9] provide support for representing crosscutting concerns in separate design modules. There are two means of designing a crosscutting concern. The first is to design it as part of the design of a concern module. Examples of this include the AODM [13] and AAM [4] approaches. The second is to design the concern specification separately. The best examples of this include UFA [8] & AML [6], Theme [1] and AVA [11]. We support the second approach as it subsumes the latter ensuring approach generality.

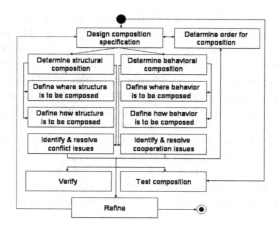

Fig. 8. Design Concern Specification

As depicted in Figure 8, this process is divided into two sub-processes. One sub-process deals with structural composition and the other deals with behavioural composition. The sub-processes in both cases are concerned with identifying where composition is required and also how composition should occur. This process also deals with the identification and resolution of conflict issues between concerns that arise during the composition. Ordering of composition is an issue that is highlighted in the AVA [11] approach. Determining the order of composition is an activity in this process. Composition specification can be designed in a test driven manner - tests can be designed after design and applied as a means to ensure design correctness.

3.6 Refinement

As described in Section 2.3.3, the design process has been engineered, such that, the products created during the process, can be used as input to the design process for refinement. We refer to this type of refinement as vertical refinement. We also recognize horizontal refinement in this process. Each activity process defined in this contains a refinement activity. Horizontal refinement is a process of improvement or fine-tuning. When designing concerns, it can be difficult to know whether the designed solution is good or not. Software metrics are used to measure properties of software, such as maintainability and/or reusability. AO metrics have been proposed [12]. These metrics have been based on the AspectJ model of AO and target implementation. Some of these metrics may be applied to particular instantiations of the AOD process that utilize AspectJ like models. However, it is difficult to apply metrics which target AspectJ models to design approaches such as Theme [1] or UFA [8] which follow different models of AO.

4   Summary and Future Work

The contribution of a generic AOD process is a consistent means for addressing all of the issues related to AOD in an extensible, customizable and independent generic process, which is easy to adopt. Our generic process is based on the approaches surveyed in [9]. In Section 2, we describe the proposed generic AOD process and illustrate how it can be flexibly configured for adoption in existing processes. In Section 3, we illustrate how each issue related to AOD is addressed in the generic AOD process that we have presented. We also describe examples of related work that may be integrated to support each process activity. In our future work, we will investigate the integration of existing research into a complete and workable generic AOD process. As there is not much literature that describes a generic AOD processes in use, we intend to evaluate and validate the generic AOD process by applying it in several case studies. An example of a case study to which we are applying different configurations of the AOD process is an Auction System[2], previously used in publications which evaluate the Fondue Method. In parallel with the AOD process, we are working on creating a common AOD language to support all of the activities in this process.

Acknowledgements

This work is supported by European Commission grant IST-2-004349: European Network of Excellence on Aspect-Oriented Software Development (AOSD-Europe), 2004-2008.

References

[1] Clarke S., Baniassad E., Aspect-Oriented Analysis amd Design the Theme Approach, ISBN: 0321246748 Addison-Wesley, 2005.

[2] Dinh-Trong T. T., A Systematic Approach to Testing UML Design Models, Doctoral Symposium, Unified Modeling Language (UML), October 10-15, 2004, Lisbon, Portugal.

[3] Elrad, T., Aldawud, O., Bader, A., Aspect-Oriented Modeling: Bridging the Gap between Implementation and Design, Generative Programming and Component Engineering Conference (GPCE), October 6-8, Pittsburgh, PA, USA, 2002.

[4] France R., Ray I., Georg G., Ghosh S., An Aspect-Oriented Approach to Early Design Modeling, IEE Proceedings - Software, vol 151, number 4, August, 2004.

[5] Fuentes L., Pinto M., Vallecillo A., How MDA Can Help Designing Component- and Aspect-based Applications, Enterprise Distributed Object Computing Conference (EDOC), September 16-19, Brisbane, Australia, 2003.

[6] Groher I., Baumgarth T., Aspect-Orientation from Design to Code, Aspect-Oriented Requirements Engineering and Architecture Design workshop, Aspect-Oriented Software Development (AOSD), March 22-26, Lancaster, UK, 2004.

[7] Grundy, J.C., Multi-perspective specification, design and implementation of components using aspects, International Journal of Software Engineering and Knowledge Engineering, Vol. 10, No. 6, December 2000.

[8] Herrmann S., Composable Designs with UFA,Workshop: Aspect-oriented Modelling, 1st International Conference on Aspect-Oriented Software Development (AOSD), University of Twente Enschede, The Netherlands, April 22-26, 2002.

[9] Chitchyan R., Rashid A., Sawyer P., Garcia A., Alarcon M.P, Bakker J., Tekinerdogan B., Jackson A., Clarke S., Survey of Aspect-Oriented Analysis and Design Approaches, http://www.aosd-europe.net/documents/analys.pdf, 2005.

---

[2] http://lgl.epfl.ch/research/fondue/case-studies/auction/

[10] Jacobson I., Ng P., Aspect-Oriented Software Development with Use Cases, ISBN: 0321268881, Addison Wesley Professional, 2005.

[11] Katara M., Katz S., Architectural Views of Aspects, Aspect-Oriented Software Development (AOSD), March 17 - 21, Boston, Massachusetts, USA, 2003.

[12] Sant'Anna C., Garcia A., Chavez C., Lucena C., Staa A. V., On the Reuse and Maintenance of Aspect-Oriented Software: An Assessment Framework XVII Brazilian Symposium on Software Engineering, Manaus, Brazil, October 2003.

[13] Stein D., Hanenberg S., Unland R., Designing Aspect-Oriented Crosscutting in UML, Workshop: Aspect-oriented Modelling, 1 Aspect-Oriented Software Development (AOSD), April 22-26, University of Twente, Enschede, The Netherlands, 2002.

[14] Workshop on Testing Aspect-Oriented Programs, http://www.cs.colostate.edu/~rta/wtaop/ Chicago, USA, March 14-18, 2005

Model Transformations in Practice Workshop

Jean Bézivin, Bernhard Rumpe, Andy Schürr, and Laurence Tratt

University of Nantes, TU Darmstadt, TU Braunschweig, King's College London
http://sosym.dcs.kcl.ac.uk/events/mtip/

1 Background

Model Transformations in Practice (MTiP) 2005 was a workshop which provided a forum for the model transformation community to discuss practical model transformation issues. Although many different model transformation approaches have been proposed and explored in recent years, there has been little work on comparing and contrasting various approaches. Without such comparisons, it is hard to assess new model transformation approaches such as the upcoming OMG MOF/QVT recommendation, or to discern sensible future paths for the area. Our aims with the workshop were to create a forum that would help lead to an increased understanding of the relative merits of different model transformation techniques and approaches. A more advanced understanding of such merits is of considerable benefit to both the model transformation and wider modelling communities.

2 Workshop Format

In order to achieve the workshops' aims, we took an unusual approach in the Call for Papers (CfP). We decided that the workshop would focus on underlying model transformations mechanisms, concepts, languages and tools, development environments, libraries, practises and patterns, verification and optimization techniques, traceability and composeability issues, applicability scope, deployment techniques, and so on. In order to achieve aim, we detailed a specific mandatory example that all submissions had to tackle (detailed in section 5), in order that it would be easier to compare and contrast submissions. Authors were asked to take a particular model transformation approach and structure their submission as follows:

1. An overview of the authors' chosen model transformation approach.
2. The required aspects of the mandatory model transformation example.
3. Optionally, additional aspects of the mandatory model transformation example.
4. Optionally, extra model transformations chosen by the authors from a list of alternatives.
5. Results and discussion.

Authors were asked to consider and discuss, where relevant, the following issues with regard to their chosen approach:

J.-M. Bruel (Ed.): MoDELS 2005 Workshops, LNCS 3844, pp. 120–127, 2006.

- Composition of transformations.
- Robustness and error handling,
- Debugging support.
- Flexibility, overall usability and power of the chosen approach.
- Whether the approach can express bidirectional and / or incremental (sometimes known as change propagating) transformations.
- Technical aspects such as the ability to deal with model exchange formats, modelling tool APIs, and layout updates.

3   Accepted Submissions

Because of the unusual demands of our CfP, we were pleasantly surprised at both the quantity and quality of submissions. In the end we accepted the following eight submissions:

Model Transformation by Graph Transformation: A Comparative Study
Gabriele Taentzer, Karsten Ehrig, Esther Guerra, Juan de Lara, Laszlo Lengyel, Tihamer Levendovszky, Ulrike Prange, Daniel Varro, Szilvia Varro-Gyapay, Technische Universität Berlin, Universidad Carlos III de Madrid, Universidad Autonoma de Madrid, Budapest University of Technology and Economics

Model Transformation with Triple Graph Grammars
Alexander Königs, University of Technology Darmstadt

Kent Model Transformation Language
D.H.Akehurst, W.G.Howells, K.D.McDonald-Maier, University of Kent

Practical Declarative Model Transformation With Tefkat
Michael Lawley, Jim Steel, DSTC, University of Rennes

Transforming Models with ATL
Frédéric Jouault, Ivan Kurtev, INRIA

Model Transformation Approach Based on MOLA
Audris Kalnins, Edgars Celms, Agris Sostaks, University of Latvia

On Executable Meta-Languages applied to Model Transformations
Pierre-Alain Muller, Franck Fleurey, Didier Vojtisek, Zoé Drey, Damien Pollet, Frédéric Fondement, Philippe Studer, Jean-Marc Jézéquel, IRISA/INRIA, France, EPFL/IC/UP-LGL, INJ, Switzerland, Université de Haute-Alsace

Model Transformation in Practice Using the BOC Model Transformer
Marion Murzek, Gerti Kappel, Gerhard Kramler, Vienna University of Technology

With so many high quality submissions to pick from, choosing only two for inclusion in these proceedings was an inevitably difficult task. However we believe that the two papers that the programme committee voted to select are indicative of the overall high quality of submissions.

4   Programme Committee

The workshop had a programme committee which reflected many of the different parts of the model transformation community. The programme committee performed sterling work in reviewing the CfP, voting on papers to accept and so on. The programme committee consists of:

Wim Bast	Compuware, Netherlands
Tony Clark	Xactium, UK
Krzysztof Czarnecki	University of Waterloo, Canada
Gregor Engels	University of Paderborn, Germany
Kerry Raymond	DSTC, Australia
Robert France	Colorado State University, USA
Jens Jahnke	University of Victoria, Canada
Jean-Marc Jézéquel	University of Rennes, INRIA, France
Stuart Kent	Microsoft, UK
Gabor Karsai	Vanderbilt University, Tennessee, USA
Gregor Kiczales	University of British Columbia, Canada
Reiko Heckel	University of Leicester, UK
Dániel Varró	Budapest University of Technology and Economics, Hungary
R. Venkatesh	Tata Consultancy Services, India
Albert Zündorf	University of Kassel, Germany

5   Mandatory Example

All submissions were asked to tackle the example as outlined in this section. The example itself is a slight variation on the well known 'class to RDBMS' transformation. This example was chosen because, despite its relative simplicity, it tends to exercise a broad class of model transformation features. Perhaps inevitably after the release of this example, prospective authors found small ambiguities, missing details, and even the odd small mistake in the specification. We kept the workshop website up to date with 'errata' on the CfP, and informally suggested to authors that in the event of doubt on their part, they were welcome to choose a particular path provided they documented it appropriately.

The rest of this section contains the model transformation specification as it was defined in the CfP which the reader will find useful when reading the two papers selected from the MTiP workshop.

5.1   Meta-models

The meta-model for class models is shown in figure 1. The following OCL constraint is also part of the model (the `allAttributes` operation returns a class's local and inherited attributes):

```
context Class inv:
    allAttributes()->size > 0 and
    allAttributes()->exists(attr | attr.is_primary = true)
```

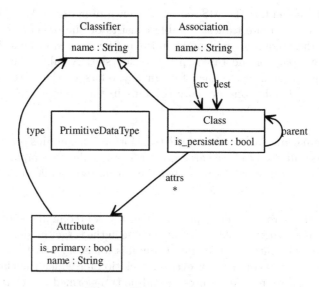

Fig. 1. Class meta-model

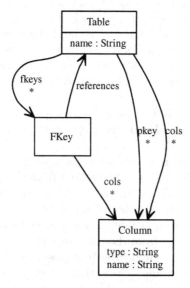

Fig. 2. RDBMS meta-model

A model consists of classes and directed associations. A class consists, possibly via inheritance, of one or more attributes, at least one of which must be marked as constituting the classes' primary key. An attribute type is either that of another user class, or of a primitive data type (e.g. String, Int). Associations are considered to have a 1 multiplicity on their destination. Submissions may assume the presence of standard data-types as instances of the `PrimitiveDataType` class.

The meta-model for RDBMS models is shown in figure 2. An RDBMS model consists of one or more tables. A table consists of one or more columns. One or more of these columns will be included in the pkey slot, denoting that the column forms part of the tables primary key slot. A table may also contain zero or more foreign keys. Each foreign key refers to the particular table it identifies, and denotes one or more columns in the table as being part of the foreign key.

Transformation. This version of the transformation contains several subtleties that authors will need to be aware of. In order to facilitate comparisons between approaches, authors should ensure that they accurately implement the transformation.

1. Classes that are marked as persistent in the source model should be transformed into a single table of the same name in the target model. The resultant table should contain one or more columns for every attribute in the class, and one or more columns for every association for which the class is marked as being the source. Attributes should be transformed as per rules 3 – 5.
2. Classes that are marked as non-persistent should not be transformed at the top level. For each attribute whose type is a non-persistent class, or for each association whose dst is such a class, each of the classes' attributes should be transformed as per rule 3. The columns should be named *name_transformed attr* where *name* is the name of the attribute or association in question, and **transformed attr** is a transformed attribute, the two being separated by an underscore character. The columns will be placed in tables created from persistent classes.
3. Attributes whose type is a primitive data type (e.g. String, Int) should be transformed to a single column whose type is the same as the primitive data type.
4. Attributes whose type is a persistent class should be transformed to one or more columns, which should be created from the persistent classes' primary key attributes. The columns should be named *name_transformed attr* where *name* is the attributes' name. The resultant columns should be marked as constituting a foreign key; the FKey element created should refer to the table created from the persistent class.
5. Attributes whose type is a non-persistent class should be transformed to one or more columns, as per rule 2. Note that the primary keys and foreign keys of the translated non-persistent class need to be merged in appropriately, taking into consideration that the translated non-persistent class may contain primary and foreign keys from an arbitrary number of other translated classes.
6. When transforming a class, all attributes of its parent classes (which must be recursively calculated), and all associations which have such classes as a src, should be considered. Attributes in subclasses with the same name as an attribute in a parent class are considered to override the parent attribute.

7. In inheritance hierarchies, only the top-most parent class should be converted into a table; the resultant table should however contain the merged columns from all of its subclasses.

Notes on the transformation:

- Rules 2, 4 and 5 are recursive – the 'drilling down' into attributes' types can occur to an arbitrary level.
- Associations do not directly transform into elements; however each association which has a particular class as a `src` must be considered when transforming that class into a table and / or columns.
- When merging the transformation of a non-persistent class, care must be taken to handle the primary and foreign keys of the transformed class appropriately.
- Foreign keys, primary keys and so on should point to the correct model elements – transformations which create duplicate elements with the same names are not considered to provide an adequate solution.

Authors are encouraged to take particular note of the following points when they create their transformations:

- The recursive nature of the drilling down.
- The creation of foreign keys.
- Associations.

Example Execution. Figures 3 and 4 show the example input and output to the class to RDBMS transformation example.

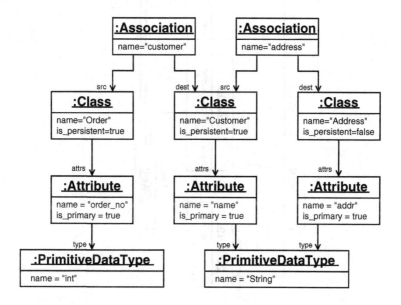

Fig. 3. Example input

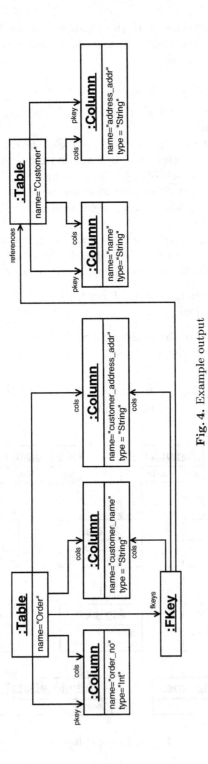

Fig. 4. Example output

6   Workshop Outcomes

The workshop itself was a lively, and well attended affair. We devoted a substantial portion of the day to discussion. Much of this related to the model transformation approaches presented, and their relation to other approaches not presented (e.g. the forthcoming QVT standard). In no particular order, some of the points raised during discussion were as follows:

- Current model transformation approaches lack scalability in two aspects: their efficiency, and their code organization. The latter would be aided by features such as modularity.
- The relationship of model transformations to normal compilers could fruitfully be explored.
- A lack of formalization of model transformation approaches, and consequent inability to reason reliably about model transformations.
- Are bidirectional transformations practical and / or desirable?
- The importance of tracing information for tool users to track their transformations.
- Difficulties in making diagrammatic syntaxes for all aspects of model transformations.
- A need for more sophisticated taxonomies of model transformation systems.
- A need to define the relationship of semantics preserving model transformations to the concept of refinement.

7   And Finally...

We would like to thank the authors of papers, the programme committee, and all those who turned up and participated on the day itself for making the MTiP workshop a success. Due to the interest in this subject, we anticipate holding another workshop on this subject to which you are all cordially invited!

Transforming Models with ATL*

Frédéric Jouault and Ivan Kurtev

ATLAS Group (INRIA & LINA, University of Nantes)
{frederic.jouault, ivan.kurtev}@univ-nantes.fr

Abstract. This paper presents ATL (ATLAS Transformation Language): a hybrid model transformation language that allows both declarative and imperative constructs to be used in transformation definitions. The paper describes the language syntax and semantics by using examples. ATL is supported by a set of development tools such as an editor, a compiler, a virtual machine, and a debugger. A case study shows the applicability of the language constructs. Alternative ways for implementing the case study are outlined. In addition to the current features, the planned future ATL features are briefly discussed.

1 Introduction

Model transformations play an important role in Model Driven Engineering (MDE) approach. It is expected that writing model transformation definitions will become a common task in software development. Software engineers should be supported in performing this task by mature tools and techniques in the same way as they are supported now by IDEs, compilers, and debuggers in their everyday work.

One direction for providing such a support is to develop domain-specific languages designed to solve common model transformation tasks. Indeed, this is the approach that has been taken recently by the research community and software industry. As a result a number of transformation languages have been proposed. We observe that, even though the problem domain of these languages is common, they still differ in the employed programming paradigm. Current model transformation languages usually expose a synthesis of paradigms already developed for programming languages (declarative, functional, object-oriented, imperative, etc.). It is not clear if a single approach will prevail in the future. A deeper understanding and more experience based on real and non-trivial problems is still necessary. We believe that different approaches are suitable for different types of tasks. One class of problems may be easily solved by a declarative language, while another class is more amenable to an imperative approach.

In this paper we describe a transformation language and present how different programming styles allowed by this language may be applied to solve different types of problems. The language is named ATL (ATLAS Transformation Language) and is developed as a part of the AMMA (ATLAS Model Management Architecture) platform [2]. ATL is a hybrid language, i.e. it is a mix of declarative and imperative constructs.

---

* Work partially supported by ModelWare, IST European project 511731.

J.-M. Bruel (Ed.): MoDELS 2005 Workshops, LNCS 3844, pp. 128–138, 2006.
© Springer-Verlag Berlin Heidelberg 2006

We present the syntax and semantics of ATL informally by using examples. Space limit does not allow presenting the full ATL grammar and a detailed description of its semantics. A simple case study illustrates the usage of the language.

The paper is organized as follows. Section 2 gives an overview of the context in which ATL is used. Section 3 presents the language constructs on the base of examples. Section 4 presents a case study that shows the applicability of ATL. Section 5 describes the tool support available for ATL: the ATL virtual machine, the ATL compiler, the IDE based on Eclipse, and the debugger. Section 6 presents a brief comparison with other approaches for model transformations and outlines directions for future work. Section 7 gives conclusions.

2   General Overview of the ATL Transformation Approach

ATL is applied in a transformational pattern shown in Fig. 1. In this pattern a source model *Ma* is transformed into a target model *Mb* according to a transformation definition *mma2mmb.atl* written in the ATL language. The transformation definition is a model. The source and target models and the transformation definition conform to their metamodels *MMa*, *MMb*, and *ATL* respectively. The metamodels conform to the *MOF* metametamodel [8].

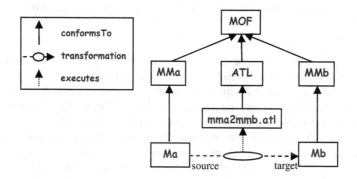

Fig. 1. Overview of ATL transformational approach

ATL is a hybrid transformation language. It contains a mixture of declarative and imperative constructs. We encourage a declarative style of specifying transformations. However, it is sometimes difficult to provide a complete declarative solution for a given transformational problem. In that case developers may resort to the imperative features of the language.

ATL transformations are unidirectional, operating on read-only source models and producing write-only target models. During the execution of a transformation the source model may be navigated but changes are not allowed. Target model cannot be navigated. A bidirectional transformation is implemented as a couple of transformations: one for each direction.

3 Presentation of ATL

In this section we present the features of the ATL language. The syntax of the language is presented based on examples (sections 3.1-3.4). Then in section 3.5 we briefly describe the execution semantics of ATL.

3.1 Overall Structure of Transformation Definitions

Transformation definitions in ATL form *modules*. A module contains a mandatory *header* section, *import* section, and a number of *helpers* and *transformation rules*.

Header section gives the name of the transformation module and declares the source and target models. Below we give an example header section:

```
module SimpleClass2SimpleRDBMS;
create OUT : SimpleRDBMS from IN : SimpleClass;
```

The header section starts with the keyword *module* followed by the name of the module. Then the source and target models are declared as variables typed by their metamodels. The keyword *create* indicates the target models. The keyword *from* indicates the source models. In our example the target model bound to the variable OUT is created from the source model IN. The source and target models conform to the metamodels *SimpleClass* and *SimpleRDBMS* respectively. In general, more than one source and target models may be enumerated in the header section.

Helpers and transformation rules are the constructs used to specify the transformation functionality. They are explained in the next two sections.

3.2 Helpers

The term *helper* comes from the OCL specification ([9], section 7.4.4, p11), which defines two kinds of helpers: *operation* and *attribute* helpers.

In ATL, a helper can only be specified on an OCL type or on a source metamodel type since target models are not navigable. *Operation* helpers define operations in the context of a model element or in the context of a module. They can have input parameters and can use recursion. *Attribute* helpers are used to associate read-only named values to source model elements. Similarly to operation helpers they have a name, a context, and a type. The difference is that they cannot have input parameters. Their values are specified by an OCL expression. Like operation helpers, attribute helpers can be recursively defined with constraints about termination and cycles.

Attribute helpers can be considered as a means to decorate source models before transformation execution. A decoration of a model element may depend on the decoration of other elements. To illustrate the syntax of attribute helpers we consider an example.

```
1. helper context SimpleClass!Class def : allAttributes :
2.    Sequence(SimpleClass!Attribute) = self.attrs->union(
3.      if not self.parent.oclIsUndefined() then
4.        self.parent.allAttributes->select(attr |
5.          not self.attrs->exists(at | at.name = attr.name))
6.      else Sequence {} endif  -- Terminating case for the recursion
7.    )->flatten();
```

The attribute helper *allAttributes* is used to determine all the attributes of a given class including the defined and the inherited attributes. It is associated to classes in the source model (indicated by the keyword *context* and the reference to the type in the source metamodel *SimpleClass!Class*) and its values are sequences of attributes (line 2). The OCL expression used to calculate value of the helper is given after the '=' symbol (lines 2-7). This is an example of a recursive helper (line 4).

3.3 Transformation Rules

Transformation rule is the basic construct in ATL used to express the transformation logic. ATL rules may be specified either in a declarative style or in an imperative style. In this section we focus on declarative rules. Section 3.4 describes the imperative features of ATL.

Matched Rules. Declarative ATL rules are called *matched rules*. A matched rule is composed of a *source pattern* and of a *target pattern*. Rule source pattern specifies a set of *source types* (coming from source metamodels and the set of collection types available in OCL) and a *guard* (an OCL Boolean expression). A source pattern is evaluated to a set of matches in source models.

The target pattern is composed of a set of *elements*. Every element specifies a *target type* (from the target metamodel) and a set of *bindings*. A binding refers to a feature of the type (i.e. an attribute, a reference or an association end) and specifies an initialization expression for the feature value. The following snippet shows a simple matched rule in ATL.

```
1. rule PersistentClass2Table{
2.    from
3.       c : SimpleClass!Class (c.is_persistent and c.parent.oclIsUndefined())
4.    to
5.       t : SimpleRDBMS!Table (name <- c.name )
6. }
```

The rule name *PersistentClass2Table* is given after the keyword *rule* (line 1). The rule source pattern specifies one variable of type *Class* (line 3). The guard (line 3) specifies that only persistent classes without superclasses will be matched.

The target pattern contains one element of type *Table* (line 5) assigned to the variable *t*. This element has one binding that specifies an expression for initializing the attribute *name* of the table. The symbol '<-' is used to delimit the feature to be initialized (left-hand side) from the initialization expression (right-hand side).

Execution Semantics of Matched Rules. Matched rules are executed over matches of their source pattern. For a given match the target elements of the specified types are created in the target model and their features are initialized using the bindings.

Executing a rule on a match additionally creates a *traceability link* in the internal structures of the transformation engine. This link relates three components: the rule, the match (i.e. source elements) and the newly created target elements.

The feature initialization uses a value resolution algorithm, called *ATL resolve algorithm*. The algorithm is applied on the values of binding expressions. If the value type is primitive, then the value is assigned to the corresponding feature. If its type is a metamodel type or a collection type there are two possibilities:

- if the value is a **target element** it is assigned to the feature;
- if the value is a **source element** it is first resolved into a target element using internal traceability links. The resolution results in an element from

the target model created from the source element by a given rule. After the resolution the target model element becomes the value of the feature;

Thanks to this algorithm, target elements can be linked together using source model navigation.

Kinds of Matched Rules. There are several kinds of matched rules differing in the way how they are triggered.

- *Standard* rules are applied once for every match that can be found in source models;
- *Lazy* rules are triggered by other rules. They are applied on a single match as many times as it is referred to by other rules, every time producing a new set of target elements;
- *Unique lazy* rules are also triggered by other rules. They are applied only once for a given match. If a unique lazy rule is triggered later on the same match the already created target elements are used;

The ATL resolution algorithm takes care of triggering lazy and unique lazy rules when a source element is referred to within an initialization expression.

Rule Inheritance. In ATL rule inheritance can be used as a code reuse mechanism and also as a mechanism for specifying polymorphic rules.

A rule (called *subrule*) may inherit from another rule (*parent* rule). A subrule matches a subset of what its parent rule matches. The source pattern types in the parent rule may be replaced by their subtypes in the subrule source pattern. The guard of a subrule forms a conjunction with the guard of the parent rule.

A subrule target pattern extends its parent target pattern using any combination of the following: by subtyping target types, by adding bindings, by replacing bindings, and by adding new target elements.

3.4 Imperative Features of ATL

The declarative style of transformation specification has a number of advantages. It is usually based on specifying relations between source and target patterns and thus tends to be closer to the way how the developers intuitively perceive a transformation. This style stresses on encoding these relations and hides the details related to selection of source elements, rule triggering and ordering, dealing with traceability, etc. Therefore, it can hide complex transformation algorithms behind a simple syntax.

However, in some cases complex source-domain or target-domain specific algorithms may be required and it may be difficult to specify a pure declarative solution for them. There are several possible approaches to this issue. We consider two of them:

- allow **native operation calls** to modules written in an arbitrary language. This solution has the drawback that it moves the control flow out of the transformation language semantics;
- offer an **imperative part** in the transformation language. In that way the control flow remains in the transformation language semantics but the developer must encode this control flow explicitly;

ATL has an imperative part based on two main constructs:

- **called rules**. A called rule is basically a procedure: it is invoked by name and may take arguments. Its implementation can be native or specified in ATL;
- **action block**. An action block is a sequence of imperative statements and can be used instead of or in a combination with a target pattern in matched or called rules. The imperative statements available in ATL are the well known constructs for specifying control flow such as conditions, loops, assignments, etc. We do not give their syntax in this paper;

If either a called rule or an action block is used in an ATL program, this program is no longer fully declarative.

3.5 Execution of Transformation Definitions

In this section we briefly sketch some aspects of the execution algorithm of ATL transformations. The execution starts by invoking an optional called rule marked as *entry point*. This rule, in turn, may invoke other called rules. Then the algorithm executes the standard matched rules (some of them may contain an action block). Rule matching and rule application are separated in two phases. In the first phase all patterns of the rules are matched against the source model(s). For every match the target elements are created. Traceability links are also created in this phase. In the second phase all the bindings for the created target elements are executed. ATL resolution algorithm and execution of lazy rules are applied if necessary.

The algorithm does not suppose any order in rule matching, target elements creation for a match, and target elements initialization. Action block (if present) must, however, be executed after having applied the declarative part of the rule.

Attribute helpers may be initialized in a pass performed before running the rest of the transformation. They may also be lazily evaluated when the helper value is read for the first time. Since the source models are read-only, the attribute helper values may be cached. Lazy evaluation and caching improve the performance.

As long as lazy rules and called rules are not used, the execution algorithm terminates and is deterministic. Although the order of execution of rules is non-deterministic, different execution orders produce the same result for a given source model. This is a consequence of the fact that source models are read-only: the execution of a rule cannot change the set of matches. In addition, target models are write-only: the initialization of a target element cannot impact the initialization of another. It is possible to have recursive helpers that do not terminate. In this case the transformation does not terminate either. Called rules use imperative constructs and the termination is not guaranteed. Lazy rules may introduce circular references to each other thus causing non-termination.

4 Case Study: Transforming Class to Relational Models

Because of the lack of space we present a rather simplified version of the case study given in the call for papers of the workshop. For the full version the reader is referred to [5]. The case study requires transformation of simple class models to relational models. The source and target metamodels are shown in Fig. 2.

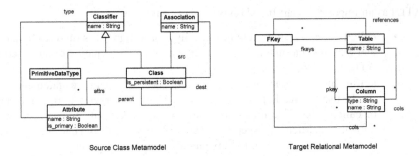

Fig. 2. Source and target metamodels

Classes in the source model have names and a number of attributes. They may be declared as persistent (attribute *is_persistent*). The type of an attribute is a classifier: either a primitive data type or a class. Attributes may be defined as primary (attribute *is_primary*). Every relational model contains a number of tables. Each table has a number of columns, some of them form a primary key. A table may be associated to zero or more foreign keys. We will focus only on two transformation rules:

- Persistent classes that are roots of an inheritance hierarchy are transformed to tables;
- Table columns are derived from the attributes of a class. Attributes of a primitive type are transformed to a single column. If the attribute is primary it results in a column from the primary key. Attributes of a non-primitive type are transformed to a set of columns derived from the type attributes. This rule is applied recursively until a set of primitive attributes is obtained (flattening);

Below we give the transformation definition for the case study.

```
1.  module SimpleClass2SimpleRDBMS;
2.  create OUT : SimpleRDBMS from IN : SimpleClass;
3.
4.  helper context SimpleClass!Class def :
5.    flattenedAttributes : Sequence(Sequence(SimpleClass!Attribute)) =
6.      self.attrs->collect(a |
7.    if a.type.oclIsKindOf(SimpleClass!PrimitiveDataType) then Sequence {a}
8.      else a.type.flattenedAttributes->collect (t | t->prepend(a))
9.    endif
10.     )->flatten();
11.
12. rule PersistentClass2Table{
13.   from
14.     c : SimpleClass!Class (c.is_persistent and c.parent.oclIsUndefined())
15.   to t : SimpleRDBMS!Table (
16.       name <- c.name,
17.       cols <- c.flattenedAttributes,
18.       pkey <- c.flattenedAttributes->select(t | t->last().is_primary)
19.   )
20. }
21.
22. unique lazy rule AttributeTrace2Column {
23.   from trace : Sequence(SimpleClass!Attribute)
24.   to col : SimpleRDBMS!Column (
25.       name <- trace->iterate(a; acc : String = '' |
26.               acc + if acc = '' then '' else '_' endif + a.name),
27.       type <- trace->last().type
28.   )
29. }
```

The transformation specification may be split into two logical parts. The first part performs decoration of the source model and the second part contains the actual transformation rules. The decoration part is based on the helper *flattenedAttributes*. In the helper every class generates a sequence of traces derived from its attributes. Every trace is a sequence of attributes and will be transformed to a column. If an attribute is of a primitive type then the trace is the attribute itself (line 7). If an attribute is of a non-primitive type then it results in a set of traces derived from the traces of its type by prepending the attribute to every trace (line 8). The traces represent the paths to the primitive attributes for a given class after application of flattening.

Transformation rules use the result of the decoration part to create the elements in the target model. Rule *PersistentClass2Table* transforms persistent root classes to tables. The interesting part of this rule is the initialization of the features of the created tables. The code in line 17 initializes the *cols* slot of the table. The value of this slot is a collection of all the columns of the table. Columns are created from traces contained in the *flattenedAttributes* helper. The value of the helper is resolved according to the ATL resolution algorithm. The resolution requires finding a rule that transforms the value of the expression into target model elements. In this case we have an implicit invocation of a transformation rule. The only suitable rule is *AttributeTrace2Column* unique lazy rule. This rule transforms traces to columns.

Furthermore the slot *pkey* contains the primary key of the table. Primary key is a subset of all the columns of the table. The columns in the key are created from the traces whose last element is a primary attribute (line 18). Similarly to the previous slot we have an implicit invocation of *AttributeTrace2Column* rule. This rule may be triggered multiple times over the same source. Since it is a unique lazy rule the invocations after the first time will return the same result.

It must be noted that this implementation relies on features of ATL that are not implemented yet. Current compiler does not fully support lazy rules, rules with multiple source elements, and source elements that are of OCL types (e.g. sequences). A working solution is available on the Eclipse GMT project site [5].

5   ATL Tools

ATL is accompanied by a set of tools that include the ATL transformation engine, the ATL integrated development environment (IDE) based on Eclipse, and the ATL debugger. ATL transformations are compiled to programs in specialized byte-code. Byte-code is executed by the ATL virtual machine. The virtual machine is specialized in handling models and provides a set of instructions for model manipulation.

The architecture of ATL execution engine is shown in Fig. 3. The virtual machine may run on top of various model management systems. To isolate the VM from their specifics an intermediate level is introduced called *Model Handler Abstraction Layer*. This layer translates the instructions of the VM for model manipulation to the instructions of a specific model handler. Model handlers are components that provide programming interface for model manipulation. Some examples are Eclipse Modeling Framework (EMF) [4] and MDR [7]. Model repository provides storage facilities for models.

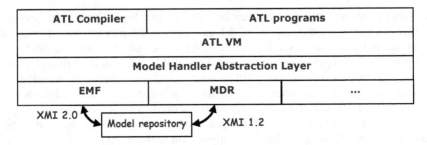

Fig. 3. The architecture of the ATL execution engine

The current ATL IDE is built on top of Eclipse platform. It includes an editor that provides view of the text with syntax highlighting, outline (view of the model corresponding to the text), and error reporting. The IDE uses the Eclipse interface to the ATL debugger.

Table 1 presents a summary of the features of the current ATL compiler and some features planned for future extensions. Stars indicate the supported features. An explanation of some of the features is given after the table.

Table 1. ATL features summary

ATL feature			Current version	Future extensions
OCL helpers	operations and attributes in the context of	metamodel types, OCL primitive and tuple types, transformation module (i.e. static)	*	
		OCL collection types		*
Code reuse	helpers libraries		*	
	rule libraries (importable modules)			*
Matched rules	standard		*	
	lazy			*
	unique lazy			*
	rule inheritance			*
	multiple source elements			*
ATL resolve algorithm	standard		*	
	with rule inheritance			*
	with lazy rules			*
Refining mode (1)			*(basic)	*(improved)
Traceability			internal	external
Imperative part	ATL called rules			*
	native called rules			*
	action blocks			*
OCL type checking			Dynamic	Static (following the specification)

(1) In ATL, source models are read-only and target models are write-only; this prohibits in-place transformations. However, such transformations are quite common in certain domains. ATL provides a mechanism to answer this need: *refining mode*. This mode can be used for transformations having the same source and target metamodel. Unmatched source elements are automatically copied into the target model, as if a default copying rule was present.

6 Related and Future Work

In the last couple of years we observed a number of proposals for model transformation languages. Some of them are a response to the QVT RFP issued by OMG [10]. As we explained in Section 2 ATL is applicable in QVT transformation scenarios where transformation definitions are specified on the base of MOF metamodels [8]. However, ATL is designed to support other transformation scenarios going beyond QVT context where source and target models are artifacts created with various technologies such as databases, XML documents, etc. In that way ATL serves the purpose of the AMMA platform as a generic data management platform. A comparison between ATL and the last QVT proposal may be found in [6].

Another class of transformation approaches relies on graph transformations theory [1][11]. ATL is not directly based on the mathematical foundation of these approaches. An interesting direction for future research is to formalize the ATL semantics in terms of graph transformation theory. The declarative part of ATL is especially suitable for this.

In [3] we present an application of ATL by showing how it can be used to check models if they satisfy given constraints. A simple specific target metamodel is defined to represent diagnostics resulting from evaluation of these constraints as a set of problems (i.e. constraint violations). OCL constraints defined on a metamodel can then be translated into ATL rules generating such problems. Diagnostic models can subsequently be transformed into any convenient representation. We plan to extend this work and show how ATL can be used to compute any kind of metrics on models.

Static type checking of OCL expressions used in ATL programs is not implemented in current compiler. It is, however, necessary to be closer to OCL 2.0 specification.

7 Conclusions

In this paper we presented ATL: a hybrid model transformation language developed as a part of the ATLAS Model Management Architecture. ATL is supported by a set of development tools built on top of the Eclipse environment: a compiler, a virtual machine, an editor, and a debugger.

The current state of ATL tools already allows solving non-trivial problems. This is demonstrated by the increasing number of implemented examples and the interest shown by the ATL user community that provides a valuable feedback.

The applicability of ATL was demonstrated in a case study. We identified alternative ways for implementing the case study. Alternatives are based of different programming styles, e.g. declarative and imperative. ATL allows both styles to be used in transformation definitions depending on the problem at hand. We encourage a declarative approach for defining transformations whenever possible. We believe that this approach allows transformation developers to focus on the essential relations among the model elements and to leave the handling of complex execution algorithms and optimizations to the ATL compiler and virtual machine.

References

[1] Agrawal A., Karsai G., Kalmar Z., Neema S., Shi F., Vizhanyo A.The Design of a Simple Language for Graph Transformations, Journal in Software and System Modeling, in review, 2005

[2] Bézivin, J., Jouault, F., and Touzet, D. An Introduction to the ATLAS Model Management Architecture. Research Report LINA, (05-01)

[3] Bézivin, J., Jouault, F. Using ATL for Checking Models. To appear in the proceedings of the GraMoT workshop of GPCE 2005 conference in Tallinn, Estonia

[4] Budinsky, F., Steinberg, D., Raymond Ellersick, R., Ed Merks, E., Brodsky, S. A., Grose, T. J. Eclipse Modeling Framework, Addison Wesley, 2003

[5] Eclipse Foundation, Generative Model Transformer Project, http://www.eclipse.org/gmt/

[6] Jouault, F., Kurtev, I. On the Architectural Alignment of ATL and QVT. Proceedings of ACM SAC 2006, Track on Model Transformations, Dijon, France, 2006, to appear

[7] Netbeans Meta Data Repository (MDR). http://mdr.netbeans.org

[8] OMG. Meta Object Facility (MOF) Specification, version 1.4, OMG Document formal/2002-04-03

[9] OMG. Object Constraint Language (OCL). OMG Document ptc/03-10-14

[10] OMG. MOF 2.0 Query/Views/Transformations RFP. OMG document ad/2002-04-10, 2002

[11] Varró, D., Varró, G., Pataricza, A. Designing the automatic transformation of visual languages. Journal of Science of Computer Programming, vol. 44, pp. 205-227, Elsevier, 2002

Practical Declarative Model Transformation with Tefkat[*]

Michael Lawley[1] and Jim Steel[2]

[1] CRC for Enterprise Distributed Systems Technology (DSTC),
Brisbane, QLD 4072, Australia
michael@lawley.id.au
[2] INRIA/Irisa, University of Rennes 1, France
jsteel@irisa.fr

Abstract. We present Tefkat, an implementation of a language designed specifically for the transformation of MOF models using patterns and rules. The language adopts a declarative paradigm, wherein users may concern themselves solely with the relations between the models rather than needing to deal explicitly with issues such as order of rule execution and pattern searching/traversal of input models. In this paper, we demonstrate the language using a provided example and highlight a number of language features used in solving the problem, a simple object-to-relational mapping.

1 Introduction

Tefkat is the result of 5 years of research and development of languages for model transformation [1, 2, 3, 4], most recently in the context of the OMG's QVT work [5]. In reaching the current point, one of the guiding principles has been that model transformation be treated as a specific problem, and that approaches treating it as a specific sub-problem of general-purpose programming will result in languages ill-suited for the specific issues that face model transformation.

Exploring different approaches to model transformations has revealed requirements, patterns and approaches in writing transformations that appeared very frequently when solving the prototypical examples of the problem space. The current approach attempts as much as possible to build these mechanisms into the language, in order that the programmer need not concern themselves with problems such as implementing algorithms for detecting input model patterns or ordering the application of their rules.

In this paper we present a summary of the language and its features, using a mandatory example to illustrate how they combine to allow users to construct model transformations.

In Section 2 we present an overview of the language. In section 3 we elaborate on some of the details of the language and how they are used in solving the mandatory example. Section 4 presents a discussion of several aspects of Tefkat's implementation,

[*] The work reported in this paper has been funded in part by the Co-operative Research Centre for Enterprise Distributed Systems Technology (DSTC) through the Australian Federal Government's CRC Programme (Department of Education, Science, and Training).

J.-M. Bruel (Ed.): MoDELS 2005 Workshops, LNCS 3844, pp. 139–150, 2006.
© Springer-Verlag Berlin Heidelberg 2006

including its concrete syntax and environment. The full text of the mandatory class-to-relational example may be found at the end of the paper following the conclusion.

2   Language Overview

The Tefkat language is declarative, logic-based, and defined in terms of a MOF meta-model. It has been specifically designed to address both the OMG's QVT RFP [6] and additional requirements identified as a result of a series of experiments with different transformation language approaches [1].

A Tefkat transformation specification effectively asserts a set of constraints that should hold over a collection of (disjoint) source and target extents (models). These constraints can:

- assert the existence of object instances in a target extent,
- assert the type of object instances in a target extent,
- assert the value(s) of object features,
- assert the relative order of values of an object's feature, and
- assert that a named relationship holds between one or more values (usually source and target object references).

A Tefkat language implementation uses these implied constraints to construct, if possible, a suitable set of target models that satisfy the constraints.

There are several aspects of the language worth noting:

- transformations do not specify a traversal order of the input models, nor an execution order for the rules – implementations must ensure that rules are executed in an order that satisfies the semantics,
- transformations are constructive – you cannot constrain an object to not exist, nor a feature to not have a particular value,
- it is not intended to describe or perform in-place model updates,
- change propagation can be supported through a model-merge process [7],
- the language is defined in terms of its abstract syntax (via a MOF metamodel). Thus, several concrete syntaxes are possible. This paper uses an SQL-inspired syntax.

Every transformation is expressed relative to three kinds of extents: one or more source extents, one or more target extents, and a single tracking extent. A transformation rule can query both source extents and the tracking extent, and can constrain/make assertions about both the target extents and the tracking extent. Thus the tracking extent is special since it is the only extent that can be both queried and constrained.

More formally, a rule, r, can be considered to have two parts: the query, src, and the constraint, tgt, and two sets of variables: those that occur in the query, $\overline{x}$, and those that occur only in the constraint, $\overline{y}$. We can then write

$$r \equiv \forall \overline{x} \; src(\overline{x}) \rightarrow \exists \overline{y} \; tgt(\overline{x}, \overline{y})$$

3 Mandatory Example

In this section we introduce various aspects of the Tefkat language via fragments of the sample solution to the mandatory example.

A transformation is a named entity with named parameters for the input and output models that participate in the transformation. Any number of metamodels may be imported by a transformation. This brings all the EClassifiers in these metamodels into consideration when class, datatype, and enum names are resolved.

```
TRANSFORMATION mtip05_class_to_relational: class -> relational

IMPORT http:///mtip05/class.ecore
IMPORT http:///mtip05/rdbms.ecore
```

The transformation specification then contains any number of class definitions, rules, pattern definitions, and template definitions.

3.1 Class Definitions

Class definitions allow for the simple specification of ECore models and are part of the concrete syntax of Tefkat, but not part of its abstract syntax. Their main use is for definition of a transformation's tracking classes. Tracking classes are part of the mechanism used to represent the named relationships between source and target elements. Valid types for the features of these classes include all the types that are in-scope as a result of IMPORT statements plus the ECore data-types corresponding to: boolean, string, int, long, float, and double.

Here we define two classes that are used for tracking relationships in the sample solution. These are discussed further in Section 3.4 below.

```
CLASS ClsToTbl {
  Class class;
  Table table;
};

CLASS AttrToCol {
  Class class;
  Attribute attr;
  Column col;
};
```

Note that for complex transformations one would normally create a separate metamodel defining these classes and import it into the transformation's namespace.

3.2 Rules

Rules are the primary action elements of the transformation. Broadly speaking, each rule consists of two constraints - source and target - that share variables. More specifically, the rule matches and then constrains a number of objects, either from the source model or from the trackings, and then *creates* (or ensures the existence of) a number of target model objects with a set of constraints.

The following rule matches all instances of Class (in the default extent, class) for which the is_persistent attribute is true. and asserts that a Table with the same name must exist and that the ClsToTbl relationship holds for the corresponding Class and Table instances.

```
RULE ClassAndTable(C, T)
  FORALL Class C {
          is_persistent: true;
          name: N;
        }
  MAKE Table T {
        name: N;
      }
  LINKING ClsToTbl WITH class = C, table = T;
```

Since the semantics of rules requires the target to always hold whenever the source holds, we can use a target of FALSE to encode constraints that input models should satisfy in order for the transformation to be valid.

For example, a non-persistent class with an association to itself would result in an infinite number of columns being created. Here is a rule whose source pattern matches this condition. Note the use of the built-in Pattern println to provide useful feedback in case the constraint is violated.

```
RULE constraint_no_reflexive_relations_on_non_persistent_classes
  FORALL Class C
  WHERE C.is_persistent = false
    AND ClassHasReference(C, C, _)
    AND println("Found a non-persistent class in relation (by
association or attribute) with itself: ", C)
  SET FALSE;
```

3.3   Pattern and Template Definitions

Pattern and template definitions are used to name and parameterise constraints that may be used in multiple rules. Pattern definitions correspond to source constraints and template definitions correspond to target constraints.

A pattern/template may be recursively defined. That is, it may directly or indirectly refer to itself. Such recursion is commonly used when matching recursive tree or graph structures like the parent reference of Class in the example.

Here are several patterns used in the solution of the mandatory example. Note the recursive nature of the pattern ClassHasAttr to *drill down* into a Class's attributes reflecting the recursive nature of the specification's rules 2, 4, and 5.

```
PATTERN ClassHasAttr(Class, Attr, Name, IsKey)
  WHERE ClassHasSimpleAttr(Class, Attr, Name, IsKey)
    OR ClassHasIncludedAttr(Class, Attr, Name, IsKey)
    OR ClassChildHasAttr(Class, Attr, Name, IsKey);
```

```
PATTERN ClassHasSimpleAttr(Class, Attr, Name, IsKey)
  FORALL Class Class {
          attrs: Attribute Attr {
            type: PrimitiveDataType _PT;
            name: Name;
            is_primary: IsKey;
          };
        };
PATTERN ClassHasIncludedAttr(Class, Attr, Name, IsKey)
  FORALL Class Class
  WHERE ClassHasReference(Class, Type, RefName)
    AND ClassHasAttr(Type, Attr, AttrName, IsKeyForType)
    AND IF Type.is_persistent = true
        THEN
          IsKeyForType = true AND
          IsKey = false
        ELSE
          IsKey = IsKeyForType
        ENDIF
    AND Name = join("_", RefName, AttrName);

PATTERN ClassChildHasAttr(Class, Attr, Name, IsKey)
  FORALL Class SubClass
  WHERE Class = SubClass.parent
    AND ClassHasAttr(SubClass, Attr, Name, IsKey)
    AND IsKey = false;
```

3.4 Trackings

Tracking classes are used to represent mapping relationships between source and target elements. While they may directly reflect a relationship established by a single rule (such as the rule ClassAndTable in Section 3.2), multiple rules may contribute to a single tracking relationship. This allows other rules that depend on that relationship to be decoupled from the details of how the relationship is established.

As discussed in [2, 4], decoupling the rules that establish a mapping relationship from those that depend on that relationship is a key aspect of supporting maintainability and re-use of rules and transformations.

3.5 FROM Clauses

For any non-trivial transformation one needs to be able to carefully control the number of objects that are created. In Tefkat this information is represented in the abstract syntax by an Injection term. The corresponding concrete syntax is the optional FROM clause. There will be exactly one object created for each unique tuple corresponding to a FROM.

In the case of MAKE clauses that do not contain explicit FROM clauses, an implicit FROM is constructed as follows: the label is the concatenation of the rule name and the name of the target instance variable, and the parameters are the set of variables corresponding to source instances in the containing rule's FORALL clause. For example, the implicit FROM clause for MAKE Table T in the rule ClassAndTable in Section 3.2 is: FROM ClassAndTable_T(C).

The following rule shows a case where an explicit FROM is required. The originating Class and the path of attributes and associations, as encoded in the name bound to N uniquely identify the Columns to be created.

```
RULE MakeColumns
  WHERE ClassHasAttr(C, A, N, IsKey)
    AND ClsToTbl LINKS class = C, table = T
  MAKE Column Col FROM col(C, N) {
        name: N;
        type: A.type.name;
  }
  SET T.cols = Col,
      IF IsKey = true
      THEN
        SET T.pkey = Col
      ENDIF
  LINKING AttrToCol WITH class = C, attr = A, col = Col;
```

The use of an explicit FROM clause allows multiple rules to separately and independently assert the existence of a target object, with only a single object being actually created. Again, this enhances the maintainability and re-usablility of rules and transformations.

4   Language Implementation

4.1   Concrete Syntax

The concrete syntax of Tefkat was initially designed to feel familiar and comfortable to programmers with experience using SQL, another declarative language, and also to suggest an intuitive semantics that help direct the writing of rules.

The only major change to the syntax since its first specification has been the introduction of *object literals*.

```
Class Class {
  attrs: Attribute Attr {
    type: PrimitiveDataType _PT;
    name: Name;
    is_primary: IsKey;
  };
}
```

Object literals are pure syntactic sugar designed to make rules more succinct and readable since, with appropriate formatting, they expose explicit structure in the constraints being specified.

Here is the equivalent constraint expressed without using object literal synyax.

```
Class Class AND
Class.attrs = Attr AND
Attribute Attr AND
Attr.type = PT AND
PrimitiveDataType PT AND
Attr.name = Name AND
Attr.is_primary = IsKey
```

Another concrete syntax feature that deserves special mention is the use of variables whose name begins with an underscore. These variables are termed *anonymous variables* and references to them are, by definition, unique. That is, if the variable name _PT, for example, is used more than once in an individual rule, patterm, or temaplate, then each reference defines and refers to a different variable.

While not an error, the parser will emit a warning when an anonymous variable (except for the variables named by a single underscore) is used more than once. The parser will also emit a warning when a variable whose name does not begin with an underscore is used only once in a given rule. By naming variables to avoid these warnings, simple spelling mistakes and some copy-and-paste errors are more easily detected, which is a real bonus for a language that does not require variables to be explicitly declared.

4.2   Advanced Language Features

Tefkat is designed to support transformations that span meta-levels. There are two key features that enable this: reflection, and the *Any Type*.

Support for reflection comes in two parts. The simplest is allowing access to the reflective features that every object implicitly inherits from EObject. For example, you can access an object's container object with O.eContainer(), all its contained objects with O.eContents(), and its meta-class object with O.eClass().

The more advanced aspect is the ability to use an arbitrary expression, prefixed by a dollar symbol, anywhere a type name or feature name may be used. In the simplest case, O.$"name" = A is equivalent to O.name = N. Other examples include O.$join("_", N1, N2) = A which gets the value of an attribute whose name is the concatenation of N1, "_", and N2, and O1.name = N AND $N O2 which binds O2 to all instances of the class named by the value of N.

The *Any Type* is represented by an underscore. It behaves like an implicit universal supertype of all types. This allows a transformation rule to match all objects regardless of their actual type and without requiring an explicit common supertype. To illustrate this, here is a transformation that makes a copy of an arbitrary input model.

```
TRANSFORMATION copy : src -> tgt

IMPORT http://www.eclipse.org/emf/2002/Ecore

CLASS ObjToObj {
  EObject src;
  EObject tgt;
};
```

```
RULE copyObjects
  FORALL _ Src
  MAKE    $Src.eClass() Tgt
  LINKING ObjToObj WITH src = Src, tgt = Tgt;

RULE copyAttributeValues
  WHERE ObjToObj LINKS src = Src, tgt = Tgt
    AND Src.eClass() = Class
    AND Class.eAllAttributes = Attr
    AND Attr.changeable = true
    AND Src.eIsSet(Attr) = true
    AND Value = Src.$Attr
  SET Tgt.$Attr = Value;

RULE copyObjectReferences
  WHERE ObjToObj LINKS src = Src, tgt = Tgt
    AND Src.eClass() = Class
    AND Class.eAllReferences = Ref
    AND Ref.changeable = true
    AND Src.eIsSet(Ref) = true
    AND Value = Src.$Ref
    AND ObjToObj LINKS src = Value, tgt = TgtValue
  SET Tgt.$Ref = TgtValue;
```

4.3   The Engine and Environment

The Tefkat engine is suitable for standalone use and is invokable from the command-line, but for most developers it will be used as part of a full-featured set of Eclipse plugins. These include a syntax-highlighting editor that is integrated with the parser to provide direct, linked feedback on parser errors and warnings. Figure 1 shows this editor, including a warning about a singleton variable use. Note the outline view to the right. Clicking on an entry in this view will cause the editor to jump to the appropriate line.

Also included with the Eclipse plugin is a source-level debugger, shown in Figure 2. Running the transformation in the debugger allows you to single step through the evaluation of each term in a rule. Variables and their bindings are shown in the view at the top right, while the stack displays the current term and the terms of the current rule that have been evaluated leading to this point.

While very useful, the debugger does suffer some limitations. Being a declarative logic-based language, the execution model is somewhat like that of Prolog. Thus the internal state is a set of trees rather than the stack of traditional procedural languages for which the Eclipse debugging framework is designed.

This, coupled with the need to re-order terms during evaluation for both efficiency and semantic correctness (for example, ensuring that a variable is bound to an object before attempting to get a feature's value), means that it can sometimes be difficult to follow a rule's execution, although the integrated source highlighting helps a great deal.

To improve the debugging experience we would like to explore the use of annotations to describe the expected behaviour of parts of rules. This would be similar to

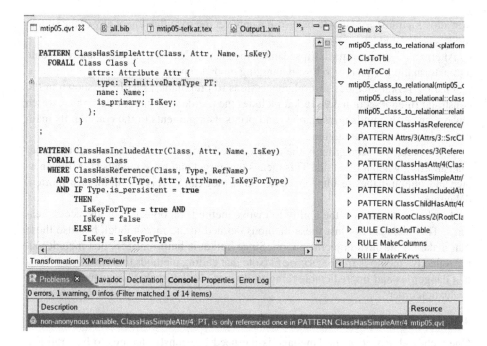

Fig. 1. The Tefkat editor for Eclipse

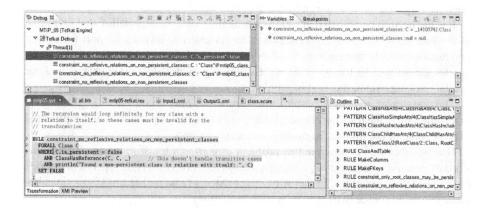

Fig. 2. The Tefkat source-level debugger for Eclipse

the determinism declarations used in Mercury [8]. In the longer term, it may also be possible to adapt concepts from declarative debugging [9].

Tefkat is integrated with the Eclipse build system. Its configuration is stored as a model in the file `tefkat.xml`. This describes one or more transformation applications in terms of source and target models, an optional trace model for recording which rules and source elements were used to create which target elements, and any mappings required to translate URIs naming meta-models to resolvable URLs. The build integration allows a transformation to be re-run whenever the specification or any of the source models is updated.

Alternatively, the normal Eclipse launch mechanism can be used to manually execute a transformation. This is also how debugging mode is entered.

Finally, Tefkat includes several concessions to pragmatics. Firstly, as shown in the constraint rule in Section 3.2, Tefkat includes the pre-defined pattern `println` which always succeeds, binds no variables, and prints its arguments to the console. Its main use is as a *probe* for debugging.

Also useful for debugging is the ability to tell Tefkat to continue executing rather than aborting when a rule fails. This means that target and trace models are still generated and, although they result from buggy rules, they can be very useful for post-mortem debugging.

Another concession is the ability to invoke methods on objects, not just access features. This includes not just those methods defined in the meta-model, but also those that make up the Java implementation. Since Tefkat is built on EMF, this includes all the reflective methods from `EObject`. Note that calling methods that have side-effects is a dangerous and unpredictable thing to do since Tefkat makes no guarantees about evaluation order.

4.4 Limitations

One technical aspect of the language is the need for transformations to be stratified. Essentially this means that a rule (or pattern) cannot depend (directly or indirectly) on its own negation. For example, a rule cannot check that there are no instances of a tracking class, and then create an instance of that tracking class.

It is the need to be able to determine stratifiability of a transformation that gives rise to the limitations on querying elements in target extents. Tefkat's support for reflection means that determining *negative dependencies* in the face of arbitrary target extent queries would impose too great a cost. By limiting queries to source extents and the special tracking extent, this cost is avoided.

The cost, however, is that complex transformations may need to store large amounts of information in the tracking classes. Future work will investigate whether it is practical to relax some of the limitations on querying target extents.

One possible way to mitigate this problem is to *stream* transformations. That is, instead of specifying a single large transformation that does everything, perform a series of smaller transformations. In this way, target extents from earlier transformations become queriable source extents in later transformations.

While this form of transformation composition can be done outside of the Tefkat language, we believe there are benefits to supporting it and other forms of composition directly in the language.

5 Conclusion

The example, typical of those used as both exemplary and motivating problems for model transformation, shows how the use of a declarative language allows transformation writers to focus their endeavours on the logic of the transformation rather than on how to facilitate its execution.

The example presented, although interesting, is by necessity small in scale. A number of other works are currently underway using the language and engine that are offering valuable feedback and serving to evaluate their ability to deal with large-scale examples. In [10], the authors have written Tefkat transformations to generate UML2 Testing Profile models from UML requirements and design models. In [7], the author addresses the problem of change propagation for Tefkat, and implements it using transformations themselves written in Tefkat. One transformation takes as input the updated source model, the original (possibly updated) target models and a newly generated target model, and the trace models for the original and new transformations and produces a delta model. The delta model represents the differences between the old and new target models. Based on heuristics and user feedback, a subsequent transformation produces a final target model that preserves any manual changes that may have been made between transformation executions.

In addition, the engine is also being used to manage the transformation between electronic health record formats and to generate Xforms for input of health record information. The metamodels and transformations in each of these examples are both large and complex. The Xform transformation is also of particular interest because it takes two meta-models as input (a reference model, and an archetype model [11]), and produces an XML Schema-based model as output. Additionally, it needs to combine implicit hints from both input models to construct a useful ordering of input fields and labels in the resulting Xform.

Our experiences with Tefkat demonstrate that declarative transformation specification is both practical and productive. A declarative specification means you can concentrate on *what* the transformation should do rather than getting caught up in *how* the transformation should do it.

References

1. Gerber, A., Lawley, M., Raymond, K., Steel, J., Wood, A.: Transformation: The missing link of MDA. In Corradini, A., Ehrig, H., Kreowski, H.J., Rozemberg, G., eds.: Proc. 1st International Conference on Graph Transformation, ICGT'02. Volume 2505 of Lecture Notes in Computer Science., Springer Verlag (2002) 90–105
2. Duddy, K., Gerber, A., Lawley, M., Raymond, K., Steel, J.: Model transformation: A declarative, reusable patterns approach. In: Proc. 7th IEEE International Enterprise Distributed Object Computing Conference, EDOC 2003, Brisbane, Australia (2003) 174–195
3. Duddy, K., Gerber, A., Lawley, M., Raymond, K., Steel, J.: Declarative transformation for object-oriented models. In van Bommel, P., ed.: Transformation of Knowledge, Information, and Data: Theory and Applications. Idea Group Publishing (2004)
4. Lawley, M., Duddy, K., Gerber, A., Raymond, K.: Language features for re-use and maintainability of MDA transformations. In: OOPSLA workshop on Best Practices for Model-Driven Software Development, Vancouver, Canada (2004)
5. DSTC, IBM, CBOP: MOF Query/View/Transformation, initial submission (2003)
6. OMG: Request for Proposal: MOF 2.0 Query/Views/Transformations RFP. OMG Document: ad/02-04-10 (2002)
7. Metke, A.: Change propagation in the MDA: A model merging approach. Master's thesis, School of Information Technology and Electrical Engineering, The University of Queensland (2005)

8. Henderson, F., Somogyi, Z., Conway, T.: Determinism analysis in the Mercury compiler. In: Proceedings of the Australian Computer Science Conference, Melbourne, Australia (1996) 337–346

9. Naish, L.: A three-valued declarative debugging scheme. Technical Report 97/5, Department of Computer Science, University of Melbourne, Melbourne, Australia (1997)

10. Dai, Z.R.: Model-driven testing with UML 2.0. In Akehurst, D., ed.: Second European Workshop on Model Driven Architecture (MDA), Canterbury, Kent, University of Kent (2004) 179–187

11. Beale, T., Goodchild, A., Heard, S.: EHR design principles. http://titanium.dstc.edu.au/papers/ehr_design_principles.pdf (2002)

Essentials of the 4th UML/MoDELS Workshop in Software Model Engineering (WiSME'2005)

Krzysztof Czarnecki[1], Jean-Marie Favre[2],
Martin Gogolla[3], and Tom Mens[4]

[1] University of Waterloo, Canada
[2] University of Grenoble, France
[3] University of Bremen, Germany
[4] University of Mons-Hainaut, Belgium

Abstract. Model-Driven Engineering is a form of generative engineering, by which all or at least central parts of a software application are generated from models. Model Driven Engineering should be seen as an integrative approach combining existing software engineering techniques (e.g., testing and refinement) and technical spaces (e.g., 'ModelWare', 'XmlWare') that have usually been studied in separation. The goal of the workshop is to improve common understanding of these techniques across technical spaces and create bridges and increase the synergies among the spaces. This year's WiSME workshop will concentrate on two complementing themes: Bridging Technical Spaces and Model-Driven Evolution. This paper reports on a workshop held at the 8th UML/MoDELS conference. It describes motivation and aims, organisational issues, and abstracts of the accepted papers.

1   Motivation and Aims

The OMG initiative Model Driven Architecture (MDA) attempts to separate business functionality specification from the implementations of that functionality on specific technology platforms. This approach is intended to play a key role in the fields of information system and software engineering. MDA is supposed to provide a basic technical framework for information integration and tool interoperability based on the separation of platform specific models (PSMs) from platform independent models (PIMs). Models of coarse granularity and high abstraction will represent the various functional and non-functional aspects of computer systems. In the long term, there will be well-defined operations on models, implemented by well-defined commercial tools, that will allow us to build, transform, merge, verify, and evolve models. Key standards in the MDA are based on OMG recommendations such as UML, MOF, XMI, CWM, QVT.

MDA can be considered an implementation of a more general trend that has been gathering momentum in recent years called Model Driven Engineering (MDE). Model-Driven Engineering is a form of generative engineering, by which all or at least central parts of a software application is generated from models. The basic ideas of this approach are close to those of other disciplines

J.-M. Bruel (Ed.): MoDELS 2005 Workshops, LNCS 3844, pp. 151–158, 2006.

of software engineering, such as Generative Programming, Domain Specific Languages (DSLs), Model Integrated Computing (MIC), and Software Factories. In this new perspective, models, metamodels, and transformations take a primary position amongst the artifacts of development. MDE aims at making models the primary driving assets in all aspects of software engineering, including system design, platform and language definition, definition of mappings among artifacts, but also design data integration, design analysis, tool specification, and product family development. Model Driven Engineering should be seen as an integrative approach combining existing techniques and technical spaces that have usually been studied in separation. The goal of the workshop is to improve common understanding of these techniques, to increase the benefits of combining approaches such as grammars, schemas, or metamodels, and to create bridges between such various technical spaces.

The workshop will concentrate this year on two complementing themes: Bridging Technical Spaces and Model-Driven Evolution. When dealing with models residing in different technical spaces (e.g., UML/MOF and XML), one encounters the problem of co-evolution or model synchronisation across technical spaces. For example, whenever a change is made to a UML model, which is also represented in another format (e.g., XMI), both models need to be synchronised. The fact that this synchronisation occurs in different technical spaces makes the problem difficult and interesting. Another topic within these themes is the problem of language evolution: How can one deal with the fact that the languages in which models are developed (e.g., UML, MOF, XML, XMI) evolve at a rapid pace? The descriptions developed in these languages need to co-evolve as well. This form co-evolution has been known in the technology space of databases as schema evolution.

The non-exhaustive list of topics included:

- Transformation systems for models; Types of transformations; Merging of a platform model and a business model
- Transformation frameworks; Transformation libraries; Transformations processes; Transformations as reuseable assets
- Operations on models: Merging, alignment, verification, validation, refactoring, refinement, abstraction, reduction, normalization, generalization
- Models, Schemas, Grammars, Meta-models and Ontologies; Reflection in meta-model architectures
- Meta-modeling frameworks and tool integration
- Modularity aspects for model organization: profiles, packages, name spaces, viewpoints, contexts; Issues of granularity for models
- Meta-data and repositories; Middleware-supported model engineering
- Requirements modeling; Know-how modeling; Architecture modeling; Service modeling; Rule modeling
- Co-evolution of and synchronization between models (including business models, requirements, analysis and design models, and source code)
- MDA and MDE industrial cases, best practices and empirical studies
- Co-evolution of meta-models and models, schema and data, meta-grammar and grammar

- Co-transformation (e.g., co-transforming database schemas and SQL expressions and applications)
- Megamodeling (i.e., defining basic MDE concepts and structure of MDE component repository structures)
- Technology spaces (e.g., MDA, GrammarWare, XmlWare) and bridges between them (e.g., the relationships between 'Grammar' and 'Class Diagram')

2   Organisational Issues

This workshop is the fourth in a series of workshops started at UML'2002 [1] and continued at UML'2003 [2] and UML'2004 [3]. The paper selection process was carefully supported by an international programme committee and additional referees. All accepted papers can be found in [4]. Revised versions of the papers will be published in Electronic Notes in Theoretical Computer Science (ENTCS), Elsevier.

Programme Committee

- Jean Bezivin, INRIA & University of Nantes, France
- Mireille Blay, University of Nice, France
- Krysztof Czarnecki, University of Waterloo, Canada
- Johannes Ernst, NetMesh, USA
- Jack Greenfield, Microsoft, USA
- Jean-Marie Favre, University of Grenoble, France
- Robert France, University of Boulder, USA
- Martin Gogolla, University of Bremen, Germany
- Pieter Van Gorp, University of Antwerp, Belgium
- Reiko Heckel, University of Manchester, Great Britain
- Gabor Karsai, Vanderbilt University, USA
- Ivan Kurtev, University of Twente, The Netherlands
- Ralf Laemmel, Microsoft, USA
- Steve Mellor, ProjTech, USA
- Tom Mens, University of Mons-Hainaut, Belgium
- Alfonso Pierantonio, University of L'Aquila, Italy
- Paul Sammut, Xactium, Great Britain
- Gabi Taentzer, Technical University of Berlin, Germany
- German Vega, University of Grenoble, France
- Jon Whittle, George Mason University, USA
- Andreas Winter, University of Koblenz, Germany

The workshop was structured into 4 thematic sessions:

- Bridging Approaches for Technical Spaces (Papers 3.1-3.3)
- Bridging Textware and Modelware (Papers 3.4-3.6)
- Modeling Approaches (Papers 3.7-3.9)
- Modeling Engineering Environments (Papers 3.10-3.11)

3 Presented Papers

3.1 Model Engineering Support for Tool Interoperability

Jean Bezivin, Hugo Bruneliere, Frederic Jouault, Ivan Kurtev

ATLAS group - INRIA - LINA, Universite de Nantes, France

Abstract: In this paper we want to show how MDE (Model Driven Engineering) approaches may help solving some practical engineering problems. Our view of MDE is not based on the usage of huge and rather monolithic modeling languages like UML 2.0 but instead on small DSLs (Domain Specific Languages) defined by well focused metamodels. As a consequence we use a rather "agile" view of MDE where each tool is characterized by one of several metamodels and where the interoperability between tools is implemented by specific model transformation operations. We base our discussion on a practical illustrative problem of bug-tracking in a collaborative project involving different partners using tools at different maturity levels. We conclude by discussing the help that MDE approaches may bring to solving these kinds of situations.

3.2 A Metamodel Refinement Approach for Bridging Technical Spaces - A Case Study

A. Staikopoulos, B. Bordbar

School of Computer Science, University of Birmingham, UK

Abstract: To benefit from positive aspects of an existing diverse set of Technical Spaces, it is important to develop methods of automated transformation of models between such domains. Sometimes it is possible to describe Technical Spaces via metamodels. In such cases, the Model Driven Engineering and Architecture pose as a natural candidate for dealing with such transformations between Technical Spaces. This paper deals with the case where the metamodel of the source Technical Space is more complex than the metamodel of the destination. Thus, the gap between the two Technical Spaces is highly non-trivial. The method presented in this paper is based on successive metamodel refinements to bridge this gap. Finally, the method is applied to the transformation from Business Process Execution Language to Petri nets.

3.3 Bridging Persistency Impacts: Towards Automatic Integration of Domain-Data Layers

Mira Balaban and Lior Limonad

Computer Science Department, Ben-Gurion University of the Negev, ISRAEL

Abstract: Domain and data layers are two different technical spaces that need to co-exist and co-evolve in integrated complex systems. The combined operation of Domain and Data modules usually suffers from model mismatch problems, and raises problems of consistency. Existing methods and technologies offer partial solutions that do not support full automation of persistency decisions. In this paper we introduce a method for automatic construction of a Data Access Layer that bridges between a Domain and a Data layers. The method is based on analysis of class navigation patterns that involve persistency stereotyping in the domain layer. Such patterns are termed Data Access Patterns. For each pattern we suggest a data access layer implementation that can be automated, and leaves the domain layer classes intact. The combined analysis of all patterns provides a complete solution for bridging persistency impacts. The current implementation handles the static aspects, i.e., schema transformation.

3.4   Bridging Grammarware and Modelware

Manuel Wimmer, Gerhard Kramler

Business Informatics Group, Vienna University of Technology, Austria

Abstract: In Software Engineering many text-based languages and sup- porting tools are used, forming the grammarware technical space. Cur- rently model driven engineering is the new emerging paradigm for soft- ware engineering, which uses modelling languages and tools, forming the modelware technical space. Transition to the new technical space and interoperability between these two technical spaces is needed in many development scenarios. Building a bridge between these two technical spaces is a tedious task, that has to be repeated for each language to be transformed. Therefore, we propose a generic bridge between gram- marware and modelware technical spaces, that can generate a specfic bridge based on the EBNF of a given language semi-automatically. The generation comprises of two steps, (1) automatic generation of meta- model corresponding to the EBNF and (2) annotations to provide the additional semantics not captured by the EBNF. The generated bridge is capable of bi-directional transformations between sentences (programs) and corresponding models and can be used in re-engineering applications and for integration of text-based and model-based tools. The benefits of this approach are rapid development and correctness.

3.5   HUTN as a Bridge Between ModelWare and GrammarWare: An Experience Report

Pierre-Alain Muller, Michel Hassenforder

IRISA/INRIA, Rennes, France

Abstract: In this paper we report on our experience using HUTN as a bridge between ModelWare and GrammarWare, to generate parsers and editors for

DSLs defined under the shape of metamodels. We describe the problems that we have encountered with the ambiguities of the current HUTN specification and discuss how this specification may be fixed to be usable with grammar- driven tools.

3.6 Specifications for Mapping UML Models to XML Schemas

Krish Narayanan, Shreya Ramaswamy

Department of Computer Science, Eastern Michigan University, General Motors Corporation

Abstract: An imminent activity in software design is to map models, either from one level of detail to another or from different perspectives of an application. It is extremely important that these models are consistent with each other in the semantics they carry for a successful software implementation. With the introduction of a number of CASE tools, this activity has been partially auto- mated with little or no human intervention. Yet, one of the major drawbacks of these tools is that the mapping process sometimes tends to loose the inherent semantics of an application. Also, for some applications, there are no such com- mercially available tools. In this paper, we focus on XML applications that use a standard structure specified by their corresponding schemas. The output of the design activity for such applications is typically, a generic model that represents the schema in an abstract way. UML being the language of choice for modeling software systems, is often used in modeling XML applications. But, the mapping from UML models to XML schemas is far from perfect. We consider the intrica- cies involved in both the forward (UML to XML) and reverse (XML to UML) engineering processes and ensure that the application's structural semantics are maintained in the mapping process. In this paper, we define the complete spec- ifications for forward engineering UML model constructs to their corresponding XML counter parts. We also share our experiences from a tool we have developed that automates the mapping process.

3.7 Navigating the MetaMuddle

Arnor Solberg, Robert France, Raghu Reddy

SINTEF/University of Oslo, Norway, Colorado State University, USA

Abstract: Developers of model transformations and other model-driven devel- opment (MDD) mechanisms that manipulate models often work at the meta- model level. The complexity of the UML metamodel can hinder the develop- ment of UML-based MDD technologies. In this paper, we identify some of the current barriers to understanding, using and evolving the UML 2.0 metamodel and present ideas on how to simplify these tasks using query based views and aspect oriented techniques.

3.8   A UML Precise Specification of Design Patterns Using Decoupling Constraints

Samir Ammour, Mikal Ziane, Xavier Blanc and Salima Chantit

LIP6, Laboratoire d.Informatique de Paris 6, Paris, France

Abstract: UML collaboration templates do not capture the problem part of design patterns. It is then possible to apply a pattern solution in contexts that are not consistent with this solution. Moreover, when the context evolves, it must stay consistent with the patterns that were previously applied. Since design problems can be quite varied, we focused on one of the most frequent design goals of design patterns: avoiding unnecessary coupling. In this paper, we adapt the notion of decoupling constraints to UML models and we express it using the Object Constraint Language. Adding decoupling constraints to collaboration templates allows checking if a context is consistent with the solution of a pattern and eases the adaption of this solution to an evolving context. These constraints must be checked before applying a pattern but also when the context evolves, to guarantee that the solution of the pattern is consistent and complete.

3.9   A Meta-model for the Problem Frames Approach

Maria Lencastre1, Juliane Boetlho1, Pedro Clericuzzi1, Joao Araojo

Pernambuco University, Brazil, Universidade Nova de Lisboa, Portugal

Abstract: Michael Jackson's Problem Frames are a well-known software engineering approach for requirements analysis and problem domain specification. This paper describes this technique through the definition of a meta-model, whose aim is to clarify the involved concepts to help the devel- opment and implementation of tool support and also to compare, transform, merge different requirement techniques.

3.10   A Presentation Framework for Metamodeling Environments

Gergely Mezei, Tihamor Levendovszky, Hassan Charaf

Budapest University of Technology and Economics, Budapest, Hungary

Abstract: Although the flexibility provided by metamodeling systems is proven to be enough in practical applications, the presentation is not supported to the same extent. The goal of this paper is to present a presentation framework which exploits the advantages of the underlying metamodeling system and provides enough flexibility to present the concrete syntax of feature models, UML 2.0 diagrams, and resource diagram for mobile telephones. The static structure as well as the behavioral aspect are described to illustrate the solutions and the design decisions related to the framework.

3.11   Some Lessons Learnt in the Building of a Model Engineering Platform

Jean Bezivin

Atlas Group, INRIA and LINA, University of Nantes, France

Abstract: As we are currently improving AMMA (ATLAS Model Management Architecture), a second generation model engineering platform installed on top of the Eclipse Modeling Framework (EMF), we borrow inspiration from a previous work undertaken fifteen years ago at the University of Nantes. This initial model engineering platform named sNets (Semantic Networks) included several functional blocks like the sMachine, the sBrowser, the sQuery, the sAction system, etc. Several parts of these tools are still in use today. At a time when we are defining the main architectural style of the new platform, it may be helpful to come back on the initial learning of this project. This paper describes the sNets project and summarizes some lessons learnt in the course of the design and utilization of this first generation modelling framework.

References

1. Jean Bezivin, Robert France: Proc. 1st UML Workshop in Software Model Engineering (WiSME'2002). www.metamodel.com/wisme-2002.
2. Jean Bezivin, Martin Gogolla: Proc. 2nd UML Workshop in Software Model Engineering (WiSME'2003). www.metamodel.com/wisme-2003.
3. Martin Gogolla, Paul Sammut, Jon Whittle: Proc. 3rd UML Workshop in Software Model Engineering (WiSME'2004). www.metamodel.com/wisme-2004.
4. Krzysztof Czarnecki, Jean-Marie Favre, Martin Gogolla, Tom Mens: Proc. 4th UML Workshop in Software Model Engineering (WiSME'2005). www.metamodel.com/wisme-2005.

Bridging Grammarware and Modelware

Manuel Wimmer and Gerhard Kramler

Business Informatics Group, Vienna University of Technology, Austria
`lastname@big.tuwien.ac.at`

Abstract. In Software Engineering many text-based languages and supporting tools are used, forming the grammarware technical space. Currently model driven engineering is the new emerging paradigm for software engineering, which uses modelling languages and tools, forming the modelware technical space. Transition to the new technical space and interoperability between these two technical spaces is needed in many development scenarios. Building a bridge between these two technical spaces is a tedious task, that has to be repeated for each language to be transformed. Therefore, we propose a generic bridge between grammarware and modelware technical spaces, that can generate a specific bridge based on the EBNF of a given language semi-automatically. The generation comprises of two steps, (1) automatic generation of metamodel corresponding to the EBNF and (2) annotations to provide the additional semantics not captured by the EBNF. The generated bridge is capable of bi-directional transformations between sentences (programs) and corresponding models and can be used in re-engineering applications and for integration of text-based and model-based tools.

1 Indroduction

The term *technical spaces* was introduced in [7] and with it the demand for bridges between several technical spaces. Manual bridging of technical spaces is a error prone and recurring task, typically relevant in model driven engineering but also in other software engineering disciplines, e.g., the migration from relational databases to XML based documents. Therefore a need for tools arises, which support and automate interoperability between technical spaces.

A bridge between grammarware and modelware is useful in many software development tasks. Not only forward engineering but also reverse engineering of existing software systems is a suitable field of application. Regarding the latter the *Object Management Group (OMG)* is working on model-based reverse engineering and software modernization. For that purpose a special work group for *Architecture-Driven Modernization (ADM,* [9]) has been initiated. The main target of ADM is to rebuild existing applications, e.g, legacy systems, as models and then perform refactorings or transform them to new target architectures. A bridge between grammarware and modelware can act as a basic infrastructure tool to support various ADM tasks.

Bridging two technical spaces involves several tasks, such as processing the artifacts in the source technical space and transforming them into new artifacts,

J.-M. Bruel (Ed.): MoDELS 2005 Workshops, LNCS 3844, pp. 159–168, 2006.

that can be processed by tools from the target technical space. Currently transformation definitions are placed at the M2 level, e.g., between Java grammar and UML class diagram metamodel. This approach has a huge drawback, because for each pair of languages exactly one bridge must be defined. For another pair a different bridge has to be developed. Generally speaking for technical space 1, which has n languages, and technical space 2, which has m languages, $n * m$ bridges are needed. Considering the huge amount of languages in the grammarware, bridging at the M2 level is not a satisfying solution. In modelware there are not existing as many languages as in grammarware existing, but it seems that many Domain Specific Modeling Languages [3] will be developed in the near future. The exploding number of language combinations between these two spaces requires a more generic approach, which allows to generate bridges for all language combinations in the same way automatically.

In this paper we propose a generic mechanism for the semi-automatic generation of a specific bridge between grammarware and modelware based on the EBNF of a given language. EBNF [13] [4] is the most used metalanguage for defining programming languages in the grammarware. However other forms of metalanguages [6] are common, and sometimes there are no formal grammar definitions available at all. It is important to note that our work does not address these problems - for more information see [5]. In the modelware our mechanism is based on MOF [8], which is the main standard for defining metamodels. The first step in the proposed process is the production of a metamodel and a transformation program for transforming programs into models. The resulting metamodels and models have some drawbacks, because of the genericity of the transformation rules. In order to eliminate these unintentional properties, we introduce a second step - the optimization of metamodels and models. Some optimization steps can be done automatically - we call this process *condensation* - but some optimizations have to be done semi-automatically by user-annotations. This optimization process is called *customization*. With manual annotations it is possible to add semantics to the metamodels that are not captured by the original grammars.

The rest of the paper uses Mini-Java [11] as an running example and is structured as follows. Section 2 provides an overview of the framework architecture. Section 3 presents details of the parsing process and the raw meta model. Furthermore mappings between EBNF and MOF concepts are discussed. In section 4 details about the optimization steps in the condensation process are shown. Section 5 represents the main features of the customization process, in particular the manual annotations. Section 6 gives an overview of the related work and how it differs from this work. Finally, section 7 draws some conclusions and outlines future work regarding implementation and application.

2   Overview of the Framework Architecture

Our proposed framework exploits the fact, that grammarware and modelware have metalanguages. The main idea is to find correspondences between EBNF and MOF concepts and to use these correspondences for defining bridges.

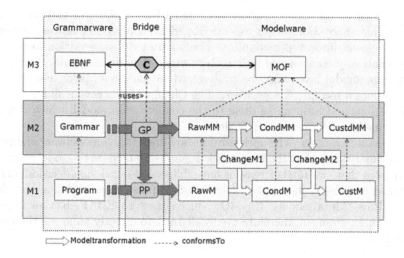

Fig. 1. Framework Overview

Figure 1 shows the main idea by a correspondence relation in the M3 layer
between EBNF and MOF. EBNF is a reflexive language, i.e., EBNF can be described in EBNF. We utilize this property for constructing an attributed grammar, which defines a grammar for EBNF and implements the correspondences
between EBNF and MOF as transformation rules. A compiler-compiler takes
the attributed grammar as input and generates a parser called *Grammar Parser
(GP)*. On the one hand the GP converts grammars defined in EBNF into *Raw
Metamodels* and on the other hand it generates a parser for programs, which are
conform to the processed grammar. This parser is called *Program Parser (PP)*.
Via the PP programs can be transformed in a *Raw Models*. The Raw Metamodel
and the Raw Model are expressed in *XML Metadata Interchange (XMI* [10]),
thus they can be processed by modelware tools. The grammar parser and the
program parser act as the main bridging technologies between grammarware and
modelware. It is important to note, that both parsers are automatically generated from grammars and from the correspondences between EBNF and MOF.

Once the Raw Metamodel and the Raw Model are created, we have reached
the modelware technical space. However the Raw Metamodel and the Raw Model
can grow very big in terms of number of classes. To eliminate this drawback, some
transformation rules for optimization are introduced, which can be automatically
executed by model transformation engines. The optimization rules are applied
to the Raw Metamodel and the outcome of this transformation is called *Condensation Metamodel*. Not only the metamodel has to be optimized, but also the
model has to be adjusted in such a way that it is conform to the Condensation
metamodel. This adjustment is defined by a *Change Model*, which includes all
required information to rebuild the Raw Model as a *Condensation Model*.

Furthermore our approach provides a mechanism to add additional semantics
to the metamodel that cannot be expressed in EBNF. These additional semantics

are attached to the Condensation Metamodel by manual annotations. In particular, this annotations cover aspects like Identification/References semantics, data types and improved readability. The annotated Condensation Metamodel is automatically transformed into a *Customized Metamodel*. Again, the changes in the metamodel layer must be propagated to the model layer. For this task we introduce a second *Change Model*. The Change Model covers all user-defined modifications and propagates them to the condensation model, which is finally transformed into a *Customized Model*.

The main reason why the optimizations are done in the modelware and not in the grammarware is that the framework is aligned to be used by model engineers. Apart from that two further reasons have influenced our design decision: (1) the optimization rules require potentially complete parse trees, which are available by the Raw (Meta)models. (2) MOF, in contrast to EBNF, has an inherent annotation mechanism, therefore we decided not to directly annotate the EBNF grammars.

3   Parsing and Raw (Meta)model

The main target of the parsing process is to transform the textual definitions of the grammarware into a format, that can be processed by model engineering tools. The first step is parsing the grammar of a given language. For our framework we decided to use EBNF as metalanguage, because it is the most used metalanguage to define grammars. In order to process each EBNF grammar identical, the syntax of the grammars must conform to the standardized EBNF syntax [4]. The Grammar Parser for processing the EBNF grammars can be generated by a compiler-compiler and an attributed grammar. The attributed grammar contains the structure and the concepts of EBNF, as well as method calls for the transformation of EBNF concepts to MOF concepts.

For the transformation of EBNF concepts into MOF concepts, the correspondences between these two metalanguages have to be clarified. This has been done in previous work - see [1], where relations between EBNF and MOF concepts are discussed. Based on this work, we constructed a complete set of transformation rules, which are summarized in the following. The transformation rules are organized along the major EBNF concepts, i.e., production rule, non-terminal, terminal, sequence, repetition, optional and alternative.

Rule 1: Represent every left hand side of a production rule as a class. The elements of the right hand side are represented as classes as defined by the following rules and are connected to the left hand side class by a containment association. An exceptional case is the first production rule of the grammar. In this case the LHS class is additionally marked with the ≪start_symbol≫ stereotype.

Rule 2: Represent every non-terminal as a class, which is called like the non-terminal name plus _REF and is marked with a ≪reference≫ stereotype. The class is connected to the corresponding left hand side class of the non-terminal by an association.

Rule 3: Represent every terminal as a class named as T plus a consecutive number and marked with the stereotype ≪terminal≫. The value of the terminal is represented as the value of the literal property.

Rule 4: Represent a sequence as an anonymous class called SEQ plus a consecutive number and marked with ≪sequence≫ stereotype. The classes representing the sequence are attached to the anonymous class by a containment association. The associations are assigned with an ≪ordered≫ stereotype and a key/value pair indicating the position of the element in the sequence.

Rule 5: Represent every repetition by an anonymous class called REP plus a consecutive number and marked with a ≪repetition≫ stereotype. The anonymous class has a one-to-many association with the class representing the repeated element. Note, that it is important to tag the association end with multiplicity many as ordered. This constraint is required to rebuild the linear order of EBNF.

Rule 6: Represent every option by an anonymous class called OPT plus a consecutive number and marked with a ≪option≫ stereotype. The anonymous class has a zero-to-one association with the class representing the optional element.

Rule 7: Represents every alternative as a subclass of an anonymous class called ALT plus a consecutive number. The anonymous class is marked with an ≪alternative≫ stereotype and is defined as an abstract class.

Mappings for the grouping concept can be ignored in the transformation process, because a group can be directly transformed in a sequence element or in an alternative element. Furthermore there is no need for a special transformation rule for recursive definitions, because this rule can be constructed from the combination of rule 2 and 7.

The Grammar Parser implements the listed transformation rules and is therefore able to generate a Raw Metamodel expressed in XMI from a grammar expressed in EBNF. Not only a Raw Metamodel is produced by the Grammar Parser, but also a Program Parser is derived from the correspondences at M3 level and the generated Raw Metamodel. The Program Parser creates a corresponding model representation in XMI - called Raw Model - from textual-based programs.

4 Condensation

The generated Raw Metamodels and Raw Models have some unintentional properties. The generic transformation rules, explained in chapter 3, let the design size of the models grow immoderate, because lots of anonymous classes were introduced. To eliminate this drawback, transformation rules for optimization of the Raw Metamodel and of the Raw Model are established, which can be executed by model transformation engines automatically. The optimization rules have to derive (1) a optimized Metamodel - called *Condensation Metamodel* - from the Raw Metamodel and (2) a *Change Model*, which includes all necessary informations to rebuild a Condensation Model from a Raw Model. From the combination of Condensation Metamodel and Change Model it is possible to rebuild a model from a Raw Model, so that it is conform to the Condensation Metamodel. The Change Model is included in the Condensation Metamodel as special marked annotations.

The optimization of the Raw Metamodel starts with the upper class in the class hierarchy - the class marked with ≪start_symbol≫. From this class the optimization rules are executed in depth-first order, because the containment hierarchy of the Raw Metamodel corresponds to the tree strucutre of the EBNF grammar and therefore can be processed like a tree. When an optimization rule matches for a given class, the children of this class must be checked, whether optimization rules can be applied on them. This has to be done recursively until a child class is found on the path, for which no optimization rules can be applied. Then all optimization rules are performed on the path in reverse order, until the class with the original match is reached. From this class the depth-first optimization is continued. It is important that the changes in the child classes are reflected in the optimization of the upper classes, because this makes it possible to execute the optimization in one step and no temporary metamodels are needed. In the following the optimization rule 1 for the Raw Metamodel is shortly quoted. The complete description of rule 2 (optimization of sequences), 3 (optimization of terminal classes) and 4 (optimization of alternatives) may be found in [12].

Rule1: Deletion of anonymous classes for options and repetitions, where precondition 1 holds. The child class in the containment hierarchy takes the place of the deleted class. The original path of the child class must be saved in the Change Model.

Precondition:
(1) The anonymous class owns only one child class and the type of the child class is either sequence or non-terminal.

Effect and Change Model for Precondition (1) shown by option-elimination:

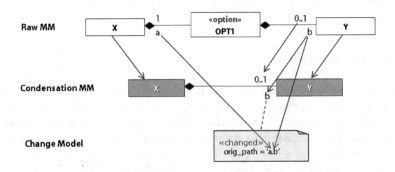

The order in which the rules are applied, must comply with the listing order of the rules. The rules do not change the semantics of the metamodel, only some anonymous classes are eliminated or some terminal classes are restructured in a more compact way. The expressiveness of the language is the same as with the un-optimized metamodel, but the size of the metamodel and of the model is reduced.

5   Customization

The aim of the generated metamodels and models is to maximize the understandability of languages and program specifications. As far as we have described, the metamodels and models are only graphical representations for the textual definitions. In this section we introduce a semi-automated mechanism to add additional semantics to the automatically generated metamodels, which cannot be expressed in EBNF. The user can attach annotations of a pre-defined set to the Condensation Metamodel. In order to enhance the quality of the generated metamodel by supporting improved readability, identification/reference semantics and data types, we propose the following manual annotations for the Condensation Metamodel. From these annotations it is possible to derive a Change Model to propagate the user-defined changes in the metamodel to model level in order to rebuild a Customized Model from the Condensation Model. The Change Model is again included in the generated Metamodel, in this case in the Customized Metamodel. The complete description of the annotation mechanism for data types and readability may be found in [12].

Identification/Reference: In metamodels the differentiation between Identification and Reference can be achieved easily. In contrast, grammars have no appropriate concepts for describing Identification or Reference in order to give a clue for the language designer's intentions. In our Mini-Java example the problem reveals with the class *Identifier*. An Identifier can be a variable, a class or a method name. If a variable is of type of a certain class, the identifier must be a class name and not a variable or method name. To indicate this constraint, we need additional information from the user in form of annotations, because this information cannot be derived from EBNF grammars.

Annotations: For this aspect two annotations are available (1) the ID annotation for defining an Identification and (2) the IDREF annotation for defining a reference. The stereotype ≪id≫ should be assigned to associations, which connect the element with the identifier class. The association end must have a multiplicity of 1. Also a new reference association to the actual referenced class is needed. This is done by marking existing associations, which should be redirected, with the stereotype ≪idref≫ and define the new target association end. The transformation has to delete the pseudo references, which become obsolete by the use of the user-created reference associations. The Change Model stores the original target of the reference association.

Effect and Change Model:

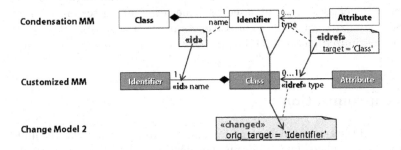

Readability: In metamodels the ability to give convenient names to elements makes it easier for the user to understand the intentions of the language designer. With annotations for names we allow the user to replace anonymous names, like OPT1 or ALT1 with convenient labels.

Data Types: MOF provides the following data types for metamodelling: string, integer and boolean. In contrast, EBNF has no concepts for data types and so they have to be described with complex expressions. These expressions result in complex class structures in the generated Condensation Metamodel. The substitution of such complex structures with data types provided by MOF leads to a more convenient metamodel.

As an example for the final output of our framework see Figure 2. In this figure an excerpt from the Customized Metamodel for Mini-Java is shown. Due to lack of space, we ignore stereotypes and tagged values concerning the concrete syntax. Note that the metamodel is completely automatically generated with our framework, except for manual annotations in the Condensation Metamodel. On the basis of Figure 2 it is readily identifiable, that the proposed optimization rules and annotations lead to a very intuitive metamodel.

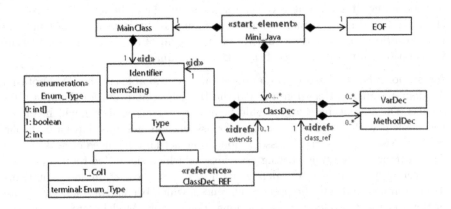

Fig. 2. Core of the Mini-Java Metamodel

6 Related Work

This section compares our work with related research activities: on the one hand approaches addressing the bridging of technical spaces and on the other hand approaches discussing the mapping between EBNF and MOF concepts.

Another mapping approach based on the M3-layer is described in [2]. In particular this work is focused on bridging model engineering and ontology engineering. Unlike our approach, only languages are transformed, which are based on MOF and have an XMI representation. Therefore it is possible to transform the XML representation with XSLT.

Alanen and Porres [1] discuss relations between context-free grammars and MOF metamodels. In contrast to our work, they only define mappings for M2 based on M3. We extend this approach by mapping not only M2, but also M1 based on M3. Furthermore, we establish various optimizations in order to get a more user-friendly metamodel. Our approach has used some mapping concepts of this previous work to define the grammar to raw metamodel transformation rules.

7 Conclusion and Future Work

In this work we have presented a generic framework, which supports the transformation of grammars into metamodels and of programs into models. The used transformation process is based on the M3 level, which allows to generate bridges between grammarware and modelware automatically. Furthermore we have described how to build a minimal and user-friendly metamodel through a number of optimization rules and user-annotations.

We are currently working on a prototype for the presented framework. As soon as our prototype is full functioning, we will use it to evaluate our framework with larger grammars and extensive programs. We hope this facility brings more insight on bridging grammarware and modelware. Therefore our next steps will be searching for additional optimization rules and user annotations, which allow a more flexible design mechanism for the final metamodel.

References

1. Marcus Alanen and Ivan Porres. A Relation Between Context-Free Grammars and Meta Object Facility Metamodels. Technical report, Turku Centre for Computer Science, 2003.
2. J. Bézivin, V. Devedzic, D. Djuric, J.M. Favreau, D. Gasevic, and F. Jouault. An M3-Neutral infrastructure for bridging model engineering and ontology engineering. In *Proceedings of the first International Conference on Interoperability of Enteprise Software and Applications, (INTEROP-ESA 05)*, 2005.
3. Krzysztof Czarnecki and Ulrich Eisenecker. *Generative Programming: Methods, Tools, and Applications*. Addison-Wesley Professional, 2000.
4. ISO. ISO/IEC 14977:1996(E), Information technology - Syntactic metalanguage - Extended BNF, 1996.

5. P. Klint, R. Lämmel, and C. Verhoef. Towards an engineering discipline for grammarware. *ACM TOSEM*, May30 2005. To appear; Online since July 2003, 47 pages.
6. K. Koskimies. Object Orientation in Attribute Grammars. *LNCS, vol. 545.* *Springer-Verlag*, pages 297–329, 1991.
7. Ivan Kurtev, Mehmet Aksit, and Jean Bézivin. Technical Spaces: An Initial Appraisal. *CoopIS, DOA2002 Federated Conferences, Industrial track, Irvine*, 2002.
8. OMG. Meta Object Facility (MOF) 2.0 Core Specification. http://www.omg.org/docs/ptc/03-10-04.pdf, 2004.
9. OMG. Architecture Driven Modernization. www.omg.org/adm, 2005.
10. OMG. *XML Metadata Interchange (XMI) Specification.* OMG, http://www.omg.org/docs/formal/05-05-01.pdf, 2005.
11. Ryan Stansifer. EBNF Grammar for Mini-Java. http://www.cs.fit.edu/~ryan/cse4251/mini_java_grammar.html, August 2005.
12. Manuel Wimmer and Gerhard Kramler. Bridging Grammarware and Modelware. Technical report, Vienna University of Technology, http://www.big.tuwien.ac.at/research/publications/2005/1105.pdf, 2005.
13. Niklaus Wirth. What can we do about the unnecessary diversity of notation for syntactic definitions. *Communications of the ACM, 20(11)*, November 1997.

sNets: A First Generation Model Engineering Platform

Jean Bézivin

Atlas Group, INRIA and LINA, University of Nantes,
2, rue de la Houssinière - BP92208, 44322 Nantes Cedex 3, France
Jean.Bezivin@univ-nantes.fr

Abstract. As we are currently improving AMMA (the ATLAS Model Management Architecture), a second generation model engineering platform installed on top of the Eclipse Modeling Framework (EMF), we borrow inspiration from a previous work undertaken fifteen years ago at the University of Nantes. This initial model-engineering platform named *sNets* (for Semantic Networks) included several functional blocks like the *sMachine*, the *sBrowser*, the *sQuery*, the *sAction* system, etc. Several parts of these tools are still in use today. At a time when we are defining the main architectural style of the new platform, it may be helpful to come back on the initial learning of this project. This paper describes the sNets project and summarizes some lessons learnt in the course of the design and utilization of this first generation modeling framework.

1 Introduction

This paper summarizes some lessons learnt in the building of a model-engineering platform fifteen years ago. Initiated in 1990 the project was concluded several years later by the PhD Thesis of Richard Lemesle in October 2000. The application we had in mind when starting the project was the reverse engineering of legacy systems, mainly COBOL programs [5], [18]. The idea was to use what is called today a COBOL metamodel or DSL (Domain Specific Language) to extract models from programs in order to facilitate many viewing, querying and transforming operations on these models. Several other metamodels were also produced and used during this work.

1.1 Context of the Project

The first idea was to use directly the facilities of an advanced object-oriented language (Smalltalk-80) for building the reverse engineering system. We wanted the system to be very evolutionary and capable of handling not only standard COBOL but other languages as well, including dialects of COBOL itself. Soon it became obvious that the advanced Smalltalk mechanisms were not sufficient to provide the needed extensibility. Starting from the Smalltalk compiler written in Smalltalk, we designed a COBOL analyzer written in Smalltalk. When dealing with all the syntactical categories found in a COBOL program, we came to the conclusion that the precise, complete and evolutionary expression of these categories and of the various relations between them needed a stronger ontological framework support. The architectural

J.-M. Bruel (Ed.): MoDELS 2005 Workshops, LNCS 3844, pp. 169–181, 2006.
© Springer-Verlag Berlin Heidelberg 2006

decision to build an intermediate layer, on top of Smalltalk, able to allow modular and changeable definitions of "domains" was rapidly taken. This layer built itself in Smalltalk was intended to facilitate the decoupling of the application from the underlying system. In retrospect, we understand this as a transition from pure object-oriented programming to domain modeling and a positioning of both technologies. The main part of the intermediate layer is the sMachine, some kind of model engineering virtual machine, functionally similar to the ATL virtual machine recently described in [25].

1.2 Inspiration

The basic inspiration in the sNets project was the PIE system defined by Bobrow and Goldstein [19]. This was one of the first important applications built in the Smalltalk-76 language. PIE was a collaborative work support system with advanced versioning capabilities. This project was later restarted at Xerox to build a new version of PIE in Smalltalk-80, but unfortunately cancelled. The study of the PIE system started in 1989 in Nantes but no code was available and a first series of prototypes had to be built in order to implement the described properties of the system. Many features were added to PIE in the first series of sNets prototypes in order to build progressively a three-level modeling framework, similar to the present MOF-based metamodeling frameworks.

1.3 Organization

This paper is organized as follows. Section 2 describes the main results achieved in the sNets project. Section 3 presents a short related work discussion. Section 4 presents some lessons learnt in this project and section 5 concludes.

2 Achievements

2.1 The sNets Conceptual Model

The basic underlying algebraic structure was directed edge-labeled graphs. From the PIE system, we kept the organization of a semantic network and the versioning system. We then added three new features that were found at this time to be essential to achieve our goals: global typing, reflectivity and partitioning. The usual definition of sNets was some kind of reflective, typed and partitioned semantic networks. A unique "meta" relation (Figure 1) was used to define the global typing system.

The lower part of Figure 1 could be interpreted as:

$$\exists\, x, \exists\, y : \mathbf{Cat}\,(x) \wedge \mathbf{Mat}\,(y) \wedge \mathbf{name}\,(x, "aCat") \wedge \mathbf{name}\,(y, "aMat") \wedge \mathbf{on}\,(x, y)$$

The global typing system defined as in the left part (a) of Figure 2 could be visually presented as in the right part (b) of the same Figure.

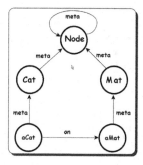

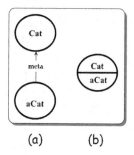

Fig. 1. Basic sNets organization

Fig. 2. Visual sNets notation for the global typing system

2.2 The "Universe" Concept

We became rapidly convinced that modularity mechanisms should be added to our modeling framework right from the start. We decided that, in the global sNets graph, we would add a notion of partition of the graph (a subgraph), captured by the concept of a "Universe" (Figure 3). Any sNets element belongs to one and exactly one such Universe.

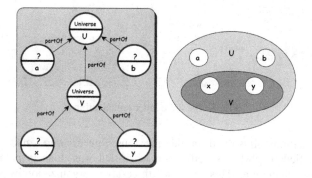

Fig. 3. Capturing graph partitions with the notion of Universe

2.3 The "Layer" Concept

The notion of universe was important to define an organization of the global modeling graph. We stated that SU is a meta-universe of U iff every element of U finds its *metaelement* in SU. This relation named "*sem*" at the time is today recognized as the "*conformsTo*" relation [13] defining the conformance between a model and its metamodel.

The conformance relation between universe U and meta-universe SU in Figure 4 captured by the "sem" relation allowed defining a three-layer system (U, SU, SSU) as illustrated by Figure 5.

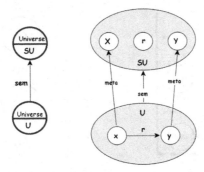

Fig. 4. Universes and meta-universes: the sem relation

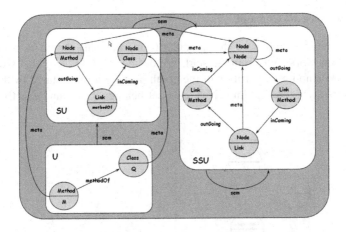

Fig. 5. The three layer organization

All the situations illustrated in the previous figures were made explicit and formally specified in [28], a specification work that was done in parallel with the Smalltalk implementation. This resulting three-layer organization was then found satisfactory and could be used for several practical experiments on various domains different from the COBOL domain (software test, languages and methods, etc.).

In the sNets organization, every node pertains to one and only one universe and has three standard links: "meta", "name" and "partOf". Some less important relations were also added in the first SSU layer (commonly called now the M3 layer), for example to express that a link represents the reverse relation of another link.

2.4 The sMachine

In order to implement this entire framework, a virtual machine was then defined and implemented in Smalltalk, with a set of APIs for accessing the various model elements [26]. Many examples of meta-universes were then built and served to experimental assessment. In some cases, universes based on these meta-universes were set up. This gave a first idea of the remaining scale-up problems. With some meta-universes of the Smalltalk system, the volume of a typical extracted universe could be of the order of more than 50.000 nodes and challenged the memory capacity and processing power of the basic desktop machines at the time (1990's).

2.5   The sBrowser

Viewing a complex graph was an important challenge. The first idea to browse such structures was to build specialized visual tools. In reason of the sNets uniform representation structure, such a visual presentation could be defined (and as a matter was defined) in specialized viewing tools (Figure 6). Note that in this view bidirectional links are automatically drawn to represent couples of unidirectional reverse links.

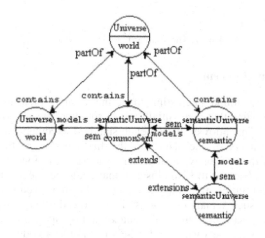

Fig. 6. Visual presentation of sNets

However, practical experience with such visual presentations shown serious limits when displaying more than 50 nodes simultaneously [10]. A new solution had to be found. Taking inspiration from the initial PIE system, a sliding window textual browsing system was then defined (Figure 7). This *sBrowser* system provided browsing capabilities that performed independently of the size of the whole graph.

The version of the sBrowser pictured in Figure 7 has the same capabilities as the original Smalltalk one, but was later redesigned in Java in [28]. The buttons at the bottom allows broadening or narrowing the window view on the graph (here the window is seven panes wide).

The sBrowser was the basis for technical observation and updating of the sNets system. However, this could not be accepted by end users that would need to access the system. Therefore, several different specialized browsers were defined for specific meta-universes at the level M2 (i.e. metamodels). Since one main application was the analysis of COBOL programs, specialized COBOL browser were programmed by hand on top of the sNets representation. No tentative was made to generate this browser semi-automatically from the COBOL semantic universe (metamodel).

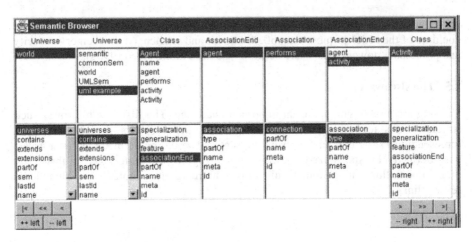

Fig. 7. The standard sBrowser system

2.6 The "sAction" Concept

Very rapidly, it was found interesting to define what is presently known as M3-executability. The name that was initially given to some special nodes was semantic actions (*sActions*). This allowed to associate standard executability to every node in any of the three layers of the sNets. In the first version of the framework, the implementation of the various types of semantic actions was done by associating them to Smalltalk blocks (similar to Lisp closure), that could be executed in the context of the Smalltalk object representing the current node. From a given node, several named links could lead to such semantics actions. This allowed a very simple and powerful mechanism of automatic definition of contextual pop-up menus (e.g. right mouse button click) displaying the various link labels leading to a node of type *sAction* like

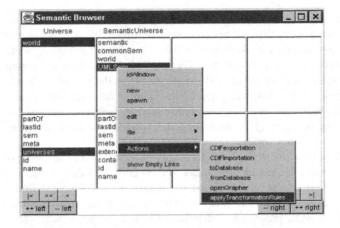

Fig. 8. Applying sActions in sNets

ioWindow, *new*, *spawn*, *edit*, *file*, *Actions*, and *show Empty Links* in the example of Figure 8. A possibility of hierarchical pop-up menus could be added without any difficulty, following a similar organization.

2.7 The "sQuery" Concept

Very soon after the start of the sNets project, the need arose for a mechanism for querying graphs. The initial specification of the project involved the use of path expressions as navigation and querying facility in these graphs. A first complete implementation was presented in [20]. This allowed to write such selection expressions as *(a.(b|c*).d)** to access a set of nodes from a given node. The vocabulary *{a,b,c,d}* corresponded in this implementation to any edge label in the graph, not only labels of a given level-2 universe. The important objective of the project described in [20] was the homogeneous representation of query expressions in the graph itself, as normal sNets expressions. This querying facility was then extended in [28] as a full model transformation facility and proposed as such in [29]. Some time later, the OMG launched the QVT request for proposal (RFP).

3 Related Work

The work on sNets was also much influenced by other important contributions in model engineering that have been very often forgotten in recent literature. It is common practice to date the beginning the modern period of model engineering at the launch of the MDA initiative by OMG in 2000. The reality is much more complex.

We have already mentioned the important impact of such proposals as PIE and Sowa graphs on the domain. Other initiatives were also very influential. We will only quote below some of those that came to our attention during the course of the sNets project. A complete review of influencing model-engineering sources is beyond the scope of the present paper, but would constitute an interesting undertaking.

Since the beginning, we have acknowledged the strong link between modern model engineering and ontology engineering. The pioneering work of Gruber was a permanent source of inspiration. The KIF (Knowledge Interchange Format [2]) had many interesting features related to modularity that comforted us in the idea of installing this notion at the hearth of the formalism with the notion of sNets Universes related to the notion of KIF "Theory". The modular organization of KIF theories is still today an example to follow. The recent work of Gruber (Every Ontology is a Treaty [23]) is completely relevant to model engineering and could be applied to metamodels.

CDIF (CASE Data Interchange Format [21]) was most influential in the period when UML and MOF were still being defined at OMG. Once again here, one of the key values of CDIF, beyond its ability to provide a standard exchange scheme between CASE tools (ako XMI without the XML lexical basis) was its strong modularity device ("Subject Areas") and the important varieties of corresponding metamodels. It is unfortunate that only a limited number of ideas made their way to the UML/MOF construction at that time.

The story of the Microsoft OIM (Open Information Model) initiative is hard to follow today since many historical traces recorded in Web sites have already been lost. Some disappeared like the one handled by the Metadata coalition. Fortunately, one may still find traces of these in such contributions as [4]. In the following organization of metamodels (Figure 9) extracted from [4], we can even see that a transformation metamodel was included. Note that in this work, the UML metamodel is the first proposal UML 1.0. OIM proposed at this time an advanced model-engineering environment that unfortunately was not pursued. Many lessons from this undertaking have probably been lost.

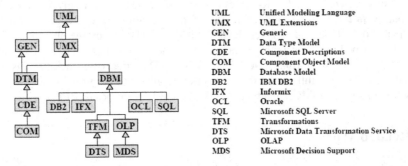

Fig. 9. The Microsoft Open Information Model (OIM)

Many CASE or MetaCASE tool builders have been very influential in the 80's, like Concerto (Edourd André), MetaEdit+ (Juha-Pekka Tolvanen), GraphTalk (Patrick Jeulin) and many more. It is surprising how the present undertakings in metamodel driven tools are ignoring the lessons of these past projects and very often reinventing the wheel. MetaEdit+ was built in Smalltalk like sNets but concentrated on graphical modeling, GraphTalk used an underlying structure of hypergraphs and Concerto initially developed most of the advanced ideas we see now appearing in modern model engineering platforms.

4   Lessons Learnt

Many lessons learnt in this project may still be of interest today. We propose some of them here as an initial list. We are still borrowing inspiration from this project when studying the design alternatives of our current AMMA platform built on top of the Eclipse project [1].

4.1   On the Need for a Conceptual Model

In retrospect what seems the most important issue when building such a platform is to define a clear and precise conceptual model -there is nothing more practical than a good theory-. This conceptual model has to be matched onto an efficient implementation. This was achieved in the sNets system through several cycles of definition/implementation.

Another requirement that is often made is the mapping onto normative recommendations. In the case of the sNets, this goal was not pursued at all. One reason is that the interesting normative recommendations (like CDIF) were not in the domain of reverse engineering. As a result, the whole sNets system relied on proprietary formats. In retrospect this was not too much of a problem since it was possible when necessary to map onto existing standards. Mapping to UML or to MOF-based system could be achieved later at a reasonable implementation cost by specific bridges.

4.2 On the Need for Minimality

One goal that was pursued since the beginning of the project was the definition of a minimal level M3 universe (SSU). We tried very hard to eliminate all that was not strictly necessary at the M3 level (domain independent) to allow this feature to be reintroduced at the M2 level (domain dependent). This permanent quest for conceptual simplicity helped us to achieve the best performance for the virtual machine. It also allowed us to provide maximum evolutivity and flexibility due to the domain-specific M2-level universes. One decision that was probably not adequately addressed in the sNets project was to implement in the sMachine a powerful version management system, based on the PIE "context" feature. Today we recognize that there are several needs for such a version management capability and this should probably be left to the M2 level. This is similar to the model transformation language. Instead of defining just only one at the M3 level, it seems wise to allow for multiple definitions of such model transformation languages at the M2 level, by defining the associated metamodel or DSL.

4.3 From Implicit to Explicit

In retrospect what seems the most important issue when building such a platform is to define beforehand a clear and precise conceptual model making explicit all the design choices. After that, the implementation decisions could be applied, even by short-circuits. For example, the fact that each node has an outgoing *name* link leading to another node of type String with the name itself as its value could be implemented in a more efficient way in associating directly the String to the node. However, to all actions implying this node, the initial specification was expected.

In the sNets system, we tried to be as explicit as possible. We realized later that we had probably not completely reached this goal. If one looks at Figure 4 for example, one may realize that there is no possibility to link physically edge *r* to node *r*. The reason is that we are working in a graph and not in a hypergraph. The conceptual cost of using a hypergraph would probably be too important. A compromise was to use Sowa graphs to make explicit the "meta" relation between an "edge" and a "node" themselves explicitly represented in the Sowa graph as described in Figure 10 extracted from [180]. It seems that this later approach of using Sowa graphs for expressing the model engineering conceptual model could be a good choice. Of course, this does not contradict the implementation choices of the sNets, but may complement it by a more general conceptual model[1].

---

[1] Another interesting property of the Sowa graph notation is that it would not need an additional assertion language like OCL because the same language may describe at the same time the structural definition part and the logical assertion part.

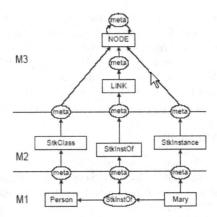

Fig. 10. A Sowa graph representation of modeling layers

4.4 Modularity Devices

As has been mentioned, the idea that model modularity mechanisms should be built from the start at the M3 level was an important design decision in sNets. A study was later conducted of the various proposed solutions (CDIF, OMG, etc.) and concluded on the high importance of this subject [27]. In retrospect, we may blame the weak definition of UML profiles, for many difficulties in present implementations of OMG recommendations. There is still a need for defining a clearer extension scheme for MOF metamodels.

4.5 Metamodels and Grammars

One feature of the original sNets system was the support for model extraction process based on a given metamodel. This was not pursued towards automatic support and was done only for the COBOL programs. The COBOL semantic universe was hand-coded into a context free grammar transformed into a "T-gen" parser recognizing input conforming to that grammar. T-gen is a Smalltalk translator generator. We know today that much more advanced automatic translation between grammars and metamodels are possible and also with other technical spaces like XML and many others.

4.6 Key Role of the Metametamodel

After observing many undertakings in the light of what was achieved in the sNets project, we are convinced of the essential role of a proper definition and implementation of the M3 level (metametamodel). With a weak definition of this key part of any model engineering framework, there is little hope to stability and convergence. On the contrary, a precisely defined and well-implemented M3-level metametamodel will allow the evolutive improvement of a library of M2-level metamodels.

5 Conclusions

As we have seen in this paper, there are many similarities between building a model-engineering platform in the present context and in a previous context. Even if this seems strange, the building of a model-engineering platform on top of the Eclipse system is very similar to the initial building of a model-engineering platform on top of the Smalltalk language. The main idea is how to map a conceptual view of such a platform onto an executable framework. Mapping to EMF is probably easier because it takes already into account some of the normative choices of the OMG for us (MOF) by providing an approximation of it with ECORE. This is the dimension we missed in the sNets: the correspondences with the normative world that did not exist at the time. However, we realize today that the price to pay for such a normative alignment may be very high. Furthermore, there are several ways to achieve this alignment: by interpretation or by transformation. Today these two possibilities still exist and should be compared when making engineering choices.

The experience in the sNets system is of high value today in the building of the AMMA platform [1]. For example, the status of the primitive types that we needed to introduce in the SSU M3-level universe is quite important and should not be confused with the similar primitive types that may be introduced in domain specific contexts at the M2-level. Another lesson is about the interest of choosing an object-oriented M3 or not. The need to introduce or not classes and attributes at the M3 level is much more accurately perceived when we have been able to experiment with a neutral M3. The sNets M3 level has no such feature and may be seen as closer to prototype-based object languages (like Self) than to class-based object languages (like Smalltalk). At a time when it may become important to evaluate and compare such different industrial choices as the OMG MOF 2.0, the Eclipse ECORE, the Microsoft DSL Tools, the experience gained with sNets is very valuable.

The most important lesson in the work on the sNets system was that it was possible to build a neutral and minimal M3-level infrastructure. The comparison with other industrial or normative M3-level solutions has still to be made on objective basis.

Acknowledgements

It is difficult to thank all the contributors to the sNets system since the beginning of the project. The main architect has been Richard Lemesle helped by Jérôme Lanneluc for the initial sMachine. While working on this project, Jérôme Lanneluc was supported by the OTI Company, Ottawa, Canada. Jérôme Cupif and Régis Cavaro implemented the initial sQuery system. The sBrowser has been implemented several times in Smalltalk by different people, each bringing iteratively new functionalities and new simplifications. The performance issues of the sBrowser and sMachine have been constantly improved through these different implementations. The present work has been supported in part by the IST European project ModelWare (contract IP #511731) and by a grant from Microsoft Research (Cambridge).

References

1. Allilaire, F., Bézivin, J., Didonet Del Fabro, M., Jouault, F., Touzet, D., Valduriez, P. **AMMA : vers une plate-forme générique d'ingénierie des modèles**. Génie Logiciel (73):8-15, (2005) see also the ATL website www.sciences.univ-nantes.fr/lina/atl

2. American National Standard, **KIF Proposed Standard Draft, Knowledge Interchange Format**, NCITS.T2/98-004, http://logic.stanford.edu/kif/dpans.html

3. Antonetti, F. **The OSMTool project**, Technical report, OSM project, University of Nantes LIST, (1994)

4. Bernstein, P.A., T. Bergstraesser, J. Carlson, S. Pal, P. Sanders, D. Shutt, **Microsoft Repository Version 2 and the Open Information Model**, Information Systems 24(2), (1999), pp. 71-98. available from http://research.microsoft.com/~philbe/

5. Bézivin, J & Lemesle, R. **sNets : The Core Formalism for an Object-Oriented CASE Tool** COODBSE'94 Proceedings of the Colloquium on Object Orientation in Databases and Software Engineering, World Scientific Publishers, ISBN 981-02-2170-3, pp 224-239, (1994)

6. Bézivin, J. & Gerbé, O. **Towards a Precise Definition of the OMG/MDA Framework** ASE'01, Automated Software Engineering, IEEE Computer Society Press, San Diego, USA, (2001).

7. Bézivin, J. & Lanneluc, J. & Lemesle, R. **A Kernel Representation System for OSM**. Rapport de recherche ERTO, Université de Nantes, (1994)

8. Bézivin, J. & Lemesle, R. **Ontology-Based Layered Semantics for Precise OAD&D Modeling** ECOOP'97 Workshop on Precise Semantics for Object-Oriented Modeling Techniques, Jyväskylä (Finland). LNCS Vol. 1357, Springer, (1998), ISBN 3-540-64039-8, pp 151-154

9. Bézivin, J. & Lemesle, R. **Reflective Modeling Schemes**, OOPSLA'99 workshop on Object-Oriented Reflection and Software Engineering, Denver. pp 107-122 (proceedings), (1999)

10. Bézivin, J. & Lemesle, R. **sBrowser : a prototype Meta-Browser for Model Engineering**, OOPSLA'98 Workshop on Model Engineering, Methods and Tools Integration with CDIF, Vancouver, (1998)

11. Bézivin, J. & Lemesle, R. **Towards A True Reflective Scheme** Reflection and Software Engineering, LNCS Vol. 1826, Springer, (2000), pp 21-38

12. Bézivin, J. Lanneluc, J. & Lemesle, R. **sNets: The Core Formalism for an Object-Oriented CASE Tool**, Object-Oriented Technology for Database and Software Systems, V.S. Alagar & R. Missaoui ed., World Scientific Publishers, (1995), p. 224-239.

13. Bézivin, J. **On the Unification Power of Models**. Software and System Modeling (SoSym) 4(2):171-188, Springer Journals, (2005)

14. Bézivin, J., Ernst, J. & Pidcock, W. **Model Engineering with CDIF** OOPSLA'98, Vancouver, post-proceedings, Summary of the workshop, (October 1998)

15. Bézivin, J., Lanneluc, J., Lemesle, R. **A Kernel Representation System for OSM**. Resarch Report, University & Nantes, (1994)

16. Bézivin, J., Lanneluc, J., Lemesle, R. **Representing Knowledge in the Object-Oriented Lifecycle** TOOLS PACIFIC'94, Melbourne, (December 1994), Prentice Hall, pp. 13-24

17. Bézivin, J., Lanneluc, J., Lemesle, R. **Un réseau Sémantique au cœur d'un AGL**. LM094, Grenoble, 13-14 (October 1994), 12 p.

18. Bézivin, J., Lennon, Y., Nguyen Huu, Ch. **From Cobol to OMT - A Reengineering Workbench Based on Semantic Networks** TOOLS USA'95, (1995), Santa Barbara.

19. Bobrow, D.G., Goldstein, I.P. **Representing Design Alternatives**, Proc. Conf. on Artificial Intelligence and the Simulation of Behaviour, Amsterdam, (July 1980)
20. Cupif, J, Cavaro, R. **Système Avancé de Navigation dans un réseau sémantique**. Report of Master Student work, (1995-1996)
21. Ernst, J. **Introduction to CDIF**, (September 1997), www.eigroiup.org/cdif/intro.html
22. Franceschini, A., Faure, L. **Study of the Personal Information Environment and second prototype implementations**, Report of Master Student work, (1992-1993)
23. Gruber, T. R. **Every Ontology is a Treaty** AIS Bulletin, Vol. 1, Issue 4, (2004), http://www.sigsemis.org/newsletter/october2004/tom_gruber_interview_sigsemis
24. Gruber, T.R. **A Translation Approach to Portable Ontologies**. Knowledge Acquisition, 5(2):199-220, (1993)
25. Jouault, F., Kurtev, I. **On the Architectural Alignment of ATL and QVT**, ACM Symposium on Applied Computing (SAC 06), Model Transformation Track, Dijon, Bourgogne, France, (2006)
26. Lanneluc, J. **The sMachine (Version 3)**, Technical report, OSM project, University of Nantes LIST, (1994)
27. Lemesle, R. **Meta-modeling and Modularity : Comparison between MOF, CDIF and sNets formalisms**, OOPSLA'98 Workshop on Model Engineering, Methods and Tools Integration with CDIF, Vancouver, (1998)
28. Lemesle, R. **Techniques de modélisation et de métamodélisation** PhD Thesis, University of Nantes, (26 October 2000)
29. Lemesle, R. **Transformation Rules Based on Meta-modeling**, Enterprise Distributed Object Computing, EDOC'98 proceedings, San Diego, (1998).
30. Lemesle, R. **Un réseau sémantique au coeur d'un AGL** Master Thesis (DEA), (September 1994)
31. Lescalier, V., Gréard, B., **Study of the Personal Information Environment and First Prototype Implementations**, Report of Master Student work, (1991-1992)

Workshop Report: Model Driven Development of Advanced User Interfaces (MDDAUI)

Andreas Pleuß[1], Jan van den Bergh[2], Stefan Sauer[3], and Heinrich Hußmann[1]

[1] Institute for Computer Science,
University of Munich, Munich, Germany
{Andreas.Pleuss, Heinrich.Hussmann}@ifi.lmu.de
[2] Expertise Centre for Digital Media,
Hasselt University, Hasselt, Belgium
Jan.VandenBergh@uhasselt.be
[3] Institute for Computer Science,
University of Paderborn, Paderborn, Germany
sauer@upb.de

Abstract. This paper reports about the workshop *Model Driven Development of Advanced User Interfaces* (MDDAUI) which was held on October 2nd, 2005 at the *MoDELS/UML 2005* conference in Montego Bay, Jamaica. We introduce the topic of the workshop and give an overview about the workshop's structure. Then we summarize the accepted contributions and finally we provide an overview about the workshop discussion and its results.

It is intended to provide a follow-up event of this workshop in the next year.

1 Workshop Topic

The user interface of an application is often one of the core factors determining its success. Existing approaches for user interface development provide abstract and platform independent models for basic widget-based user interfaces. This workshop deals with model driven development of advanced user interfaces.

Today there is an increasing demand for user interfaces with high usability whereas the covered functionality gets more and more complex. Applications often provide more intuitive interaction techniques as well as tailored and customizable representations of information. Complex information is presented in individual and interactive graphic objects. Techniques like animation or 3D visualization are used to achieve a more comprehensive or attractive presentation. Some user interfaces also use additional perception channels beside graphics, e.g. speech or haptic output. In addition, the usage of temporal media types, like animation or sound, and the combination of different modalities lead to synchronization and dependency issues. Moreover, even within a single modality, different devices are used for different purposes.

While on the one hand such a broad spectrum of presentation, perception, and representation media has been established, it is on the other hand necessary

J.-M. Bruel (Ed.): MoDELS 2005 Workshops, LNCS 3844, pp. 182–190, 2006.

to figure out a possible configuration which best addresses the user's needs. An appropriate level of usability often requires customization of the user interface. Some applications also require an automatic adaptation to their current runtime context, like location or available devices.

Significant work has been done addressing these issues for an advanced development of user interfaces and further research is still under progress. For application development in general, some of the most important state-of-the-art concepts are the Unified Modeling Language and the Model Driven Development (MDD) paradigm. Thus, the workshop involves the areas of software engineering and human-computer interaction and aims to integrate the required methods and concepts of advanced user interface development into MDD. The goal is to support a model driven development of applications under comprehensive consideration of features of advanced user interfaces. The target application area is not limited to classical business applications and may include for example games, simulations, and infotainment or edutainment applications.

2   Spectrum of Submissions and Participants

Interested participants were asked to submit a short position paper of four pages length in double-column format. We received 13 submissions from which 9 have been accepted according to the reviews of the program committee. As various work has already been done in the area of user interface development, we concentrated on papers which demonstrate the experience of the authors in this field and clearly focus on the workshop topic.

The resulting spectrum of participants included people from human-computer interaction domain as well as people working mainly in the field of model driven development. Besides people from academia, we had also participants working in industrial context.

As a result, the presentations included a broad spectrum of views on the workshop topic. In particular the literature references in the accepted papers provide a very comprehensive overview over existing work relevant in this research area. Most accepted papers propose a concrete solution for some of the open problems while a few are position papers which summarize the state-of-the art and outline critical problems and challenges in model driven user interface development.

3   Workshop Schedule

The workshop took one day during the week of the MoDELS/UML 2005 conference. We provided sufficient time for in-depth discussion, scheduling the presentation of papers mainly within the two morning sessions. A selected number of papers were presented as long presentations while all other accepted papers were presented in short presentations.

The talks in the two morning sessions were structured according to the following scheme: The first session was used for the presentation of approaches with a more general usage of models and model-based techniques for user interface development. The second session was used for papers which address more explicitly the techniques and standards of model driven development like *model driven architecture* (MDA). Finally, two short talks which presented more specific approaches opened the discussion sessions in the afternoon.

The detailed program can be found on the workshop webpage [1].

4   Presented Papers

The following section summarizes the papers presented on the workshop. All papers are published in [2].

4.1   A. Boedcher, K. Mukasa, D. Zuelke: Capturing Common and Variable Design Aspects for Ubiquitous Computing with MB-UID

This paper describes a model-based development process for useware, i.e. hardware and software components used for operating technical systems, e.g. in a factory. The process allows developing the user interface for different devices in a consistent way by identifying commonalities and variabilities of the interfaces. The models in the process are described using an XML language called UseML.

4.2   A. Wolff, P. Forbrig, D. Reichart: Tool Support for Model-Based Generation of Advanced User-Interfaces

The paper shows a model driven approach for user interface development under consideration of existing models like task models, dialogue models, and abstract user interface models. In particular, the paper focuses on the tool chain to support the models and the transformations between them. To enable an evolutionary development process, the tools apply to an "edit by replacement" approach which allows the developer to keep the connections of model elements throughout the different levels of abstraction in the development process.

4.3   S. Basnyat, R. Bastide, P. Palanque: Extending the Boundaries of Model-Based Development to Account for Errors

This approach addresses the domain of safety-critical interactive systems by integrating information about possible erroneous user behavior into the models. Therefore, the authors introduce an extension for task models. As an extended system model they use an existing approach called ICO (Interactive Cooperative Objects). Finally, they define the relationships between the extended task models and the ICOs.

4.4 N. Sukaviriya, S. Kumaran, P. Nandi, T. Heath: Integrate Model-Driven UI with Business Transformations: Shifting Focus of Model-Driven UI

This position paper provides an overview about current problems and challenges in practical application of model driven user interface development. Therefore, the authors explain several problem fields based on their experience with the integration of user interface design with model-based approaches. For the goal of integrating user interface development and model-based business process modelling, the authors show commonalities between these two tasks and conclude that business analysis can act as a useful starting point for user interface development.

4.5 J.S. Sottet, G. Calvary, J.M. Favre: Towards Model Driven Engineering of Plastic User Interfaces

This paper presents a model driven approach for the development of plastic user interfaces. With the term plasticity the authors refer to user interfaces which are adaptable to the context of use specified by the respective target platform, user, and environment. They consequently apply the state-of-the-art techniques of model driven development. In this way, they aim on the one hand to overcome known problems of monolithic code generators for user interfaces but on the other hand also to gain new insights – with user interfaces development as a very complex application domain – in the research area of model driven engineering.

4.6 T. Schattkowsky, M. Lohmann: Towards Employing UML Model Mappings for Platform Independent User Interface Design

This paper introduces a model driven approach for the development of user interfaces based on an extended UML class diagram, called information model. The information model contains the information to be provided by the system augmented with abstract information whether the user is allowed e.g. to create, delete or edit this information during runtime. On that base, transformation rules are described which finally lead to the specification of a concrete platform specific user interface.

4.7 J. Van den Bergh, K. Coninx: Using UML 2.0 and Profiles for Modeling Context-Sensitive User Interfaces

The paper presents a UML profile for context-sensitive user interfaces. It introduces stereotypes to support the modelling of common user interface models, like task models and dialogue models, with UML 2.0. In addition, it presents a context model to specify the context of the application, like the user and the environment. The elements from the context model can then be used to specify the influence of the application's context on its behaviour.

4.8   R.I. Bull, J.M. Favre: Visualization in the Context of Model Driven Engineering

The paper proposes a model driven approach to realize complex visualizations of large data. Therefore, it provides explicit metamodels for common complex graphical visualizations. A complex graphical visualization of a system's data can thus be generated by defining transformations between the models of the source data and the target graph. As an example, the authors show the generation of visualizations for source code.

4.9   C. Nill, V. Sikka: Modeling Software Applications and User Interfaces Using Metaphorical Entities

The paper discusses the use of metaphors to design interactive software. In this way it proposes to combine the concepts from user interface metaphors and the concepts from the "Tools and Materials" approach from software engineering domain. The authors propose to use the metaphors as a kind of conceptual patterns for an application's user interface.

5   Workshop Discussions

The sessions in the afternoon were mainly used for discussions. The discussions started with a collection of relevant general research questions in the whole group. We considered three complexes of questions as most relevant for the model driven development of (advanced) user interfaces:

- Models: Which are the adequate models? Which models are more important in which situation and what are some important points of attention?
- Process: What is an adequate development process? How to integrate prototypes? How to incorporate the user?
- Validation: How to validate the proposed approaches? How to validate the models?

On that base we formed two discussion groups to go more into the details. Each group consisted of eight workshop participants. The first group discussed on models for advanced user interfaces, the second group discussed on the model driven development process for (advanced) user interfaces. The third topic, validation, was not further discussed at this workshop.

5.1   Models

The discussion about the kind of models that are adequate in model driven development of advanced user interfaces was started by the observation that the answer to this question would probably be dependent on the kind of application. Therefore an attempt was made to define a limited number of categories of user interfaces. The discussion resulted in three categories identified by typical examples: "wordprocessor", "website", "first person shooter".

The first category, identified by the wordprocessor, has a user interface built around a document or object. Other examples are graphics editors, spreadsheets or integrated development environments. The manipulation of a central object or document is the main purpose of an application. Much of the functionality is dependent on the state of the object (e.g. selection of a word, paragraph, figure, table or no selection at all).

The second category, identified by the website (but also database applications), has a central role in the interface for different kinds of user-tasks. When lots of tasks are available, they are probably arranged around user roles or user interests, not around a central object.

The third category, identified by the first-person shooter, contains applications that are proactive, and often offer an immersive experience. These applications typically do not wait for user interaction, but rather act on their own and the user reacts to changes. Simulation software, action games and role playing games can be put in this category.

The discussion then continued on what makes the user interfaces of these applications inherently different. Four different criteria were determined: the influence of time on the behaviour of the application, the importance/structuring of user-tasks, the line between application logic and user interface, and the nature of the "controls".

Table 1 gives an overview of the perceived characteristics for each combination of categories and criteria. The score given for task importance should be regarded as follows: High task importance denotes that one can easily establish a number of steps or actions that have to be taken to reach a certain goal. One can therefore create a clear and highly structured task models organized in a tree structure for the given category of application. The medium score is given to applications like the word processor, which typically offer a lot of functionality. A task model of such an application would consist of a lot of tasks that can be executed in parallel or in an order-independent way. Such tasks typically have one or more preconditions which depend on the results of tasks that are performed at an earlier moment in time, such as a piece of text has to be selected before it can be made bold. Another example can be that some information had to be put on the clipboard (precondition) before it can be pasted somewhere in the document. A low score is given for user interfaces where it is very hard to establish a direct correlation between the high-level goals and the low-level actions. One could say that the scores are inverse proportional to the number of ways to solve a problem through the user interface of the application.

Table 1. Characteristics for the different categories

	Category 1	Category 2	Category 3
Task importance	medium	high	low
Time dependency	low	low	high
Separation of UI	medium	high	low
Controls	specialized, standard	standard	custom, no direct clues

The timing of interactions has different importance for different types of applications. The time it takes to do a certain action is in general not very important in the first two categories of user interfaces/applications, while this is in many cases crucial for applications of the last category, since the state of the application changes whether or not a user interacts with it.

The degree of separation between the user interface and the application logic also depends on the category of application. This is also shown by the type of controls that are used to realize the user interface of applications in each category. The applications in the second category can do with standards controls. Applications of the first category require a single specialized and complex control. In the last category of applications, the user interface is usually for the greatest part custom-made, with highly specialized controls or actions that are only accessible through short-cuts (no visual or other clues that those actions are available).

During the discussion it became clear that different categories of user interfaces can be discerned which have different requirements for models that would be used to describe them. It was, however, noted that the categorization that was made is not absolute and that it would need additional research to confirm that these categories are really different. A last remark was that one application can have different parts that belong to different categories. For example, the general configuration part of a 3D racing game application is part of category 2, while the part responsible for game play is of category 3 and the part to configure the car is of category 1.

As a general conclusion we can say that it is very probable that there is no single set of models optimal for every kind of user interface. It is however necessary to investigate the compatibility of the models to enable model driven development of complete applications, including the user interface.

5.2   Process

The discussion about the model driven development process for (advanced) user interfaces focused on problems of the practical application of model driven approaches. Thereby we considered the knowledge of those participants with experience as user interface designer in industrial context. We found the following research question as an extract of the most important issues regarding the model driven development process in practice:

> In the field of human-computer interaction and user interface design, well-established techniques exist to incorporate on the one hand creativity and on the other hand the user into the user interface development process. This observation yields the question how to incorporate the user/prototypes/creativity into the model-based development process?

In this view, we have elaborated the following properties of the model driven development process for user interfaces:

Models as Transmitter of Information. The role of models from the viewpoint of user interface design is to act as a kind of transmitter for the essential information about the user interface. A first aspect here is the transmission of information between different tools in the development process. With regard to user interface design, the involved tools here are not only modelling tools, but also tools to support the creative aspects mentioned in the question stated above. These are not only common user interface builders; often more sketching and drawing oriented tools like Photoshop are used to freely create ideas about a possible user interface design.

A second, possibly closely related, aspect is the transmission of information between different stakeholders within the development process. The supposed user of the system is often interested in the concrete layout, represented e.g. by screenshot-like images or prototypes, to discuss ideas and details about the system. The software developer, however, is interested in an abstract view on that part of the user interface which interrelates with the application logic.

In such a scenario, the models can act as the common information base for all the different representations and views on the user interface, containing the important essence of the overall decisions and hiding irrelevant or too much detailed information of respective development artefacts. For example from a screenshot of the user interface, the involved abstract user interface elements may be the only important information to be provided for further development steps. Other models may specify the number of different presentation units (e.g. screenshots) required for the overall system and the links between them.

Resulting Benefits. The discussion above led us to the core benefits of a model driven process in the view of such a design-oriented process. As the models act as transmitter for information, they can increase efficiency by preventing to create very similar information many times during the development process. Examples are hi-fi mock-ups or prototypes which build up on low-fi mock-ups like sketches: While the concept is derived from foregoing low-fi mock-ups, the realization itself has to be started from scratch again. If the required essence of the earlier development steps is captured within models, it will be possible to generate starting points for the next development steps.

Another benefit of models is their potential as communication tool between different stakeholders. This is especially important the context of user interface development, as it usually involves additional stakeholders (in addition to the software designer and the customer) like e.g. a user interface designer or, more specifically, a graphic designer. The models can also act as a kind of contract between them.

Certainly, general advantages of models are likewise significant for user interface development, like quality assurance, model-based validation, and documentation.

Requirements on Models. Finally, we discussed the resulting requirements on models to achieve a process which integrates experts, methods, and tools from user interface design area into model driven development. First, the models have to be flexible enough. This means in particular that models are allowed to be incomplete during the development process, to enable the creative design process and not to force designers to make decisions earlier than necessary.

Second, the modelling language must provide a high degree of usability for stakeholders who have to deal with the respective model. For example, models which have to be read or created by user interface designers should not base too much on technical concepts. A possibly intuitive notation and the recognition of well-known concepts in the modelling language can strongly increase the general acceptance of the language and thus the success of the whole process.

6   Conclusion

The workshop about Model Driven Development of Advanced User Interfaces was a first event to bring together knowledge from the fields of user interface development and model driven engineering. We received a broad spectrum of high quality contributions from people with very different backgrounds within this area. Thus, the submitted papers provide a comprehensive overview about work and literature relevant in this field.

Based on the success of this workshop, it is intended to aim for a follow-up event in the next year. A possible future direction is a more detailed analysis of the differences and commonalities between the available concepts.

Acknowledgements

We thank the workshop participants for their high quality contributions as well as the program committee members for their valuable reviews.

References

[1] MoDELS 2005 Workshop on Model Driven Development of Advanced User Interfaces, Workshop Webpage, 2005 http://www.edm.uhasselt.be/mddaui2005/
[2] Pleuß, A., Van den Bergh, J., Hußmann, H., Sauer, S.: Proceedings of Model Driven Development of Advanced User Interfaces. CEUR Workshop Proceedings, Vol. 159, 2005, http://ceur-ws.org/Vol-159

Towards Model Driven Engineering
of Plastic User Interfaces

Jean-Sébastien Sottet, Gaëlle Calvary, Jean-Marie Favre,
Joëlle Coutaz, Alexandre Demeure, and Lionel Balme

University of Grenoble, France
{Jean-Sebastien.Sottet, Gaelle.Calvary, Jean-Marie.Favre,
Joelle.Coutaz, Alexandre.Demeure, Lionel.Balme}@imag.fr

Abstract. Ubiquitous computing has introduced the need for interactive systems to run on multiple platforms in different physical environments. Providing a user interface specially crafted for each context of use (<user, platform, environment>) is costly, may result in inconsistent behaviors [5] and above all is limited to the contexts of use that have been envisioned at design time. Opportunistic interaction in a changing environment requires enabling approaches and techniques for gracefully adapting the interactive system to its context of use. In Human-Computer Interaction, this ability of an interactive system to withstand variations of context of use while preserving its quality in use is called *plasticity* [7]. This paper shows how Model Driven Engineering is suited for supporting plasticity both at design time and run time.

1 Introduction

In 1990s, Human Computer Interaction (HCI) promoted *model-based approaches* for automatically generating the code of the User Interface (UI) from more abstract descriptions. A plethora of Model-Based Interface Development Environments (MB-IDE) appeared, killing the approach by the poor quality of the generated UIs. In 2001, models come back [17] empowered by a taxonomy of transformations encompassing the seminal automatic forward engineering, and acting as a framework for reasoning about UIs engineering [6].

In the meantime, Software Engineering (SE) was advancing in Model Driven Engineering (MDE) [20], promoting networks of "productive" models, i.e. models that can be processed by the machine and that are interconnected through explicit mappings and transformations [12]. The cornerstone is the definition of explicit *metamodels*, i.e. models of the modeling languages used to describe the models. Actually, the focus is mostly set on transformation and traceability rather than on runtime productive models.

This paper bridges the gap between SE and HCI, envisioning MDE for both the design and run time of advanced UIs called *plastic UIs*. In HCI, plasticity refers to the ability of an interactive system to mould itself to a range of contexts of use while preserving its quality in use [7]. A *context of use* is defined as a triplet <user, platform, environment > respectively depicting the end user of the interactive system, the hardware and software resources that sustain the interaction, and the physical space in which the interaction takes place. With ubiquitous computing, UIs are no longer con-

J.-M. Bruel (Ed.): MoDELS 2005 Workshops, LNCS 3844, pp. 191–200, 2006.

fined to a unique desktop. They may be distributed and migrate across a dynamic set of possibly heterogeneous interaction resources that are opportunistically composed, borrowed and lent. For instance, because the battery of the PC gets low, the interactive system fully migrates to the nearest platform: another PC, a PDA, or a phone. But, of course, the UI cannot be the same on a PC and a PDA or a phone. As a result, the UI has to be *remold* to gracefully target such an other platform. Distribution, migration and molding are the three fulcra of plasticity [2].

Plasticity has first been addressed from the *multi-targeting* perspective, investigating design processes for producing UIs fitted for a range of targets (i.e., explicit contexts of use). Section 3 presents a MDE framework that, like SE, focuses on transformation and traceability. But, in ubiquitous computing, the changing and not always foreseeable context of use requires to go beyond multi-targeting. Both the vision and a research agenda are provided in section 4 for supporting a full plasticity. The paper is illustrated on a simple case study presented in section 2.

2 Case Study: Home Heating Control System

Basically, a Home Heating Control System (HHCS) makes observable and modifiable the temperature at home. In the case study, two rooms (the living room and the wine cellar) are equipped with a thermostat that can be set through different UIs (Figure 1). In a/, the screen size is comfortable enough to display the two thermostats. In b/, c/ and d/, the system shows a single thermostat at a time. The other one is accessible through a navigation task supported by a button in b/, a combo box in c/ and hyperlinks in d/. In e/, the watch is so small that the HHCS is limited to the most important room: the living room.

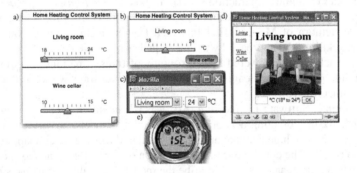

Fig. 1. Variants of a Home Heating Control System UI depending on the screen size

Experience shows that code-centric engineering is not suited for product line approaches: it induces extra-cost in development and maintenance, and does not prevent ergonomic inconsistencies [5].

3 From Mono- to Multi-targeting

The European CAMELEON project [8] produced a model-based framework for structuring the development process of UIs. This section proposes an improved version, compliant with the MDE backbone: design processes, metamodels, mappings and transformations.

3.1 Development Process

Whilst current industrial practice is still mostly code-centric (right bottom of Figure 2), MDE processes are based on successive refinements of models with the integration of new information at each step. ArtStudio [22] and Teresa [16] exemplify forward engineering processes. Conversely, Vaquita [4] and WebRevenge [18] build abstract models from implementations. Such reverse engineering tools are valuable for both dealing with legacy systems and facilitating the elaboration of abstract models. Figure 2 proposes a MDE CAMELEON-based framework that covers both forward and reverse engineering. In practice, processes are iterative rather than straightforward, mixing forward and reverse engineering, the number of steps and the entry point may vary [14].

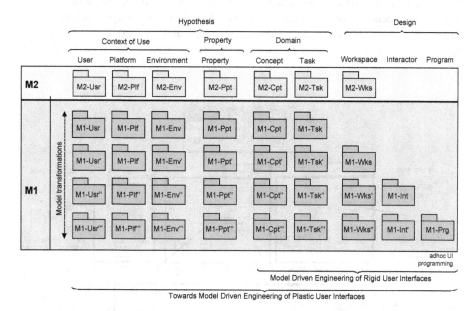

Fig. 2. A Model Driven Engineering framework for the development of UIs. For clarity, mappings and transformations are not shown.

The framework makes explicit the two levels, M1 and M2, of the *metapyramid* [13]. The top layer corresponds to the M2 level: each package represents a *metamodel*. As the reader can see, many facets have to be made explicit comprising design hypotheses and design decisions. Design hypotheses include the definition of the

target (<user, platform, environment>), the elicitation of required properties (typically, the quality in use), and the applicative domain in terms of both concepts and
user tasks. Design decisions cope with the structure of the UI in *workspaces*, its rendering with *interactors*, and its coding as an executable/interpretable *program*.

The models representing a specific interactive system (e.g., HHCS in Figure 1c)
belong to the M1 layer. The set of columns represent different points of view on a
same UI. In a given column, all models *conform to* [13] the same metamodel. A line
is the result of a (reverse) engineering step. The framework makes explicit the need
for revising models during the engineering process to fit in new constraints. For instance, an initial task model (M1-Tsk) might be tuned into another version (M1-Tsk')
for replacing a tasks interleaving (Figure 1a) with a sequence (Figure 1b) due to a too
small screen size.

3.2 (Meta)Models

Metamodels are keys to Model Driven Engineering. To be productive, each model
must be accompanied with a precise and explicit metamodel. Otherwise the model
cannot be interpreted and transformed by a machine. As historically speaking, the
backbone of model-based approaches was limited to the domain and design models,
their metamodels are of course more advanced than the innovative metamodels of
target (M2-User, M2-Platform, M2-Environment) and properties (M2-Property).
Figure 3 introduces very basic metamodels for demonstrating the framework on the

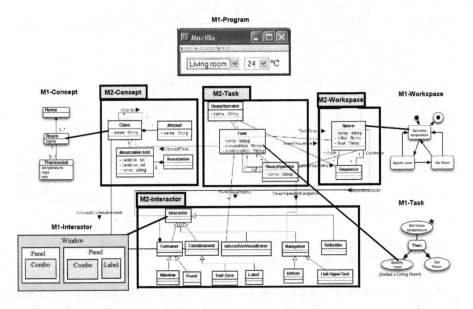

Fig. 3. Models conform to Metamodels for the UI (*M1-Program*) presented in Fig1c. For clarity, few mappings (at the M2 level only) are shown.

case study depicted in Figure 1c. The concepts (M1-Concept) are limited to the notions of "home", "room" and "temperature". They are written as an UML class diagram. The task model (M1-Task) decomposes the root task "control the temperature at home" in first "specify the room" then "set its thermostat". A workspace is created per task (M1-Workspace), and the navigation between workspaces complies with the task decomposition. At the interactor level (M1-Interactor), the root task is mapped to a window that contains the two panels corresponding to the sub-tasks. The selections (room and temperature) are done through combo boxes whilst a label makes observable the temperature unit. The program model (which metamodel describes the HTML language) is not shown.

Obviously, metamodels are connected together. For clarity, few links are drawn in Figure 3. They express that:

- Tasks may manipulate concepts (mapping between M2-Concept and M2-Task). For instance, the task "control the temperature at home" manipulates the concept of "home";
- Tasks are performed in workspaces which navigation may be driven by the operators between tasks (mapping between M2-Task and M2-Workspace);
- Tasks, workspaces and concepts are rendered by interactors (mappings between M2-Task, M2-Concept, and M2-Interactor).

3.3 Mappings and Transformations

With metamodels, mappings and transformations are the cornerstones of MDE. Without them, all the models would be isolated. On the contrary, the idea is to incrementally transform abstract models (Platform Independent Models, PIM in MDE jargon) into Platform Specific Models (PSM). This is obviously an over simplification. Monolithic code generators are not suited for advanced UIs. An alternative comes from libraries of small composable and extensible transformations. The designer selects and if necessary tunes the appropriate transformations. If no transformation is appropriate, a new one can be written thanks to transformation languages. It can then be added to a library for further use. In this way, expertise can be captured and packaged into transformation libraries.

Quite often, transformation engines are associated to specific modeling environments based on a given set of metamodels for UI development. This is the case for TransformiXML in the UsiXML environment [15]. While this kind of approaches is worth, it is specific to UI development. It does not cover the whole software engineering process.

The core idea of our approach is to use generic MDE techniques and extensive libraries of metamodels. This approach is being investigated in the Zooomm project [23]. While emerging standards for expressing MDE transformations are under active development (e.g. QVT), we are investigating the appropriateness of the ATL generic MDE transformation language [3] for plasticity. The following piece of code is an example of transformation written in ATL based on the metamodels of Figure 3. It describes very simple rules transforming tasks (M1-Task) into workspaces (M1-Workspace):

- The rule *TaskToSpace* creates one workspace *w* per user task *t*. The workspace takes the name of the task;
- The rule *OrOperatorToSequence* applies to the task model. It transforms all OR operators *o* between two user tasks (*o.leftTask* and *o.rightTask*) into two sequence operators (from o.*motherTask* to o.*leftTask*, and o.*leftTask* to o.*rightTask*).

```
module M2TaskToM2Workspace {
    from M1Task : M2Task
    to   M1Workspace : M2Workspace
    -- One workspace per task
    rule TaskToSpace {
      from t : M2Task!Task
      to w : M2Workspace!Space (
        name <- t.name )
    }
    -- OrOperator to SequenceOperators
    rule OrOperatorToSequence{
      from o : M2Task!BinaryOperator (
        o.name = "or"
      )
      to motherToLeft : M2Workspace!Sequence (
        origin<- [TaskToSpace.w]o.motherTask,
        destination<-[TaskToSpace.w]o.leftTask)
    ...
```

As pointed out by the MDE framework, mappings and transformations must be further explored to convey both their validity domain (i.e., the contexts of use in which they make sense) and their rationale (e.g., the properties they preserve). This is necessary for promoting transformations libraries, and envisioning their use at runtime. More generally, this vision of prefabricated hand-made models, selected, transformed, and linked at runtime is the approach we promote for supporting a full plasticity.

4   From Multi-targeting to Plasticity

The "no limit" vision of ubiquitous computing compels to *open* approaches capable of adapting the UI to unforeseen contexts of use. Services discovery calls for this same openness. However, experience shows that on the fly generated UIs do not compete with the quality of "hand made" UIs. As a result, a mix of prefabrication and creation on the fly rises as a valuable approach. The milestones are: ecosystems for an extensive use of productive models, a mix of open and close adaptations, and a meta-UI for providing the end user with the observability and control of plasticity.

4.1   Towards Ecosystems

An *ecosystem* refers to the complex of organisms and their environment interacting as a unit. By analogy, plastic interactive systems and the surroundings in which they evolve form an ecosystem, i.e., an islet in which physical and digital resources are borrowed and lent. The metaphor of octopuses that cling to rocks may be taken for conveying the opportunistic deployment of plastic interactive systems among the available resources. An octopus can stick to a unique rock, or on the contrary take benefit from its elasticity to spread on a set of rocks. Its deployment depends on the surroundings (the topology, other organisms, undercurrents, etc.). The approach we promote for enabling this full plasticity takes advantage of the MDE framework but goes one step further: the deployment of the interactive system is finer described, its evolution is integrated, and models and mappings have an existence at runtime.

As explained in [9], the key activities in software architectural design include: functional and modular decompositions, functions allocation to modules, processes identification, mapping modules with processes and mapping processes with processors. From a plasticity perspective, adaptation may change both the identification of software architecture *elements* (functions, modules, processes and processors) and their mappings (functions and modules, modules and processes, processes and processors). Typically, when a PDA arrives, the availability of this new processor may trigger a reshuffling of any element and/or mapping, for instance a migration. Yet, the framework is limited to the UI perspective (it does not take into account the functional core) and covers neither the modules nor the processes (the UI is directly mapped on the platform). This calls for an extension of the framework to integrate the functional, modular and coordination structures [9]. The physical structure [9] requires more advanced platform and environment models. This is challenging as platform and environment tend to blend together [2]. For instance, augmented tables and rain curtains may serve as display surfaces. As a consequence, the physicality of an entity (physical, digital and spiritual) and its role become central and might be modeled [11].

As pointed out in CAMELEON, additional metamodels are required for modeling the *transformation* of the interactive system when the context of use changes. CAMELEON distinguishes the *evolution* and *transition* models. Whilst the evolution model prescribes the reaction to perform in case of change of context of use, the *transition* model deals with the continuity of interaction for accompanying the end user in the change. Pick and Drop [21] provides an example of transition: yellow lines are projected on the table to make observable the platform to which the UI is migrating.

Thus, an interactive system becomes a "cobweb" made of interconnected models. For instance, the combo-box "Living room" in Figure 3 knows to which task it corresponds (i.e., "specify the room"). If this task t is optional, then a strategy may be to suppress t if the user shrinks the window. Suppressing t will be "simply" done by deleting all the interactors that are mapped on t. As shown in [11], this approach is powerful for reasoning about UIs. Traditional usability properties such as *observability* [1] and more advanced properties such as distribution, replication and migration can be formally defined and checked [11].

4.2 Towards a Mix of Close and Open Adaptation

Close-adaptiveness refers to the ability of an interactive system to handle a set of contexts of use alone. A close adaptive interactive system embeds mechanisms for sensing the context of use, detecting the need of adaptation, computing and executing the most appropriate reaction. The reaction may be dictated by an internal evolution model or computed on the fly. In the opposite, *open-adaptiveness* makes reference to adaptation processes that are taken over by tier components, for instance the DMP middleware [2]. To that end, the interactive system provides the world with management mechanisms: self-descriptive meta-data (such as the current state and the services it supports and requires), and the methods to control its behavior such as start/stop and get/set-state. Active models are a good option for a meta-description at runtime.

Between these two extremes of *full close* and *full open* adaptations, hybrid allocations distribute the four steps of the adaptation process (sensing the context of use, detecting the need of adaptation, computing and executing the reaction) in a slinky way to either the interactive system or tier components. Typically, if the interactive system does not embed all the components necessary for its adaptation, then an external components manager may be used to retrieve existing reusable components in a components storage [8]. To do so, components are self-descriptive: they indicate the function they support, the context of use they require, the properties they satisfy, etc. Obviously, MDE approach is fine for such a metadescription.

4.3 Towards a Meta-user Interface

From the end user perspective, the future heads for *interactive spaces* that harmoniously combine the physical space, the computing, networking and interaction resources available at this place and the digital world [2]. M*eta-user interfaces* (meta-UI) will be to interactive spaces what the desktop is to conventional workstations. They will bind together the activities that can be performed within the interactive space and provide users with the means to configure, control and evaluate the state of the space. Typically, the interaction techniques used to couple two surfaces, detach part of the UI, migrate UIs and accompany the end user in the change will be part of the meta-UI. Dash styles and scissors may convey the *detachability* of UIs elements; polylines may afford their *tearability* (the detachment is possible but not recommended); magnets could solve the dropping and reattachment of UIs elements, etc. Such techniques are nothing else than the UI of the MDE revised framework: any model, any mapping, any transformation should be under the control of the end user.

5 Conclusion

Models are not new in HCI. First attempts focused on full automatic generation of UIs, but the quality of both code and usability was poor. Moreover, the use of quite monolithic code generators made impossible the UIs customization and the integration of specific heuristics based on application domains. Finally, existing environments were not designed with interoperability in mind.

The approach presented in this paper is quite different. Instead of focusing on the UI only, general MDE techniques are investigated. The key idea is to merge the experience of both MDE and HCI communities. Instead of developing specific model based tools such as transformation languages for HCI, reusing emerging MDE technologies is promising. First versions might not be fully suited to UI development specificities, but if this is the case, this would lead to new requirements for MDE.

More generally, let us remember the unifying feature of the approach: HCI and MDE, design time and run time, remolding and redistribution. This last point is quite innovative as migration is considered as a quite heavy development process in the MDE community.

Acknowledgements

This work has been supported by the SIMILAR European Network of Excellence.

References

1. Abowd G., Coutaz J., Nigay L., "Structuring the Space of Interactive System Properties", Proceeding of the IFIP, 1992.
2. Balme, L., Demeure, A., Barralon, N., Coutaz, J., Calvary, G. CAMELEON-RT: A Software Architecture Reference Model for Distributed, Migratable, and Plastic User Interfaces, Lecture Notes in Computer Science, Volume 3295 / 2004, Ambient Intelligence: Second European Symposium, EUSAI 2004, Markopoulos P., Eggen B., Aarts E. *et al.* (Eds), Springer-Verlag Heidelberg (Publisher), ISBN: 3-540-23721-6, Eindhoven, The Netherlands, November 8-11, 2004, pp 291-302.
3. Bézivin, J., Dupé, G., Jouault, F., Pitette, G., Rougui., J. "First Experiments with the ATL Transformation Language: transforming XSLT into Xquery", in OOPSLA Workshop, Anaheim California USA, 2003.
4. Bouillon, L., Vanderdonckt, J., Retargeting Web Pages to other Computing Platforms, Proceedings of IEEE 9th Working Conference on Reverse Engineering WCRE'2002 (Richmond, 29 October-1 November 2002), IEEE Computer Society Press, Los Alamitos, 2002, pp. 339-348.
5. Calvary, G., Coutaz, J., Thevenin, D. A Unifying Reference Framework for the Development of Plastic User Interfaces, Proceedings of 8th IFIP International Conference on Engineering for Human-Computer Interaction EHCI'2001 (Toronto, 11-13 May 2001), R. Little and L. Nigay (eds.), Lecture Notes in Computer Science, Vol. 2254, Springer-Verlag, Berlin, 2001, pp. 173-192.
6. Calvary, G., Coutaz, J., Thevenin, D., Limbourg, Q., Souchon, N., Bouillon, L. Vanderdonckt, J. Plasticity of User Interfaces: A Revised Reference Framework, First International Workshop on Task Models and Diagrams for User Interface Design TAMODIA'2002, Bucarest, 18-19 July 2002, pp 127-134.
7. Calvary, G., Coutaz, J., Dâassi, O., Balme, L., Demeure, A. Towards a new generation of widgets for supporting software plasticity: the « comet », EHCI-DSVIS'2004, The 9th IFIP Working Conference on Engineering for Human-Computer Interaction Jointly with The 11th International Workshop on Design, Specification and Verification of Interactive Systems, Bastide, R., Palanque, P., Roth, J. (Eds), Lecture Notes in Computer Science 3425, Springer, ISSN 0302-9743, Hamburg, Germany, July 11-13, 2004, pp 306-323.
8. CAMELEON (Context Aware Modelling for Enabling and Leveraging Effective interactiON) project: http://giove.isti.cnr.it/cameleon.html.
9. Coutaz, J. Architectural Design for User Interfaces; The Encyclopedia of Software Engineering, J. Marciniak Ed., Wiley & Sons Publ., seconde édition, 2001.
10. Coutaz, J., Lachenal, C., Dupuy-Chessa, S. Ontology for Multi-surface Interaction. Proc. Interact 2003, M. Rauterberg et al. Eds, IOS Press Publ., IFIP, 2003, pp.447-454.
11. Demeure, A., Calvary, G., Sottet, J.S., Vanderdonckt, J. A Reference Model for Distributed User Interfaces, International Workshop on Task Models and Diagrams for User Interface Design, September 2005, Gdansk, Poland, pp 79-86.
12. Favre J.M., "Foundations of Model (Driven) (Reverse) Engineering", Dagsthul Seminar on Language Engineering for Model Driven Development, DROPS, http://drops.dagstuhl.de/portals/04101, 2004.

13. Favre J.M., "Foundations of the Meta-pyramids: Languages and Metamodels", DROPS, http://drops.dagstuhl.de/portals/04101, 2004.
14. Limbourg, Q. "Multi-path Development of User Interfaces", PhD of University of Louvain La Neuve, Belgium, 2004.
15. Limbourg Q., Vanderdonckt J., Michotte B., Bouillon L., Lopez-Jaquero, V., "UsiXML: a Language Supporting Multi-Path Development of User Interfaces", Working Conference on Engineering for Human-Computer Interaction, 2004.
16. Mori G., Paternò F., Santoro C. "Design and Development of Multidevice User Interfaces through Multiple Logical Descriptions" IEEE Transactions on Software Engineering, August 2004.
17. Myers B., Hudson S.E., Pausch R. "Past, Present, and Future of User Interface Software Tools", Transactions on Computer-Human Interaction (TOCHI), Vol 7, Issue 1, 2000.
18. Paganelli, L., Paternò, F. A Tool for Creating Design Models from Web Site Code, International Journal of Software Engineering and Knowledge Engineering, World Scientific Publishing 13(2), pp. 169-189, 2003.
19. Paternò, F. ConcurTaskTrees: An Engineered Notation for Task Models, Chapter 24, in Diaper, D., Stanton, N. (Eds.), The Handbook of Task Analysis for Human-Computer Interaction, pp. 483-503, Lawrence Erlbaum Associates, 2003.
20. Planet MDE, "A Web Portal for the Model Driven Engineering Community" http://planetmde.org.
21. Rekimoto, J.: Pick and Drop: A Direct Manipulation Technique for Multiple Computer Environments. In Proc. of UIST97, ACM Press, (1997) 31-39.
22. Thevenin, D., Coutaz, J., Calvary, G. A Reference Framework for the Development of Plastic User Interfaces. In Multi-Device and Multi-Context User Interfaces: Engineering and Applications Frameworks. Wiley Publ., H. Javahery Eds, 2003.
23. Zooomm, "Zooomm, The International ZOO Of MetaModels, Schemas and Grammar for Software Engineering", http://zooomm.org.

UML Model Mappings for Platform Independent User Interface Design

Tim Schattkowsky[1] and Marc Lohmann[2]

[1] C-LAB, Fürstenallee 11, 33102 Paderborn, Germany
`tim@c-lab.de`
[2] University of Paderborn, Department of Computer Science, Warburger Str. 100,
33098 Paderborn, Germany
`mlohmann@uni-paderborn.de`

Abstract. While model based design of platform independent application logic
has already shown significant success, the design of platform independent user
interfaces still needs further investigation. Nowadays, user interface design is
usually platform specific or based on C-level cross-platform libraries. In this
paper, we propose a MDA like design approach for user interfaces based on the
transformation of UML models at different levels of abstraction. This enables
platform independent design of user interfaces and a clear separation of UI and
application logic design while enabling full use of native controls in the actual
user interface implementation.

1 Introduction

Today, user interface development is still dominated by platform-dependent GUI
builders like those provided by the leading development environments. These tools
are suitable for building prototypes and real UIs at a very low level of abstraction.
Normally, they can only be used to design a user interface for one specific platform
and one specific programming language. Usually a user interface designer who devel-
ops a user interface for an application has to understand the relationship between the
different elements of his user interface, the implementation specific classes of the
application and the specific characteristics of a target platform. Furthermore, lack of
abstraction in UI design often forces large parts of the UI implementation in the responsibility of the software engineer rather than enabling the UI designer to work
concurrently.

Nowadays, these problems are getting even more important as contemporary applications are developed for different target platform. Modern information and communication systems have to present their UI on different devices with different capabilities. Thus, providing individual user interfaces for different target platforms becomes
an increasing burden as the number of platforms as well as the size of the applications
increases.

UI Models can provide an abstraction from the detailed problems of the implementation technologies and specific platform characteristics and can allow user interface
designers to focus on the conceptual tasks. In the software engineering community
model-driven development has become very successful. Especially the diagrams of
the industry standard UML (Unified Markup Language) [5] have become very suc-

J.-M. Bruel (Ed.): MoDELS 2005 Workshops, LNCS 3844, pp. 201–209, 2006.
© Springer-Verlag Berlin Heidelberg 2006

cessful and accompanying software development tools are available. Models are an established part of modern software development processes and thus a manual implementation of user interfaces becomes more and more undesirable. Furthermore, designing the interfaces on a higher abstraction level allows a clear separation of UI and application logic design. Thus, using models we can improve both productivity and software quality.

The problem with using models for the development of user interfaces is that we still face the problem that we have to generate user interface implementations for different platforms. Again, we can find a solution for this problem in the field of software engineering. The OMG has proposed the Model Driven Architecture (MDA) [6] that allows for deriving code from stable models even if the underlying infrastructure shifts over time. The idea is to distinguish between platform-independent models (PIMs) that are refined into platform-specific models (PSMs) which carry annotations for the generation of platform-specific code.

We propose an approach that adapts the MDA to the development of user interfaces. Our approach starts with the development of a platform independent model that describes the information to be displayed on a user interface. Designing the displayed information on such a high abstraction level allows for a complete separation of the user interface and application logic design. This platform independent model is refined at multiple levels to a platform specific model from which can be employed to generate an implementation for a specific target platform. The transformation steps between the different models are described by graph transformation rules.

The remainder of this paper is organized as follows: The next section discusses related work before section 3 introduces our approach. Finally, section 4 closes with a conclusion and future work.

2 Related Work

UI design has been subject to research for quite some time now. However, model based methods are largely discussed in the context of XML.

The User Interface Markup Language (UIML) [1] is an XML language that aims at providing a meta language for the declarative description of UIs. UIML maps abstract UI elements to actual platform widgets and describes events on these elements. The mapping is based on identifiers with no additional semantics and must be done by the application. UIML does not provide a generic mapping approach from a single abstract specification to different platforms. Instead, it is not independent from the target platform and the event mapping mechanism is quite limited. This latter is addressed by [2] where a similar UI description is complemented by more sophisticated behavior specification. However, this is not comparable to the expressiveness of UML's behavior models.

The User interface eXtensible Markup Language (UsiXML) [4] addresses the need for more abstraction in UI design, but still in an XML context. However, it introduces the idea to create an abstract UI model based on a domain model that is later refined to a concrete UI model consisting of existing widgets. This model is the basis for generating the final UI implementation. The whole approach is based on XML and graph transformations [3]. It is not aligned with the UML or behavior modeling in general. However, the approach could produce UML compliant output and a UI design tool based on the approach is available [11].

Finally, [7] discusses UI modeling using the UML. Different levels of abstraction exist in the form of a fixed simple model for abstract UIs that are the foundation for manual refinement of the abstract model to the actual application model.

3 Design Approach

Our approach is driven by the idea to allow for a complete separation of the UI and application logic design. As in MDA, our approach starts with the creation of a plat-form independent model. Before generating a platform specific UI implementation, the designer can configure the UI on multiple levels of PIMs, each independent of a target platform. From the most detailed PIM we can generate a platform specific UI implementation (see Fig. 1). Transformation rules between the different models facili-tate tool support for our UI development approach.

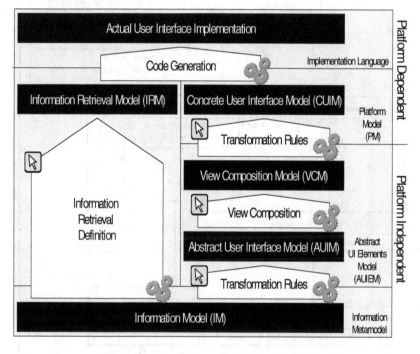

Fig. 1. Platform Independent UI Design Flow

3.1 Information Model

Our basic PIM is the Information Model (IM). This class diagram provides an abstract definition of the information and their logical dependencies that should be presented and modified through a UI. It is undistorted by technology information. Therefore, it allows business experts to ascertain much better than with a platform specific model and it provides an early starting point for user interface design.

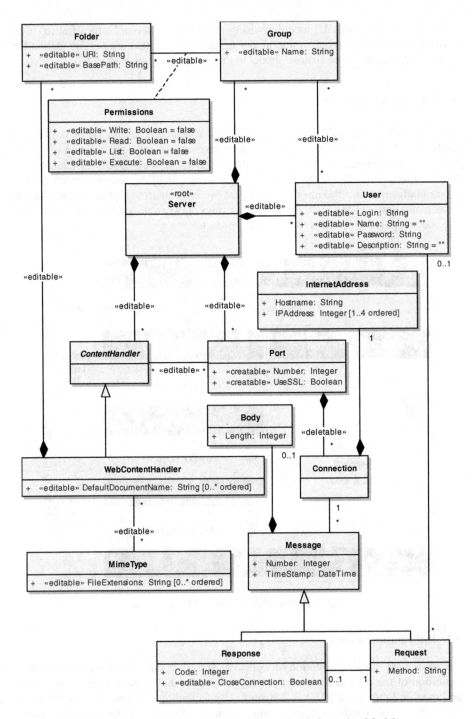

Fig. 2. Web Server Configuration UI Example - Information Model

Figure 2 shows the IM of an administration interface of a simple Web server. The Web Server may have a ContentHandler at a certain Port to which a Connection can be made by a User to access the content of a Folder if he has the necessary Permissions according to his Group memberships. Furthermore, the pending Requests and Responses are represented.

The associations and attributes in the IM are marked to indicate different kinds of data. Generally, the stereotypes <<readonly>> and <<editable>>, are used to mark associations and attributes as only displayable or editable. Attributes marked <<editable>> may have their values altered at runtime while such associations may have links added and removed. If an association is marked as <<deletable>>, links may only be removed in contrast to attributes, which may instead be marked as <<creatable>> indicating that their value may only be set by the constructor, i.e., when creating a new instance. If no stereotype is provided for an attribute or association, <<readonly>> is assumed.

The data types used by the attributes in the IM are fixed and range from primitive types (e.g. Integer, Float) to complex types defined by classes. Operations may be defined to interface application logic that cannot be captured by the data model, e.g., to send explicit messages to the application aside from persistent data.

The whole IM is a composition tree starting by a <<root>> class whose only instance represents the whole systems. This enables inference of aggregations to automatically generate all levels of abstraction from the IM without the need for user interaction. However, usually this is not desirable and the UI designer wants to provide these decisions manually at each level of abstraction.

3.2 Abstract User Interface Model

The PIM at the next level is the Abstract User Interface Model (AUIM). It includes some aspects of UI technology event though platform-specific details are absent. Essentially, the AUIM combines the data from the IM with abstract UI elements to access and manipulate that data. We have developed a metamodel –Abstract User Interface Elements Model (AUIEM)–that defines different UI elements at an abstract level in terms of related data sets and triggers. This Metamodel can be extended to project-specific needs by using the UML profiling mechanism.

Figure 3 shows an excerpt from the AUIEM employed in our example. This excerpt defines the Choice UIElement for selecting one Item from a Set. Furthermore, it provides the necessary elements to employ the Choice to select an Instance of a Class or a Link from a Property.

These elements are used in a set of graph transformation rules [8] that facilitate tool support for our approach. Each rule consists of a left hand side (subgraph of the IM) and a right hand side (subgraph of the respective AUIM to be created). In Fig. 4 an <<editable>> association is mapped to a set of UIElements for deleting and adding links on the association. The basic intuition is that every object or link, which is only present in the right hand side of the rule, is newly created and every object or link, which is present only in the left hand side of the rule, is being deleted. Objects or links which are present on both sides are unaffected by the rule.

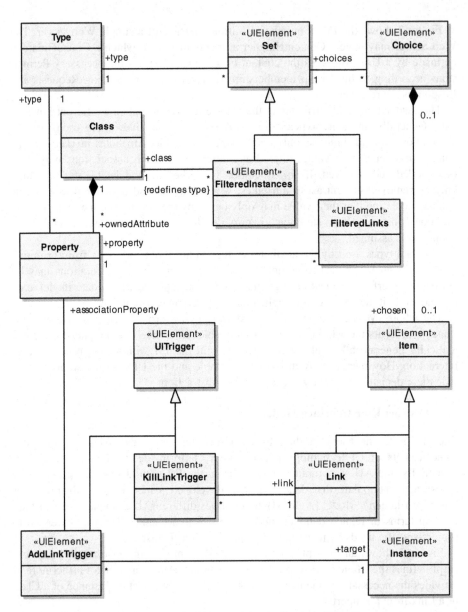

Fig. 3. Excerpt from the AUIEM used for the Example Transformations

The application order of rules is not determined. Furthermore, different rules with the same left-hand side may exist to provide alternative UI elements for the same structure. The actual choice of the desired mappings is an interactive design decision that can be supported by tools. However, complete generation of the AUIM based on the rules is possible. This could be interesting in the context of an UI style defining the actual mappings to be applied.

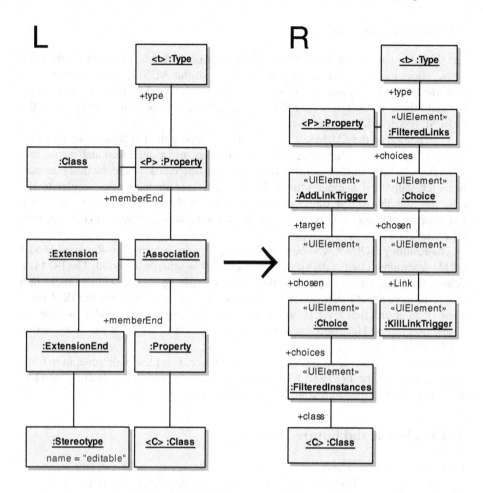

Fig. 4. IM-AUIM Mapping Rule Example

3.3 View Composition Model

The most detailed PIM is the View Composition Model (VCM). It partitions the AUIM into several overlapping and navigable Views. Each of these Views provides the scope of a Class instance for the contained UIElements. Thus, master-detail-like views can be implemented. Furthermore, navigation along Links can be defined. Finally, Views can be composed. Each contained view either inherits the scope from the containing view or has the scope provided by links selected in the containing View. A root View must be defined. Views enable the purposeful selection of different platform UI elements for the same UIElement depending on the overall context of a View while deriving the Concrete User Interface Model (CUIM) representing the actual platform dependent user interface.

3.4 Concrete User Interface Model

The CUIM is defined by the Platform Model (PM), which contains a set of available native UI elements on the target platform. Like in the AUIEM, these elements are combined with the elements form the Information Metamodel. Thus, the translation between these models is based on the substitution of the UIElements from the AUIEM by native UI elements from the PM.

The creation of the CUIM not only involves mapping the UIElements to actual UI controls (widgets) on the target platform, but also providing additional layout and decoration. A GUI builder tool should support the whole task where the designer may handpick individual mappings for UIElements. Transformation rules similar to the rules for the IM-AUIM transforamtion can be employed here. These rules map UIElements and their context to attributed and annotated instances of platform specific UI classes.

The resulting CUIM has to be complemented by the Information Retrieval Model (IRM) describing how the data processed by the UI is actually accessed. The IRM is a behavioral UML model (e.g. an activity diagram) giving an operational description how to retrieve the IM elements from the actual implementation. Thus, the IRM functions as an abstraction layer between the UI and the application similar to database abstraction layers. However, the actual implementation of the IRM may vary and is not discussed here.

To create an Actual User Interface Implementation, complete code generation takes place combining the IRM and CUIM information to a working platform dependent UI. Again, a set of transformation rules is used here.

4 Conclusion and Future Work

In this paper, we have proposed a model-driven design approach for user interfaces based on the UML. This approach allows for concurrent development of UI and application logic by starting from a common platform independent information model. Furthermore, due to our code generation mechanisms we can support different target platforms from the same abstract model. The approach has been outlined and discussed on the context of a real world Web server administration interface example.

We are currently implementing the results of the manual execution of our approach for this example. Future work will include a prototype implementation in the context of our work in the fields of executable models [10] and concurrent software components [9].

References

1. Abrams, M., Phanouriou, C., Batongbacal, A. L., Williams, S. M., Shuster, J. E.: UIML: an appliance-independent xml user interface language. In Computer Networks 31, Elsevier Science, 1999
2. Bleul, S., Schäfer, R., Müller, W.: Multimodal Dialog Description for Mobile Devices. In Proc. Workshop on XML-based User Interface Description Languages at AVI 2004, 2004.

3. Limbourg, Q., Vanderdonckt, J.: Addressing the Mapping Problem in User Interface Design with UsiXML. In Proc. of 3rd Int. Workshop on Task Models and Diagrams for user interface design TAMODIA'2004, ACM Press, New York, 2004.
4. Limbourg, Q., Vanderdonckt, J., Michotte, B., Bouillon, L., Lopez-Jaquero, V.: UsiXML: a Language Supporting Multi-Path Development of User Interfaces. In Proc. EHCI-DSVIS'2004, 2004.
5. Object Management Group, The: Unified Modeling Language: Infrastructure. OMG ad/2004-10-02, 2004.
6. Object Management Group, The: Model Driven Architecture (MDA). OMG ormsc/2001-07-01, 2001.
7. Pinheiro da Silva, P., Paton, N.: User Interface Modelling with UML. In Proc. of the 10th European-Japanese Conference on Information Modelling and Knowledge Representation, 2000.
8. Rozenberg, G. et al (eds.): Handbook of Graph Grammars and Computing by Graph Transformation, Vol. 1. World Scientific, Singapore, 1997
9. Schattkowsky, T., Förster, A: A generic Component Framework for High Performance Locally Concurrent Computing based on UML 2.0 Activities. In Proc. 12th Annual IEEE International Conference and Workshop on the Engineering of Computer Based Systems (ECBS), 2005.
10. Schattkowsky, T. Müller, W.: Model-Based Design of Embedded Systems. In Proc. 7th IEEE International Symposium on Object-oriented Real-time distributed Computing (ISORC), 2004.
11. Vanderdonckt, J.: A MDA-Compliant Environment for Developing User Interfaces of Information Systems. In Proc. of 17th Conf. on Advanced Information Systems Engineering CAiSE'05 (Porto, 13-17 June 2005), O. Pastor & J. Falcão e Cunha (eds.), Lecture Notes in Computer Science, Vol. 3520, Springer-Verlag, Berlin, 2005.

Workshop on Models for Non-functional Properties of Component-Based Software – NfC

Geri Georg[1], Jan Øyvind Aagedal[2], Raffaela Mirandola[3], Ileana Ober[4], Dorina Petriu[5], Wolfgang Theilmann[6], Jon Whittle[7], and Steffen Zschaler[8]

[1] Colorado State University, Computer Science Department, Fort Collins, USA
[2] SSINTEF ICT and Simula Research Laboratory, Oslo, Norway
[3] Dipartimento di Elettronica e Informazione, Politecnico di Milano, Milano, Italy
[4] IRIT - Université Paul Sabatier, France
[5] Carleton University, Systems and Computer Engineering Dept., Ottawa, Canada
[6] SAP Research, Belfast, UK
[7] George Mason University, Fairfax, USA
[8] Technische Universität Dresden, Fakultät Informatik, Dresden, Germany

Abstract. Developing reliable software is a complex, daunting, and error-prone task. Many researchers are interested in improving support for developers creating such software. Component-based software engineering has emerged as an important paradigm for handling complexity. In addition, using models to raise the level of abstraction when reasoning about systems, is another technique to lower complexity. The goal of the NfC series of workshops is to look at issues related to the integration of non-functional property expression, evaluation, and prediction in the context of component-based software engineering and find the best techniques to deal with non-functional properties in a model based approach. Approaches need to include semantic issues, questions of modeling language definition, and also support for automation, such as analysis algorithms, MDA-based approaches, and tool-support for refinement steps. Since models are only really meaningful if used in the context of a software development process, the workshop also welcomes work in this area. The aim of the 2005 NfC workshop was to bring together practitioners and academics that are currently working with these topics and highlight the ongoing solutions and problems still remaining. The 2005 NfC workshop was organized as two half-day sessions: The morning session was dedicated to presentations and discussion of papers, followed in the afternoon by working sessions. The topics of the working sessions were derived from the morning discussions, and from topics discussed in the 2004 NfC workshop.

1   Introduction

The workshop on Models for Non-Functional Properties of Component-Based Software (NfC Workshop) was held at MoDELS 2005, and was the second such workshop held in conjunction with the UML series of conferences. Four papers were presented in the morning, each followed by discussion and questions. Discussion topics were collected during this time, and grouped into four categories for

J.-M. Bruel (Ed.): MoDELS 2005 Workshops, LNCS 3844, pp. 210–216, 2006.

small-group discussion in the afternoon. We also reviewed the discussion outcomes from last year's workshop, and added them to the discussion topics for the afternoon. We noted that we were continuing discussion in some areas from last year, while others no longer appeared to be issues. In particular the area of non-functional property (nfp) conflict identification and resolution is still very much a concern.

The workshop held at UML 2004 [1] produced results in four areas. These are summarized below:

- In the area of *domain limits* we agreed that by starting at the requirements stage and moving toward code, functional properties are identified first, and non-functional properties are identified later. Properties are not functional or non-functional by themselves, but rather depend on the point of view, or intent of the system.
- In the area of *non-functional property support*, we agreed that they need to be considered throughout the entire development process. We also noted that for verification purposes, many non-functional properties require separate analysis models to be constructed and analyzed. The results of such analyses need to feed back into the development process. Most of the time, the properties are verified at several steps of the development process and thus at several levels of abstraction. Analysis results and models are usually not maintained over functional refinement steps, but rather must be recreated at each different level of abstraction. Representation of non-functional properties is often different at different stages in the development process. For example, properties are expressed very explicitly in the requirements, but can be represented by certain structures in the architecture, or by a middleware configuration. This requires sophisticated notions of refinement and traceability.
- We also discussed *resources as components* versus these being two different concepts. The general conclusion was that there is no formal difference between components and resources. However, it may be practical to distinguish them for hiding implementation details and complexity. They can be distinguished based on usage, where resources represent an encapsulation of lower-level components. This issue did not come up at all in the 2005 workshop, and we did not include it in any discussions at the recent NfC Workshop.
- We identified different *composition dimensions*. These were: 1) the semantics of model composition versus composition of e.g. components executing in a container 2) the way in which properties of individual components contribute to the properties exhibited by the composed system 3) the semantics of composition when the constituent properties are not orthogonal. Note that the papers presented at NfC 2005 did not address composition; it remains an open and actively researched area.

Four papers were presented at the workshop, using the following format. First the author made a presentation regarding the paper, then a workshop organizer made a very short presentation of related ideas or questions, then we discussed the paper, ideas, and questions. This format generated many additional ideas which were captured for the afternoon discussions.

2 Overview of the Papers Presented at the 2005 NfC Workshop

The complete papers and slides presented at the workshop are available on the workshop website, at http://www.comquad.org/nfc05/. Two of the papers are also published in this workshop satellite proceedings. This section therefore presents an overview of the papers.

2.1 Adding Behavior Description Support to COTS Components Through the Use of Aspects [4]

The authors discuss the need for flexibility when adding new features to reusable components. They present a method that is based on aspect-oriented techniques to add such features to COTS components. An example is given for a stack component by using state machines to describe the various features and their composition. The paper also discusses the issue of having insufficient behavioural descriptions of COTS components, and the generally unsatisfactory situation this leaves. There does not appear to be a systematic way to approach this problem. In fact, this issue led to one of the afternoon discussions.

2.2 Abstraction-Raising Transformation for Generating Analysis Models [5]

The paper presents a graph grammar based model transformation technique, focused on abstraction-raising to remove information in a model and to bring it into an analysable notation. This is accomplished using graph-based transformations coupled with relational transformations to map from a source UML activity model to Klaper, a performance analysis language. A brief example is given to demonstrate the graphical rule-based transformations and mapping to Klaper. Two rules are presented, SEQ and COND which are defined to transform specific UML activities into the more abstract concepts needed by Klaper.

2.3 Explicit Architectural Policies to Satisfy NFRs Using COTS [2]

This paper presents an approach to extend MDA to take into account "concern-specific" non-functional requirements (NFRs). The underlying idea is to exploit architectural policies and mechanisms, and a multidimensional description of components to consider a non-functional requirement starting at the architectural level. The paper describes a framework under development that extends MDA to deal explicitly with non-functional requirements. The key ideas are: 1) the representation of concern-specific NFRs using architectural policies, 2) the systematic reification of policies into mechanisms and 3) a description of the ways in which different components implement the said mechanism.

2.4 Extending Security Requirement Patterns to Support Aspect-Oriented Risk-Driven Development [3]

The paper extends previous work of the authors in the area of aspect-oriented risk-driven development (AORDD), which combines two approaches, risk-driven analysis and aspect-oriented development, with the purpose of enabling software designers to trade off between alternative security design solutions. More specifically, the paper describes an extension to a security pattern profile that supports AORDD. The paper starts from a UML profile for security requirement patterns, a profile defined by the authors previously, which is extended to support aspect-oriented risk-driven development approach for designing security solutions.

3   Discussions at the 2005 NfC Workshop

We identified four areas to stimulate discussions in the 2005 workshop. These were:

- Technical issues dealing with non-functional properties such as how to obtain a behavioral description of a component, and what to do when components affect more than one non-functional property.
- Users and practicality including handling incomplete or imprecise models, and addressing the gap between architectural levels of abstraction and development.
- Property composition, specifically identifying and resolving conflicts between non-functional properties.
- Other applications of techniques dealing with non-functional properties such as creating self-modifying systems.

The resulting discussions actually produced results in six areas: 1) obtaining information about a component and describing that information, 2) specifying what is needed in a component, 3) a small discussion on systems development using components, including legacy systems re-engineering, 4) bridging the abstraction gap between architecture and development with respect to non-functional properties, 5) conflict identification and resolution between non-functional properties, and 6) areas of particular interest for discussions at a future workshop.

3.1   Obtaining Information About a Component

We came to the conclusion that component developers are unlikely to begin completely characterizing their components in the near future. We therefore need to identify other methods to characterize component behavior. A first step in this process is probably to define certain dimensions that need to be described. Some non-functional properties are fairly well defined and therefore their dimensions have been identified.   Examples of such non-functional properties include security, fault tolerance, and quality of service (QoS).

Once dimensions are identified, there appear to be only a few viable ways to determine a component's characteristics. One is via reverse engineering and the other is via experimentation and tracing. Interviews with component developers can be used in conjunction with these methods to characterize component behaviour. Functional behaviour can then be described using state machines or state charts, while some non-functional property behaviour must be reported via metrics or benchmarks. It was generally agreed that some sort of middle-man or institution that compiled and catalogued this information into a readily available medium (like a TTL book in the semi-conductor world) would be very useful. The existence and widespread use of such a catalogue could also influence component developers to better characterize the components they provide.

Describing the non-functional property behaviour of a component goes hand-in-hand with obtaining information about that behaviour, so we also discussed this issue. We noted that notations for describing component behaviour will vary, but in all cases non-functional property behaviour is to some extent dependent on the execution environment, and the support provided by middleware. We hypothesized that the internal properties of a component could be described, and then the effect of middleware support on those properties could be specified. We agreed that the context or support provided by middleware really had to be understood before it was possible to reason about non-functional properties.

3.2 Defining What Non-functional Properties Are Needed in a Component

Another topic related to component non-functional property description is specifying what non-functional properties are needed in a component. We believe demand-driven models that only describe the necessary properties will be used to specify components. These models will vary in their type and detail. Examples of the range of model complexity are simple ATAM or SAM models all the way to UML/state charts or semantic meta-models. The key will be being able to adequately specify the required non-functional property behaviour. In some cases, a simple model may need to be augmented to convey the specification. We again noted that non-functional properties which have been studied in depth (e.g. security, fault tolerance, and QoS) will be initially easier to specify since the dimensions involved in characterizing the property are well defined. In many cases the developer may have to do more work to adequately specify the component. This specification must be complete with respect to the developer's expectations, including expectations about the execution context. We noted that profiles may be useful in this space, but profiles require that non-functional properties are described as objects, which may not be possible or feasible depending on the non-functional property. The new OMG profile on Quality of Service (QoS) for component software, and QoS Enabled Distributed Objects (Qedo), may be useful for component non-functional property specification.

3.3 Systems Development Relative to the Non-functional Properties of Components

We briefly discussed systems development and its relation to the non-functional properties of components. We noted that there is usually a metaphor used to describe a system solution, and that component descriptions must be mapped into this higher level metaphor. The solution metaphor must also identify and describe non-functional properties. Legacy systems re-engineering presents interesting situations since often non-functional properties can be removed from legacy code and middleware components can be used to provide these properties. In some cases it may not be possible to completely refactor the legacy system, but it may be possible to reorganize it so that components can provide some non-functional properties. We discussed the issue of components that provide more non-functional properties than are strictly needed, and noted that it is often possible to configure components so they only provide the desired non-functional properties. In other cases, extra non-functional properties can be ignored. However, in all cases it is necessary to trace what non-functional properties of the components are being used and why, so that if in the future a different component is used, the required non-functional properties are still included in the system.

3.4 Bridging the Abstraction Gap Between Architecture and Development

We spent quite awhile discussing the abstraction gap between what an architect decides is needed in a system and what components developers add to a system to achieve the architectural goals. Several alternatives emerged from our discussion. On the one hand we discussed mechanisms to bridge the gap between abstract models and code, and on the other hand we discussed mechanisms to identify portions of code responsible for implementing various architectural behaviors.

Mechanisms to bridge the gap between abstract models and code include refining models and then eventually generating code from models, defining policies for templates to create mechanisms, and using domain-specific solutions to implement architectural behaviour. Such solutions generally exist within technology domains and also within non-functional property domains.

Mechanisms to identify code related to architectural behaviour include pattern searching to find patterns of code often used to implement a behaviour, e.g. caching in web applications, and using traces to identify code related to particular behaviours. Architect interviews may also be helpful in determining code that implements a part of the architecture. Once such areas of code are identified, they can be removed, and the remaining code can be analyzed further to determine if it is architecturally consistent with the initial intent of the architects. This ability is especially important since systems tend to diverge from architectural standards over time. We noted that finding patterns can be difficult if the pattern is cross-cutting. This observation led to a discussion regarding the use of aspects. Aspects are one way to represent the design of a non-functional property and allow it to be integrated into a system design. An alternative is to use overriding and inheritance to configure and choose between different non-functional property behaviors.

3.5 Non-functional Property Conflict Identification and Resolution

We discussed non-functional property conflict identification and resolution and noted that these conflicts usually occur because of underlying conflicts in requirements that need to be resolved. Luckily, components are often highly configurable and this can help resolve system non-functional property conflicts. The Kestrel algebraic specification language was discussed. This language is used to specify and resolve conflicts in functionality. The Kestrel group is working on adapting the language to be used in the non-functional property space, and it remains to be seen if they are successful.

3.6 Future Workshop Topics

Finally, we noted that an area of particular interest for research and discussion for the next NfC workshop is that of dynamic analysis of non-functional properties, and changing a running system to effect different non-functional properties.

4 Conclusions

The creative environment during the workshop discussions and the interest in the discussed topics convinced us one more time, how much dealing with non-functional properties is an open research area. With respect to last year's edition, we perceived a gain in maturity of the NfC community towards some issues, while a great deal of work remains in other areas.

The workshop organizers would like to thank all the participants in this year's workshop, and invite you to help organize another workshop on this topic in the future. Suggestions for topics in the next call for papers, invited talks, and workshop organization are welcome. Feedback on the usefulness of this workshop is also welcome.

References

[1] Jean-Michel Bruel, Geri Georg, Heinrich Hussmann, Ileana Ober, Christoph Pohl, Jon Whittle and Steffen Zschaler: *Models for Non-functional Aspects of Component-Based Software* (NfC'04), in: Nuno Jardim Nunes, Bran Selic, Alberto Rodrigues da Silva, et al. (eds.), UML Modeling Languages and Applications: 2004 Satellite Activities, Springer 2005 (LNCS 3297), pp. 62-66

[2] C. López, H. Astudillo. *Explicit Architectural Policies to Satisfy NFRs using COTS*

[3] G. Georg, S. Hilde Houmb, D. Matheson. *Extending Security Requirement Patterns to Support Aspect-Oriented Risk-Driven Development*

[4] A. Moreira, J.-M. Bruel, and J. Araújo. *Adding Behavior Description Support to COTS Components through the Use of Aspects*

[5] A. Sabetta, D. C. Petriu, V. Grassi, R. Mirandola. *Abstraction-Raising Transformation for Generating Analysis Models*

Abstraction-Raising Transformation for Generating Analysis Models

Antonino Sabetta[1], Dorina C. Petriu[2], Vincenzo Grassi[1], and Raffaela Mirandola[1]

[1] University of "Tor Vergata", Dept. of Informatics,
Systems and Production, Rome, Italy
{sabetta, vgrassi, mirandola}@info.uniroma2.it
[2] Carleton University, Department of Systems and Computer Engineering,
Ottawa, ON Canada, K1S 5B6
petriu@sce.carleton.ca

Abstract. The verification of non-functional requirements of software models (such as performance, reliability, scalability, security, etc.) requires the transformation of UML models into different analysis models such as Petri nets, queueing networks, formal logic, etc., which represent the system at a higher level of abstraction. The paper proposes a new "abstraction-raising" transformation approach for generating analysis models from UML models. In general, such transformations must bridge a large semantic gap between the source and the target model. The proposed approach is illustrated by a transformation from UML to Klaper (Kernel LAnguage for PErformance and Reliability analysis of component-based systems).

1 Introduction

OMG's Model Driven Architecture (MDA) promotes the idea that software development should be based on models throughout the entire software lifecycle [13]. This change of focus from code to models raises the need for formal verification of functional and non-functional characteristics of UML software models. Over the years, many modeling formalisms (such as queueing networks, Petri nets, fault trees, formal logic, process algebras, etc.) and corresponding tools have been developed for the analysis of different non-functional characteristics (such as performance, reliability, scalability, security, etc.). The challenge is not to reinvent new analysis methods targeted to UML models, but to bridge the gap between UML-based software development tools and different existing analysis tools.

Each of these analysis models and tools is suited for the evaluation of different non-functional software properties. In general, an analysis model abstracts away many details of the original software model, emphasizing only the aspects of interests for the respective analysis. A transformation whereby a more abstract target analysis model is generated from a source software model is called here "abstraction-raising" transformation, as opposed to a "refining" transformation that produces a more detailed target model (such as the transformations used in MDA).

Traditionally, analysis models were built "by hand" by specialists in the field, then solved and evaluated separately. However, with the change of focus on models brought by MDA, a new trend started to emerge, whereby software models are auto-

J.-M. Bruel (Ed.): MoDELS 2005 Workshops, LNCS 3844, pp. 217–226, 2006.
© Springer-Verlag Berlin Heidelberg 2006

matically transformed into different analysis models. For example, this kind of approach was used to obtain a formal logic model for analyzing security characteristics in [7]. Transformations from UML into different performance models have been surveyed in [1]. Examples of such transformations are from UML to Layered Queueing Networks in [10, 11], to Stochastic Petri Nets in [2], and to Stochastic Process Algebra in [3]. More recently, a transformation framework from multiple design models into different performance models was proposed in [17].

Different kinds of analysis techniques may require additional annotations to the UML model to express, for instance non-functional requirements and characteristics, or the user's directives for the desired analysis. OMG's solution to this problem is to define standard UML profiles for different purposes. Two examples of such profiles are the "UML Profile for Schedulability, Performance, and Time"[14] and "UML Profile for Modeling Quality of Service and Fault Tolerance Characteristics and Mechanisms"[15].

The paper proposes a new approach for developing abstraction-raising transformations from UML to different kind of analysis models in different formalisms (such as Petri nets, queueing networks, fault trees, formal logic, etc.) In general, such transformations must bridge a large semantic gap between the source and the target model, which represent the system at different abstraction levels. The proposed approach is illustrated by a transformation from UML to Klaper (Kernel LAnguage for PErformance and Reliability analysis of component-based systems) [6].

2   Conceptual Description of the Transformation Approach

The proposed approach combines two methods that, so far, have been used separately in model transformations: relational and graph grammar-based transformations [5]. In the relational approach, used in the proposal for the QVT standard [12], the source and target models are each described by its own metamodel; a transformation defines relations (mappings) between different element types of the source and target (meta)models. According to [12], a *Transformation* is a generalization of both *Relation* and *Mapping*. Relations are non-executable bi-directional transformation specifications, whereas Mappings are unidirectional transformation implementations used to generate a target model from the source model.

The graph-transformation and relational approaches are compared in [8]. While the former is based on *matching and replacement*, the latter is based on *matching and reconciliation*. The conclusion is that, is spite of their differences, advantages and disadvantages, the two approaches are rather similar. More research is needed to identify which one is more suitable for certain kinds of applications.

In our proposed approach, we keep the idea that the source and target models are described by separate metamodels, between which transformations must be defined. However, in our case the target metamodel represents analysis domain concepts, which are usually at a higher-level of abstraction than the source model concepts. In order to define mappings between the source and target models, sometimes it is necessary to group (aggregate) a large number of source model elements according to certain rules, and to map the whole group to a single target element. The aggregation

rules correspond to the raising in the abstraction level necessary for bridging the semantic gap between the source and the target model. Such rules are dependent on the
semantic differences between the source and target model, and are not represented in
the source metamodel.

Therefore, a new mechanism is needed to express the aggregation rules, in addition
to the mechanism for defining the transformation from source to target. We propose
to use a graph grammar [16] for describing the aggregation rules; the terminals of the
graph grammar correspond to metaobjects from the source model, whereas the non-
terminals correspond to more abstract concepts that will be transformed directly in
target model concepts. The proposed transformation approach is illustrated in Fig.1.
Some target model elements can be obtained by a direct mapping from source models
elements, like in a relational transformation, whereas other target elements, representing more abstract concepts, correspond to graph-grammar non-terminals obtained by
parsing the source model. According to the taxonomy of model transformations proposed in [9], the abstraction-raising transformation discussed in this paper is both
exogenous (i.e., the source and target models are different) and vertical (the abstraction level is different).

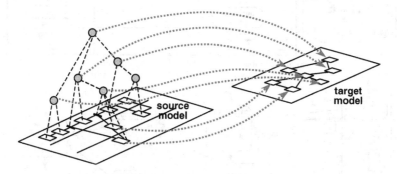

Fig. 1. Principle of the proposed "abstraction-raising" transformation approach

3   Analysis Model for Component-Based Systems

In this section, the abstraction-raising transformation approach presented in section 2
is illustrated by applying it to the transformation of a UML model extended with the
SPT Profile to an analysis model named Klaper (Kernel LAnguage for PErformance
and Reliability analysis of component-based systems) [6].

3.1   Description of the Source Model

We assume that the source UML model describes the high-level software architecture
as a component diagram, and the key scenario(s) for performance/reliability analysis
as activity diagram(s), as in Fig. 2.a. We also assume that the information required for
the generation of the analysis model is available from the source UML model, possibly by means of annotations compliant with one or more profiles [14, 4].

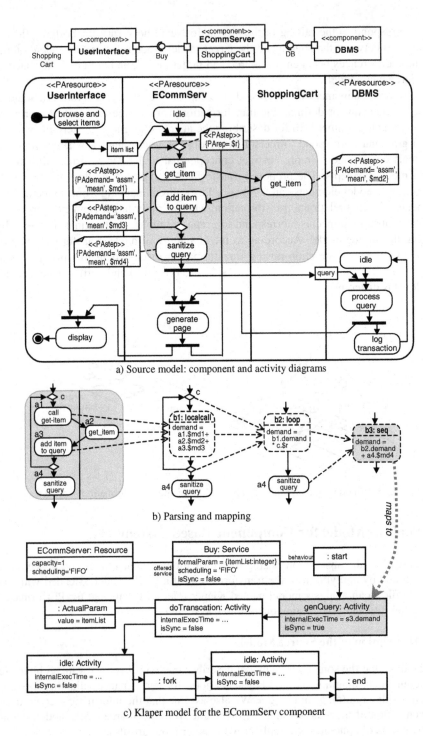

a) Source model: component and activity diagrams

b) Parsing and mapping

c) Klaper model for the ECommServ component

Fig. 2. Example of abstraction-raising transformation from UML to Klaper

Although both the parsing and the mapping implied by the proposed transformation are defined at the abstract syntax level based on the metamodel representation of the source model, the paper uses only the graphical UML notation for the sake of conciseness. The example is an e-commerce application designed as a client/server system with three basic components: a user interface, an e-commerce server component and a database (at the top of Fig. 2.a). Due to space limitations, we consider a single usage scenario, which is part of the checkout procedure, given as an activity diagram in Fig. 2.a. After the user has selected one or more items, the first client-server interaction takes place, with UserInterface acting as client of the EComm-Server. We assume that a server component waits for requests in the "idle" state. After accepting a client request, ECommServer loops through the items in the shopping cart to prepare a database query, and acts in turn as client in another client-server interaction, where the DBMS is the server. After getting the required information, ECommServer generates a page with the checkout information, sends it to the User-Inteface for display and returns to the "idle" state, where it can accept a new request.

The SPT Profile is used to identify the main basic abstractions for performance analysis in the UML model from Fig. 2.a. *Scenarios* define response paths through the system, and can have QoS requirements such as response times or throughputs. Each scenario is executed by a *workload*, which can be closed or open. Scenarios are composed of scenario *steps* that can be joined in sequence, loops, branches, fork/joins, etc. A step (stereotyped as <<PAstep>>) may be an elementary operation at the lowest level of granularity, or a complex sub-scenario. Each step has a mean number of repetitions, a host execution demand, other demand to resources and its own QoS characteristics, which are given as tagged value. *Resource* is another basic SPT abstraction; it can be active or passive, each with its own attributes.

Not all SPT annotations are shown in Fig. 2.a, just a few <<PAStep>> stereotypes applied to different activities. The tagged value PAdemand gives the CPU demand for a step. For instance, "PAdemand ='assm', 'mean', \$md1, 'ms'" means that the step has an assumed mean execution time of \$md1 ms (where \$md1is a variable). The tagged value "PArep =\$r" gives the average number of loop repetitions. Such quantitative annotations will be used during the transformation process to compute the parameters of the target model. A more detailed description of the use of SPT profile for performance analysis is given in [11].

3.2 Description of the Target Model

The target model in this case study is an abstract analysis model expressed in Klaper, a Kernel Language for Performance and Reliability analysis of component-based systems [6]. Its purpose is to capture in a lightweight and compact model all the relevant information for the performance and reliability analysis of component-based systems, while abstracting away irrelevant details. Klaper was designed as an intermediate "distilled" language to help bridge the large semantic gap between design-oriented and analysis-oriented notations, and to mitigate the "*N-by-M*" problem of translating *N* design notation types into *M* performance/reliability model types.

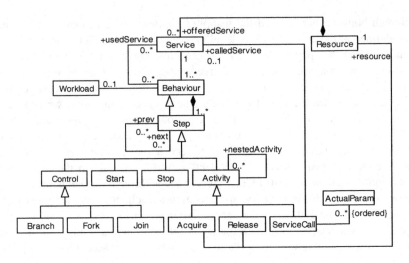

Fig. 3. Klaper metamodel (adapted from [6])

This "*N-by-M*" problem is reduced to a less complex task of defining *N+M* transformations: *N* from different design notations to Klaper, and *M* from it to different analysis models. (In this paper, we consider only one transformation, from UML 2 to Klaper). Klaper has been defined in [6] as a MOF-compliant metamodel to allow the exploitation of existing transformation facilities in the context of MDA. A diagram of the metamodel is shown in Fig.3. The domain model underlying Klaper considers that a system is an assembly of interacting *Resources*, where a resource may offer (and possibly require) *Services*. Thus, Klaper Resources can represent both software components and physical resources like processors, communication links or other physical devices. Each offered Service is characterized by a list of *formal parameters* that can be instantiated with actual values by other resources requiring that service. The *Behaviour* of (offered) services is modeled as a graph of *Steps* that can be simple "internal" *Activities* (i.e. operations that do not require any services offered by other resources), or *Activities* with one or more associated *ServiceCalls* addressed to other Resources, or *Control nodes* (Begin/End, Fork/Join, etc.). An interesting feature of Klaper is that service parameters are meant to represent abstractions (for example expressed in terms of random variables) of the "real" service parameters (see [6] for more details).

3.3 Model Transformation

From a high level perspective, the mapping from UML to Klaper can be described as follows. UML components (from component diagrams) and nodes (from deployment diagrams) are mapped onto Klaper *resources*. The corresponding offered and required *services* are derived from the provided and required interfaces for each component. The *behaviour* of each offered service is derived from a suitable UML activity or state diagram, that either specifies the local component behaviour or the global system behaviour. Due to space constraints, we do not describe in this example the mapping of UML nodes to Klaper resources, nor the derivation of the behaviour that models the interactions between components (i.e. connectors). The attributes of Klaper elements defined in [6] are mainly derived from the information provided by the SPT [14] and reliability stereotypes [4] given in the UML source model.

Many of the mappings from UML to Klaper are straightforward, in that they can be described as one-to-one relations between elements of the two metamodels; for instance each UML *component* is mapped to a Klaper *resource*, each provided interface of a UML component is mapped to a *service* offered by the *resource* corresponding to that component, each required interface is mapped to a *service call*, and so on. However, there are cases where a group of elements in the source model represents, as a whole, an abstraction that will be mapped to a single Klaper element. To illustrate more clearly this idea, let us examine the derivation of the Klaper model for the ECommServ component (see Fig. 2.c).

In general, the behaviour is represented in the analysis model at a higher level of abstraction than in the source model; this comes from the nature of the transformation from a software design to a performance model. Thus, we do not need to translate each and every UML activity to a Klaper step, but would like to aggregate unnecessary details. For instance, we may decide that all the activities executed in a single swimlane between the receiving of a message and the sending of the next message (as shown in the shaded fragment in Fig. 2.a) should be grouped and mapped, as a whole, to a single Klaper *activity* (shown by the "maps-to" arrow in Fig. 2). We may also want to aggregate, in the same block, calls to local passive objects. The fragment shown in Fig. 2.a is rather simple, but in principle can have any number of activities connected in different ways in sequence, branches, loops, etc. Since the UML metamodel does not define a concept (metaclass) corresponding to a "block of activities" as described above, there is no single element in the source metamodel that can be mapped to an element in the target metamodel. We propose to describe the above aggregation rules by the means of a few graph grammar rules (see Fig. 4).

By applying the grammar rules in an appropriate order, we can eventually reduce a "correct" activity diagram to the starting symbol 'AD'. In the parsing process, a set of non-terminals are generated, which correspond to more "abstract" constructions found in the source model. The rules are applied for reduction as follows: when a subgraph matching the right hand side (rhs) of a rule is found in the host graph (i.e., in the source model possibly rewritten by previous rules), the matching subgraph is removed and is replaced by the left hand side (lhs) of the rule, according to the embedding policy. More precisely: a) the edges attached to nodes of the rhs that are kept in the lhs are preserved (they represent the "context"); b) the edges that are left dangling (because of the removal of some node from the lhs) are removed; c) if a node in the rhs is rewritten as one node in the lhs, then all the edges attached to the former are redirected to the latter (this applies to non-injective morphisms too). The graph grammar is structured so that high level constructs, such as loops, conditional constructs, sequences and client-server interactions, are discovered through parsing. To this purpose the concept of a "block" has been introduced and formally defined in the grammar by rule 2. Most of the rules are recursive, raising the abstraction power of the proposed technique.

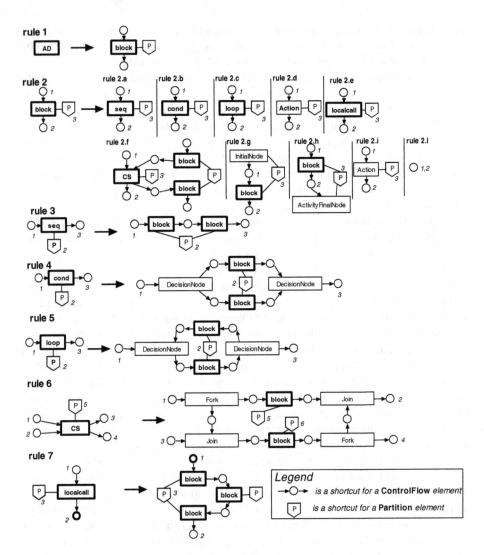

Fig. 4. Graph grammar

Basic constructs such as sequences, conditional blocks and loops are defined, in terms of blocks and terminal symbols, by rules 3, 4 and 5. Rule 6 is used to recognize the asynchronous client-server interactions and rule 7 reduces calls to passive objects. Remarkably, each of the *blocks* in the right hand side of the grammar rules can represent structures as simple as an elementary action or as complex as a big block that could contain in turn other client-server interactions and arbitrarily nested conditions, loops and sequences.

Fig. 2.b illustrates how the rules are applied in order to aggregate the activities from the shaded fragment to a single block. In order to keep the figure clear, a few details of the transformation steps were omitted. In the first step, rule 2.d is applied to each of the actions to rewrite them as blocks. Then blocks a1, a2 and a3, are reduced by rule 7 to a *localcall* non-terminal (b1). Non-terminal elements have their own attributes, computed from the elements in the right-hand side of the reduction rule, possibly by considering also the stereotypes and tagged values attached to them. In this example, the attribute *demand* of *b1* (which represents the average CPU execution time required for this block) is computed as the sum of the mean execution times for the activities *a1 a2* and *a3* (given as SPT performance annotations in Fig.2.a). In the second step, rule 2.e transforms the *localcall* non-terminal into a block, and then the loop can be parsed by rule 5 yielding *b2*. The attribute *demand* for *b2* is computed, by multiplying the demand of the loop body with the number of repetitions. In step 3 the *loop* is rewritten as a block (rule 2.c) and then rule 3 collapses the sequence of blocks (*b2, a4*) into *b3*.

This node, obtained by parsing a complex structure, will be mapped to a *single* Klaper element (also given in grey in Fig. 2.c). A simplified Klaper model of the component ECommServer offering the service Buy, is described by the graph of steps from *start* to *end* given in Fig. 2.c. After the service, the component will remain *idle*.

The example shows that the abstraction-raising transformation from UML to Klaper aggregates away details that are not important for performance/reliability analysis, but maintains enough information so that the analysis results (such as response times for services under different workloads, throughputs, utilization of different resources, queue lengths, time to failure, etc.) can be imported back in the UML models, by using the mapping between the elements of the source and target models. The example also illustrates how the graph grammar rules can be used to impose and verify additional well-formedness constraints on top of the standard UML metamodel.

4 Conclusions

This paper tackles the problem of abstraction-raising transformation for deriving analysis-oriented models from design specifications of component-based software systems. The proposed approach addresses the need to bridge the significant semantic gap that usually exists between the software design domain (source) and the performance/reliability domain (target). We propose to separate the concern of parsing the source model for extracting higher-level of abstraction concepts from the concern of mapping between the source and target model, which could be realized by traditional MDA techniques. A graph grammar is used to parse the source model and to extract higher-level of abstraction constructs that are semantically closer to the target domain. Our proposal can be seamlessly integrated into standard MOF-based transformation frameworks, as the parsing and the extension of the source model can be realized as a pre-processing step of a "conventional" model transformation pipeline.

Acknowledgements

This work was done during Antonino Sabetta's visit to Carleton University, Ottawa, with the financial support of NSERC Canada through its Discovery and Strategic Grants, of the MIUR-FIRB project "PERF: Performance evaluation of complex systems" and of the MIUR project "Model driven design and analysis of adaptable software architectures".

References

1. Balsamo, S., Di Marco, A., Inverardi, P., Simeoni, M., "Model-based performance prediction in software development: a survey" IEEE Transactions on Software Engineering, Vol 30, N.5, pp.295-310, May 2004.
2. S. Bernardi, S. Donatelli, and J. Merseguer, "From UML sequence diagrams and statecharts to analysable Petri net models," in Proc. of 3rd Int. Workshop on Software and Performance (WOSP02), Rome, July 2002, pp. 35-45.
3. C. Cavenet, S. Gilmore, J. Hillston, L. Kloul, and P. Stevens, "Analysing UML 2.0 activity diagrams in the software performance engineering process," in Proc. 4th Int. Workshop on Software and Performance (WOSP 2004), Redwood City, CA, Jan 2004, pp. 74-83.
4. V. Cortellessa, A.Pompei, "Towards a UML profile for QoS: a contribution in the reliability domain", In Proc. 4th Int. Workshop on Software and Performance WOSP'2004, pp.197 - 206, Redwood Shores, California, 2004
5. K. Czarnecki and S. Helsen, "Classification of Model Transformation Approaches", OOPSLA'03 Workshop on Generative Techniques in the Context of MDA, 2003.
6. V. Grassi, R. Mirandola, A.Sabetta, "From Design to Analysis Models: A Kernel Language for Performance and Reliability Analysis of Component-based Systems", In Proc. 5th Int. Workshop on Software and Performance WOSP'2005, pp. 25-36, Palma, Spain, July 2005.
7. J. Jürjens, P. Shabalin, "Automated Verification of UMLsec Models for Security Requirements", Proceedings of UML 2004, Lisbon, Portugal Oct. 11–15, 2004.
8. J.M. Kuster, S. Sendall, M. Wahler, "Comparing Two Model Transformation Approaches", Proc. Workshop on OCL and Model Driven Engineering, October, 2004.
9. T. Mens, K. Czarnecki, P. Van Gorp, "A Taxonomy of Model transformations", in Proc. of Dagstuhl 04101 Language Engineering for Model-Driven Software Development (J. Bezivin, R. Heckel eds), 2005.
10. D.C. Petriu, H.Shen, "Applying the UML Performance Profile: Graph Grammar based derivation of LQN models from UML specifications", in Computer Performance Evaluation: Modelling Techniques and Tools, (T. Fields, P. Harrison, J. Bradley, U. Harder, Eds.) LNCS 2324, pp.159-177, Springer, 2002.
11. D. C. Petriu, C. M. Woodside, "Performance Analysis with UML," in UML for Real, (B. Selic, L. Lavagno, and G. Martin, eds.), pp. 221-240, Kluwer, 2003.
12. OMG, QVT-Merge Group, "Revised submission for MOF 2.0 Query/Views/Transformations RFP", version 1.0, April 2004.
13. OMG, "MDA Guide", version 1.0.1, June 2003.
14. OMG, "UML Profile for Schedulability, Performance, and Time", version 1.0, formal/03-09-01, September 2003.
15. OMG, "UML Profile for Modeling Quality of Service and Fault Tolerance Characteristics and Mechanisms (QoS)", Adopted Specification, ptc/2004-06-01, June 2004.
16. Schürr, A., Programmed Graph Replacement Systems, in G.Rozenberg (ed): Handbook of Graph Grammars and Computing by Graph Transformations, pp. 479-546, 1997.
17. Woodside, C.M, Petriu, D.C., Petriu, D.B., Shen, H, Israr, T., and Merseguer, J. "Performance by Unified Model Analysis (PUMA)", In Proc. 5th Int. Workshop on Software and Performance WOSP'2005, pp.1-12, Palma, Spain, July 2005.

Explicit Architectural Policies to Satisfy NFRs Using COTS

Claudia López and Hernán Astudillo

Universidad Técnica Federico Santa María, Departamento de Informática,
Avenida España 1680, Valparaíso, Chile
clopez@inf.utfsm.cl, hernan@inf.utfsm.cl

Abstract. Software architecture decisions hinge more on non-functional requirements (NFRs) than on functional ones, since the architecture stipulates *which* software to build. Model-Driven Architecture (MDA) aims to automate the derivation/generation of software from high level architectural specifications, but most current MDA implementations start from software design (i.e. *how* to build a software piece) rather than software architecture. This article presents an approach to extend MDA through the concepts of *architectural policies and mechanisms*. The key ideas are representation of NFRs through architectural concerns using architectural policies, systematic reification of policies into mechanisms, and multi-dimensional description of components as implementations of mechanisms. A detailed illustrative example is provided. Azimut framework realizes these ideas, supports larger-scale work through catalogs of policies, mechanisms and components, and allows traceability and reuse of architecture by enabling these architecture-level descriptions and reasoning using incomplete characterizations of requirements and COTS.

1 Introduction

Model-driven Software Development and Model-driven Architecture (MDA) [1] arise from the possibility of building software systems through systematic transformations of high level models. Most proposed approaches emphasize modeling and transformations that address functional requirements, but in practice Non-Functional Requirements (NFRs) such as reliability, performance and stability are much harder to satisfy, and therefore the ones that require most attention from software architects.

Some proposals [2–8]extend MDA to deal explicitly with NFRs, especially from a perspective of components more than from detailed software design. Yet remains much work to be done: there is no traceability of decisions from NFRs to architecture to design and to final implementation, nor techniques to generate hybrid solutions that combine pre-existing components and ad-hoc development.

This article presents the key ideas of a Azimut framework that extends MDA with explicit modeling of architectural policies and their derivation into implementation. The key framework ideas are representation of NFRs with architectural policies, mapping and systematic refinement of architectural policies into

J.-M. Bruel (Ed.): MoDELS 2005 Workshops, LNCS 3844, pp. 227–236, 2006.

mechanisms, multi-dimensional description of pre-existing components (herein labeled COTS) and specific products insofar as they implement architectural mechanisms, and ongoing development of a multi-dimensional catalog of components. The Azimut allow to systematically select feasible architectural solutions using incomplete characterizations of the system requirements and available COTS.

The reminder of this paper is structured as follows: Section 2 provides a brief overview of related work on NFRs in MDA; Section 3 introduces the Azimut Framework and the concepts of *Platform-Independent Architecture Model* (PIAM), *Architecture Reification Model* (ARM), and *Policies-Specific Platform-Independent Model for Concern v* (PIM^v); Section 4 illustrates Azimut and its concepts with a detailed example; and Section 5 and 6 discusses further work and conclusions, respectively.

2   MDA, NFRs, and Component-Based Development

Software architects focus more on NFRs than on functional requirements because the former are much harder to satisfy in large and distributed systems. NFRs cannot be satisfied with local design decisions, but require global solutions because they correspond to systemic properties; for example, security and stability usually cannot be added ex-post-facto to an already running system without large effort and risk. Software architecture focuses on reasoning about *which* software to build or to include, and not necessarily about *how* to build it. Therefore, system NFRs are key since they determine the nature of the solution.

Despite having architecture in their name, most proposed MDA methods and tools (e.g. [9–12]) take as starting point a description in terms of functional components at *design* level, leaving the resolution of NFRs to prior steps.

Some recent projects [2–8]have addressed explicit mechanisms to satisfy NFRs through MDA transformations. From a component-based standpoint, some projects [2–4]try to satisfy system NFRs through a model-driven process for selecting components to achieve systemic NFRs, and later configuring and deploying the selected components. Other projects from a more design-oriented approach [5–8]aim to generate implementations that satisfy multiples NFRs at once, starting out from design description at platform-independent (PIM) level; thus, NFRs must be modeled and solved at prior stages.

Other researches deal with NFRs on MDA, but focus on only one NFR [13–15], on code generation to monitor NFRs [17], or use MDA to analyze NFRs at design time [16]. We focus on implementing solutions to multiple NFRs.

3   Architectural Policies to Implement NFRs Through MDA and COTS

Our research goal is developing tools to describe, automate and keep traceability of architectural decisions from NFRs into implementations that satisfy them, using COTS whenever possible. The key conceptual feature is descriptions using *architectural policies and mechanisms*. The process supported by these tools is an iterative exploration of design spaces by human architects. The approach and tools lend themselves to use incomplete and architecture-oriented information on requirements and COTS; we speak of "characterizations" rather than "specifications".

3.1 Architectural Policies and Mechanisms

Architects may reason about the overall solution properties using architectural policies, and later refine them (perhaps from existing policy catalogs) into artifacts and concepts that serve as inputs to software designers and developers, such as component models, detailed code design, standards, protocols, or even code itself. Thus, architects define policies for specific architectural concerns and identify alternative mechanisms to implement such policies. For example, an availability concern may be addressed by fault-tolerance policies (such as master-slave replication or active replication) and a security concern may be addressed by access control policies (such as identification-, authorization- or authentication-based) [19].

Each *reification* yields more concrete artifacts; thus, architectural decisions drive a process of successive reifications of NFRs that end with implementations of mechanisms that do satisfy these NFRs.

To characterize such reifications, we use concepts from the distributed systems community [18], duly adapted to the software architecture context:

Architectural Policy: The first reification from NFRs to architectural concepts. Architectural policies can be characterized through specific concern dimensions that allow describing NFRs with more details.

Architectural Mechanism: A construct that satisfies architectural policies. Several mechanisms may satisfy the same architectural policy; and can also be characterized with concern dimensions.

As a brief example (expanded in Section 4), consider inter-communication among applications. An architectural concern is the communication type, which might have the dimensions of sessions, topology, sender, integrity v/s timeliness and synchrony [20]. Then, the requirement *send a private report to subscribers by Internet* might be mapped in some project (in architectural terms) as requiring communication "asynchronous, with 1:M topology, with a push initiator mechanism, and priorizing integrity over timeliness". Based on these architectural requirements, an architect (or automated tool!) can search a catalog for any existing mechanisms or combination thereof that provides this specified policy; in our case, lacking additional restrictions, a good first fit is SMTP (the standard e-mail protocol), and thus any available COTS that provide it.

3.2 Generation of Policies-Specific PIMs

Figure 1 gives an overview of the Azimut framework. We distinguish two *PIM* levels, *Platform-Independent Architecture Model* (*PIAM*) and *Platform-Independent Model for Concern v* (*PIM^v*).

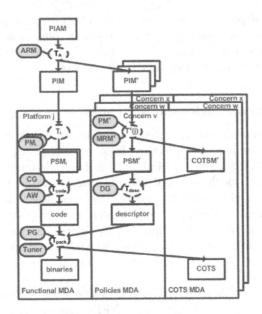

Fig. 1. Azimut Framework for NFRs and COTS

The *PIAM* characterizes platform-independent architectural policies and their dimensions, and the PIM^v characterize platform-independent mechanisms satisfying the required architectural policies. The *PIAM*'s elements are transformed to *PIM*'s and PIM^v's using the *Architectural Reification Model (ARM)*, which provides guidelines to go from architectural policies to architectural mechanisms. The *ARM* indicates which combinations satisfy each policy, and may have rules about mechanism combinations (e.g. potential restrictions).

The transformation process determines feasible sets of mechanisms that provide specific architectural policies, and propose them to the architect for validation or correction; supported mechanisms are presented according to the policies they satisfy (possibly several), and are grouped into PIM^v for each concern v.

3.3   Treatment of Policies-Specific PIMs

The previous process generates platform-independent models (a *PIM* for functional domain components and a PIM^v for components supporting policies for each concern v) that must be implemented on specific platforms.

The *PIM* is transformed into a set of *PSM*; this is encoded by the platform mappings *PM*. The generated *PSM* can be transformed to code using conventional MDA approaches such as [9, 10, 11, 12].

The platform-independent model PIM^v for each concern v may also be implemented with a MDA approach for NFRs [5, 6, 7, 8], or may be mapped to selected COTS. In the former case, each PIM^v generates a PSM^v as encoded in the PM^v. Since each PSM^v gives place to code and deployment descriptors, they are weaved with the PIM-derived code using an aspect weaver (AW). Deployment descriptors are generated by a descriptor generator (DG), and guide the deployment process for the code.

Implementing a PIM^v with COTS requires other selection/transformation step. If one or more of the selected mechanisms are implemented by an available COTS (or set thereof), the process identifies them and the parameters they should take to implement the intended mechanism. This step is codified in a *Mechanism Reification Mappings* (MRM), which uses a COTS catalog that describes available components, the mechanism(s) that each one implements, and their required parameters. In addition, the MRM contains rules about the possible combinations of COTS and the platforms where they can be implemented. The process uses several algorithms to determine the best combination of available components to implement the required mechanisms in PIM^v under the MRM constraints.

The $COTSM^v$ (COTS Model) describes the components to be assembled and deployed to satisfy policies for concern v, and is shown in Figure 1 by the right-most column. The $COTSM^v$ are used to generate deployment descriptors, just like the to PSM^v. The deployment descriptors include information about the actual COTS parameters.

The last transformation includes a *COTStuner* that allows configuring COTS, finally yielding deployable work sets consisting of generated code, deployment descriptors and configured components.

4   Example

Let's explore an example with a requirement about extraction and propagation of information on stocks behavior. A requirement might be:

The system must collect data for a customers portfolio and report back with it. The system extracts information from several sources according to portfolio, summarizes it into a report, and sends this report to the customer. The service must have 99.9% availability and provide security through access control.

This requirement can be decomposed into functional and non-functional requirements. The former can be *Extract information*, *Synthesize information* and *Send information*. The service *Send information* has the NFRs of *availability=99,9%* and *security by access control*.

From these requirements it is possible to identify *architectural concerns* as the `communication type` architectural concern relates to *the system must extract information from different sources* and *the system must send such reports to the client*; other architectural concerns are `security` and `availability`.

Without loss of generality, we will focus on the requirement *Send information* to show our derivation process for all identified architectural concerns in this example. *Extract information* can be dealt with a similar process considering only `communication type` concern, and *Synthesize information* can be used to guide software development in traditional MDA approach.

Figure 2 shows the architectural concerns related to the requirements of this example, and the valid values for the dimensions of `communication type`, `security` [21, 22] and `availability` [21, 23, 24] concern.

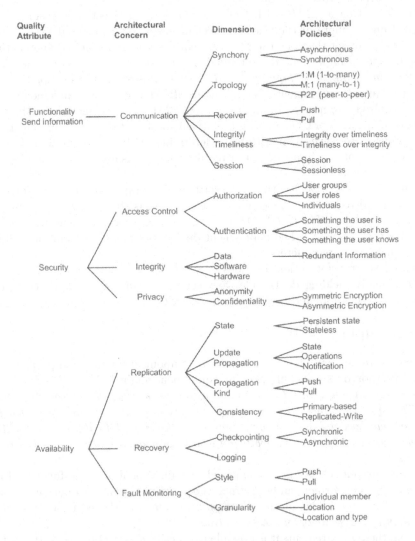

Fig. 2. Partial content of the Architecture Reification Mappings (*ARM*)

Thus, we can specify a requirement for `Communication Type` being *asynchronous*, with *1:M topology* and *Push* initiator kind; also, the communication must privilege *integrity over timeliness*. `Security` requirements are focused on access control, and we assume that these requirements are *individual authorization* and *authentication based on something that user knows*[22], as usual. `Availability` may be reified to several architectural concerns, such as *replication, recovery* and *fault monitoring*, but we only will focus on *replication* concern. To meet a high availability requirement, we specify that it needs replica with *persistent state* and *primary-based consistency.*

Once requirements for architectural concerns are defined by specifying theirs dimensions, we need to reify these architectural policies to mechanisms. Table 1, 2 and 3 show several architectural mechanisms that satisfy some of the architectural policies for the `communication type`, `security` and `availability` concerns, respectively. Notice that in this example, architectural mechanisms are specifications of communication protocols, security mechanisms and tactics to meet availability goals, and therefore they are platform-independent just like architectural policies, although at a lower abstraction level. These mechanisms are available as targets for the *ARM*-guided reification process that maps architectural policies for the each concern into specific mechanisms.

With the available *ARM* information (shown in Table 1, 2 and 3), the framework can recommend to the architect several possible mechanisms to satisfy the specified architectural policies. For example, the policies related to `Communication Type` for *Send information* can be reified to the protocols NNTP (used for client-initiated subscription-based articles reading) or SMTP (used to send e-mail); on the client side, IMAP (used for read news), or POP3 and IMAP (both widely used for e-mail reading).

We need to select among these alternative mechanisms. In practice the actual choice among alternative mechanisms is usually taken using information not available in Table 1 (such as cost or simplicity), but this rationale can be recorded to provide traceability and support the selection process.

On the other concerns, requirements for access control policies can be addressed with a password mechanisms, and `availability` requirements with passive replication of servers.

Once mechanisms are chosen, they are reified by choosing specific components that implement them. Figure 3 shows a (part of the) *MRM*'s catalog

Table 1. Partial content of the *ARM* for Communication Type

Mechanism	Synchrony	Topology	Initiator	Integrity/Timeliness	Sessions
SMTP	Asynchronous	1:M	Push	Integrity	Yes
NNTP	Asynchronous	1:M	Push	Integrity	Yes
RSS	Asynchronous	1:M	Pull	Integrity	Yes
SIP	Synchronous	P2P	Pull	Timeliness	No
POP3	Synchronous	M:1	Pull	Integrity	Yes
IMAP	Synchronous	M:1	Pull	Integrity	Yes

Table 2. Partial content of the *ARM* for Access Control

Mechanism	Authorization	Authentication
Personal Password	Individual	Something the user knows
ID Card	Individual	Something the user has
Fingerprint	Individual	Something the user is

Table 3. Partial content of the *ARM* for Node Replication

Mechanism	State	Update Propagation	Propagation Kind	Consistency
Active Replication	Persistent State	Operations	Push	Replicated-write
Passive Replication	Persistent State	State	Push	Primary-based

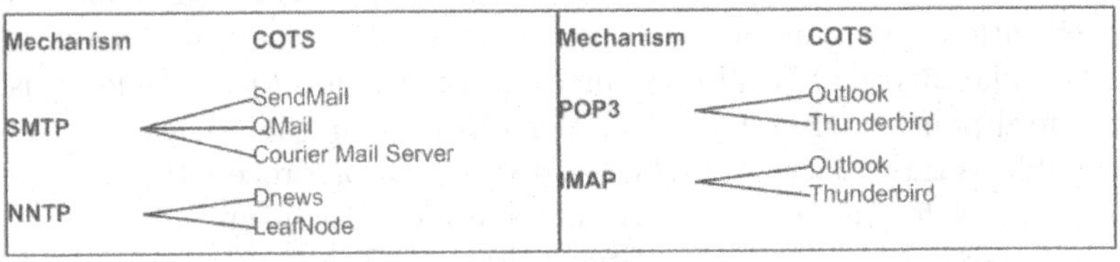

Fig. 3. Partial content of COTS Catalog in the *MRM*

COTS components that describes available options to implement these particular communication mechanisms.

If SMTP and IMAP or POP3 are chosen, the *MRM*-known available COTS alternatives are SendMail, QMail and Courier Mail Server (for SMTP) and Outlook and Thunderbird (for POP3 and IMAP). We also need to select implementations for selected *access control* and *replication* mechanisms. For instance, SMTP-AUTH protocol can implement access control for SMTP, and therefore we need to identify COTS that implement SMTP-AUTH, such as SendMail (8.1 and later), QMail (with qmail-smtpd-auth patch) and Courier Mail Server; both, Outlook and Thunderbird implement POP-AUTH and IMAP-AUTH to support access control mechanisms for sending mail. Regarding replication, there are several possibilities as well: passive replication achieving SMTP server replication and related policies with ad-hoc development; purchasing/adquiring COTS with this capabilities (e.g. LifeKeeper for Linux, SMTP.NET for Windows); or outsourcing this service to third parties defining SLA (availability=99,9%).

At this point, the architect makes the first decision about platform, in this case picking one on which both products run; the known choices are Windows (a gamut of choices itself) and Linux (likewise). We leave that last leg of the exercise to the reader.

5   Further Work

Work in progress includes expanding the policies catalog by adding more concerns and their dimensions, extending the framework to allow generation and comparison of alternative combinations of mechanism to satisfy a given problem, and identifying constraints on mechanism combinations. Hard problems that are being jointly studied with combonatorial optimization researchers are exploration and selection of mechanism combinations that are optimal according to second-order non-technical criteria (such as purchase cost, deployment risk, and development complexity) and their trade-off analysis; support for architectural what-if analysis (impact of requirement changes) and backwards questions (from available COTS or their providers, to original requirements that they satisfy); and exploration of the solutions space through incomplete and imprecise characterizations of COTS, mechanisms, or both.

Currently, Azimut models describing each abstraction level are tagged UML models, used as direct input to and output from the Azimut prototype, based on AndroMDA [9]. Applications of the aspect oriented approach are being considered as alternative representations of the policies and mechanisms dimensions and the mappings among them. Also, parallel work is starting to be able to predict, assess and measure quality attributes of the system to be built.

6   Conclusions

This article presents NFRs and their satisfaction using the Azimut framework and the process it supports. Azimut extends MDA for reasoning about architectural policies, preserving traceability of architectural decisions, and generating hybrid solutions with COTS and ad-hoc development.

The key framework ideas are representation of NFRs with architectural policies, multi-dimensional description of components as implementations of specific architectural mechanisms, systematic refinement and mapping from architectural policies into mechanisms and COTS, and development of catalogs of policies, mechanisms and COTS. The systematic use of architectural policies and mechanisms allows describing and reasoning architectural decisions at an architecture level, i.e. determining which software to build rather than how to build it, to provide certain required systemic properties (NFRs).

The Azimut approach avoids the complexity that would come from demanding correct, complete and consistent descriptions for NFRs and COTS, by using incomplete descriptions of NFRs and of available COTS ("characterizations" rather than full specifications) and by supporting the architect in the systematic exploration of the design space with automated COTS search and selection.

References

1. *Object Management Group: MDA Guide Version 1.0.1* (June 2003). http://www.omg.org/cgi-bin/doc?omg/03-06-01
2. Gokhale, A., Balasubramanian, K., and Lu, T. *CoSMIC: Addressing Crosscutting Deployment and Configuration Concerns of Distributed Real-Time and Embedded Systems.* OOPSLA 2004, ACM Press, p. 218-219.
3. Solberg A., Huusa K. E., Aagedal J. ., Abrahamsen E: *QoS-aware MDA.* Workshop SIVEOS-MDA 2003, ENTCS Journal.
4. Cao, F., Bryant, B., Raje, R., Auguston, M., Olson, A., Burt. C: *A Component Assembly Approach Based on Aspect-Oriented Generative Domain Modeling.* ENTCS 2005, pp.119-136.

5. Burt, C., Bryant, B., Raje, R., Olson, A., Auguston, M.: *Quality of Service Issues Related to Transforming Platform Independent Models to Platform Specific Models.* EDOC 2002, pp.212-223.

6. Silaghi, R., Fondement, F., Strohmeier, A.: *Towards an MDA-Oriented UML Profile for Distribution.* EDOC 2004, pp.227-239.

7. Simmonds, D., Solberg, A., Reddy, R., France, R., Ghosh, S.: *An Aspect Oriented Model Driven Framework.* EDOC 2005, to appear.

8. Weis, T., Ulbrich, A., Geihs, K., Becker, C.: *Quality of Service in Middleware and Applications: A Model-Driven Approach.* EDOC 2004, pp.160-171.

9. AndroMDA website. http://www.andromda.org/

10. OptimalJ website. http://www.compuware.com/products/optimalj/

11. ArcStyler website. http://www.interactive-objects.com/

12. SosyInc Modeler and Transformation Engine website. http://www.sosyinc.com/

13. Almeida, J.P.A., van Sinderen, M.J., Ferreira Pires, L. and Wegdam, M.: *Handling QoS in MDA: a discussion on availability and dynamic Reconfiguration.* Workshop MDAFA 2003, TR-CTIT-03-27, pp. 91-96.

14. Basin, D., Doser, J., and Lodderstedt, T.: *Model driven security for process-oriented systems.* SACMAT 2003, pp.100-109.

15. Lang, U., and Schreiner, R.: *OpenPMF: A Model-Driven Security Framework for Distributed Systems.* Presented at ISSE 2004

16. Skene, J., and Emmerich, W.: *A Model Driven Architecture Approach to Analysis of Non-Functional Properties of Software Architectures.* ACE 2003, pp.236-239.

17. Pignaton, R., Villagra, V., Asensio, J., Berrocal, J.: *Developing QoS-aware Component-Based Applications Using MDA Principles.* EDOC 2004, pp.172-183.

18. Policy and Mechanism Definitions. http://wiki.cs.uiuc.edu/MFA/Policy+and+Mechanism

19. Firesmith, D.: *Specifying Reusable Security Requirements.* Journal of Object Technology, Vol. 3, N° 1, (Jan-Feb 2004), pp.61-75.

20. Britton, C.: *IT Architectures and Middleware: Strategies for Building Large, Integrated Systems.* Addison-Wesley Professional (Dec 2000).

21. Bass, L., Clements, P., Kazman, R.: *Software Architecture in Practice, Second Edition* Addison-Wesley Professional (Apr 2003).

22. http://sarwiki.informatik.hu-berlin.de/Authentication_Mechanisms

23. OMG Specification : *UML Profile for Modeling Quality of Service and Fault Tolerance Characteristics and Mechanisms,* (Jun 2004) http://www.omg.org/docs/ptc/04-06-01.pdf

24. Tanenbaum, A., Van Steen, M.: *Distributed Systems Principles and Paradigms* Prentice Hall (2002)

Workshop 9 Summary

MDD for Software Product-Lines: Fact or Fiction?

Douglas C. Schmidt[1], Andrey Nechypurenko[2], and Egon Wuchner[2]

[1] Vanderbilt University, Nashville, TN, USA
[2] Siemens AG, CT SE 2, Munich, Germany

1 Workshop Synopsis and Goals

Software product-lines are an important technology for meeting the growing demand for highly customized - yet reusable - solutions. Commonality-variability analysis (CVA) is a well-known approach to address the challenges of software product-line development. The goal of CVA is to identify (1) what aspects of a software system are stable across multiple variants or over time, (2) what aspects of a software system vary across multiple variants or over time, and (3) the development techniques that best address specific commonalities and their variabilities, e.g., to allow substitution of custom variable implementations via a common interface. Model-driven development (MDD) provides effective techniques for documenting and conveying the results of a CVA by combining

- **Metamodeling**, which defines type systems that precisely express key abstract syntax characteristics and static semantic constraints associated with product-lines for particular application domains, such as software defined radios, avionics mission computing, and inventory tracking.
- **Domain-specific modeling languages (DSMLs)**, which provide programming notations that are guided by and extend metamodels to formalize the process of specifying product-line structure, behavior, and requirements in a domain.
- **Model transformations and code generators**, which ensure the consistency of product-line implementations with analysis information associated with functional and quality of service (QoS) requirements captured by structural and behavioral models.

Key advantages of using MDD in conjunction with CVA are (1) rigorously capturing the key roles and responsibilities in a CVA and (2) helping automate repetitive tasks that must be accomplished for each product instance. Often, however, new customer requirements invalidate the results of earlier CVAs, such that a CVA and its derived meta-models, DSMLs, and generators must be modified invasively and intrusively to reflect these new requirements.

For example, previous generations of automotive audio output systems (*e.g.*, radio, CD) did not have to share the audio output channel, *e.g.*, only one audio source could be active at the same time (*i.e.*, either radio or CD). The introduction of built-in mobile phone and traffic messaging systems require sharing

J.-M. Bruel (Ed.): MoDELS 2005 Workshops, LNCS 3844, pp. 237–246, 2006.
© Springer-Verlag Berlin Heidelberg 2006

and switching ownership of the audio output channel and must be managed correspondently. This new feature can cause changes to the set of entities defined by the metamodel. In addition, the set of composition and collaboration rules can undergo significant changes. These modifications can significantly complicate product-line evolution and maintenance efforts, which may outweigh the advantages of product- line development and automation compared to single product instance development.

The focus this workshop was on new theory and methods to reduce the impact of the new unanticipated requirements on the (meta)models and model interpreters to improve the (re)usability of model-based technologies in production large-scale applications. In particular, the papers (1) explored the pros and cons of current model-based technologies for software product-line development, validation, and evolution, (2) summarized the state of the current research on solution approaches regarding the problem of stabilizing meta-models, model-transformations, and code generators non-intrusively, and (3) analyzed the impact of promising relevant software development methodologies and techniques for software product-lines on industrial software development.

2   Workshop Organization

The workshop was organized into two parts. In the first part, a representative from each paper presented the material in the paper and the audience asked questions. During each paper presentation, the workshop organizers summarized the set of problems addressed by the authors and the corresponding set of suggested solutions. As a result, we collected an interconnected set of problem/solution pairs.

In the second part of the workshop, the organizers conducted a moderated discussion session to evaluate the maturity level of the R&D approaches with respect to solutions available for identified problems. To reach this goal, the moderator presented each problem statement, then the statement were refined during interactive discussion. Suggested solutions based on the workshop papers were discussed, followed by an evaluation of the maturity level of these solutions.

The remainder of this document is divided into sections corresponding to each identified problem. There are also subsections that outline suggested solutions and present the maturity level mark we agreed upon during the workshop discussions. Due to time restrictions, we did not discuss and evaluate all problem/solution domains in detail.

The figures shown in this document use ovals to depict the problem and boxes represent the proposed solution. As mentioned above, some solutions were evaluated. We used the range 1 to 5 where 5 means "very mature" and 1 corresponds to the "very immature."

The suggested approaches are not evaluated or commented. They are also not presented in detail level to avoid duplication of each paper where the corresponding approach is described. The goal of our workshop discussion was to simply summarize the suggested solutions to the identified problems and roughly determine the maturity level of the model-based approaches.

3 Metamodel Definition

Several authors [1, 2, 5] identified that having a high-quality metamodel is a key factor for successful and productive use of Domain Specific Languages (DSL). It is not yet clear, however, what are the most flexible and productive ways to define metamodels. The following solutions were suggested by workshop paper authors:

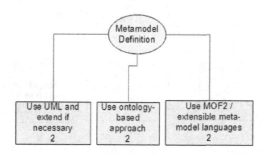

Fig. 1. Suggested Solution for Metamodel Definition

- *Use UML and extend it if necessary.* UML provides several extension mechanisms, such as stereotypes and tagged values, that can be used to define metamodels via pure UML notation, and if necessary extend it using provided extension mechanisms [6]. Maturity level: 2.
- *Use an ontology-based approach.* The problem of metamodeling can be treated as a detailed problem domain analysis, *i.e.*, identification of the domain-specific entities and their relationships. An ontology graph is the set of interconnected domain specific entities. It may be possible and helpful to apply ontology-based approaches to define metamodels since they are ontologies of the problem domain [4]. Maturity level: 2.
- *Use the OMG Meta-Object Facility (MOF2) and extensible metamodeling languages.* The OMG MOF2 www.omg.org/technology/documents/formal/mof.htm provides an extensible, flexible, and standardized way to define, access, and maintain (meta)models. These standardized mechanisms can improve modeling experience in cases where different modeling tasks could be accomplished with different modeling tools that interoperate using MOF2. There is not yet much support for this standard from tool vendors, however. Maturity level: 2.

4 Maintenance and Improvement of Code Generators

In large-scale applications, *i.e.*, with thousands of components, the complexity and related maintenance problems of the code generators and other types of required model interpreters/transformations can quickly outweigh the advantages of a generative approach. This problem becomes even more complicated

in product-line architecture development, where unexpected changes in requirements for new product instances can yield complicated changes propagated from
the metamodel level down to models, and then down to code generators and
model validation algorithms. Workshop participants made the following suggestions to overcome these types of problems:

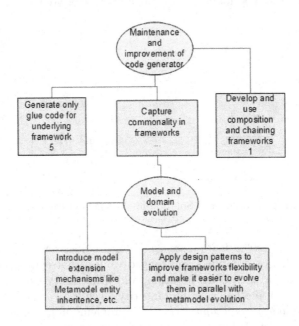

Fig. 2. Maintenances of Model Interpreters (Generators) and Model Evolution

- *Generate only glue code for underlying framework.* Early generations of *Computer Aided Software Engineering* (CASE)-based tools often failed because
  of attempts to generate the **complete** application. As a result, the generated
  code was suboptimal, hard to understand and debug, and hard to integrate
  into common runtime platforms, such as middleware and application frameworks. Experience shows that it might be more effective to generate only
  glue-code and configuration layers for existing middleware and frameworks.
  In this approach, the complexity of code generators could be significantly
  reduced and quality of the generated code improved. Maturity level: 5.
- *Capture commonality in frameworks.* The workshop participants generally
  agreed that model-driven tools (and related overhead compared to traditional handcrafted development) is most effective where many product instances with a high degree of commonality and certain variabilities must be
  produced (generated) and maintained. In such cases, workshop participants
  [2] recommended that common functionality should be captured in reusable
  software frameworks instead of trying to increase the complexity of code
  generators.

- *Develop and use composition and chaining frameworks.* Chaining and composing reusable components can also be challenging *e.g.*, due to ensuring end-to-end QoS of component assemblies in distributed real-time and embedded systems. The are also often certain semantic constraints and rules how to compose certain components which need to be enforced (ideally before the runtime) to avoid run-time errors. Certain related problems can be solved by development of specialized infrastructure (*e.g.*, frameworks, components, libraries, etc.) that help to connect available software artifacts together to produce runnable applications [2]. The implementations of CORBA Component Model (CCM) Deployment and Configuration specification www.omg.org/cgi-bin/doc?mars/2003-05-08 is an example of this approach, though it is just reaching critical mass in terms of multiple interoperable implementations and adoption by industry. Maturity level: 2.

5   Model and Domain Evolution

Evolution in understanding of the key problem domain aspects and relationships between different entities reflected in DSLs could lead to changes in formalized knowledge representation, which is typically exposed in form of metamodels. In turn, these changes can invalidate the existing set of models that are build under certain assumptions (*i.e.*, in conformance with metamodels). To provide an effective model-driven development cycle, the solution to model and domain evolution should be found. The following solution approaches were discussed during the workshop:

- *Capture commonality in frameworks.* As shown in Figure 2, the idea of using frameworks to capture commonalities between product-line members could also help while evolving and changing models as a result of evolution of the domain understanding [2].
- *Introduce model extension mechanisms.* Certain evolution and reusability problems at the metamodel level can be solved applying well-known techniques from the domain of object-oriented analysis. For example, introducing metamodel entity inheritance relationships in metamodeling environment could encapsulate certain common properties in common base entities. As a result, the change that will affect all derived entities can be localized [2, 5].
- *Apply design patterns to improve reusability of underlying frameworks.* A typical source of problems during model evolution is the mismatch between required flexibilities at the problem domain level and the configuration and adaptation mechanisms available at the solution level, *i.e.*, at the level of frameworks used in the generated code. Applying patterns for framework development can help improve the reusability and configuration of provided building blocks. In turn, this can help reduce the amount of work required to reflect (meta)model evolution at all levels of a model-driven tool chain [2].

6   Complexity at the Solution Level

To perform automatic mapping (*e.g.*, code generation) from the problem domain described as model(s), the solution domain should also be modeled and/or certain assumptions about the solution space should be made. The complexity of modern technologies typically used as a solution domain has increased to the level where it is hard to understand and use these technologies properly to solve certain problems. Without clear understanding how the solution space is defined, however, it is hard to develop (or generate) high quality solutions. The following solution approaches were discussed during the workshop:

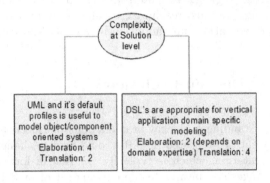

Fig. 3. Dealing with Complexity at the Solution Level

- *UML and its default profiles can be used to model object-/component-oriented systems.* If the solution space can be described using object-oriented methodologies and corresponding languages (such as C++ or Java) then UML can be used to model the problem domain. Maturity level: elaboration: 4, translation: 2.
- *DSMLs are appropriate for vertical application domain-specific modeling.* Often, domain experts describe the solution using terminology and abstractions different from the object-oriented paradigm. In such cases, the use of DSLs is preferable because it bridges the gap between domain experts and software engineers. Multiple transformations may be necessary to convert high-level models to lower-level source code. For example, the first transformation (manual or automatic) could represent the solution in DSL and then the second transformation can treat the DSL as a problem domain at lower level and consider an object-oriented framework as a target solution domain. Maturity level: elaboration - 2 (depends on domain expertise), translation - 4.

7   How to Enforce Constraints

Certain sets of rules for modelers can be exposed in metamodels. Often, however, there is a set of logical constraints that restrict how certain model elements can be configured or interact with each other. These constraints should be enforced automatically via a modeling environment. The following solution approach was discussed during the workshop:

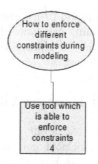

Fig. 4. Enforcing Constraints

- *Use tools that can enforce constraints.* It is responsibility of the modeling environment to provide the possibility to specify constraints and then check and enforce these constraints [5]. An example of such constraints are the Object Constraint Language (OCL) www.omg.org/technology/documents/formal/uml.htm provided by the Generic Modeling Environment (GME) www.isis.vanderbilt.edu/Projects/gme/. Maturity level: 4.

8   How to Transform Variation Points to Code

Often DSLs are designed in such a way that each DSL element could be parameterized and configured to reflect the variability presented in the subject of modeling. Due to typical paradigm mismatches between concepts described

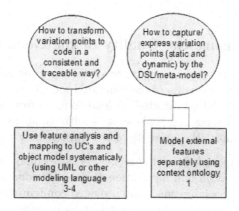

Fig. 5. Capturing and Transforming Variation Points to Code

in DSL and concepts available in modern programming languages, however, it is often hard to identify how DSL variation points should be transformed or implemented with concrete programming language [3]. The following solution approach was discussed during the workshop:

- *Use feature analysis and mapping to use cases.* Systematic feature analysis together with use case modeling can help identify the right set of software components or any other artifacts required to implement certain functionality (features). Maturity level: 3-4.

9   How to Capture and Express Variation Points

There are many ways to capture variability at the problem domain level and express them in DSL building blocks. For example, customization properties, DSL elements, inheritance, and customized reactions on user actions (such as resizing and moving) can help make DSLs easier to understand for domain engineers. These capabilities can also improve the reusability of DSL entities. In contrast to the object-oriented technologies, however, there are few well-defined rules and patterns that can help DSL developers decide which way is preferable in certain situations. For instance, in object-oriented design there is a set of patterns, such as Strategy, Service Configurator and Template Method, that help enhance flexibility. The following solution approaches were discussed during the workshop:

- *Use feature analysis and mapping to use cases.* As shown in Figure 5, systematic feature analysis and mapping to use cases can help identify the variation points and the proper way to express them in DSLs [3]. Maturity level: 3-4.
- *Model external features separately using context ontology.* It is helpful to distinguish between internal and external features, *e.g.*, to track the relationships between different features and functionality supposed to be provided by application. To simplify these tracking and maintenance tasks, the ontology-based analysis and modeling of external features could be used [4]. Maturity level: 1.

10   How to Ensure the Quality of the Generated Code

The fact that the source code or any other artifacts are generated cannot be used as an excuse for the poor quality of the generated code. For example, redundancy, lack of proper encapsulation, bloated or dead code is often as problematic with code generated from modeling tools as it is with manually written code. The following solution approaches were discussed during the workshop:

- *Use framework specialization techniques.* These techniques include (1) framework instrumentation and annotation to simplify code generation and customization, (2) specialization using provided configuration options and customization hooks, and (3) evolution driven by changing requirements or improved problem or solution domain understanding. These techniques can be

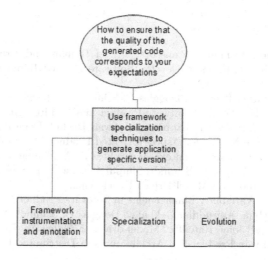

Fig. 6. How to Ensure the Quality of the Generated Code

used to generate application-specific versions where one side is based on a solid framework foundation, whereas the other side consists of application-specific functionality to ensure that all specific requirements are met [7].

11   Dealing with Overhead to Build the Model-Driven Infrastructure

Infrastructure that supports model-driven development of concrete product instances should be developed in advance and is rarely available off-the-shelf. For example, DSLs should be designed carefully based on extensive domain analysis. The result of this analysis should be documented formally using metamodeling. Code generators should be developed to automate the transformation from previously designed DSLs. All these activities require considerable up-front investments and need to be performed carefully to ensure that the overhead of building the modeling infrastructure does not offset the benefits of using it.

The following solution approach was discussed during the workshop:

- *Use compositional metamodeling techniques.* Compositional metamodeling is a key idea to simplify the construction of DSML metamodels. This technique provides a metamodel composition capability by reusing existing metamodel language concepts. When building complex metamodel for large-scale DSMLs, such metamodels can be built by reusing existing metamodel languages as libraries. Apart from being read-only, all objects in the metamodel imported through the library are equivalent to objects created from scratch. Metamodel designers can then create subtypes and instances from the metamodel library and refer library objects through references. Maturity level: 2-3.

References

[1] Vikram Bhanot, Dominick Paniscotti, Angel Roman and Bruce Trask: Using Domain-Specific Modeling to Develop Software Defined Radio Components and Applications

[2] Gan Deng, Gunther Lenz and Douglas C. Schmidt: Addressing Domain Evolution Challenges in Model-Driven Software Product-line Architectures

[3] Neil Loughran, Am=E9rico Sampaio and Awais Rashid: From Requirements Documents to Feature Models for Aspect Oriented Product Line Implementation

[4] Dennis Wagelaar: Towards Context-Aware Feature Modelling using Ontologies

[5] Jules White and Douglas C. Schmidt: Simplifying the Development of Product-line Customization Tools via Model Driven Development

[6] Hassan Gomaa: Variability Management in Software Product Lines

[7] Arvind S. Krishna, Aniruddha Gokhaley, Douglas C. Schmidt, Venkatesh, Prasad Ranganathz and John Hatcliffz: Model-driven Middleware Specialization Techniques for Software Product-line Architectures in Distributed Real-time and Embedded Systems

[8] OMG: "Meta-Object Facility, version 2.0",=20 url.

Addressing Domain Evolution Challenges in Software Product Lines

Gan Deng[1], Gunther Lenz[2], and Douglas C. Schmidt[1]

[1] Department of EECS, Vanderbilt University,
Nashville, Tennessee, USA 37203
{dengg, schmidt}@dre.vanderbilt.edu
[2] Siemens Corporate Research, Princeton, NJ 08540
lenz.gunther@siemens.com

Abstract. It is hard to develop and evolve software product-line architectures (PLAs) for large-scale distributed real-time and embedded (DRE) systems. Although certain challenges of PLAs can be addressed by combining model-driven development (MDD) techniques with component frameworks, domain evolution problems remain largely unresolved. In particular, extending or refactoring existing software product-lines to handle unanticipated requirements or better satisfy current requirements requires significant effort. This paper describes techniques for minimizing such impacts on MDD-based PLAs for DRE systems through a case study that shows how a layered architecture and model-to-model transformation tool support can reduce the effort of PLA evolution.

Keywords: Model-driven development, Product-line Architectures, Model Transformation.

1 Introduction

Software *product-line architectures* (PLAs) [20] are a promising technology for industrializing software development by focusing on the automated assembly and customization of domain-specific components, rather than (re)programming systems manually. Conventional PLAs consist of *component frameworks* [29] as core assets, whose design captures recurring structures, connectors, and control flow in an application domain, along with the points of variation explicitly allowed among these entities. PLAs are typically designed using *common/variability analysis* (CVA) [23], which captures key characteristics of software product-lines, including (1) *scope*, which defines the domains and context of the PLA, (2) *commonalities*, which describe the attributes that recur across all members of the family of products, and (3) *variabilities*, which describe the attributes unique to the different members of the family of products.

Despite improvements in third-generation programming languages (such as Java, C#, and C++) and runtime platforms (such as component and web services middleware), the levels of abstraction at which PLAs are developed today remains low relative to the concepts and concerns within the application domains themselves. A promising means to address this problem involves developing PLAs using *model-driven*

J.-M. Bruel (Ed.): MoDELS 2005 Workshops, LNCS 3844, pp. 247–261, 2006.

development (MDD) [9] tools. As shown in Figure 1, MDD tools help raise the level of abstraction and narrow the gap between problem and solution domain by combining (1) metamodeling and model interpreters to create domain-specific modeling languages (DSMLs) with (2) CVA and object-oriented extensibility capabilities to create domain-specific component frameworks. DSMLs help automate repetitive tasks that must be accomplished for each product instance, e.g., generating code to glue components together or synthesizing deployment artifacts for middleware platforms Domain-specific component frameworks factor out common usage patterns in a domain into reusable platforms, which help reduce the complexity of designing DSMLs by simplifying the code generated by their associated model interpreters.

To use MDD-based PLA technologies effectively in practice, however, requires practical and scalable solutions to the *domain evolution problem* [30], which arises when existing PLAs are extended and/or refactored to handle unanticipated requirements or better satisfy current requirements. Although PLAs can be enhanced by combining component frameworks with DSMLs, existing MDD tools do not handle the domain evolution problem effectively since they require significant manual changes to existing component frameworks and metamodels. For example, changing metamodels in a PLA typically invalidates models based on previous versions of the metamodels. While software developers can manually update their models and/or components developed with a previous metamodel to work with the new metamodel, this approach is clearly tedious, error-prone, and non-scalable.

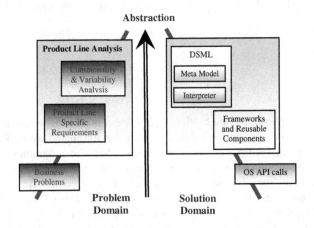

Fig. 1. Using DSMLs and Component Middleware to Enhance Abstraction and Narrow the Gap between Problem and Solution Domain

This paper describes our approach to PLA domain evolution. We use a case study of a representative MDD-based tool for DRE system to describe how to evolve PLAs systematically and minimize human intervention for specifying model-to-model transformation rules as a result of metamodel changes. Our approach automates many tedious, time consuming, and error-prone tasks of model-to-model transformation to reduce the complexity of PLA evolution significantly.

The remainder of this paper is organized as follows: Section 2 describes our vision of the architecture of PLA for DRE systems, and introduces our case study, which applies the *Event QoS Aspect Language* (EQAL) MDD tool to simplify the integration and interoperability of diverse publish/subscribe mechanisms in the Bold Stroke PLA; Section 3 describes challenges we faced when evolving models developed using EQAL and presents our solutions to these challenges; Section 4 compares our work on EQAL with related research; and Section 5 presents concluding remarks.

2 Overview of MDD-Based PLA and Case Study (EQAL)

This section presents an overview of an MDD-based PLA for DRE systems, focusing on the design concepts, common patterns, and software architecture. We then describe the structure and functionality of EQAL.

2.1 Design Concepts of MDD-Based PLAs for DRE Systems

The MDD-based design and composition approach for embedded systems in [10] describes the benefits of combining DSML and reusable component frameworks. We believe this approach also applies to the design of PLAs for large-scale DRE systems. Figure 2 illustrates the high-level design principle and overall architecture of an MDD-based PLA solution that exploits a *layered* and *compositional* architecture to modularize various design concerns for DRE systems.

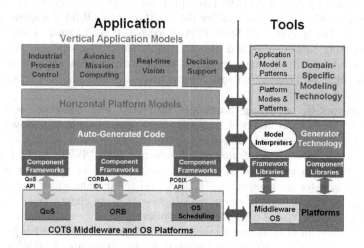

Fig. 2. MDD-Based Product-line Architecture for DRE Systems

MDD-based PLAs for DRE systems are based on a core set of platforms, frameworks, languages, and tools. DRE systems increasingly run on commercial-off-the-shelf (COTS) middleware and OS platforms. Middleware platforms include *Real-time Java, Real-time CORBA, Real-time CCM*, and the *Data Distribution Service* (DDS) and OS platforms include *VxWorks, Timesys Linux*, and *Windows CE*. Since many DRE systems require a loosely-coupled distribution architecture to simplify extensibility, COTS middleware typically provides publish/subscribe-based communication mechanisms where application components communicate anonymously and asynchronously by defining three software roles: *publishers* generate events that are transmitted to *subscribers* via *event channels* that accept events from publishers and deliver events to subscribers. Event-based communication helps developers concentrate on the application-specific concerns of their DRE systems, and leaves the connection, communication, and QoS-related details to middleware developers and tools. An event-based communication model also helps reduce ownership costs since it defines clear boundaries between the components in the application, thereby reducing dependencies and maintenance costs associated with replacement, integration, and revalidation of components. Moreover, core components of event-based architectures can be reused, thereby reducing development, quality assurance, and evolution effort.

Component frameworks provide reusable building blocks of PLAs for DRE systems. These frameworks are increasingly built atop COTS middleware and OS platforms. Since the philosophy of COTS middleware and OS platforms catered to maintaining "generality, wide applicability, portability ad reusability," customized frameworks are often desired in DRE software product-lines to (1) raise the level of abstraction, and (2) offer product-line specific runtime environments. Examples of component frameworks include *domain-specific middleware services* layer in the Boeing Bold Stroke PLA [26], which supports many Boeing product variants, such as F/A-18E, F/A-18F, F-15E, and F-15K, using a component-based, publish/subscribe platform built atop *The ACE ORB* (TAO) [27] and *Prism* [28], which is QoS-enabled component middleware influenced by the *Lightweight CORBA Component Model* (CCM) [19]. The Boeing Bold Stoke PLA supports systematic reuse of avionics mission computing functionality and is configurable for product-specific functionality (such as heads-up display, navigation, and sensor management) and execution environments (such as different networks/buses, hardware, operating systems, and programming languages).

Domain-specific modeling languages (DSMLs) and patterns facilitate the model-based design, development, and analysis of *vertical application domains*, such as industrial process control, telecommunications, and avionics mission computing. Example DSMLs the include *Saturn Site Production Flow* (SSPF), which is a manufacturing execution system serving as an integral and enabling component of the business process for car manufacture industry [11] and the *Embedded System Modeling Language* (ESML) [12], which models mission computing applications in the Boeing Bold Stroke PLA. DSMLs are also applicable to *horizontal platform domains*, such as the domain of component middleware for DRE systems, which provide the infrastructure for many vertical application domains. Examples of DSMLs for horizontal platforms include *Platform Independent Component Modeling Language* (PICML) [13], which facilitates the development of QoS-enabled component-based DRE systems and J2EEML [17], which facilitates the development of EJB applications. Regardless of whether the DSMLs target vertical or horizontal domains, model interpreters can be used to generate various artifacts (such as code and metadata descriptors), which can be integrated with component frameworks to form executable applications and/or simulations.

As shown in Figure 2, MDD-based PLA defines a framework of components that adhere to a common architectural style with a clear separation of commonalities and appropriate provisions for incorporating variations by integrating vertical/horizontal DSMLs, component frameworks, middleware and OS platforms. In this architecture, MDD technologies are used to model PLA features and glue components together, e.g., they could be utilized to synthesize deployment artifacts [13] for standard middleware platforms.

2.2 The Design of EQAL

The *Event QoS Aspect Language* (EQAL) is an MDD tool designed to reduce certain aspects of component-based publish/subscribe PLA-based DRE systems, such as the Boeing Bold Stroke PLA described in Section 2.1. EQAL is implemented using the Generic Modeling Environment (GME) [5], which is a toolkit that supports the development of DSMLs. The EQAL DSML provides an integrated set of metamodels, model interpreters, and standards-based component middleware that allowing PLA developers to visually configure and deploy event-based communication mechanisms in DRE systems via models instead of programming them manually. EQAL is an example of a DSML that supports a horizontal platform domain, i.e., it is not restricted to a particular vertical application domain, but instead can be leveraged by multiple vertical domains.

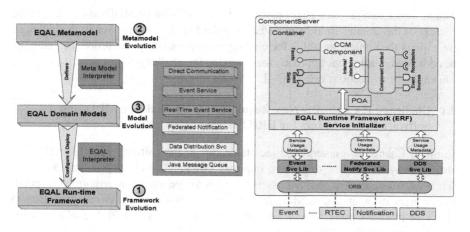

Fig. 3. EQAL MDD Tool Architecture   **Fig. 4.** EQAL Framework Evolution

As shown in Figure 3, EQAL is a layered architecture that supports several types of abstractions, which are subject to change stemming from domain evolution, as discussed in Section 3. The bottom layer is the *EQAL Runtime Framework*, which is a portable, OS-independent framework built atop the *Component-Integrated ACE ORB* (CIAO) QoS-enabled implementation of the Lightweight CCM specification. The EQAL Runtime Framework provides an extensible way to deploy various event-based communication mechanisms, including a two-way event communication mechanism based on direct method invocation, the CORBA Event Service, and TAO's Real-time Event Service [24].

The middle layer in the EQAL architecture is a set of domain models that represent instances of modeled DRE systems. These models are created by the EQAL DSML and are used to capture the structural and behavioral semantic aspects of event-based DRE systems.

The top layer of the EQAL MDD architecture consists of metamodel that enables developers to model concepts of event-based DRE systems, including the configuration and deployment of various publish/subscribe services and how these services are used by CCM components. This layer also contains several model interpreters that synthesize various types of configuration files that specify QoS configurations, parameters, and constraints. The EQAL interpreters automatically generate publish/subscribe service configuration files and service property description files needed by the underlying EQAL Runtime Framework and CIAO middleware.

Although the EQAL MDD tool could be used to simplify the integration and interoperability of diverse publish/subscribe mechanisms in some PLAs, evolving such a MDD-based PLA would often bring additional challenges.

3   Resolving Challenges of MDD-Based PLA When Facing Domain Evolution

This section examines challenges associated with evolving an MDD-based PLA in the context of the Boeing Bold Stroke PLA and the EQAL DSML. For each challenge, we explain the context in which the challenge arises, identify key problems that must be addressed, outline our approach for resolving the challenges, and describe how we can apply these solutions using EQAL.

3.1   Challenge 1: Capturing New Requirements into Existing MDD-Based Software Product-Lines for DRE Systems

Context. Change is a natural and inevitable part of the software PLA lifecycle. The changes may be initiated to correct, improve, or extend assets or products. Since assets are often dependent on other assets, changes to one asset may require corresponding changes in other assets. Moreover, changes to assets in PLAs can propagate to affect all products using these assets. A successful process for PLA evolution must therefore manage these changes effectively [15].

Problem → New Requirements Must Be Captured into Existing PLAs. DRE systems must evolve to adapt to changing requirements and operational contexts. In addition, when some emerging technologies become sufficiently mature, it is often desirable to integrate them into existing PLAs for DRE systems. For example, depending on customer requirements, different product variants in the Bold Stroke PLA may require different levels of QoS assurance for event communication, including timing constraints, event delivery latency, jitter, and scalability. Even within the same product variant, different levels of QoS assurance may be required for different communication paths, depending on system criticality, e.g., certain communication paths between components may require more stringent QoS requirements than other ones.

The event communication mechanisms currently supported by EQAL include: (1) two-way based event communication based on direct method invocation, (2) CORBA event service, and (3) TAO's Real-time Event Service [24]. Although the communication mechanisms provided by EQAL are applicable to many types of event-based systems, with the evolution in a domain and new technologies emerging, other event communication mechanisms may be needed. For example, TAO's reliable multicast *Federated Notification Service* is desired in certain DRE systems to address scalability and reliability. Likewise, the OMG's *Data Distribution Service* (DDS) [25] is often desired when low latency and advanced QoS capabilities are key product variant concerns. When these two new publish/subscribe technologies are added into the existing EQAL MDD tool, all layers in EQAL MDD architecture must change accordingly, including EQAL Runtime Framework, EQAL DSML and EQAL Domain Models. Moreover, since EQAL models have already been used in earlier incarnations of a PLA, such as Bold Stroke, we must minimize the effort required to migrate existing EQAL models to adhere to the new metamodels.

Solution → Evolve PLA *Systematically* Through Framework and Metamodel Enhancement. Although a layered PLA can significantly reduce software design complexity by separating concerns and enforcing boundaries between different layers, since different layers in PLA still need to interact with each other through predefined interfaces, therefore, to integrate new requirements into a PLA, all layers must evolve in a *systematic* manner. As shown in Figure 3, for most PLAs for DRE systems we generalized this evolution to the following three ordered steps:

1. **Component framework evolution.** As discussed in Section 2.1, frameworks are often built atop middleware and OS platforms and provide the runtime environment to DRE systems. As a result, whenever the DRE systems must evolve to adapt to new requirements, component frameworks are often affected since they have *direct* impact on the system.
2. **DSML evolution.** DSML metamodels and interpreters are often used to capture the *variability* and *features* of DRE systems so a system can expose different capabilities for different product variants. Often, DSMLs are used to glue different component framework entities together to form a complete application. Hence, typically DSML evolution should be performed after framework evolution is completed.
3. **Domain model evolution.** The DSML metamodel defines a type system to which domain models must conform to. Since the changes to the metamodel of a DSML often invalidate the existing domain models by redefining the type system, domain model evolution must be performed after the DSML evolution.

We discuss the challenges and solutions associated with component framework and DSML evolution in the Section 3.1.1 and then discuss the challenges and solutions associated with domain model evolution in Section 3.1.2.

3.1.1   EQAL Framework Evolution

In our case study, the EQAL Runtime Framework provides a set of service configuration libraries that can configure various publish/subscribe services. Since these middleware services can be configured using well-defined and documented *interfaces*, we can formulate the usage patterns of such middleware services easily. The EQAL Runtime Framework can encapsulate these usage patterns and provide reusable libraries that (1) contain wrapper façades for the underlying publish/subscribe middleware services to shield component developers from tedious and error-prone programming tasks associated with initializing and configuring these publish/subscribe services and (2) expose interfaces to the external tools to manage the services, so that service configuration and deployment processes can be automated, as shown in Figure 3. I. To incorporate these new publish/subscribe technologies and minimize the impact on existing DRE systems, we used the *Adapter* and *Strategy* patterns so all event communication mechanisms supported by EQAL provide the same interface, yet can also be configured with different strategies and QoS configurations.

3.1.2   EQAL DSML Evolution

The EQAL metamodel must be enhanced to incorporate these new requirements, so system developers can model the behavior of new event-based communication mechanisms visually. For example, to enhance EQAL to support DDS and TAO's Federated Notification Service, the metamodel of the EQAL DSML must be changed. Since the EQAL metamodel defines the language to describe EQAL domain models, it is essential to minimize the impact on EQAL domain models, so that the EQAL domain models can be transformed easily to comply with the new EQAL metamodel.

Compositional metamodeling is a key idea to make metamodel scalable and easier to evolve. This technique provides a metamodel composition capability for reusing and combining existing modeling languages and language concepts. Since EQAL is implemented with GME, when new publish/subscribe services are integrated, we could design a new DSML within GME and import the old EQAL metamodel as a "library".. Apart from being read-only, all objects in the metamodel imported through the library are equivalent to objects created from scratch.   Since the new publish/subscribe services share much commonality between the exiting publish/subscribe services that EQAL already supports, when the old EQAL metamodel is imported as library, we could create subtypes and instances from the metamodel library and refer library objects through references.

3.2   Challenge 2: Migrating Existing Domain Models with MDD-Based PLA Evolution

Context. The primary value of the MDD paradigm stems from the models created using the DSML. These models specify the system, and from the models the executable system can be generated or composed. Changes to the computer-based system can be modeled, and the resulting executable model is thus a working version of the actual system. Unfortunately, if the metamodel is changed, all models that were defined using that metamodel may require maintenance to adapt to the semantics that represent the computer-based system correctly. Without ensuring the correctness of the domain models after a change to the domain, the benefits of MDD will be lost. The only way to use instance models based on the original metamodel is to migrate them to use the modified metamodel. During this migration process, we must preserve the existing set of domain model assets and allow new features to be added into domain models; ideally with as little human intervention effort as possible.

Problem → Existing Domain Models Evolution Techniques Require Excessive Human Intervention. To address the challenge of preserving the existing set of domain model assets, old domain models must be transformed to become compliant with the changed metamodel. In the MDD research community, particularly in the DSML community, research has been conducted on using model transformation to address metamodel evolution. Since the underlying structure of models, especially visual models, can be described by graphs, most of the model transformation research has been conducted in the context of graph transformation. In particular, recent research [1,2] has shown that graph transformation is a promising formalism to specify model transformations rules.

Most existing model transformation techniques, however, require the transformation be performed *after* the domain metamodel has changed. For example, when an old metamodel is modified and a new metamodel based on it is created, the model transformation designer must take both the old metamodel and new metamodel as input, and then manually specify the model transformation rules based on these two metamodels by using the "transformation behavior specification language" provided by the transformation tool. Although such a design approach could solve the model transformation problem, it introduces additional effort in specifying the model transformation rules, even if the metamodel evolution is minor (e.g., a simple rename of a concept in the metamodel). This additional effort is particularly high when the metamodels are complex, since the transformation tool must take both complex metamodels as input to specify the transformation.

Solution → Tool-Supported Domain Model Migration. To preserve the assets of domain models, our approach is to bring *model migration* capabilities online, i.e., embed domain model migration capabilities into the metamodeling environment itself. This approach is sufficiently generic to be applied to any existing metamodeling environment. A description of the change in semantics between an old and a new DSML is a sufficient specification to transform domain models such that they are correct in the new DSML. Moreover, the pattern that specifies the proper model migration is driven by the change in semantics, and may be fully specified by a model composed of entities from the old and new metamodels, along with directions for their modification [6].

3.2.1 Integration of Syntactic-Based and Semantic-Based Domain Model Migration

Based on the characteristics of metamodel change, researchers have shown that 14 "atomic" types of metamodel changes can be defined [6], as shown in Table 1.

Table 1. Changes that Require a Paradigm Shift [6]

Type of metamodel change	Affected domain models (of this type) are present?	Change is Required?
Additions		
1 Addition of new type A	No	No
2 Addition of new attribute of type A	Yes	No
3 Addition of association between types B and C	Yes	No
4 Addition of type(s) E derived from type D	Yes	No
5 Addition of constraint on type F	Yes	Yes
Deletions		
6 Deletion of an attribute of type A	Yes	Yes
7 Deletion of an existing type B	Yes	Yes
8 Deletion of association between types D and E	Yes	Yes
9 Deletion of constraint on type F	Yes	No
Modifications		
10 Renaming type A	Yes	Yes
11 Renaming attribute of type A	Yes	Yes
12 Changing type of B	Yes	Yes
13 Addition of type(s) E derived from type D, that replaces D in a certain context(s)	Yes	Yes
14 Modification of constraint on type F	Yes	Yes

These results provide us the intuition into the problem. In some cases, the semantics can be easily specified. For example, if the metamodel designer deletes an atom called "foo" in the metamodel and creates a new atom called "bar" we can then specify the semantics of the change as:

$$replace(Atom("foo") \rightarrow Atom("bar"));$$

Syntactic metamodel changes, however, can often affect semantic changes, which results in a highly challenging task in model migration, i.e., *semantic migration*. Semantic migration requires that the meaning of the old domain models is preserved after the transformation, and that the new domain models conform to the entire set of static constraints required in the new domain. In these cases, it is quite challenging to discover the semantics of the change. To make such algorithms provide actual "semantic migration" capabilities, human input will be necessary since semantic changes in metamodels can not be captured through syntactic changes alone.

For model migration, we generalized two approaches to perform model transformation with semantic migration. In the first approach, given two *distinct* metamodels, old and new, we can perform a transformation that converts the old model in entirety to the new one. This means one will have to write a complete set of rules to convert each entity in the models. In the second approach, we create a *unified* metamodel (old + new), such that both old and new models are valid in it. Developers can then write transformation translators that convert those parts of the model belonging to the old part of the paradigm to equivalent models in the new part of the paradigm.

It is evident that the second approach is much cleaner and user-friendly than the first approach since it requires much less human effort. We are therefore investigating the second model migration approach. In our approach, after the unified metamodel is formulated, we use an "SQL-like" declaratively language that allows one to query and change the model to define model transformation rules. The *Embedded Constraint Language* (ECL), used by the C-SAW GME plug-in [2], seems to be a good candidate for such a language. The ECL is a textual language for describing transformations on visual models. Similar to the Object Constraint Language (OCL) defined in OMG's UML specification, the ECL provides concepts such as collection and model naviga-tion. In addition, the ECL also provides a rich set of operators that are not found in the OCL to support model aggregations, connections, and transformations. ECL is an imperative language that allows one to specify procedural style transformation rules of the syntax translator to capture the semantic migration.

3.2.2 EQAL Domain Model Evolution

Figure 5 illustrates the BasicSP application scenario in the Boeing Bold Stroke PLA, in which two component instances named BMDevice and BMClosedED are con-nected with each other through real-time event channel provided by TAO's Real-time Event Service. An event channel consists of one RTEC_Proxy_Consumer module and RTEC_Proxy_Supplier module, which could be configured with various QoS settings. Consider a domain evolution scenario, where the Real-time Event Ser-vice is not the desired choice for a particular Bold Stroke product variant, so it must be replaced with TAO Federated Notification Service. In this case, the current domain model below will become invalid and must be migrated to the new EQAL DSML that supports the configuration of TAO's Federated Notification Service.

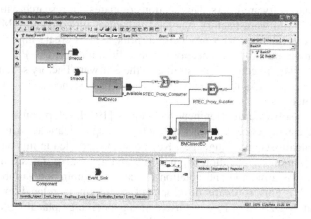

Fig. 5. EQAL Configuring Real-time Event Service between Two Components

With ECL declarative language, we could create a model translator by defining strategies as below:

```
strategy ChangeToFNS() {

    declare FNS_Proxy_Consumer,
            FNS_Proxy_Supplier : model;

    // Find interested model elements...
    if(atoms()->select(a | a.kindOf() =
        "RTEC_Proxy_Consumer")->size() >= 1) then

    //get the RTEC_Proxy_Consumer model element
    //and its connections
        ...
    //delete the RTEC_Proxy_Consumer model element
    RTEC_Model.deleteModel(
        "RTEC_Proxy_Consumer",
        "RTEC_proxy_consumer");

    //add the FNS_Proxy_Consumer model
    FNS_Proxy_Consumer:=
        addModel("FNS_Proxy_Consumer",
            "FNS_proxy_consumer");
    FNS_Proxy_Consumer.setAttribute("Reactive", "1");
    FNS_Proxy_Consumer.setAttribute("LockType",
    "Thread Mutex");

    //add the connections
    RTEC_Model.addConnection(
        "Event_Source_Proxy_Consumer",
        event_source,
        FNS_Proxy_Consumer);
    RTEC_Model.addConnection(
        "Proxy_Supplier_Event_Sink",
        FNS_Proxy_Consumer,
        event_sink);

    //do similar to the FNS_Proxy_Supplier model
        ...
    endif;
};
```

The semantic meaning of this translator is straightforward, i.e., first find the interested model elements and their associations that are based on TAO's Real-time Event Service and replace these model elements and associations with TAO's Federated Notification Service.

4 Related Work

Software product-line is a viable software development paradigm that enables order-of-magnitude improvements in time to market, cost, productivity, quality, and other business drivers [20]. As MDD technology becomes more pervasive, there has been an increase in focus on technologies, architecture, and tools for applying MDD-based techniques into software PLAs. This section compares our research with related work.

Microsoft's Software Factory scheme [9] focuses on combining MDD- and component-based techniques with product-line principles to create highly extensible development tools quickly and cheaply for specific domains. The PLAs for DRE systems we describe in Section 2 are similar to the Software Factory scheme, but focuses on how aspects of PLAs for DRE systems should be designed and evolved throughout a system's lifecycle.

Generative software development techniques [19] develop software system families by synthesizing code and other artifacts from specifications written in textual or graphical domain-specific languages. Key concepts and idea in this paradigm include DSML, domain and application engineering, and generative domain models. Feature modeling [18] is a method and notation for capturing common/variable features in a system family. This software development paradigm is related to our approach, though in our MDD-based PLA we use domain-specific graphical DSML notations to describe the application semantics, instead of using a universal feature modeling notation since the latter is too restrictive for many DRE systems. .

Significant efforts have focused on evolution problems of model-based legacy systems. The *Atlas Transformation Language* (ATL) developed in the *Generative Model Transformer* project [22] aims to define and perform general transformations based on OMG's MDA technology. Atlas is a model transformation language specified both as a metamodel and as a textual concrete syntax, and a hybrid of declarative and imperative language. The *Graph Rewriting and Transformation* (GReAT) [21] tool provides a model transformation specification language to handle the model migration problem by explicitly defining complex graph patterns and pattern matching algorithms through models. While the methods mentioned above are powerful, they are also labor-intensive since transformations must be defined manually, which does not scale up for large-scale DRE systems. In contrast, our approach enables automatic transformation with limited human intervention that eliminates much of the tedious tasks of model evolution. C-SAW [2] is a general model transformation engine developed as a GME [5] plug-in and is compatible with any metamodel, i.e., it is domain-dependent and can be used with any modeling language defined within the GME. C-SAW, however, can only handle domain model transformations when the metamodel is not changed, while our approach can be used even when the metamodel has changed.

5 Concluding Remarks

Large-scale DRE systems are hard to build. Software product-line architectures (PLAs) are an important technology for meeting the growing demand for highly customized and reusable DRE systems. MDD-based PLA provides a promising means to develop software product-lines for DRE systems by combining metamodeling, DSMLs, interpreters, frameworks, and COTS middleware and OS platforms.

Software product-lines must inevitably evolve to meet new requirements. Adding new (particularly new unanticipated) requirements to MDD-based PLAs, however, often causes invasive modifications to the PLA's component frameworks and DSMLs to reflect these new requirements. Since these modifications significantly complicate PLA evolution efforts, they can outweigh the advantages of PLA development compared to one off development. To rectify these problems, a layered and compositional architecture is needed to modularize system concerns and reduce the effort associated with domain evolution. This paper illustrates via a case study how (1) structural-based model transformations help maintain the stability of domain evolution by automatically transforming domain models and (2) aspect-oriented model transformation and weaving helps reduce human effort by capturing model-based structural concerns.

References

[1] Jonathan Sprinkle, Aditya Agrawal, Tihamer Levendovszky, Feng Shi, Gabor Karsai, "Domain Model Translation Using Graph Transformations," *ECBS 2003*: 159-167

[2] Jeff Gray, Ted Bapty, Sandeep Neema, James Tuck, "Handling Crosscutting Constraints in Domain-specific Modeling," *Communicaton of ACM* 44(10): 87-93 (2001)

[3] Jayant Madhavan, Philip A. Bernstein, Erhard Rahm: "Generic Schema Matching with Cupid," *VLDB 2001*: 49-58, Roma, Italy

[4] Frank Budinsky, David Steinberg, Ed Merks, Ray Ellersick, Timothy Grose, *"Eclipse Modeling Framework"*, Addison-Wesley 2004

[5] Ledeczi A., Maroti M., Bakay A., Karsai G., Garrett J., Thomason IV C., Nordstrom G., Sprinkle J., Volgyesi P., "The Generic Modeling Environment," *Workshop on Intelligent Signal Processing*, Budapest, Hungary, May 17, 2001.

[6] Jonathan Sprinkle, Gabor Karsai, "A Domain-Specific Visual Language for Domain Model Evolution", *Journal of Visual Language and Computation*, vol. 15, no. 3-4, pp. 291-307, Jun., 2004.

[7] Gan Deng, Jaiganesh Balasubramanian, William Otte, Douglas C. Schmidt, and Aniruddha Gokhale, "DAnCE: A QoS-enabled Component Deployment and Conguration Engine," *Proceedings of the 3rd Working Conference on Component Deployment*, Grenoble, France, November 28-29, 2005.

[8] Gan Deng, "Supporting Configuration and Deployment of Component-based DRE Systems Using Frameworks, Models, and Aspects," *OOPSLA '06 Companion*, October 2005, San Diego, CA, to appear

[9] Jack Greenfield, Keith Short, Steve Cook, Stuart Kent, John Crupi, *Software Factories: Assembling Applications with Patterns, Models, Frameworks, and Tools*, Wiley 2004

[10] Gabor Kasai, Janos Sztipanovits, Akos Ledeczi, and Ted Bapty, "Model-Integrated Development of Embedded software", Proceedings of the IEEE number 1, volume 91, Jan. 2003

[11] Karsai G., Sztipanovits J., Ledeczi A., Moore M., "Model-Integrated System Development: Models, Architecture and Process," *21st Annual International Computer Software and Application Conference (COMPSAC)*, pp. 176-181, Bethesda, MD, August, 1997

[12] http://www.isis.vanderbilt.edu/Projects/mobies/.

[13] Krishnakumar Balasubramanian, Jaiganesh Balasubramanian, Jeff Parsons, Aniruddha Gokhale, and Douglas C. Schmidt, "A Platform-Independent Component Modeling Language for Distributed Real-time and Embedded Systems," *Proceedings of the 11th IEEE Real-Time and Embedded Technology and Applications Symposium*, San Francisco, CA, March 2005

[14] George Edwards, Gan Deng, Douglas C. Schmidt, Anirudda Gokhale, and Balachandran Natarajan, "Model-driven Configuration and Deployment of Component Middleware Publisher/Subscriber Services," *Proceedings of the 3rd ACM International Conference on Generative Programming and Component Engineering*, Vancouver, CA, October 2004

[15] John D. McGregor, "The Evolution of Product-line Assets," Technical Report, *CMU/SEI-2003-TR-005m ESC-TR-2003-005*

[16] David Sharp. "Avionics Product-line Software Architecture Flow Policies," In *Proceedings of the Digital Avionics Systems Conference*, 1999

[17] Jules White, Douglas Schmidt, and Aniruddha Gokhale, "Simplifying Autonomic Enterprise Java Bean Applications via Model-driven Development: a Case Study", *Proceedings of ACM/IEEE 8th International Conference on Model Driven Engineering Languages and Systems*, Montego Bay, Jamaica, October 5-7, 2005.

[18] Krzysztof Czarnecki, Simon. Helsen, and Ulrich. Eisenecker, "Staged configuration using feature models", In *Proceedings of the Third Software Product-Line Conference*, Robert Nord, 2004

[19] Krzysztof Czarnecki, Ulrich Eisenecker, *Generative Programming: Methods, Tools, and Applications*, Addison-Wesley 2000

[20] Paul Clements, Linda Northrop, *Software Product-lines: Practices and Patterns*, Addison-Wesley, ISBN 0201703327, August 20, 2001

[21] Aditya Agrawal, Gabor Karsai, Ákos Lédeczi, "An End-to-end Domain-driven Software Devel opment Framework," *Proceeding of ACM SIGPLAN OOPSLA 2003 Domain Driven Design session* , Anaheim, CA, 2003

[22] Available at Generative Model Transformer project website, http://www.eclipse.org/gmt/

[23] James Coplien, Daniel Hoffman, and David Weiss, "Commonality and Variability in Software Engineering" *IEEE Software*, 15(6) November/December, 37—45, 1998

[24] Tim Harrison and David Levine and Douglas C. Schmidt, "The Design and Performance of a Real-time CORBA Event Service", *Proceedings of OOPSLA '97*, ACM, Atlanta, GA, October 6-7, 1997

[25] OMG's "Data Distribution Service for Real-time Systems Specification", version 1.0, Dec.2004. http://www.omg.org/docs/formal/04-12-02.pdf

[26] David Sharp and Wendy Roll, "Model-Based Integration of Reusable Component-Based Avionics System," in *Proceedings of the Workshop on Model-Driven Embedded Systems in RTAS 2003*, May 2003

[27] Douglas Schmidt, David Levine, and Sumedh Mungee, "The Design and Performance of Real-Time Object Request Brokers", *Computer Communications*, vol. 21, pp. 294–324, Apr. 1998

[28] Wendy Roll, "Towards Model-Based and CCM-Based Applications for Real-Time Systems," in *Proceedings of the International Symposium on Object-Oriented Real-time Distributed Computing (ISORC)*, Hokkaido, Japan, IEEE/IFIP, May 2003

[29] Clemens Szyperski, *"Component Software: Beyond Object-Oriented Programming"*, Addison-Wesley, Dec. 1997

[30] Randall R. Macala, Lynn D. Stuckey, Jr. David C. Gross, "Managing Domain-Specific, Product-Line Development", *IEEE Software*, Vol.14, No. 13, May 1996

From Requirements Documents to Feature Models for Aspect Oriented Product Line Implementation

Neil Loughran, Américo Sampaio, and Awais Rashid

Computing Department, InfoLab 21, Lancaster University, Lancaster LA1 4WA, UK
{loughran, a.sampaio, awais}@comp.lancs.ac.uk

Abstract. Software product line engineering has emerged as an approach to developing software which targets a given domain. However, the processes involved in developing a software product line can be time consuming and error prone without adequate lifecycle tool support. In this paper we describe our approach, NAPLES, which uses natural language processing and aspect-oriented techniques to facilitate requirements analysis, commonality and variability analysis, concern identification to derive suitable feature oriented models for implementation.

1 Introduction

Software product line engineering [19] promotes an architecture centric approach to developing software, which targets a particular domain or market segment. Software can then be created that is customizable to the particular requirements of different customers. Utilizing such an approach can yield high quality, optimized software with an increase in productivity and consistency as well as reductions in time to market, costs and error rates. Among the influencing factors that may necessitate the move to a product line architecture are identification of new market trends and their domains, business mergers and the encapsulation of multiple but overlapping existing products that a company may have in their itinerary. However, software product lines are difficult to develop with many of the activities (e.g., domain analysis, modeling and implementation) being time consuming and error prone. Lifecycle tool support and an associated methodology which aims to address these problems are therefore essential.

In this paper we present our approach, NAPLES (**N**atural language **A**spect-based **P**roduct **L**ine **E**ngineering of **S**ystems), a product line engineering approach that provides life cycle tool support for taking requirements documents and other textual assets (e.g. documentation and user manuals) and analyzes them for potential features and aspect candidates as well as commonalities and variabilities within a given domain. We demonstrate the approach by taking an existing set of requirements and performing analysis on them in order to mine for key domain concepts, viewpoints and aspects as well as variabilities, which can then be mapped to a suitable feature model.

The next section provides an overview of NAPLES. Section 3 demonstrates how NAPLES provides guidance and tool support to effectively mine concepts (e.g., concerns, commonalities, variabilities) as well as facilitates to produce the models in further phases. Section 4 demonstrates how framed-aspect models can be systematically delineated from the previous identified concepts and how they can map to a modularized implementation. Section 5 provides discussion on the process and

J.-M. Bruel (Ed.): MoDELS 2005 Workshops, LNCS 3844, pp. 262–271, 2006.

explains how it could be utilized for different contexts such as building a product line from scratch or from existing systems. Section 6 briefly describes related work while section 7 concludes the paper.

2 Natural Language Aspect-Based Product Line Engineering for Systems (NAPLES)

The NAPLES approach addresses product line (PL) engineering throughout the lifecycle by using different techniques, e.g., natural language processing (NLP) and aspect-oriented software development (AOSD), to provide automated support and separation of concerns during the PL lifecycle. For example, during requirements activities, tool support based on natural language processing techniques and aspect-oriented requirements engineering (AORE) [1, 2] is provided to mine for different concepts and help the developer to build models from these concepts. The tools used with the approach do not automate 100% of the engineering tasks but they aim to provide effective support for product line engineering in a cost-effective way, which is vital for product line engineering. Fig. 1 presents the NAPLES approach showing its activities and input/output artifacts.

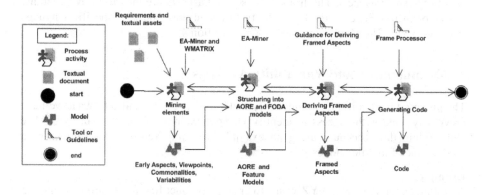

Fig. 1. An overview of the NAPLES approach

The approach starts with the *Mining Elements* activity which identifies important concepts (e.g., early aspects [1-3], viewpoints [4], commonalities and variabilities) from the requirements documents used as input, and presents them to the user in a format that can be used to produce a structured model (AORE model [1, 2] and feature model). The EA-Miner [3, 5] tool uses the WMATRIX [6, 7] natural language processor to pre-process the input documents and get relevant information. WMATRIX provides part-of-speech and semantic tagging, frequency analysis and concordances[1] to identify concepts of potential significance in the domain. Part-of-

---

[1] Concordance is a way of presenting a list of chunks of text containing a specific word and its surrounding text. The word of interest is highlighted and separated from the rest of the text (e.g., centered). Example: text... vehicle ....text.

speech analysis automates the extraction of syntactic categories from the text (e.g., nouns and verbs).

The information produced by the NLP processor is then used by EA-Miner to help list possible key domain concept candidates. For example, for the identification of viewpoints, the tool lists the most frequently occurring nouns in the text, and for Early Aspects it lists words whose meaning resembles a broadly scoped concern (e.g., security, performance, parallel, logon, authorize, and so forth) Details on how EA-Miner performs its identification can be found in [3, 5]. Commonalities and variabilities are also identified in a similar fashion, and this is detailed in Section 3.

After the software developer has identified and selected the concepts of interest in the previous activity, EA-Miner helps to build structured models during the *Structuring into Models* activity. The tool enables the application of *screen out* functionalities (e.g., add, remove, check synonyms) to discard irrelevant concepts, add new ones and check if the same concepts are identified as different ones. The output is an AORE model showing the viewpoints, early aspects and composition rules as well as a feature model showing features alongside their commonalities and variabilities.

The *Deriving Framed Aspects* activity uses the previous models (AORE and feature model) and provides guidance on how to delineate an aspect-oriented model based on framed aspects. The framed classes and aspects are then used by the frame processor in the *Generating code* activity to create the code in a specific language (e.g., AspectJ [17]). More details are given in Section 4.

3   Commonality and Variability Analysis

The process for identifying commonality and variabilities is similar to what we have previously done with success to identify viewpoints and early aspects in [3, 5]. We will explain the procedure using an example of a requirements description for a product line of mobile phones.

Example:
A mobile phone company XYZ wants to create a product line for its products aiming at reducing the costs of its operations. The phones will have similar features that can vary according to the model. Some details of the product line are:

- The phone models are: Model A, Model B and Model C.
- The feature game will be present in all models. For models A and B the games are already installed and the difference is that model B has games G3 and G4 in addition to G1 and G2 also found in A. Model C has all the previous games and also the option to download more games. For all gaming features, it is important to offer good performance to the users. Each game provides some facility to store high scores.
- The feature list of contacts is offered in all 3 models and varies in the capacity of the numbers of contacts that can be stored. For models A and B up to 50 contacts can be saved while for model C up to 100.

- Model C is the only one to offer a web browser and chat functionalities for real-time communication over the web. There is provision for the user to store the URLs of their favorite web pages.
- All mobile phones offer a password protection mechanism that is requested when the phone is turned on. The password is stored in the phone in an encrypted manner.

The identification of commonalities is based on a lexicon of relevant domain concepts for mobile phones (e.g., model, game, contacts, chat and calendar). The task of the tool is to compare if each word in the document is "equalTo" a domain concept. The "equalTo" procedure is defined as: *if a word is lexically equal, ignoring case and suffixes, to the word in the lexicon AND the word has same semantic class as a word in the lexicon.* The comparison after the AND avoids identifying words in the text that have the same spelling but are used in a completely different meaning (e.g., the word *performance* can be used to indicate a constraint on a software or to indicate the act of a dancer or artist in a show). The meaning of the words are attributed by the tagging feature of WMATRIX which tags each word in the input file with its part-of-speech and semantic categories (e.g., <w id="8.25" pos="VVN" sem="A9+"> *stored* </w>). This means that the word *stored* is a verb (VVN) whose meaning belongs to the class of "Getting and giving; possession" (A9).

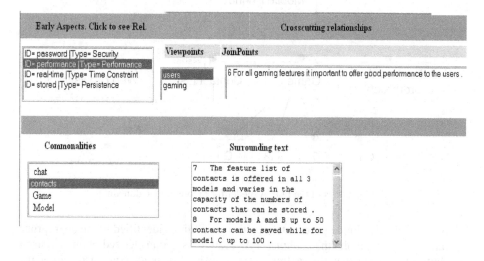

Fig. 2. A screenshot depicting the EA-Miner tool

The EA-Miner tool helps the user to identify variabilities by providing the surrounding text in which the word occurs. In figure 2, after the user selects the "contacts" commonality, the right-hand side shows in which sentences (i.e., sentences 7 and 8) of the document the word appears. The rules of thumb for identifying commonalities and variabilities are:

- The tool lists the commonalities on the left-hand side and the user searches for possible variabilities by looking at the surrounding context of a specific commonality (e.g., *contacts*);
- The user looks at the details on the right-hand side and identifies concepts that modify the commonality in some way (e.g., the *size* of the list of contacts is variable depending on the model).

Another example would be to select the word 'game' which would result in the display of the following sentences:

⇒ *4 Some details of the product line are: The phone models are: Model A, Model B and Model C. The feature game will be present in all models.*

⇒ *5 For models A and B the games are already installed and the difference is that model B has games G3 and G4 in addition to G1 and G2 also found in A. Model C has all the previous games and also the option to download more games.*

This information then helps to identify 'game' as a commonality and that each model can offer different games. Figure 3 shows a feature model based on FODA [18] which can be easily built from the information previously described.

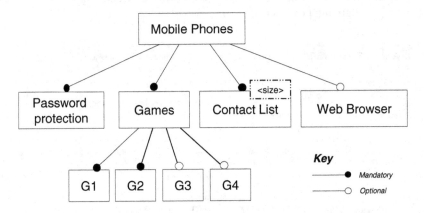

Fig. 3. Part of the FODA model for mobile phone domain

It is a relatively simple process to map the variabilities identified to the appropriate features. For example the *Contact List* feature is parameterized with a <size> attribute to indicate that this a fine grained variability point contained *within* the feature itself. An optional feature such as *Web Browser* is coarser grained in nature so is given its own feature space.

The benefits of using the tool are more evident when considering situations where the input files contain masses of information of a varying nature such as manuals, legacy documents, and previous requirements. This kind of situation is common to occur in company mergers where a wide variety of documents exist. In such situations, tool support would be very helpful in order to mine for the key concepts that will aid the construction of assets for the merged product line. Another benefit of the tool is that it is scalable. We have previously run the tool with several requirements documents in [5] and the tool takes just a few minutes to process and display the results even considering large documents (tens of thousands of words).

The process for identifying early aspects and viewpoints, shown in figure 2, is detailed in [3, 5] and is briefly mentioned here. Viewpoints represent stakeholders' intentions and also are the base decompositions of our RE model. They are identified by getting a list of the most frequent nouns from WMATRIX and their structure groups the requirements needed to satisfy specific stakeholder goals.

The early aspects seen on top of figure 2 represent crosscutting concerns (e.g., system properties such as security) that crosscut the viewpoints. The crosscutting points are also listed by the tool (e.g., "performance" crosscuts viewpoint "users" at sentence 6 in figure 2).

The identification of viewpoints will drive the implementation of the functional requirements of the features and the early aspects will help to point out some crosscutting concerns (as we will discuss for persistence in Section 4) that can affect multiple features and are not captured by the FODA model in figure 3. The next section shows how the list of viewpoints, early aspects and the FODA model built by the EA-Miner tool will be useful for delineating the models in the next stages.

4 Delineating Implementation from Feature Models

The previous stages involved searching for key domain concepts, identifying possible aspects and their variabilities and modeling them appropriately. In this section we describe how we might go about implementing the various concerns in our product line.

In [15] a process called *framed aspects* is described which unifies frame technology [16], a language independent meta-language for implementing variability, with aspect languages such as AspectJ [17]. Frame technology implements useful conditional compilation, parameterization and code refactoring techniques along with a configuration language. The framed aspects process uses AOP to modularize crosscutting and tangled concerns and utilizes framing to allow those aspects to be parameterized and configured to different requirements. An important contribution of framed aspects is the provision of a methodology for development.

The framed aspect approach involves a number of key stages:

1) Variability modeling using FODA (as done in figure 3).
2) Frame delineation of feature model (as done in figure 4)
3) Creation of parameterized, generalized aspects within the delineated frames.
4) Creation of composition rules for composing the required frames together and imposing constraints.
5) Development of specification templates for developers.

From the derived feature model in figure 3 we can now clearly delineate *coarse grained* common features in our product line from the variant ones. This is illustrated in figure 4. Mandatory features are always included in every product instantiation so these form part of the commonality set and are delineated as such. Optional features are variants and are therefore delineated separately. The fine grained variability point <size> is a simple parameter which is *internal* to a common feature, but the feature

Contact List itself is mandatory, and therefore delineated as a common feature. In other words, at this level of abstraction we are only really interested in delineating *coarse grained features*.

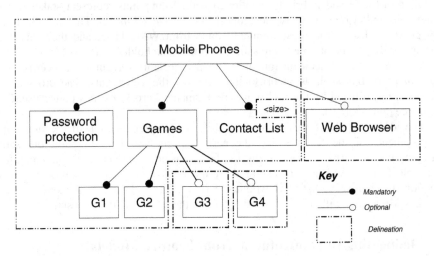

Fig. 4. Delineating common and variable parts of the mobile phone feature model

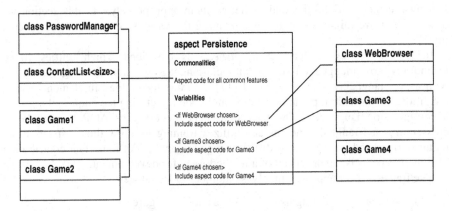

Fig. 5. The persistence concern and its crosscutting common and variable features

The feature diagram approach, used alone in isolation, does not provide an obvious implementation strategy, as it focuses on providing a commonality and variability model, which can be used to delineate features and create the appropriate configuration rules and constraints. However, by using the guidelines previously identified in the mining and structuring activities, as described in section 3, we can make a sound judgment as to what aspects and classes will be used in our architecture. Then we can combine this with the feature diagrams in order to generalize those concerns using frame technology.

An example of a concern we identified at the mining activity was *persistence*. This was identified due to the words 'storage' and 'stored' being used in the document. Because these words crosscut multiple features (e.g. password protection, games, contact list and web browser) we knew that this was a potential candidate for an aspect. Moreover, we could identify from the feature model that some of these features, where the persistence aspect crosscut, were optional (e.g. web browser), therefore the persistence aspect itself needed to be generalized using the variability mechanisms available in framed aspects. Figure 5 illustrates how an implementation of the persistence concern might proceed with this in mind. Note that in the figure we have simply mapped non crosscutting features to a single class implementation although in reality each feature may consist of multiple classes.

5 Discussion

The process we have described in this paper considered an example where a product line would be created from scratch. However, in many cases this approach might not be the most practical. A product line could be the merging of existing overlapping products in order to better manage them. Alternatively a product line may be taking an existing product and generalizing so that it can be adapted to different requirements. The question is, *can we still apply the processes of NAPLES to these situations?* We believe the answer is yes.

With respect to multiple overlapping systems, textual assets (e.g. the original requirements documents, user manuals, legacy documentation and so forth) can be processed with EA-Miner in order to find common and variable parts which will facilitate redesign. The redesign can enable the construction of a new product line since early stages of development (e.g., requirements, design) mining the existing assets and restructuring them according to NAPLES models (e.g., AORE, framed aspects). The approach will minimize the effort in structuring the existing information into a new product line by offering the automated support described before and also facilitate further evolution by means of separation of concerns.

Similarly, in the process of making a single existing product into a software product line, domain concepts can be mined using the domain lexicon and can also help with the identification of possible future places for variability. The viewpoint and aspect identification models can lead to better modularized designs which are more conducive to software product line development. For example, considering the description of a specific mobile phone we could see that possible candidates for common features would be games, list of contacts, chat, web browser, video, camera, etc. Each of these features would be identified by the tool alongside the possible aspects that affect them such as security, persistence and performance. The processes described in sections 3 and 4 would then help to restructure the current assets into the basis of a product line architecture with less effort compared to manual approaches.

6   Related Work

The use of natural language processing techniques in automation of some tasks in requirements engineering has been discussed in [8-10]. Most of these approaches focus on identifying abstractions in requirements documents and building models from them. NAPLES differs by adding semantic tagging and AORE to address crosscutting concerns and issues pertinent to product lines e.g. domain analysis, commonality and variability and lifecycle variability management.

One approach that addresses crosscutting concerns throughout the lifecycle is the Theme [11] analysis and design method;   Theme/Doc [12] is the requirements modeling approach within this method while Theme/UML is the design mechanism. Some support for package parameterization exists in Theme/UML and one can also map Theme/UML designs to multiple AOP languages. However, Theme has not been designed for product line engineering and as such does not support variability and commonality identification and analysis. Like our approach, Theme/Doc has support for lexical analysis to identify aspects in requirements. However, the developer has to read through the whole set of input documentation and manually identify a list of action words and entities that are provided as input to the Theme/Doc tool. This has the potential of becoming a bottleneck in case of large documents used for input (e.g., tens of thousands of words). Our approach, however, is based on the WMATRIX NLP tool suite which has been shown to work for large document sets [7].   The approach in [13] considers the identification of variabilities in code using concern graphs [14]. After the variabilities are found a list of refactorings are applied in the code to factor out the variabilities into aspects. A key difference that NAPLES addresses is that product lines are not only about code level assets and therefore other assets such as requirements documents and design models can also be considered and receive their proper treatment.

7   Conclusions

In this paper we have described NAPLES, our approach for taking textual assets (e.g. requirements documents, user manuals, interview transcripts, legacy documents and so forth) and deducing concerns, aspects, feature commonalities and variabilities so that an implementation can follow. Utilizing tool support saves time and effort, reducing errors and provides a holistic treatment of concerns and variability across the software lifecycle aiding traceability of requirements to their implementation. The semi-automated approach we have outlined provides guidelines for designs, which will inevitably help to drive the implementation phase and ease the creation of generalized code assets. Improving the identification of early aspects, commonalities and variabilities, as well as evolution issues pertaining to the product line, will be a focus of future work. Additionally, the guidelines applied to the delineation of feature models and their realization with the framed aspects approach will also be investigated in greater depth. The processes in NAPLES provide a systematic approach to creating a software product line architecture from requirements through to implementation. The approach automates many of the tasks which consume time and effort thus cutting costs.

Acknowledgments

This is supported by European Commission grant IST-2-004349: European Network of Excellence on Aspect-Oriented Software Development (AOSD-Europe), 2004-2008.

References

1. Rashid, A., A. Moreira, and J. Araujo. Modularisation and Composition of Aspectual Requirements. in 2nd International Conference on Aspect Oriented Software Development (AOSD). 2003. Boston, USA: ACM.
2. Rashid, A., et al. Early Aspects: a Model for Aspect-Oriented Requirements Engineering. in International Conference on Requirements Engineering (RE). 2002. Essen, Germany: IEEE.
3. Sampaio, A., et al. Mining Aspects in Requirements. in Early Aspects 2005: Aspect-Oriented Requirements Engineering and Architecture Design Workshop (held with AOSD 2005). 2005. Chicago, Illinois, USA.
4. Finkelstein, A. and I. Sommerville, The Viewpoints FAQ. BCS/IEE Software Engineering Journal, 1996. 11(1).
5. Sampaio, A., et al. EA-Miner: A tool for automating aspect-oriented requirements identification. in 20th IEEE/ACM International Conference on Automated Software Engineering (ASE2005) 2005. Long Beach, California, USA.
6. Rayson, P., UCREL Semantic Analysis System (USAS). 2005: http://www.comp.lancs.ac.uk/ucrel/usas/.
7. Sawyer, P., P. Rayson, and R. Garside, REVERE: Support for Requirements Synthesis from Documents. Information Systems Frontiers, 2002. 4(3): p. 343-353.
8. Ambriola, V. and V. Gervasi. Processing natural language requirements. in International Conference on Automated Software Engineering. 1997. Los Alamitos: IEEE Computer Society Press.
9. Burg, F.M., Linguistic Instruments in Requirements Engineering. 1997: IOS Press.
10. Goldin, L. and D. Berry, AbstFinder: A Prototype Natural Language Text Abstraction Finder for Use in Requirements Elicitation. Automated Software Engineering, 1997. 4.
11. Baniassad, E. and S. Clarke. Theme: An Approach for Aspect-Oriented Analysis and Design. in International Conference on Software Engineering. 2004. Edinburgh, Scotland, UK.
12. Baniassad, E. and S. Clarke. Finding Aspects in Requirements with Theme/Doc. in Workshop on Early Aspects (held with AOSD 2004). 2004. Lancaster, UK.
13. Alves, V., et al. Extracting and Evolving Mobile Games Product Lines. in 9th International Software Product Line Conference (SPLC-EUROPE 2005) 2005. 26-29 September 2005 Rennes, France
14. Robillard, M. and G. Murphy. Concern graphs: Finding and describing concerns using structural program dependencies. in 24th International Conference on Software Engineering. 2002.
15. Loughran, N., Rashid A. (2004) *Framed Aspects: Supporting Variability and Configurability for AOP*. International Conference on Software Reuse, Madrid, Spain.
16. Bassett, P. *Framing Software Reuse: Lessons From the Real World*: Prentice Hall, 1997.
17. "AspectJ Home Page http://www.eclipse.org/aspectj/," 2005.
18. Kang, K, S. Cohen, J. Hess, W. Novak, and A. Peterson, "Feature Oriented Domain Analysis Feasibility Study," SEI Technical Report CMU/SEI-90-TR-21 1990.
19. Clements, P and L. Northrop, "Software Product Lines - Practices and Patterns," Addison Wesley, 2002.

Use Cases in Model-Driven Software Engineering

Hernán Astudillo[1], Gonzalo Génova[2], Michał Śmiałek[3],
Juan Llorens[2], Pierre Metz[4], and Rubén Prieto-Díaz[5]

[1] Universidad Técnica Federico Santa María, Chile
[2] Universidad Carlos III de Madrid, Spain
[3] Warsaw University of Technology, Poland
[4] SYNSPACE, Germany
[5] James Madison University, USA
`hernan@inf.utfsm.cl`, `ggenova@inf.uc3m.es`,
`smialek@iem.pw.edu.pl`, `llorens@inf.uc3m.es`,
`pmetz@fbi.fh-darmstadt.de`, `prietorx@cisat.jmu.edu`
`http://www.ie.inf.uc3m.es/wuscam-05/`

Abstract. Use cases have achieved wide use as specification tools for systems observable behavior, but there still remains a large gap between specifying behavior and determining the software components to build or procure. WUsCaM 05 – "Workshop on Use Cases in Model-Driven Software Engineering" – brought together use case and MDSE experts from industry and academia to identify and characterize problem areas and promising approaches.

1 Motivation and Goals

This workshop was the second in the series of Workshops on Use Case Modeling (WUsCaM-05). The first one took place in 2004 in conjunction with the UML'04 Conference, under the name "Open Issues in Industrial Use Case Modeling". The success of the first edition encouraged us to continue the series within the MoDELS Conference, focusing the workshop on the more specific topic of "Use Cases in Model-Driven Software Engineering", which was one of the main concerns of last year workshop discussions.

The integration of use cases within Model-Driven Software Engineering requires a better definition of use case contents, in particular description of behavior through sequences of action steps, pre- and post- conditions, and relationship between use case models and conceptual models. The UML2 specification allows for several textual and graphical representations of use cases, but does not provide any rules for transformations between different representations at the same level of abstraction. It does not provide either any rule for transformations of these representations to other artifacts at levels closer to implementation. This workshop aims to show how the resourceful application of use case models may help to bridge the "requirements gap" in current research and practice of model-driven methodologies.

J.-M. Bruel (Ed.): MoDELS 2005 Workshops, LNCS 3844, pp. 272–279, 2006.
© Springer-Verlag Berlin Heidelberg 2006

1.1 Open Areas for Research

As a result of last year workshop discussions, we identified before the workshop a set of open areas for research, which can be grouped in two main topics: semantics of use cases, and pragmatics of use cases.

Semantics of use cases
- Semantic connection between the use case model and other software models (static and dynamic).
- Appropriateness of the UML 2.0 meta-model for supporting use case semantics and transformation into other models.
- Adding traceability information to use case models and their specification items.
- Refinement of collaboration and participation of actors in a use case.
- Precise notation (functional and structural) for use case specification items enabling model transformation.
- Clarification of relationships between use cases in the context of their transformation into other models.

Pragmatics of use cases
- Methods for use case application in a model-driven software lifecycle.
- Automatic transformations of use case model and its items into other models (analytical, architectural, design).
- Use case views and model views.
- Use cases composition.
- Tools supporting precise use case specification and transformation.
- Tools for use case verification and execution.
- Novel applications of use case models in model-driven development.

1.2 Organization

The workshop has been organized by Hernán Astudillo (Universidad Técnica Federico Santa María, Chile), Gonzalo Génova (Universidad Carlos III de Madrid, Spain), Michał Śmiałek (Warsaw University of Technology, Poland), Juan Llorens (Universidad Carlos III de Madrid, Spain), Pierre Metz (SYNSPACE, Germany), and Rubén Prieto-Díaz (James Madison University, VA, USA).

Submitted papers were reviewed by an international team of experts composed by the organizers and Bruce Anderson (IBM Business Consulting Services, UK), Guy Genilloud (Universidad Carlos III de Madrid, Spain), Sadahiro Isoda (Toyohashi University of Technology, Japan), Joaquin Miller (X-Change Technologies, USA), and Anthony Simons (University of Sheffield, UK). Each paper received between 2 and 4 reviews before being accepted.

2 Initial Positions of the Participants

The two initial sessions of the workshop were devoted to presentation of the accepted position papers, which represented a good mixture of experiences and researches both from academia and industry, as was one of the goals of the workshop. The authors came to the workshop with the following positions:

- **Guy Genilloud, William F. Frank, Gonzalo Génova.** *Use Cases, Actions, and Roles.* Use Cases are widely used for specifying systems, but their semantics are unclear in ways that make it difficult to apply use cases to complex problems. The authors suggested clarifications to use case semantics so that use case modeling can be applied to relate automated systems to business processes and process specifications, particularly in situations where it's necessary to integrate multiple systems in support of a single business process. They discussed the original intentions of Ivar Jacobson and UML and found out that use case specifications, whether written in natural language or as interaction diagrams, are misleading as to what is a use case (instance). They considered then a more natural modeling technique, and established a relation between a use case, a joint action, and a role.

- **Rogardt Heldal.** *Use Cases Are more than System Operations.* Correctly written use cases can be an important artifact for describing how a software system should behave. Use cases should be informal enough to permit anyone in a software project to understand them, in particular the customer (often lacking a formal background). One consequence of adopting use cases to, for example, MDA (Model Driven Architecture) can be an increasing level of formalism, which can severely limit understanding of use cases. Also, too few guidelines for how to write use cases make them both hard to write and understand. Finding the right level of formalism was the topic of this paper. Heldal suggested a new way of writing the action steps of use cases by introducing "action blocks". The introduction of action blocks makes use cases more formal, but still understandable. In addition, action blocks support the creation of contracts for system operations. He also argued that treating system operations as use cases is a misuse of use cases —system operations and use cases should be separate artifacts. One should be able to obtain several system operations from a use case, otherwise there is no dialog (process) between actors and use cases. He believes that having a clear distinction between use cases and contracts will improve the quality of both.

- **Claudia López, Hernán Astudillo.** *Use Case- and Scenario-Based Approach to Represent NFRs and Architectural Policies.* Software architecture decisions pay primary attention to nonfunctional requirements (NFRs), yet use cases normally describe functional requirements. This article presented scenario-based descriptions of "Architectural Concerns" to satisfy NFRs and of "Architectural Policies" to represent architectural choices to address such concerns. The Azimut framework combines these modeling abstractions with "Architectural Mechanisms" to enable iterative and traceable derivation of COTS-based software architectures. An example was shown using an inter-application communication problem, and its use in an MDA context was explored.

- **Hassan Gomaa, Erika Mir Olimpiew.** *The Role of Use Cases in Requirements and Analysis Modeling.* The authors described the role of use cases in the requirements and analysis modeling phases of a model-driven software engineering process, built on previous work by distinguishing between the black box and white box views of a system in the requirements and analysis phases. Furthermore, this paper described and related test models to the black box and white box views of a system.

- **Michał Śmiałek.** *Can Use Cases Drive Software Factories?* Contemporary software systems are becoming more and more complex with many new features reflecting the growing users needs. Software development organizations struggle with problems associated with this complexity, often caused by inability to cope with constantly changing user requirements. Supporting efforts to overcome these problems, miałek proposed a method for organizing the software lifecycle around precisely defined requirements models based on use cases that can be quickly transformed into design level artifacts. The same use cases with precisely linked vocabulary notions are the means to control reuse of artifacts, promising the lifecycle to become even faster and more resourceful. With properly applied use case models practitioners can significantly improve the concept of "software factories" that newly emerges in the area of model driven software engineering.

- **Jon Whittle.** *Specifying Precise Use Cases with Use Case Charts.* Use cases are a popular method for capturing and structuring software requirements. The informality of use cases is both a blessing and a curse. It enables easy application and learning but is a barrier to automated methods for test case generation, validation or simulation. Whittle presented "use case charts", a precise way of specifying use cases that aims to retain the benefits of easy understanding but also supports automated analysis. The graphical and abstract syntax of use case charts were given, along with a sketch of their formal semantics.

Besides the previous authors, two other participants at the workshop asked for a slot to make short presentations on-the-fly, which were very much related to the ongoing discussions:

- **Pascal Roques** talked about how to derive use cases from business process activity diagrams.
- **Richard Sanders** presented research on using UML2 Collaborations to model Use Cases, showing benefits gained by Composite Structure diagrams compared to Use Case diagrams in UML2 («extend» and «include» being poorly integrated in the UML language).

3   Workshop Results

The remaining two sessions of the workshop were devoted to discussions and synthesis work, trying to reach agreement wherever possible. We first established a list of open issues and prioritized them for the discussion. The discussion was then centered around three main topics: *use case-driven development, some misuses of use cases* (and how to avoid them by adequate teaching), and *non-functional requirements and use cases.* We identified other interesting issues but we had not time to discuss them in-depth: business process modeling, use cases and UML, use cases and aspects, the gap between theory and practice, project size estimation (use case points have been unsuccessful), and completeness of use cases. The following subsections summarize the discussions and agreements about the three main issues.

3.1 Use Case Driven Development

Use case-driven software development is an idea present and applied for many years in several methodologies (with UP being the most prominent). Unfortunately, use case models themselves cause many problems in applying them as true software development artifacts. These problems seem to arise from the fact that use cases are usually developed for multiple purposes: they should be well understandable by the users, enable good understanding of the system's external behavior, be coherent with the system's conceptual model, and finally, be easy to apply in the development process leading to the final software system. These highly diverse applications get reflected in a plethora of notations ranging from very informal "paragraphs of text" to perfectly formal "use case programming languages".

During the discussion we identified three topics which would allow us to resolve the ambiguity problem associated with use cases and would make the idea of use case development more efficient. These topics are:

- Differences and translation between use case representations for different purposes.
- Translation of use cases into design level artifacts.
- Reuse management on the use case level.

The first topic comes from noting that use cases could be represented by several notations at the same time. Each of these notations could be used for different purposes. The notations would include semi-formal text (subject-verb-object sentences) or graphs (activity diagrams, sequence diagrams). These notations would allow for different views of a particular use case for a specific reader (customer, developer, etc.). However, two important prerequisites need to be met. First of all, we should have an automatic transformation that would allow for instantaneous change of the view. Second, when writing use cases with any of the notations we should build a separate, independent vocabulary that would constitute a conceptual model of the specified system.

The second discussed topic derives from a statement that there still exists a significant gap between requirements and software being developed on the basis of these requirements. There is no "seamless transformation" path between requirements artifacts (like use cases) and design and implementation artifacts. This path can be significantly supported by introducing certain transformation mechanisms in accordance with the general ideas of model-driven software development. It can be argued that this transformation cannot be fully automatic. Design models need certain design decisions that can be made only by skillful architects and designers. However, certain tools can support developers in developing a first draft of the design model and in keeping the design model constantly coherent with the requirements model and vice-versa.

The third topic, maybe the most important among all three, comes from observing very low levels of requirements-driven reuse in software development. This might be caused also by lack of satisfactory solutions in the previous two topics which are closely related. Requirements-driven reuse can be organized around precisely formulated use cases closely mapped (transformed) onto design, implementation and testing level artifacts. The discussion showed two possible approaches to use case driven reuse. One approach is associated with already widely known method of *software product lines*. With this approach, the reuse process would be organized around specifying commonality and variability of use cases. Another approach would be to treat use case models together with other, precisely related software artifacts (design, code, …) as complete cases. These cases could then be kept in libraries ready for future reuse. In this approach, all the effort associated with reuse is deferred until there arises a possibility of actual reuse.

It can be noted that all three of these topics are closely dependent on developments in model transformations. We stress the need to define precise transformations and mappings between artifacts on the requirements level (use cases, conceptual models, non-functional requirements) and from requirements to design.

3.2 Misuse of Use Cases

In spite of their having been around for years, we identified some common misuses of use cases among practitioners:

- *Reducing use cases to system operations.* There was general agreement that use cases and system operations should be separate artifacts at different levels of abstraction. Confusing them leads to use case models with too many use cases which are too small. A system operation is invoked by a message from an actor to the system. A use case typically contains invocations of several system operations, otherwise there is no dialog (process) between actors and use cases. Use cases are the starting point for identifying system operations, which is an important step in the design of the system.
- *Relationships between use cases.* Practitioners encounter real difficulties in distinguishing and properly applying «include» and «extend» relationships. Moreover, included and, more frequently, extending use cases are not usually full use cases, but mere fragments. Inheritance between use cases has not a better condition, since its meaning is not defined for the various existing use case representations (what parts of a textual specification are inherited, and how? what about graphical representations?). All of this often leads to vane uses of these relationships.
- *Describing business processes instead of use cases.* A use case describes an interaction between the actor(s) and the system which yields a valuable result. A use case does not describe a whole business process, it describes only that part of the business process where the system has a contribution. The distinction is more necessary when we want to integrate several systems in a single business process.
- *Applying use cases even when they are not suitable.* Use cases are not adequate for describing the requirements of any kind of system. Use cases are good for dialog-driven systems, i.e. when the description of system-user

interactions are useful to extract functional requirements. However, use cases are not adequate for event-driven systems, or for extraction of non-functional requirements.

- *Finding the appropriate level of detail.* Maybe this is one of the most difficult points about use cases. There is no universal solution, since the level of detail depends on the audience: it should not be the same for users and stakeholders, than for analysts and developers. A principal problem here is that use cases cannot be recursively decomposed into smaller use cases, which would ease the use of the same concept at different levels of abstraction. Besides, practitioners risk to confuse between *refinement* (evolving the use case description, e.g. by adding details, into a new version that still fulfills the same purpose) and *realization* (creation of new artifacts in the following software development steps that implement the services identified by use cases).

3.3 Non-functional Requirements

Non-functional requirements (NFRs) are system-wide requirements that correspond to systemic properties, usually run-time (e.g. availability, reliability, security) or deployment-time (e.g. portability). The NFRs topic brought up a lovely discussion as well, which yielded several consensus ideas.

- *NFR cross-cut many use cases.* In general, NFRs do not pertain to a single individual task to be realized by a user, and cannot be specified with use cases since they aim to describe such individual tasks. We need a consistent way to indicate NFRs as related use cases (e.g. availability requirements for specific use cases).
- *Consistency among views.* There are several ways of describing requirements, and we need better correspondences between artifacts at the requirements level (use cases, conceptual models, non-functional requirements).
- *Taking NFRs from requirements into design.* NFRs are a key input to the architecture and design tasks, so they must be gathered and collected like functional requirements are. A problem is how to preserve and transmit forward such requirements through a phase (use case modeling) that has no major use for them.
- *Appropriateness of recording NFRs in use cases.* There were differing opinions regarding the convenience of describing NFRs in, or associated to, use cases. One position paper had explained two (existing) notations to record NFRs alongside use cases. Some felt that allowing this mix may pollute the "business task of value" sense of use cases, by forcing to consider and record system-wide assertions instead of focusing on the task being described. Others argued that this may be so, but since in practice many analysis teams collect only use cases, it would be beneficial to associate NFRs to them, with the proviso that this information can be separated and recovered later for design (see above).
- *Formalism.* Whilst several more-or-less formal semantics have been proposed for use cases, they do not account for the complexity of describing

NFRs as well. More formal notations for use cases-with-NFRs will be necessary to implement MDA's goal of (semi-)automated model translation.

- *Aspects.* Aspect-oriented modeling may be a good to describe NFRs in a use case context. One of the workshop papers had presented an approach based on architectural policies rather than aspects, and the participants wondered whether policies and aspects are congruent; work remains to be done in that regard. The interaction of aspects and use cases remains an interesting area, with some work already existing on Aspect-Oriented Requirements.

4   Conclusions and Future Work

The workshop discussions leave quite clear that use cases are the main way to specify functional requirements in modern systems development, yet some non-trivial problems remain to be addressed by the community vis-à-vis the representation of target problems, the supported processes, and the actual use by humans. These points were addressed above ("non-functional requirements and use cases", "some misuses of use cases", and "use case-driven development", respectively).

The two best papers presented at the workshop are also published in this volume along with the workshop report. To select these two papers, we had into account mainly the opinions of the reviewers, but we also considered the opinions of the other workshop participants (authors and attendants). The two chosen papers were "Specifying Precise Use Cases with Use Case Charts", by Jon Whittle, and "Use Cases, Actions, and Roles" by Guy Genilloud, William F. Frank and Gonzalo Génova.

Given the success of this scientific meeting, we hope there will be a third edition of this workshop series in the next MoDELS Conference. More information can be found at the workshop web site (http://www.ie.inf.uc3m.es/wuscam-05/).

Use Cases, Actions, and Roles

Guy Genilloud[1], William F. Frank[2], and Gonzalo Génova[3]

[1,3] Departamento de Informática, Universidad Carlos III de Madrid,
Avda. Universidad, 30 – 28911 Leganés, Madrid, Spain
`guy.genilloud@ie.inf.uc3m.es, ggenova@inf.uc3m.es`
[2] X-Change Technologies Group, 363 7th Avenue, Floor 11, New York, NY 10001
`wfrank@xtg.bz`

Abstract. Use Cases are widely used for specifying systems, but their semantics are unclear in ways that make it difficult to apply use cases to complex problems. In this paper, we suggest clarifications to use case semantics so that use case modeling can be applied to relate automated systems to business processes and process specifications, particularly in situations where we need to integrate *multiple systems* in support of a business process. We discuss the original intentions of Ivar Jacobson and UML and we find out that use case specifications, whether written in natural language or as interaction diagrams, are misleading as to what is a use case (instance). We consider then a more natural modeling technique, and establish a relation between a use case, a joint action, and a role.

1 Introduction

Use Cases are widely used in software engineering for specifying the observable behavior of systems. However, there is still controversy among practitioners about a number of issues, for example whether or not internal actions of the system should be described at all [1], and what to think of actions by actors [2, 3]. In Section 2, we find answers to these questions by looking at the main definitions of a use case, both by Ivar Jacobson and in UML. While the answers are easy to obtain, they are also surprising because most, if not all, use case specifications are misleading in this respect.

Nothing is said in UML-2 [4] about the semantic relation between a use case and an action in an activity diagram, even though activity diagrams may be used to model business processes. May a use case correspond to such an action? And what would be the correspondence? We answer this question by considering the modeling technique of the RM-ODP, rather than that of UML (see Sections 3 and 4).

2 What Is a Use Case?

For understanding the semantic of use case specifications, or in other words, for knowing what is a *use case* (in this paper, we follow ODP and Jacobson's original terminology; so by use case, we mean use case instance), we look at some of the most important definitions and explanations by both UML and Ivar Jacobson. In the quotes below, the emphasis is ours. We start with the definition in UML-2:

J.-M. Bruel (Ed.): MoDELS 2005 Workshops, LNCS 3844, pp. 280–289, 2006.

"A use case is the specification of <u>a set of actions performed by a system</u>, which yields an observable result that is, typically, of value for one or more actors or other stakeholders of the system." [4]

Before UML, Ivar Jacobson provided several definitions of a use case, and some explanations:

"A use case is <u>a sequence of transactions performed by a system</u>, which yields a measurable result of values for a particular actor." [5]

"A use case is <u>a sequence of transactions in a system</u>, whose task is to yield a result of measurable value to an individual actor of the system." [6]

"Use case: the definition above is really <u>a specific flow of events through the system</u>, that is, an instance. There are great many possible courses of events, many of which are very similar. To make a use case model meaningful, you usually group the courses of events and call each of the groups a use case class. ..." [6]

"In the system: <u>when we say 'transactions in a system', we mean that the system supplies the use cases. The actors communicate with the system's use cases.</u>" [6]

"Transaction: a transaction is an atomic set of activities that are performed either fully or not at all. It is invoked by a stimulus from an actor to the system or by a point in time being reached in the system. <u>A transaction consists of a set of actions, decisions and transmission of stimuli to the invoking actor, or to some other actor(s).</u>" [6]

The main difference between UML's definition and Jacobson's is that, before being influenced by UML and the meta-modeling approach to language definition, Ivar Jacobson was not thinking of a use case as a *specification*, but rather as the *real thing* that the system *does*. This point is of little importance for this paper, as is the difference between "a sequence of transactions" and "a set of actions."

Rather, what matters to us right now is what has remained constant across all definitions and explanations. From the sentences we have underlined, it is very clear that Jacobson and UML intend use cases to include exclusively actions performed by the system, and no other actions performed by actors. In all the above definitions, actions performed by actors are not mentioned, and this cannot be by omission.

Note also that the two sets of definitions share a view of the use case as a *sequence* of actions, rather than as an action. Since most any action is decomposable into smaller groups of actions, and any sequence of actions is considered as such only because the entire sequence is considered to be a manifestation of some higher level action, as the single action of playing a baseball game is a sequence of playing some innings, the sharp distinction between a sequence of actions and an action is only one of viewpoint, and makes inter-viewpoint communications difficult.

Jacobson, like UML, considers the stimuli sent by actors to the system as being events outside of use cases. Likewise for the stimuli received by actors. The actual communication of stimuli is not modeled – they are simply assumed to arrive at the receiver some time after having been sent by the sender (without any action taking place).

2.1 Actions by Actors

The above observation (that a use case includes exclusively actions performed by the system) is likely to surprise many practitioners. Indeed, most if not all use case textual specifications describe actions by actors: for example, "the clerk inputs customer information in the system", "the customer selects one of the presented options", "the system manager confirms her entries," etc (some authors even recommend using multiple columns for textual use case specifications, one column for the actions of the system, the other(s) for the actions of the actors).

Describing actor's actions is in fact just a way of describing that the system will receive the corresponding stimuli and input values. It is more important to write use case specifications such that they are an easy read for users and stakeholders (untrained in computing science or object modeling), than to write a use case specification so that it fits exactly its intended semantics. The question of whether an actor's actions of sending information to the system belongs or not to a use case is important to methodologists, and perhaps to analysts or to programmers, but not to their customers.

Some use cases are specified with an interaction diagram, showing the system interacting with its actors. In this case, it is the limitations of the graphical notation that make it necessary to represent actors and their actions of sending and receiving messages. In this case, it is a lot simpler to teach readers of specifications that the only actions relevant to the use case are those of the system, than to extend the interaction diagram notation.

2.2 Internal Actions of the System

Does a use case include internal actions by the system? Of course, it does, or there would be no relevant actions in it.

Following the classical object modeling technique (in which objects communicate exclusively by exchanging messages between them) assumed by UML and by Ivar Jacobson, sending a message is an internal action of the sender, and receiving it is an internal action of the receiver (when an object's state machine receives/accepts a message as an input event, no other object observes or controls that action). Such actions of the system clearly belong to the use case, but what about other actions, such as recording a customer's address, or erasing the data of its credit card?

They do. Read the quotes in Section 2.1: both UML and Jacobson speak of a set of actions performed by a system, without insisting that they should be actions of either sending or receiving a message. Again, this cannot be by accident.

In an old Objectory manual (1994), it is written:

"In the description of a use case, there are descriptions of what happens in the system. The use case description does not define how tasks are performed in the system."

This is a clear confirmation that a use case includes actions of changing the system's state, and that use case specifications describe them. Of course, the level of granularity of the actions should be such no unnecessary details are revealed (or rather, that programmers are not excessively constrained).

It would be a big mistake to omit such actions in the use case description. Think of yourselves as an analyst, who faces the question of whether or not to write, "The system erases the customer's credit card information" (assuming that no confirmation of this fact is to be given to the actor). Do you want to tell programmers that the system must erase credit card information, or leave the decision to them? Therefore, a use case description should include those internal actions of the system whose effects can be observed or inferred by the actors.

Lesley Lamport explains in [7] that it is almost necessary to mention internal actions in a (black box) system specification, and not just the system interactions. While it is possible to write specifications without mentioning any internal actions (Lamport calls such specifications *purely temporal*), it is not desirable to do this: the specifications so obtained would be much more complex. Doing so would of course be totally against the philosophy of use cases, that specifications should be easy to read, even by non-professionals. Indeed, for knowing what the system does in a particular use case, a reader would potentially need to read all the use case specifications, instead of just one.

2.3 The Actor's Task and the Use Case

Jacobson explains his important idea that a use case should yield a result of measurable value to its primary actor:

"A measurable value: this expression is a very important key to finding the correct level of a use case, that is, one that is not too detailed. A use case must help the actor to perform a task that has identifiable value. It may be possible to assess the performance of a use case in terms of price or cost. For example, applying for a loan in a bank is something that is of value for a customer of a bank."[6]

Jacobson explanations are such that the actor alone is performing this task, for which it receives help from the system. The task of the use case is to help the actor, and it is entirely separate from the actor's task. It seems therefore that the responsibility of the actor's task lies squarely with the actor, not at all with the system.

But do human actors see things in this way? If we were to ask some actors about the task they are performing, many of them would tell us that their task actually requires them to use the computer – they would not see the computer as just a help tool. With respect to taking responsibility, they would tell us that they do not feel responsible if the system makes incorrect actions, or gives them incorrect values (she is not checking calculations received from the system, and she is not asked to doing it). In many cases, the system's availability is essential for the actor's task to be performed. For all these reasons, it would seem reasonable to say that the actor and the system are performing the task together. But Ivar Jacobson assumed a modeling technique in which the system and its actors perform all their actions alone, and communicate exclusively by exchanging messages. Since a use case consists exclusively of actions by the system, it cannot be a part of the actor's task. However, it can be part of means by which the actor might achieve his goals, if the actor is a primary one (an actor for whose benefit the system exists).

In the second part of this paper, we will look at this same issue from a different perspective, that of the ODP modeling technique [8].

3 Use Cases from an ODP Perspective

3.1 ODP Basic Modeling Concepts

In an ODP model, entities in the real world can be modeled by objects, including the system, no matter if it is an IT centralized system, a distributed IT system, or a business system. The ODP notion of object is much more general than that of most OO specification or programming languages, in particular because an object may participate in all kinds of interactions (see below), instead of just communicating with other objects by exchanging messages.

8.1 Object: A model of an entity. An object is characterized by its behaviour (see 8.6) and, dually, by its state (see 8.7). An object is distinct from any other object. An object is encapsulated, i.e. any change in its state can only occur as a result of an internal action or as a result of an interaction (see 8.3) with its environment (see 8.2). ... [8]

8.3 Action: Something which happens.

Every action of interest for modeling purposes is associated with at least one object.

The set of actions associated with an object is partitioned into internal actions and interactions. An **internal action** *always takes place without the participation of the environment of the object. An* **interaction** *takes place with the participation of the environment of the object.*

NOTES

1 - "Action" means "action occurrence". Depending on context, a specification may express that an action has occurred, is occurring or may occur.

2 - The granularity of actions is a design choice. An action need not be instantaneous. Actions may overlap in time. ... [8]

An action of an object is either an *internal action* or an *interaction* of that object. The discriminator between these two categories is rather subtle, because an object may interact with itself [9]. So, for the purpose of this paper, we will adopt a simpler classification. Borrowing the terminology from Catalysis [10], we speak of *localized actions* for those actions which have just one participating object, and of *joint actions* for those actions in which several objects participate (so, every joint action is an interaction, but not every interaction is a joint action). An object which participates in an action is a *participant* in that action.

The ODP modeling technique is such that the actor's task is preferably modeled as a single joint action in which the system is also a participant. This joint action is composite, since it is specified as a configuration of simpler (joint or localized) actions[1]. Communication of information between objects is explained by joint actions of the communicating objects, either directly between themselves, or with intermediate objects [9, definition 8.8]. See [11] for a discussion and examples of joint actions at the granularity level of use cases.

The ODP modeling technique makes it easy and natural to model the task of a primary actor, but what is a use case? To answer this question, we investigate the notion of role in a joint action.

---

[1] In Catalysis, all joint actions are specified atomically (using pre- and post-conditions on the participant states) before being decomposed. However, an "atomic" specification is only valid under the assumption that no other joint action, happening concurrently, interferes with this joint action. We do not propose adopting this practice, as it is not realistic for actions at the granularity of use cases. For example, an actor may receive an urgent call and decide not to complete a task.

3.2   Joint Actions and Roles

A fundamental characteristic of ODP interactions, and therefore of joint actions, is that they have roles ("*An object may interact with itself, in which case it is considered to play at least two roles in the interaction.*" [8, Definition 8.3, Note 4]). For any joint action that we imagine, we can always find two or more roles.

Unfortunately, the RM-ODP explanations of the concept of role let much to be desired (they might be changed in the next revision of the standard). So we provide here a different explanation[2]: actions are decomposed in different parts that are played (in principle) by different objects; a *role* (of an action) is that part of an action that is played by an object, i.e., the contribution of that object to the action. Thus, a role is a part of an interaction, in a non-recursive decomposition of that action[3]. This decomposition is *non-recursive* in that the parts obtained, the roles, are not all actions. It is different from the typical *recursive* decomposition of an action, which yields sub-actions. We call the decomposition of an action that yields its roles the *role decomposition* of the action.

A role decomposition may be applied to an action seen as a whole, in which case it simply yields the roles of the action. For example, in an action in which a message is communicated, there is a sender and a receiver.

A role decomposition may also be applied to an action seen as a configuration of simpler actions (sub-actions) with constraints between them (e.g., the sequential constraint that an action occurs before another). In this case, the decomposition yields the relevant roles of the joint sub-actions, and the relevant localized sub-actions. As for the constraints between actions, they remain. For example, the role of accepting a proposal includes receiving the proposal (a role in a joint action), reading it (a localized action), and giving back a notification of acceptance to the counter-party (a role in another joint action).

A *role* is therefore a subset of the behavior of an object, that is, a role is a collection of more primitive roles (of joint actions) and localized actions with a set of constraints between them. The *behavior of an object* is then the union of all its roles. It is also a collection of roles and localized actions with a set of constraints between them. The difference between role and behavior is that a role is a contribution to some joint action, whilst no such constraint applies to the behavior of an object.

3.2.1   Difference with the Behavior of an Object in the RM-ODP

The interested reader should note that the following definition in the RM-ODP is flawed.

8.6 Behaviour (of an object): A collection of actions with a set of constraints on when they may occur. ... [8]

The problem is in fact obvious (so much that one may make the definition right without even thinking about it). For knowing what an object does, that is, its behavior, it is not enough to know all the actions in which this object participates. One must also know which roles the object performs in those actions. For example, consider a joint action in which two people get married, in front of two witnesses (as illustrated

---

[2] The concept of role, being *primitive*, cannot be defined on the basis of other concepts, but it can be explained (much like the RM-ODP does for objects and actions).

[3] We would define a role of a link in the same way.

in Fig. 2). If you were only told that a person participated in the action, you would not know whether he or she got married or was simply a witness.

3.3 Use Cases and Actors Are Roles

Having explained the concepts of joint action and role, we are now in a position to provide an alternate definition of a use case, which assumes the ODP modeling technique:

Use Case: The system role in a joint action (among the system, its actors, and possibly additional participants) that is intended by the system's designer, and expected by some actor or other stakeholder, when circumstances are appropriate, to yield a particular observable result that is of value to one or more actors or other stakeholders of the system.

Our definition makes it clear that IT systems, not just people, perform some of the actions of a business process (remember that the original vision is for a use case to help an actor perform a task, which might be an action in a business process). Likewise, IT systems (or in fact their providers), rather than their actors, may need to assume the responsibility when an action fails to provide the expected results. In other words, business processes are not composed of actors' actions (performed with the "help" of the system), but of actor-system joint actions.

Defining a use case as a role of a joint action is also interesting because it makes the notion of actor easier to understand. In UML-1.5, an actor was defined as "*A coherent set of roles that users of use cases play when interacting with these use cases. An actor has one role for each use case with which it communicates.*" But UML 1.5 did not provide one compatible, good explanation of the concept of role. And it failed to point out that a use case is a role of the system [3].

No real progress has been made in UML-2 with respect to the concepts of actor and role. In fact, the new definition of actor in UML-2 speaks of just one role for an actor, which makes the notion of an actor harder to understand. The definition may still be considered to be correct, if one sees this single role as a composite of the actor's roles in the use cases in which it participates. For further explanations of the concept of actor, see [12] and [11].

4 Applications to Business Processes

Support for a business process by IT systems becomes particularly clear, when one understands the idea that the IT system is performing roles (use cases) in the actions.

A business process is a configuration of localized and joint actions (e.g., a sequence of actions). Typically, people are involved in many actions, and more and more they perform their tasks by using an IT system. It is even possible that one person uses several systems in support of a single joint action.

Unfortunately, some notations for business process modeling work under the assumption that all actions are localized to just one participant (e.g., UML activity diagrams with swimlanes). They do not support representing joint actions with their multiple participants, much less indicating which specific role each participant performs in the joint action[4] (see Section 4.2). So a specifier faces a problem whenever she wants to describe an action that happens to have multiple participants (e.g., a primary actor, a system and a secondary actor). She may decide to aggregate all the action participants as a group, but she may end up having too many groups, some of which unnatural. She may represent only one action participant and omit others (in particular the system that helps the primary participant perform her task). Or she may decompose the action into sub-actions, such that all actions are localized, and participants (supposedly) communicate by exchanging messages). She would therefore go at a much lower level of abstraction than she originally intended to. In any case, these notations make it unnecessarily difficult to relate use cases to the actions of the business process (i.e., in Jacobson's terms, to the tasks of the primary actors).

The problems that we mentioned here are compounded when one wants to examine how several systems might be used jointly for supporting a same actor in a same business process. Indeed, one needs then not just to relate each system's use cases to the business process, but also to relate them to use cases of other systems. The following method, based on the concept of joint action, solves all these problems: first specify the business process (once and for all) as a configuration of joint actions, then find the participants in each action, and find their roles (or contributions in the action). Use cases are then given by the roles of the systems in the joint actions.

4.1 Making Use of the Use Case Specification Technique

The use cases graphical notation may be used to support our approach, as Wegmann and Genilloud showed in [11]. Fig. 1, taken from that paper, can be produced using most UML case tools on the market. Ovals represent joint actions, and actors represent participants. The role of a participant is represented using a rolename of the association between the actor and the use case. The related mutiplicity indicates how many roles of the type (say sender) might be in the joint action.

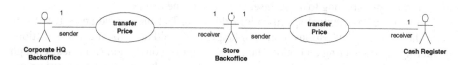

Fig. 1. The Use Case Notation may be used for representing joint actions and roles

Fig. 2. A joint action with four roles of two types, spouse and witness

---

[4] Such notations may nevertheless have a concept of role, much like the use cases notation has the concept of actor (see Section 0). But they lack support for the more fundamental concept of a joint action's role.

Joint actions may be specified textually, just like use cases. The difference is that the (sub-)actions of all participants must be mentioned, not just those in which the system participates. The use case specification(s) may then be obtained by projection of this joint action specification, i.e., by removing all the actions in which the system does not participate.

4.2 Improving the Activity Diagrams Notation

UML activity diagrams might be improved for supporting joint actions. It should be possible to indicate that actions have multiple participants, each playing one or more roles in the action. For a participant in an action, it should be possible to indicate the type of role that it performs, with a name (much like a role name of an association in UML).

We stress that this name should denote a type of role rather than a role (a role is not a type, but a kind of part of a joint action). It is indeed possible for several participants to perform roles of the same type (for example, a "Get married" joint action with two identical roles of spouse, and two identical roles of witness). If we were to name roles rather than their types, the notation might be unnecessarily restrictive and unnatural. For example, UML insists that all rolenames of associations be different, which rules out the possibility of having symmetric associations in a model [13]. See [12] for a discussion of the relation between the notions of role, type of role, and type of object.

5 Summary and Conclusions

In this paper, we set out to answer the question of what is a use case. We had in mind settling two issues often debated by use case methodologists and practitioners. We found that Jacobson's and UML definitions of a use case provide authoritative answers: (1) all the system's actions, not just those of sending or receiving messages, should be described (to some extent) in a use case specification; and (2), only the actions of the system belong to a use case, and none of the actors.

Common use case textual specifications do not reflect the second answer, but it is all for the better. Specifications in natural language should describe the actors' actions of entering data, selecting an option, etc., as a matter of convention (it is clear enough that the system receives those data), and so that they can be easily read by system users and other stakeholders. Likewise, interaction diagrams should describe the actors sending and receiving messages, because doing otherwise would require complicating the current notation.

In the second part of the paper, we considered use cases in the light of the ODP modeling technique. That is, we replaced the message passing hypothesis with joint actions [10], in which several participants may change state. This modeling technique is more natural than that of UML, since joint actions can model actions in natural language, given by verbs. All joint actions come with multiple roles; e.g., the buy action has the roles of buyer, seller, the sold entity, and its counterpart.

We then explained *a use case* as *a role in a joint action*, an important idea when one is attempting to relate IT systems to business processes, or to integrate multiple systems in support of a business process.

We showed that the use cases specification technique (i.e., the use cases graphical notation together with textual specifications) is applicable to modeling joint actions, and we indicated how the activity diagrams notation should be extended in support of the same cause.

Acknowledgements

We acknowledge the contributions of Joaquin Miller and Alain Wegmann to the years of discussions that led to this paper. We are also grateful to the anonymous reviewers for their valuable comments and suggestions.

References

1. Anderson, B. *Formalism, technique and rigour in use case modelling.* in *UML2004 Workshop on Open Issues in Industrial Use Case Modeling.* 2004. Lisbon, Portugal.
2. Isoda, S. *On UML2.0's Abandonment of the Actors-Call-Use-Cases Conjecture.* in *UML2004 Workshop on Open Issues in Industrial Use Case Modeling.* 2004. Lisbon, Portugal.
3. Génova, G. and J. Llorens. *The Emperor's New Use Case.* in *UML2004 Workshop on Open Issues in Industrial Use Case Modeling.* 2004. Lisbon, Portugal.
4. OMG, *Unified Modeling Language: Superstructure (version 2.0).* 2004, OMG.
5. Jacobson, I., et al., *Object-Oriented Software Engineering--A Use Case Driven Approach.* 1992, Reading, Massachusetts: Addison-Wesley, 1992. 524.
6. Jacobson, I., M. Ericsson, and A. Jacobson, *The Object Advantage: Business Process Reengineering with Object Technology.* ACM Press Books. 1995: Addison-Wesley. 347 pp.
7. Lamport, L., *A simple approach to specifying concurrent systems.* Communications of the ACM, 1989. **32**(1): p. 32-45.
8. ISO/IEC and ITU-T, *Open Distributed Processing - Basic Reference Model - Part 2: Foundations,* in *Standard 10746-2, Recommendation X.902.* 1995.
9. Genilloud, G. and G. Génova. *On Interactions in the RM-ODP.* in *submitted to the Workshop on ODP for Enterprise Computing (WODPEC 2005).* 2005. Enschede, The Netherlands.
10. D'Souza, D.F. and A.C. Wills, *Objects, Components and Frameworks With UML : The Catalysis Approach.* Addison-Wesley Object Technology Series. 1998: Addison-Wesley. 912.
11. Wegmann, A. and G. Genilloud. *The Role of "Roles" in Use Case Diagrams.* in *Third International Conference on the Unified Modeling Language (UML2000).* 2000. York, UK: Springer-Verlag.
12. Genilloud, G. and A. Wegmann. *A Foundation for the Concept of Role in the RM-ODP.* in *4th International Enterprise Distributed Object Computing Conference (EDOC 2000).* 2000. Makuhari, Japan: IEEE Computer Society.
13. Génova, G., *Interlacement of structural and dynamic aspects in UML associations (Ph. D. Thesis).* 2003, Carlos III University of Madrid: Madrid, Spain.

Specifying Precise Use Cases with Use Case Charts

Jon Whittle

Dept of Information & Software Engineering,
George Mason University,
4400 University Drive,
Fairfax, VA 22030
jwhittle@ise.gmu.edu

Abstract. Use cases are a popular method for capturing and structuring software requirements. The informality of use cases is both a blessing and a curse. It enables easy application and learning but is a barrier to automated methods for test case generation, validation or simulation. This paper presents *use case charts*, a precise way of specifying use cases that aims to retain the benefits of easy understanding but also supports automated analysis. The graphical and abstract syntax of use case charts are given, along with a sketch of their formal semantics.

1 Use Case Charts

Use cases are a popular way of structuring and analyzing software requirements but are usually written informally as a set of use case diagrams and text-based templates. This makes them very easy to use but is a barrier to the application of automated analysis methods such as test case generation, simulation and validation. More precise formalisms for specifying use cases are needed but the advantages of informal notations should not be sacrificed in the process. In this paper, *use case charts*, a 3-level notation based on extended activity diagrams, is proposed as a way of specifying use cases in detail, in a way that combines the formality of precise modeling with the ease of use of existing notations. The primary purpose of use case charts so far has been to simulate use cases but use case charts are also precise enough for test case generation and automated validation. With respect to simulation, use case charts provide sufficient detail that a set of communicating finite state machines can be generated automatically from them. These state machines can then be simulated using existing state machine simulators.

The idea behind use case charts is illustrated in Figure 1. For the purposes of this paper, a use case is defined to be a collection of scenarios, where a scenario is an expected or actual execution trace of a system. A use case chart specifies the scenarios for a system as a 3-level, use case-based description: level-1 is an extended activity diagram where the nodes are use cases; level-2 is a set of extended activity diagrams where the nodes are scenarios; level-3 is a set of UML2.0 ([1]) interaction diagrams. Each level-1 use case node is defined by a

J.-M. Bruel (Ed.): MoDELS 2005 Workshops, LNCS 3844, pp. 290–301, 2006.

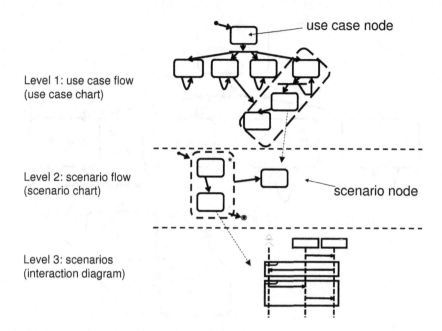

Fig. 1. Use Case Charts

level-2 activity diagram (i.e., a set of connected scenario nodes). This diagram is called a *scenario chart*. Each level-2 scenario node is defined by a UML2.0 interaction diagram.

Semantically, control flow of the entire use case chart starts with the initial node of the use case chart (level 1). When flow passes into a use case chart node at level-1, the defining level-2 scenario chart is executed with flow passing from the scenario chart's initial node in the usual manner. Flow exits a scenario node when a final node is reached. Note that there are two types of final nodes for scenario charts: those that represent successful completion of the scenario chart and those that represent completion with failure. Flow only continues beyond a scenario chart if a final success node is reached. If a final failure node is reached, the use case thread to which the scenario chart belongs is terminated. A formal semantics for use case charts is sketched in Section 3.

Figures 2, 3 and 4 give an example of how use case charts can be used to precisely describe use cases. The system under development is an automated train shuttle service in which autonomous shuttles transport passengers between stations [2]. When a passenger requires transport, a central broker asks all active shuttles for bids on the transport order. The shuttle with the lowest bid wins. A complete set of requirements for this application is given in [2]. Figure 2 shows a use case chart that includes use cases for initialization of the system, maintenance and repair of shuttles, and transportation (split into multiple use cases). Figure 3 is a scenario chart that defines the Carry Out Order use case. Figure 4 is an interaction diagram forming part of the definition of the use case Make A Bid.

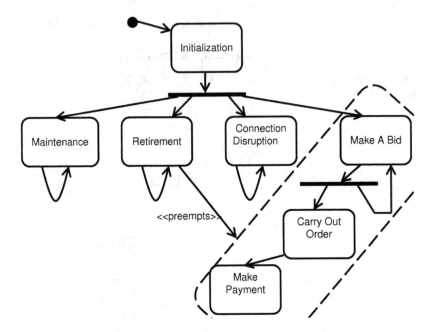

Fig. 2. Shuttle System Use Case Chart

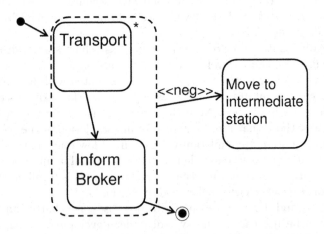

Fig. 3. Shuttle System Scenario Chart for Carry Out Order

The use case chart in Figure 2 shows the main use cases for the shuttle system and the relationships between them. As stated previously, a use case chart is an extended activity diagram. Note that the usual ⟨⟨includes⟩⟩ and ⟨⟨extends⟩⟩ relationships from use case diagrams are not part of use case charts. If desired, these can be represented independently on a conventional use case diagram. Figure 2 shows that the shuttle system first goes through an Initialization use

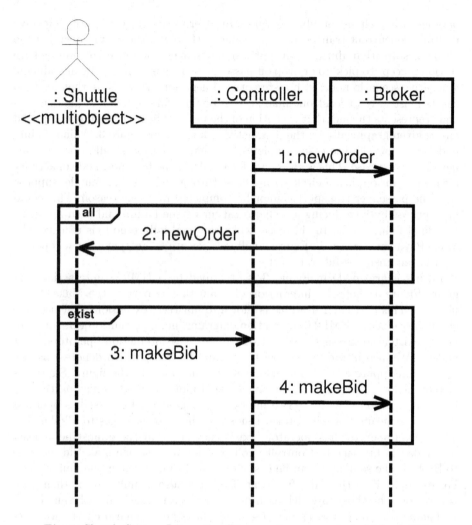

Fig. 4. Shuttle System Interaction Diagram for a scenario in Make A Bid

case. After that, four use cases execute in parallel. If the Make A Bid use case is successful, it can be followed by Carry Out Order or another bidding process (executed in parallel). The Retirement use case represents the case when the shuttles are shut down. It preempts any activity associated to Make A Bid. This is represented by a stereotyped preemption relationship that applies to a region. A region is a set of nodes enclosed in a dashed box. Note that, in the figure, a region is syntactic sugar and can be replaced by multiple preemption arrows, one to each node in the region.

Figure 3 is a description of what happens in the Carry Out Order use case. Transportation of passengers takes place and the broker is informed of success. The asterisk in the region represents the fact that the region may execute in parallel with itself any numbers of times. In other words, the use case may involve multiple concurrent transports of passengers. However, the requirements of the problem state that during transport, shuttles may not move to intermediate stations except to pick up or drop off passengers. This is captured by introducing a negative scenario node with a stereotyped negation arrow. Note that scenario charts must have at least one final success or final failure node. A final success node represents the fact that execution of the use case has successfully completed and is given graphically by the final activity node as in Figure 3. A final failure node says that the use case completes but that execution should not continue beyond the use case. This is given graphically using the final flow node of activity diagram notation, i.e., a circle with a cross through it[1]. As an example, suppose that the passenger transport cannot be completed for some reason. This could be captured by introducing a scenario capturing the failure and then an arrow to a final failure node. In this case, when the final failure node is reached, the Make Payment use case in Figure 2 will not execute — i.e., payment will not be paid for an unsuccessful transport.

Each scenario node in Figure 3 is described by a UML2.0 interaction diagram. Figure 4 shows an interaction diagram that is part of the Make A Bid use case. This particular example is shown to illustrate extensions that use case charts introduce to UML2.0 interaction diagrams, namely, multiobjects and universal/existential messages. We introduce two new interaction operators, exist and all. We also introduce a stereotype ⟨⟨multiobject⟩⟩ which denotes that an interaction applies to multiple instances of a classifier. In the figure, Shuttle is stereotyped as a multiobject which means that multiple shuttles may participate in the interaction. There are two interaction fragments. The first has operator "all". This means that the Broker sends the enclosed messages to all shuttles. The second operator has operator "exist" meaning that there must be at least one makeBid message to Controller followed by at least one makeBid message to Broker. The semantics can be easily extended to more than one multiobject. For example, if in the "all" fragment, Broker is also a multiobject, then legal traces would be those in which each broker sends a message to each shuttle.

The activity diagrams used in use case charts and scenario charts are a restricted version of UML2.0 activity diagrams but with some additional relationships between nodes. They are restricted in the sense that they do not include object flow, swimlanes, signals etc. They do include additional notations, however. The abstract syntax is defined in Section 2. The concrete syntax reuses as much of the activity diagram notation as possible. Informally, the allowed arrow types between nodes (either in use case or scenario charts) are given as follows, where, for each arrow, X and Y are either both scenario nodes or both use case nodes:

1. X continues from Y (i.e., the usual activity diagram arrow)
2. X and Y are alternatives (the usual alternative defined by a condition in an activity diagram)
3. X and Y run in parallel (the usual activity diagram fork and join)

---

[1] Note that this is not the standard UML2.0 interpretation for the final flow node.

4. X preempts Y — i.e., X interrupts Y and control does not return to Y once X is complete. This is shown graphically by an arrow stereotyped with $\langle\langle$preempts$\rangle\rangle$ from X to Y.

5. X suspends Y — i.e., X interrupts Y and control returns to Y once X is complete. This is shown graphically by an arrow stereotyped with $\langle\langle$suspends$\rangle\rangle$ from X to Y.

6. X is negative — i.e., the scenarios defined by X should never happen. This is shown graphically by an arrow stereotyped with $\langle\langle$neg$\rangle\rangle$ to X and where the source of the arrow is the region over which the scope of the negation applies.

7. X may have multiple copies — i.e., X can run in parallel with itself any number of times. This is shown graphically by an asterisk attached to node X.

8. X crosscuts Y — X is an aspect that crosscuts Y. This is shown graphically by an arrow stereotyped with $\langle\langle$aspect$\rangle\rangle$ from X to Y.

Discussion of aspects is outside the scope of this paper. The interested reader is referred to [3]. Briefly, a use case node is an aspect if it crosscuts other use cases. Similarly, a scenario node is an aspect if it crosscuts other scenarios. Use case charts contain well-defined notations for representing and composing aspects.

In addition, use case charts and scenario charts may have regions (graphically shown by dashed boxes) that scope nodes together. Arrows of type (4), (5), (8), in the preceding list, may have a region as the target of the arrow. Arrows of type (7) may have a region as the source of the arrow. All other arrows do not link regions.

Arrow types (4), (5), (6) and (8) are not part of UML2.0 activity diagrams (although there is a similar notation to (4) and (5) for interruption). Activity diagrams do have a notion of region for defining an interruptible set of nodes. Regions in use case charts are a general-purpose scoping mechanism not restricted to defining interrupts. Note that the semantics for use case charts is, in places, different than UML2.0 activity diagrams and is sketched in section 3. In addition to the arrow and region extensions, there are minor extensions to interaction diagrams.

The graphical notation for use case charts is similar to notations such as UML2.0 interaction overview diagrams (IODs) and high-level message sequence charts (hMSCs). Use case charts are a hierarchical approach to defining use cases. In IODs, there are only two levels of hierarchy — activity diagrams connect references to interaction diagrams but use cases are not incorporated. In hMSCs, nodes can be references to other hMSCs so there is an unlimited number of hierarchical levels. However, all references in hMSCs ultimately are to interaction diagrams (MSCs) so, once again, the third use case level is not captured. Modeling use cases with either IODs or hMSCs would require, in addition, the usual use case diagrams. The use case chart approach also extends both activity diagrams and interaction diagrams to increase the expressive power of use case charts. The key goal of use case charts is to support use case simulation. This cannot be done with existing use case modeling notations.

2   Use Case Chart Syntax

2.1   Abstract Syntax for Scenario Charts

The abstract syntax of a scenario chart is given first.

Definition 1. *A scenario chart is a graph of the form $(S, R_S, E_S, s_0, S_F, S_{F'},$ $L_S, f_S, m_S, L_E)$ where S is a set of scenario nodes, $R_S \subseteq \mathcal{P}(S)$ is a set of regions, $E_S \subseteq (\mathcal{P}(S \cup R_S) \times \mathcal{P}(S \cup R_S) \times L_E)$ is a set of edges with labels from L_E, $s_0 \in S$ is the unique initial node, $S_F \subset S$ is a set of success final nodes, $S_{F'} \subset S$ is a set of failure final nodes, L_S is a set of scenario labels, $f_S : S \to L_S$ is a total, injective function mapping each scenario node to a label and $m_s : S \cup R_S \to \{+, -\}$ is a total function marking whether each scenario or region can have multiple concurrent executions. The labels in L_S are references to an interaction diagram. L_E is defined to be the set $\{normal, neg, preempts, suspends\}$. L_S is the set of words from some alphabet Σ.*

This definition describes a graph where edges may have multiple sources and targets. This subsumes the notion of fork and join from activity diagrams which can be taken care of by allowing edges to have multiple source nodes and/or multiple target nodes. Multiple source nodes lead in the use case chart graphical notation to a join and multiple target nodes lead to a fork.

Regions are a scoping mechanism used to group nodes. For the most part, they are simply syntactic sugar and can be eliminated by replacing each outgoing edge with outgoing edges for each node in the region, and each incoming edge with incoming edges for each node in the region. For example, a region with an incoming preemption edge can be replaced with edges that preempt each node in the region. A region with a normal outgoing edge (i.e., no stereotypes) is equivalent to normal edges leaving each node in the region, i.e., a join.

The only case when regions cannot be viewed as syntactic sugar is when a region is marked to have concurrent executions (graphically, an asterisk). This case cannot be eliminated (without changing the semantics) by projecting the concurrent executions inside the region.

As stated previously, the intuition behind success final and failure final nodes is that a success final node denotes successful completion of the scenario chart — and hence that the current "thread" in the enclosing use case chart continues; a failure final node denotes that the scenario chart completes but unsuccessfully — and hence that the current "thread" in the enclosing use case chart terminates.

This paper omits the notion of condition but it is enough to say that guards could be placed on arrows leaving a node.

2.2   Abstract Syntax for Use Case Charts

The abstract syntax for a use case chart is almost identical except that a use case chart has only one type of final node (for success) and each use case node maps to a scenario chart not an interaction diagram. Only one type of final node is required for use case charts because there is no notion of success or failure — either a use case chart completes or it does not.

Definition 2. *A use case chart is a graph of the form* $(U, R_U, E_U, u_0, U_F, C, f_U,$ $m_U, L_E)$ *where* U *is a set of nodes,* $R_U \subseteq \mathcal{P}(U)$ *is a set of regions,* $E_U \subseteq$ $(\mathcal{P}(U \cup R_U) \times \mathcal{P}(U \cup R_U) \times L_E)$ *is a set of edges,* $u_0 \in U$ *is the unique initial node,* $U_F \subset U$ *is a set of final nodes,* C *is a set of scenario charts,* $f_U : U \rightarrow$ *is a total, injective function mapping each use case node to a scenario chart and* $m_U : U \cup R_U \rightarrow \{+, -\}$ *is a total function marking whether the use case or region can have multiple concurrent executions.*

A 3-level use case chart is well-formed if all edges map use case nodes to use case nodes or scenario nodes to scenario nodes. In other words, there should be no edge that links a use case node and a scenario node. Formally, $dom(f_S) \cap dom(f_U) = \emptyset$.

3   Use Case Chart Semantics

This section sketches a trace-based semantics for use case charts. A trace semantics is used to achieve consistency with existing semantics for sequence chart notations. A trace is a sequence of events where an event may be a send event, $!x$, or a receive event, $?x$. The semantics of a 3-level use case chart is defined as follows.

Definition 3. *The semantics of a 3-level use case chart,* U, *is a pair of trace sets,* (P_U, N_U), *where* P_U *is the set of positive traces for* U *and* N_U *is the set of negative traces for* U.

Positive traces are traces that are possible in any implementation of the use case chart. Negative traces may never occur in a valid implementation of the use case chart. An implementation satisfies a use case chart if every positive trace is a possible execution path and if no negative trace is a possible execution path.

The details of the semantics are given in stages — first, the semantics of UML2.0 interaction diagrams is given, followed by the semantics for scenario charts, and finally, use case charts.

3.1   Semantics of UML2.0 Interaction Diagrams

A message in a UML2.0 interaction has two events — a send event and a receive event. The send event must come before the receive event. In UML2.0, as shown in Figure 4, messages are composed using interaction fragments, where a fragment has an interaction operator and a number of interaction operands. For example, Figure 4 has two unary-operand fragments — one with the **all** operator and one with the **exist** operator.

The default operator is **seq** which represents weak sequencing. Any messages not explicitly contained within a fragment are by default assumed to be contained within a **seq** fragment. **seq** fragments are defined in UML2.0 to have a weak sequencing semantics ([1]):

- The ordering of events within each operand is maintained.
- Events on different lifelines from different operands may come in any order.
- Events on the same lifeline from different operands are ordered such that an event from the first operand comes before an event from the second operand.

Any **seq** fragment joins two traces — one from each of its operands – in a way that satisfies these three constraints. The positive traces for **seq** are all possible ways of joining a positive trace from the first operand and a positive trace from the second operand. The negative traces for **seq** are those derived from joining a positive trace from the first operand with a negative trace from the second, or a negative trace from the first with either a positive or negative trace from the second.

A trace semantics for the other interaction operators can be given in the same way. For example, for **alt**, the set of positive traces is the union of the set of positive traces from each operand. Similarly, the set of negative traces is the union of the set of negative traces from each operand. **par** is defined by interleaving traces from each of its operands. Its positive traces are the interleavings of positive traces from both operands. Its negative traces are the interleavings of negative traces from both operands, or a positive trace from one operand with the negative trace from the other operand. The **neg** operator simply negates all traces — its set of negative traces is the union of the positive and negative traces of its operand. This captures the fact that the negation of a negative trace remains negative. These notions are based on the formalization of UML2.0 interaction diagrams given in [4].

The semantics for the multiobject extensions are now given. Multiobjects cannot be used unless either an existential or universal operator is also used. Hence, only the semantics for the operators **exist** and **all** need be given. Suppose that an **all** fragment is applied to a positive trace of events, $t_1, t_2, \ldots$. The resulting positive traces are all those that can be derived by replacing each t_i by its image under **all**. Suppose that t_i is a receive event where the receiving instance is stereotyped as a multiobject. Then the image under **all** is given as the trace $t_{i_1}, t_{i_2}, \ldots$ where each t_{i_j} is the same event but received by instance j. The corresponding send event is also replaced by a set of send events, one for each instance j. The same logic applies if t_i is a send event where the sending instance is a multiobject. In this case, t_i is replaced by a set of send events, one for each instance of the multiobject, and the corresponding receive events for the new send events are added. If, for a message, both its sending and receiving instances are multiobjects, the preceding rules result in duplication which is just removed.

When an **all** fragment is applied to a negative trace of events, the semantics is derived in the same way as in the previous paragraph. For example, a negative send event is replaced with multiple negative send events, one for each instance of the multiobject, and the corresponding negative receive events are added.

The case for **exist** is the same except that positive (alternatively, negative) traces for the **exist** fragment are those in which t_i is replaced by a trace for just one of the multiobject instances, not all of them.

3.2 Semantics of Scenario Charts

As stated in the previous section, the semantics of an interaction diagram is given as a pair of sets of traces. The semantics is extended to scenario charts in the natural way — the semantics of a scenario chart is also given by a set of positive traces and a set of negative traces.

Edges of type *normal* in scenario charts can be given a semantics by "flattening" the edge — i.e., create a new interaction diagram that takes the interaction diagrams represented by the source and target and connects them using an interaction fragment with a particular interaction operator. Normal edges with only one source and target edge are flattened using the **seq** interaction operator for sequential composition. This captures the weak sequential semantics of one-to-one *normal* edges. Many-to-many *normal* edges are flattened using the **par** interaction operator. This is because the semantics of a one-to-many edge is defined to be a forking and that of a many-to-one edge is defined to be a joining of "threads". Hence, a many-to-many edge can be replaced by a fork and join in the usual activity diagram notation. Since *normal* edges can be eliminated in this way, their semantics is not explicitly given here but the semantics is assumed to be that of the equivalent "flattened" interaction diagram. This leaves only edges of type *neg*, *preempts* and *suspends* to be dealt with.

In what follows, c_1 **preempts** c_2 informally means that scenario c_1 preempts c_2. c_1 **suspends** c_2 means that c_1 suspends c_2 and c_1 **negative during** c_2 means that c_1 can never happen during the execution of c_2.

The semantics for preemption, suspension and negation are given only for one-to-one edges, but can be extended in the obvious way to many-to-many edges: for example, if there is a preemption edge with multiple target nodes, it means that all those nodes are preempted by the source(s) of the preemption edge.

For preemption, a positive trace for c_1 **preempts** c_2 is any trace made up of a prefix of a positive trace of c_2 concatenated with a positive trace of c_1. Note that a preempting scenario cannot have negative traces (if it does, they are simply ignored). Furthermore, c_1 **preempts** c_2 does not introduce any new negative traces because preempting traces have no effect on the original negative traces. The case for suspension is similar except that control returns to the suspended scenario once the suspending scenario is complete.

For the negation case, the positive traces of c_1 **negative during** c_2 are simply the positive traces of c_2. Negative traces, however, can be any trace that is an interleaving of a positive trace of c_2 with a positive trace of c_1. This, in effect, defines a monitor for traces of c_1 — if a c_1 trace occurs at any point, even with events interleaved with its own events, then an error state has been entered. Note that c_1 cannot have negative traces.

The semantics for multiple concurrent executions (the asterisk notation) is given by interleaving and hence can be described in terms of flattening using **par** operators. The number of **par** operators is unbounded since there can be any number of executions of the node.

For the most part, regions are merely syntactic sugar. The exception is when a region is defined as having multiple concurrent executions. In this case, the traces of the region are given by the semantics of multiple executions as described in the previous paragraph.

The semantics for final success and final failure nodes are given in the following subsection.

3.3   Semantics of Use Case Charts

The semantics for use case charts is essentially the same as for scenario charts because both a scenario and a use case are given meaning as a set of traces. For use case charts, however, the meaning of a *normal* edge is given by strong not weak sequential composition. This means that before execution can continue along an edge to the next use case, *all* instances of participating classifiers must complete (where completion is defined below). In contrast, in scenario charts, some instances may complete and continue to the next node while others remain in the current node. Strong composition is chosen to define use case charts because nodes represent use cases. Use cases are considered modular functional units in which the entire unit must complete before control goes elsewhere. Strong composition enforces the modularity and, in most cases, is probably adequate. However, the author acknowledges that, in certain situations, weak composition may be desired and future versions of use case charts may allow the modeler to choose the type of composition. Semantically, strong composition of traces is just concatenation.

A use case chart node completes if and only if its defining scenario chart reaches a final success or final failure node. If the scenario chart reaches a final success node, control continues to the next use case node. If the scenario chart reaches a final failure node, the use case "thread" terminates. Semantically, each trace in a scenario chart is either infinite, ends with a final success node (a success trace) or a final failure node (a failure trace). Suppose a use case chart has two nodes, U_1 and U_2, connected by a single edge from U_1 to U_2. Then the positive trace set of the use case chart is the union of three trace sets: the positive infinite traces of U_1, the set of traces formed by concatenating positive success traces from U_1 with positive traces from U_2, and the set of positive failure traces from U_1. The extension to negative traces is straightforward.

4   Related Work and Conclusion

A variety of notations for scenario-based definitions exist, such as UML2.0 interaction overview diagrams, high-level message sequence charts (hMSCs) and approaches based on activity diagrams (e.g., [5]). Notationally, the extensions that use case charts provide are relatively minor. The notation is based on UML2.0 activity diagrams and some extensions have been suggested by other authors — e.g., [6] deals with preemption for hMSCs. The contribution is that use case charts are a usable yet precise notation that can be directly executed. Work towards simulating use case charts is currently underway. A state machine-based simulator for interaction diagrams has already been defined [7] and a simulator for the remaining parts of use case charts is being developed.

Use case charts are intended to be used as a way to rapidly simulate use case scenarios. As such, they can be used either during requirements engineering or early design. Clearly, the appropriateness of their use depends on the application and they are more suited to complex, reactive systems. For example, so far they have been used to model air traffic control and telecommunication applications. In such applications, the sequence of interactions in use cases quickly becomes very complex and stakeholders quickly question the validity of the interactions they have developed. By using use case charts, these interactions can be simulated either during requirements gathering or early design. The focus on reactive, concurrent and distributed systems means that interaction diagrams are the most suitable notation for the level 3 models although, in principle, there is no reason why level 3 could not be based on activity diagrams as well. Note that use case charts are not meant to be a substitute for use case diagrams. The two diagram types are usually used together — use case diagrams focus on the actors whereas use case charts focus on the interactions (the initiating actors are implicitly defined at level 3).

References

1. OMG: Unified modeling language 2.0 specification (2005) http://www.omg.org.
2. Software Engineering Group, University of Paderborn: Shuttle system case study (2005) http://www.cs.uni-paderborn.de/cs/ag-schaefer/CaseStudies/ShuttleSystem/.
3. Whittle, J., Araújo, J.: Scenario modelling with aspects. IEE Proceedings — Software **151** (2004) 157–172
4. Haugen, O., Husa, K.E., Runde, R.K., Stølen, K.: Stairs: Towards formal design with sequence diagrams. Journal of Software and System Modeling (2005) To Appear.
5. Smialek, M.: Accommodating informality with necessary precision in use case scenarios. In: Proceedings of Workshop on Open Issues in Industrial Use Case Modeling at UML2004. (2004)
6. Krueger, I.: Distributed System Design with Message Sequence Charts. PhD thesis, Technische Universitaet Muenchen (2000)
7. Whittle, J., Schumann, J.: Generating statechart designs from scenarios. In: ICSE '00: Proceedings of the 22nd international conference on software engineering, New York, NY, USA, ACM Press (2000) 314–323

Summary of the Educator's Symposium

Holger Giese[1], Pascal Roques[2], and Timothy C. Lethbridge[3]

[1] University of Paderborn, Germany
hg@uni-paderborn.de
http://www.springer.de/comp/lncs/index.html
[2] Valtech Training, France
pascal.roques@valtech-training.fr
[3] University of Ottawa, Canada
tcl@site.uottawa.ca

Abstract. This first Educators' Symposium of the conference on Model Driven Engineering Languages and Systems (MoDELS - formerly the UML series of conferences) was intended as a forum to foster discussion and the exchange of information on education and training concerning model-driven engineering. This summary reports about the workshop and the results of the discussions during the workshop.

1 Introduction

Model-driven development approaches and technologies for software-based systems, in which development is centered round the manipulation of models, raise the level of abstraction and thus, improve our abilities to develop complex systems. A number of approaches and tools have been proposed for the model-driven development (MDD) of software-based systems. Examples are the UML, model-driven architecture (MDA), and model-integrated computing (MIC).

Initiating the model-driven development vision into common practice requires not only sophisticated modeling approaches and tools, but also considerable training and education efforts. To help developers adopt MDD, its principles and applications need to be taught to practitioners in industry, incorporated in university curricula, and probably even introduced in schools for primary education.

The educator's symposium at the MoDELS conference, the premier conference devoted to the topic of model-driven engineering of software-based systems, served as a forum in which educators and trainers met to discuss pedagogy, use of technology, and to share their experience pertaining to teaching modeling techniques and model-driven development. The symposium also facilitated the sharing of project ideas, exemplar models, and other teaching materials.

The symposium had 16 submissions from which only 9 papers were accepted. All papers presented during the symposium have been published in a technical report [1]. The areas addressed by the papers of this symposium include experience reports from academia, industry, and primary schools regarding issues related to teaching modeling and model-driven development in particular. The covered topics were MDD with UML [2,4,5,6,8,9,10], MDD in general [3,7], course design issues [3,4,5,6,7,8,10], and design patterns [4,8,9]. Additionally, methodology issues as well as the

J.-M. Bruel (Ed.): MoDELS 2005 Workshops, LNCS 3844, pp. 302–305, 2006.

integrating of modeling and model driven development into the curriculum are discussed. Extended versions of the two best papers [5, 10] are included in this volume.

In addition to the presentations, the symposium included time slots for working groups. Two possible working group themes were presented: Timothy C. Lethbridge proposed to discuss the role that modeling should play in the curriculum for software engineering and Pascal Roques proposed to discuss the differences and commonalities of teaching students and training professionals in the field.

In an initial discussion these two working group themes were slightly adjusted to also include other topics of interest. In the following we will outline the results obtained during the discussions.

2 Results of the Working Group on Modeling in the Curriculum

Tim Lethbridge first presented some information about the modeling content in SE-2004 [11]. The group members in this session then brainstormed for answers to two questions. The following are edited versions of the answers they produced:

The first question was: "What should be the goals and outcomes of modeling aspects of curricula?" The conclusions were as follows, most important first:

- Students should **be able to communicate effectively using abstractions**: They should be able to understand abstractions (beyond those found in programming languages), create new abstractions and validate abstractions.
- Students should **be able to model heterogeneously**: They should be able to find the right abstraction for the problem at hand, create different models for different audiences, and be able to work with different views of the same system. They should know the properties of each type of model, and should be able to choose the level of formalism so as to be cost-effective and balance costs and quality
- Students should **be able to model in at least one "real" domain**. They need to have knowledge of both the domain and ways to model in that domain. Since it is impossible to educate students in a large number of domains, they need to be able to have the flexibility to choose their specialty. Finally, they should be able to develop and work with domain-specific models and languages in their domain(s).
- Students should **be able to apply a wide variety of patterns** in their models, particularly design patterns. Patterns are widely recognized as effective expressions of expert knowledge. Applying patterns will result in better models.
- Students should **have a deep understanding of quality**. They need to understand how their modeling work influences the quality of the final product, and they need to be able to certify that models have certain properties.
- Students should **be able to create 'models that count'**: i.e. not just diagrams, but models that are formally analyzable, executable and/or used to generate final code of the system. Students should also be able to transition models to design and code, extract a model from code, and understand what a compiler and model compiler do.
- Students should **know the importance of keeping models updated.**
- Students should **know the basics of creating modeling tools and metamodelling**.

The second question addressed was, "What do we need to do to improve model education?" The answers fall into the following three themes:

- We should **confront students with complex models they have to change**, rather than having them create models from scratch. This will teach by example and help students learn about scalability. One strategy is to have students build systems using frameworks, and with models of the frameworks. Models should also be used as building blocks to build other models: i.e. students should re-use models as components. Students should also model with COTS components.
- We should **expose students to modeling in a variety of domains**, including in other types of engineering. For example, we can demonstrate electrical, mechanical and software modeling in the automotive and aeronautical industries, and teach about the types of analysis these models permit – such as performance, safety, etc.
- We should **ensure students learn the benefits of modeling**. In particular we must demonstrate that good modeling makes systems easier to change and can lead to improved performance. At the same time students must understand the limitations of modeling. This can be accomplished using well-designed case studies.

3   Differences and Commonalities of Teaching Students and Training Professionals in the Field

To start the discussion, Pascal Roques made a short presentation of his activities as a modeling consultant and trainer for a French training company called Valtech Training. He focused on the use of adult learning theory [12] in Valtech's courses: Key tenets of this are: a) Create a positive environment, b) Disseminate information, c) Exercise knowledge, and d) Provide feedback. The main goal is to provide trainees with confidence and the ability to apply course concepts outside the classroom.

The group tried to figure out the main differences and commonalities between teaching students and training professionals in the field. The following are some of the conclusions reached by the group:

Firstly, adult learners are *volunteers*. They need the knowledge for their daily work and their company is paying for it, so they want a concrete return on investment, and *practical* training is also required. Students don't have the "context", adults have: very often, professionals want to see examples in their domain. But real-life examples are very difficult to elaborate.

Adult learners are often already experts in their field. They may be even more experienced than the teacher. People who have a lot of experience and expertise are often more reluctant to change. In particular, there is an important difficulty for the teacher if the trainees have been "forced" to go to the training to reconvert (example: COBOL programmers taking UML and Java courses).

In adult courses, there is often no exam at the end. The exception is for certification courses. Sometimes adults simply want to improve their C.V., and in such cases have a similar motivation to students regarding succeeding in exams.

Other differences relate to logistics. Groups of trained professionals are usually smaller (3 to 12), but may be very heterogeneous regarding their experience in the topic, group interaction, career background, etc. Training courses are short (1 to 5 days), compared to a semester with 2 to 6 hours a week. So training for professionals must be efficient and fast. The intensity is different; there is less time to digest. One consequence is that professionals usually do not have enough time to use modeling tools, whereas students have time to master them and indeed specifically want to.

To sum up the main differences, one could say that professionals need state-of-the-art skills, while students want knowledge that will survive the next 10 years.

4 Conclusion

The symposium attracted more than 20 participants, including researchers and instructors with various interests and backgrounds in modeling and MDD. The working group discussions benefited greatly from this mixture of the two perspectives provided by the two categories of attendees. We hope that this first Educators' Symposium initiates what will become a permanent offering at future MoDELS conferences such that it can serve as a starting point for building an active community that addresses the specific problems of teaching and training issues related to modeling and the model-driven paradigm.

References

[1]   Holger Giese and Pascal Roques (Editors). Proceedings of the Educators' Symposium of the ACM / IEEE 8th International Conference on Model Driven Engineering Languages and Systems, Half Moon Resort, Montego Bay, Jamaica. October 3, 2005. Technical Report tr-ri-05-260, Department of Computer Science, University of Paderborn. A4:   http://models05-edu.upb.de/proceedings/models05-edu-proceedings-a4.pdf   Letter: http://models05-edu.upb.de/proceedings/models05-edu-proceedings-letter.pdf

[2]   Jörg Niere, Carsten Schulte. Avoiding anecdotal evidence: An experience report about evaluating an object-oriented modeling course. In [1].

[3]   Pádua, Paula Filho. A Model-driven Software Process for Course Projects. In [1].

[4]   Kendra Cooper, Jing Dong, Kang Zhang, Lawrence Chung. Teaching Experiences with UML at The University of Texas at Dallas. In [1].

[5]   Ludwik Kuzniarz, Miroslaw Staron. Best Practices for Teaching UML based Software Development. In [1].

[6]   Shayne Flint, Clive Boughton. Three years experience teaching Executable/Translatable UML. In [1].

[7]   Anirudha S. Gokhale, Jeff Gray. Advancing Model Driven Devlopment Education via Collaborative Research. In [1].

[8]   Eduardo B. Fernandez, María M. Larrondo Petrie. Teaching a course on data and network security using UML and patterns. In [1].

[9]   Claudia Pons. Basis for a Course on Design Patterns: going beyond the intuition. In [1].

[10] Gregor Engels, Jan Hendrik Hausmann, Marc Lohmann, Stefan Sauer. Teaching UML is Teaching Software Engineering is Teaching Abstraction. In [1].

[11] IEEE and ACM: Software Engineering 2004 Curriculum Recommendations: http://sites.computer.org/ccse.

[12] William A. Draves, How to Teach Adults, 2nd edition, LERN, 1997.

Teaching UML Is Teaching Software Engineering Is Teaching Abstraction

Gregor Engels, Jan Hendrik Hausmann, Marc Lohmann, and Stefan Sauer

Universität Paderborn, Germany
{engels, hausmann, mlohmann, sauer}@upb.de

Abstract. As the Unified Modeling Language (UML) has by now seen widespread and successful use in the software industry and academia alike, it has also found its way into many computer science curricula. An outstanding advantage of teaching UML is that it enables an illustration of many crucial concepts of software engineering, far beyond its concrete notation. Most important among these concepts is that of abstraction. We present a course design which demonstrates the use of UML as a vehicle for teaching such core concepts of software engineering. Multimedia elements and tools help to efficiently convey the course's message to the students.

1 Introduction

What shall we teach undergraduate computer science (CS) students? This question has plagued our profession for decades now. Possible answers range over several dimensions from principles ("Programming first!") over different application fields ("Compiler construction!"), technologies ("Java!"), and paradigms ("OO!"). And for the last five years, another big player has entered the contest for the students' attention: UML [10]. Being widely used in industry by now, proficiency in UML is certainly a valuable asset for every CS student. The widespread academic interest is also a factor in integrating this topic in the curriculum.

Evidence for the rapid increase in the importance of UML can be gained from the IEEE/ACM's computing curricula project, which mentioned UML only in passing in 2001 (amongst CRC cards and other data modeling techniques) [11] and which explicitly places UML as a central component in the core course in software engineering (SE) in 2004 [12].

The incorporation of UML in a curriculum can and should not happen by adding a separate "UML" course. UML is nothing but a means to reach an end (the end in this case being the expression of software models). And there should not be courses purely on means in an academic setting. On the one hand, there is clear and present danger that the knowledge gained in such a course is outdated before the graduation day (UML 2, anyone?). On the other hand, university graduates are expected to know the 'why' and not only the 'how'.

J.-M. Bruel (Ed.): MoDELS 2005 Workshops, LNCS 3844, pp. 306–319, 2006.

Fortunately, UML has a very natural application context and that is software development. In the context of a stepwise refinement from problem to program, one cannot only showcase UML's various features, but one can also demonstrate how these features are employed in a practical and meaningful context. The teaching of structured development itself (also a fundamental concept which should appear in every CS education) also benefits from employing UML diagrams as they help to make the various stages of development more tangible.

Another benefit of teaching UML to undergraduates goes even beyond software development: UML is a set of notations for modeling. The core of modeling is abstraction; and abstraction is the principle which is right at the heart of software engineering and in fact of computer science in general. According to Hoare: *"In the development of our understanding of complex phenomena, the most powerful tool available to the human intellect is abstraction."* [6].

However, as Jeff Kramer repeatedly pointed out in a recent series of keynotes [8], abstraction is as hard to teach as it is important. His solution, as well as ours, is the use of modeling. Modeling languages provide a fixed structure in which to express certain aspects of a domain or idea. Thus, the creation of UML diagrams always implies abstracting from the concrete instance and recognizing the more abstract core of the matter.

The notion of abstraction is not absolute, but depends on a particular purpose. Abstractions of the same subject can vary in the aspect they represent and their level of detail. The relations between these abstractions are captured by the notions of consistency and refinement. Decomposition and synthesis are techniques to elicit new abstractions. All of these very general concepts appear naturally in the context of UML-based development. Since UML is a family of diagrams rather than a single diagram, students also very naturally learn about different possible aspects and their interrelations.

In this paper we make the case that teaching UML is teaching Software Engineering and is teaching abstraction at the same time. As such, teaching UML is not just "another language course" but it can and should play a central role in each undergraduate CS education.

The presentation of the paper proceeds in three sections. We start by laying out the recently remodeled CS program in Paderborn, which implements the points made in this paper. Focusing more concretely on a single course, we show the concept of the course Softwareentwurf (translates to software design), which is the fundamental SE/UML course for undergraduate students (Sect. 3). Here, we illustrate the integrated teaching of software development principles along a simplified software development process together with extensive UML modeling. We point out how fundamental concepts can be elicited in this structure. Even the best teaching concepts fail without a proper operationalization. Thus in Sect. 4, we present some of the practices which we have found useful in conveying our intentions to the students. Our experiences with the course are briefly reported in Section 5.

2   The Paderborn CS Curriculum

Due to the switch to the Bachelor/Master structure, the Paderborn CS department has recently restructured its academic program.

In the Bachelor CS program, four different thematic columns are integrated (see Figure 1): Software Engineering and Information Systems (SE/IS), Algorithms and Models (AM), Embedded Systems and System Software (ESS), and Human Computer Interaction (HCI). In addition, the curriculum covers courses in mathematics as well as a limited number of courses in a minor subject (like economics, engineering or natural sciences). This overall structure as well as the concrete courses implementing this structure have not only been accredited by the German ASIIN accreditation agency, but have also formed the basis for a national recommendation for a well-structured CS curriculum.

In the first term of the Bachelor curriculum, CS students have to take a course on object-oriented programming (with an introduction to the Java programming language) as well as a course on foundations of modeling concepts. Topics which are taught in this course cover basic structuring means like sets, trees, terms, graphs, and basic modeling instruments like predicate logic, finite automata, Petri Nets, and ER models.

This emphasis on programming and modeling concepts right from the beginning distinguishes the Paderborn CS curriculum from most other CS curricula of German universities. Intentionally, this choice led to a reduction of general

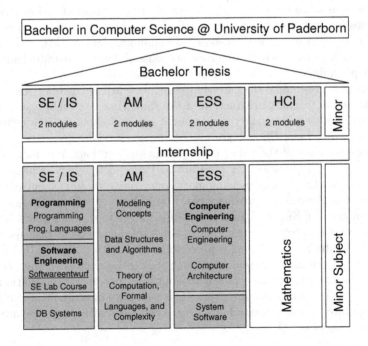

Fig. 1. Paderborn CS curriculum

mathematics courses. Rather emphasizing the modeling aspect right from the beginning yields the advantage that CS students are dealing with computer science
issues from the first day of their studies and are focusing more on formalisms
and abstractions that are directly applicable in CS.

The programming education is continued in the second term by introducing
advanced programming concepts (e.g., concurrency), different paradigms (e.g.,
functional programming), and the wealth of fundamental data structures and
algorithms. All of these courses provide the students with solid programming
skills but the scope of examples and exercises is limited to the implementation
of search algorithms and the like, i.e., tasks which have a clear structure and
require neither teamwork nor extensive planning.

In the third term, the students take the course *Softwareentwurf*, which is the
running example of this paper. The objective of the course is to introduce the
students to the problems of industrial-strength software development and supply
them with knowledge about software engineering techniques (especially UML)
to overcome these problems. The course is also intended to build on, recall, and
expand basic OO principles from the fundamental programming courses.

Based on this introduction to SE, all CS students have to take part in a lab
course during the fourth term. In this lab course, a complex software development
project has to be solved by small teams of students (cf. [5] for details on this
course). The skills and knowledge acquired during the Softwareentwurf course
are applied here in a practical setting. Upon finishing this lab, the students
have to apply their skills in the industrial reality during a mandatory 8-week
internship in a software company.

The overall structure of the program is thus to start from initial programming
experience and to continually refine this experience in eliciting more abstract
concepts on the one hand and practically applicable skills on the other hand.
Teaching UML works towards both of these ends.

3   Embedding UML in a Software Development Process for Teaching - The Softwareentwurf Course

In this section we focus on the course Softwareentwurf. The presentation here is
not intended to completely reflect the contents of the course (nor is the course
intended to cover all topics of Software Engineering) but rather to point out how
fundamental CS concepts are embedded in this course.

The course is oriented along a simplified software development process which
starts with a requirements specification phase and moves over analysis and design
phases towards actual implementation. The different models and UML diagrams
employed during this process and a selection of their relations are depicted in Figure 2. We omitted all relations which are not mentioned in the following sections.

3.1   Building Abstractions - The Domain Model

The first model which is being built in our development process is the so-
called domain model, a class diagram representing concepts and relations in the

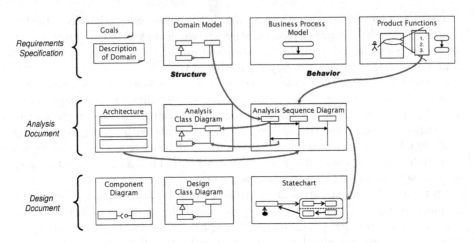

Fig. 2. Concepts underlying the Paderborn Softwareentwurf course

problem domain of the software system. Domain models help us to thoroughly understand the structure of the problem we face and thus aid us in building the right system for the user's needs.

Creating such a model requires two different kinds of knowledge: *what* is to be modeled and *how* is the model to be expressed. The latter kind of knowledge comprises the actual UML syntax symbols and is the 'easy' part of teaching as students quickly pick up the notations and tools can be used to aid them in drawing diagrams. What to model is actually the hard part as this question involves understanding of object-oriented structures and *abstractions*.

There are actually two steps of abstraction required for eventually achieving the domain class model. At first, situations in the problem domain have to be interpreted in terms of relevant objects and relations (we cannot-in general-assume a generalized description of the domain to be readily available, see Sect. 4.1 and 4.2). Irrelevant details have to be discarded and relevant information has to be notated using an object diagram.

The second abstraction generalizes these instance models towards the type level (Figure 3 shows a slide from the lecture exemplifying this distinction). Its result is expressed by a UML class diagram. Note that the notion of abstraction in these cases is not the same: while an object diagram is a token model, i.e., a projection of an observed situation, the class diagram is a type model, i.e., a generalization which only corresponds indirectly to real situations [9].

Experienced modelers actually perform both of these abstraction tasks at the same time, i.e., they can formulate a class diagram directly on the basis of concrete situations, but it is easier for students to separate these tasks.

Except for trivial cases, both abstraction tasks can yield a number of different actual results for a given problem. Typical questions are: "What is relevant?", "Which entities belong to the problem domain, which are outside of it?", and "Which level of detail is detailed enough?". Furthermore, information can often

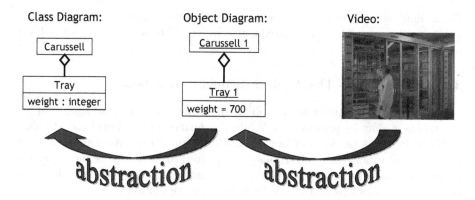

Fig. 3. Slide of lecture Softwareentwurf

be encoded in a number of ways in a UML diagram. Elements of the problem domain can for instance become classes of their own or they may become part of another class as its attributes. Structural relations can be encoded as object-valued attributes, associations, association classes or classes representing the relation explicitly.

Students need to be provided with a set of guidelines which help them to decide such questions. Scott Ambler's UML Style [2] is a collection of such general modeling guidelines, others are suitable for the didactic context only. For instance, we explicitly interdict object-valued attributes since the elicitation of domain structures and their visual representation are the main purpose of the domain model and using object-valued attributes defies this purpose. However, such rules can only be guidelines and students often feel very uncomfortable in facing the unavoidable ambiguities in building abstractions.

3.2 Separation of Concerns - The Business Activities

The documentation of the problem domain also covers the description of important business processes. This is the second modeling perspective of the software's context description and it is separated from the domain model as another concern. While the domain model represents the structure of the problem domain, the business process model describes the relevant behavior. We use UML activity diagrams to represent the business processes.

The hard part here is once again not the UML syntax (which is fairly easy for basic activity diagrams) but realizing what to model. In the domain model we forced students to concentrate on the structural aspect only. Now, only activities are in the focus of the model. It is often surprising for students that the same domain descriptions which already yielded a detailed domain model also contain the information to build an equally detailed process model which is (at least notationally) completely independent from the domain model. The realization of multiple aspects which transcend most problem situations is very important as it allows for immense reduction in problem complexity. Structure and behavior are actually an easy case as they are intuitively orthogonal, later phases in the process will pose much closer related concerns (e.g., inter-object and intra-object behavior).

3.3 OO at Work - The Analysis Sequence Diagram

Moving from the requirements specification to the analysis phase again implies a significant shift in perspective. While the former phase forces the students to think in terms of the problem domain only and discourages all premature notions of solutions, the analysis phase works towards shaping a solution for the given problem. This entails a number of different concepts which coincide in the central diagram of this phase: the analysis sequence diagram.

The first concept that underlies this diagram is *integration*. Following the object-oriented paradigm of integration of structure and behavior, the different concerns of the requirements specification need to be brought together in a meaningful way. In addition, we need to account for the overall structure of the chosen architecture.

Another underlying principle of analysis is *decomposition*: the responsibilities of the software system are partitioned among interacting objects. This relates to architecture again. For example, following a three-layer architecture we can distinguish between Entity, Boundary, and Control classes (as introduced in the Unified Process [7]). Entity classes are derived from the domain model, Control classes represent the execution of product functions (modeled as use cases in the requirements specification), and Boundary classes encapsulate the communication with external entities. The interaction between these objects is depicted by a sequence diagram.

Building the analysis sequence diagram forces students to recall the basic principles of object-orientation. Distributed data and localized behavior on this data are principles which lead them to a suitable solution. In each step of the construction, one needs to decide which step in the overall task is to be carried out next, which object is best suited to carry out this task, and how can this object be accessed from the current object. Even though the students should be aware of these principles from previous courses, applying them in this abstract fashion is rather challenging.

A further complication is that-at this point of the course-students have become rather familiar with thinking in terms of the type level, i.e., classes. Analyzing a single scenario with a sequence diagram forces them to work on the instance level again. The ability to mentally switch between these levels seamlessly is a very important capability for a software engineer. To quote Donald Knuth on this: *"Computer scientists see things simultaneously at the low level and the high level"* [14].

The overall effort for students to cope with tying information from three different sources together and eliciting new structures under the OO paradigm is very high. Again, not a unique diagram can be designated to be the only correct solution for a given problem, there is rather a space of equivalent acceptable solutions, differing in the level of detail or in some decisions taken.

3.4   Refinement - How Class Diagrams Change

As emphasized in the last section, analysis works along the scenarios of the system on the instance level. The information distributed over the various analysis sequence diagrams needs to undergo a *synthesis* into a single diagram. For this purpose we use the analysis class diagram. Information regarding objects, their operations and properties are collected from the sequence diagrams and combined in a class diagram. Especially the derivation of associations is not straightforward as associations denote a permanent relationship between objects of two classes (in contrast to temporary relationships by parameter or result passing). Whether an established relationship is permanent can only be decided by taking *all* sequence diagrams into account, i.e., we have a global criterion.

Up to this point in the course, the students could identify UML notations and their purpose by their use in the process. The analysis class diagram breaks this mapping up as its intention differs significantly from that of the domain model, even though both employ the notation of a UML class diagram. Eliciting the connections and distinctions between these two kinds of class diagrams gives rise to the notion of *refinement*. The refinement notion in this case is that classes of the domain model that are not used in an analysis sequence diagram will not appear in the analysis class diagram; classes that are used might be extended with new information. The classes conceived during the analysis phase (Control and Boundary classes) and their relationships are added, and operations and navigation directions of associations can now be used. Later in the process, a further class diagram will be introduced for gathering the results of the design phase. With this overloading of the class diagram notation, the students realize that modeling notations can be used in a number of contexts and that knowledge about the context is essential for their interpretation.

3.5   A Different Perspective - Statecharts

Introducing the statechart notation during the design phase enforces once more a change of perspective. While sequence diagrams depict system behavior in terms of object interaction, statecharts concentrate on invocation sequences on a single object. These two views on object behavior have close connections, thus the problem of *consistency* needs to be addressed. In the Softwareentwurf course, we use statecharts in the sense of protocol statecharts, i.e., every invocation sequence on an object in a sequence diagram must be permitted by the transitions of the statechart of the object's class. This notion of consistency facilitates the construction of statecharts from sequence diagrams and vice versa.

3.6   Summary

In this section we have shown how teaching the different diagrams of UML in the context of a software development process can demonstrate a number of fundamental concepts related to abstraction. If students understand these concepts, they acquire knowledge which is neither bound to our particular instance of a process, nor to the use of UML as a modeling notation (as, e.g., pointed out in [3]). Using models in this way is not without its problems, however. As emphasized above, the necessary creativity and ambiguity in finding the 'right' abstraction is an uncomfortable process for students. Keeping track of the different relations between the produced diagrams is also challenging. For these and other problems, practical measures need to be taken to actually achieve the course's goals. The next section is devoted to such more practical teaching concepts.

4   Getting the Show on the Road - Didactics, Exercises, Tools and Tricks

Planning an educational course has a strategic as well as a tactical level. On the strategic level, the learning targets are determined and the general structure of the course is derived from them. This has been covered in the previous section. On the tactical level, one needs to address the more detailed issues of how to realize the strategies in a successful way. While general didactic principles can often be applied here, we are aware of a number of issues which are rather specific for the teaching of UML as we perform it. In this section we highlight four of these specific issues and outline our solutions for them.

4.1   Feigning Incompetence for Requirements Capture - The Use of Multimedia

In teaching requirements engineering, we can identify an inherent obstacle. Most of the problems in gathering the requirements stem from the fact that the requirements are formulated and posed by persons who are unfamiliar with the process of requirements capture, have no knowledge of the technical terminology used in computer science, and cannot distinguish requirements towards a software system from the working context surrounding it. There is furthermore the problem that the input is typically incomplete and can even be contradictory if multiple stakeholders have been interviewed.

Good software engineering teachers, however, are always trying to present consistent, precise and complete information to their students. They are aware of the technological terms and automatically categorize information according to their knowledge. If such teachers do now try to present a requirements engineering problem, they will find it very hard, if not impossible, to keep this knowledge from influencing the presentation in a way as to give students hints on the solution of the problem. In other words, it is impossible for them to feign the required incompetence.

For instance, consider most textbook examples for descriptions underlying the construction of class diagrams (exceptions notwithstanding). The text usually comprises clear entities with elaborated relationships. ("An elevator serves a number of floors. Each elevator has a maximal load capacity. On each floor there is one calling button.") Expressing this information in the form of a UML class diagram can be no more than a simple translation and is not necessarily modeling. All necessary abstractions have been already made by formulating the text.

A possible solution for this dilemma is the use of video techniques. By relying on an external medium for the presentation of the problem domain, the lecturer can be sure that no solution hints slip into the presentation. This effect is maximized if videos can be obtained from external sources which are not influenced by the intentions of requirements engineering. Thus the influence of the lecturer is eliminated from both the production and the presentation of the example.

A video does furthermore present the full complexity of realistic work surroundings and the activities carried out there. To handle this audiovisual complexity, to avoid information overload, and to form the right abstractions are important parts of requirements engineering. If the problem domain is presented by a text instead of a video, this complexity is vastly reduced.

In our Softwareentwurf course, we make heavily use of video techniques to present concrete and realistic problem domains with a sufficient complexity. For example, we were able to obtain a video from a machine manufacturer (originally intended for marketing purposes) which describes the operations of an automated storage system for a hospital. We use this video in the lecture to present the domain as a foundation for the domain and business models (cf. Sect. 3.1 and 3.2).

4.2   Listening Is Not Nearly Enough - Exercises and Examples

A central problem of teaching modeling (and thus abstraction) is that the process of abstraction cannot be formalized, but relies on creativity and intuition. Consequently, no unique model can be designated in practice as the optimal abstraction for a given problem, but there is rather a space of good solutions. Building abstractions can thus not be learned by following a deterministic recipe. It rather requires a certain skill and intuition to detect relevant information, settle on the correct level of abstraction, and choose adequate representations for the information. Such skills cannot be effectively taught in lectures. They have to be based on experience (see also [4]). Thus, exercises are absolutely crucial for the teaching of modeling.

In the Softwareentwurf course we employ two different kinds of exercises: group sessions where the students solve small problems in teams under the guidance of a tutor and home exercises where the students have to tackle more complex assignments over the course of a week. Especially for the (unguided) home exercises, it is essential to provide examples which are complex enough to actually allow for non-trivial abstractions, but which also have enough limitations to prevent students from getting lost in the task. We found board games to be a very good domain for such examples. Board games comprise domain structures and business processes (game rules) which are partially documented in the instructions and can partially be elicited by actually playing the game. Especially this hands-on experience allows the students to engage in much more detailed discussion on the relevance of certain elements. Disagreement in interpreting rules gives rise to sometimes rather different models and sparks debates on the comparability of different solutions. Board games also have a reduced complexity, clear context delimitations, and a high motivational factor for students. A rich variety of examples ranging from the very simple to the very complex can be gained from this general domain.

4.3   Modeling at Hand - How Tools Can Help

Employing modeling tools in the educational setting comprises advantages and disadvantages which need to be carefully weighted. Advantages are that (1) modeling tools allow for incremental development of complex models, (2) changes are facilitated easily, and (3) the resulting models are not only cleaner than many scribbled paper-and-pen solutions, but also better thought out as students are unburdened from looking up notations and can concentrate on the content of the model rather than its form. Experience with modeling tools is also a benefit for students who start working in industry after their graduation.

Unfortunately, modeling tools typically used in industry, such as IBM's Rational Rose or Borland's Together, have significant drawbacks when applied in an educational setting. These drawbacks stem from the fact that professional modeling tools are rather *heavyweight* pieces of software in several aspects. From an organizational point of view, licensing and cost questions need to be addressed as well as support for their installation and operation (in the rather diverse configurations of the students' computers).

Other issues stem from the didactical point of view: the tools' user interfaces are quite complex and their rich set of features can distract inexperienced users. Using such tools entails the risk that the students concentrate on the tool usage rather than the particular modeling exercise. Additionally, confusion arises if the

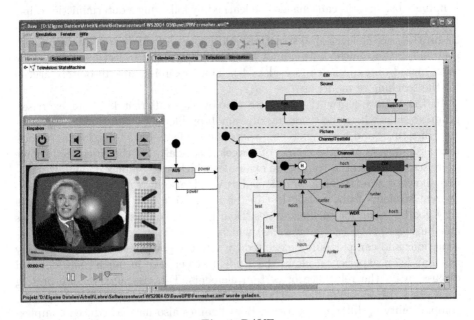

Fig. 4. DAVE

modeling tools do not follow the standard UML notation (e.g. great variety can be observed in displaying an association's reading direction).

Heavyweight tools furthermore enforce certain consistency notions in the models, for example object diagrams can only be drawn if an according class diagram is present. The consistency in this case is intended for enabling automatic code generation and does not necessarily conform to the notions of consistency that we introduce in the lecture.

For educational purposes it is desirable to have rather *lightweight* tools that allow the students to concentrate on modeling instead of tool handling. The Dortmund Automaton Visualizer and Editor (DAVE) [13] developed in the eLearning project MuSofT [1] is such a lightweight tool for modeling statecharts. A screenshot of this tool is displayed in Figure 4.

Explicitly designed for eLearning purposes, DAVE not only supports the modeling of statecharts, but also includes a simulation engine. Students can thus get direct feedback on the semantics of their models when they are doing their homework. We observed a significant improvement of the students' understanding of statecharts due to the adoption of DAVE in the exercises while the organizational effort was reasonable.

4.4 Holding Things Together - On the Importance of Documents

From previous courses we knew that the students had huge problems with the large amount of different UML notations and their application in a software development process. Diagrams were regarded as separate entities and their interrelations were not comprehended by the students.

As a remedy for this problem, we introduced documents as a further structuring means in our process. The main idea of this document-centric approach is that documents incorporate the different diagrams of a development phase, thus clarifying their relations. We designed templates for the documents which do not only predefine the structure, but also provide guidelines for constructing the models and ensuring their consistency. Document templates are complemented by review guidelines and checklists in order to let the students review and improve the quality of their respective documents. The document structure is also used in guiding the lecture, thus students have now an improved understanding about where to apply which technique (according to our empirical evaluations, the number of students who reported problems with the mapping of lecture and exercise topics was reduced by 70%).

5 Findings

Taking one's own medicine is always bitter. As the students need time to learn the abstract concepts behind software engineering, we needed time to recognize the abstract concepts behind our teaching of UML as well. The current form of the Softwareentwurf course as presented in this paper is the result of 7 years of teaching UML to more than 2000 students. The process of reflection upon our teaching was fueled and guided by closely monitoring our recipients, the students. This monitoring included direct feedback from the students collected, e.g., by questionnaires as well as our examination of their performance. Obtaining meaningful quantified evaluation results has proven to be hard as different student groups were exposed to multiple different factors which cannot be reliably separated (e.g., changes in the overall curriculum, lecture times, lecturers, examples used etc.).

More important than our own judgement of our teaching success is the fact how well our course prepares the students for the challenges ahead of them, i.e., the lab course and the internship. By using video observations of software development teams in the lab course we could ascertain that the students followed the structured development process that we taught and used the UML diagrams accordingly. When faced with new requirements (in the lab course they have to extend an existing system [5], thus use re-engineering techniques) they were able to adopt the process and the documents and showed (sometimes surprisingly good) ideas how to employ UML diagrams for this new task. We see this flexible handling as an indication that the students' understanding does indeed transcend the concrete notations and methodology that we teach them and extends to the concepts behind it. It is this understanding of principles which will be most beneficial for CS students in the long term, whether they choose to continue with the Master program or begin a career in industry.

6   Conclusions

In this paper we have argued that—from an educational perspective—UML is not "just another modeling notation", but an excellent vehicle to demonstrate some of the very core principles behind computer science in general and software engineering in particular. Our Softwareentwurf course implements this idea of combining the usually competing goals of eliciting abstract concepts and training practical skills. In our experience, the combination of these goals is beneficial for learning and acquiring both concepts and skills since the abstract concepts become more tangible and the practical skills become more transferable by this combination.

For educators who teach UML and software engineering, we hope to have provided some new insights on the strategic and some useful tips for the tactical planning of their own course.

References

1. Klaus Alfert, Ernst-Erich Doberkat, Gregor Engels, Marc Lohmann, Johannes Magenheim, and Andy Schürr. MuSoft: Multimedia in der Softwaretechnik. In *Software Engineering im Unterricht der Hochschulen*, pages 70–80. dpunkt Verlag, 2003.
2. Scott W. Ambler. *The Elements of UML Style*. Cambridge University Press, New York, NY, USA, 2002.
3. Kim Bruce. Thoughts on computer science education. *ACM Computing Surveys*, 28(4es):93, 1996.

4. Philip J. Burton and Russel E. Bruhn. Using UML to facilitate the teaching of object-oriented systems analysis and design. *Journal of Computing Sciences in Colleges*, 19(3):278–290, 2004.
5. Matthias Gehrke, Holger Giese, Ulrich A. Nickel, Jörg Niere, Matthias Tichy, Jörg P. Wadsack, and Albert Zündorf. Reporting about industrial strength software engineering courses for undergraduates. In *ICSE '02: Proceedings of the 24th International Conference on Software Engineering*, pages 395–405, New York, NY, USA, 2002. ACM Press.
6. C.A.R Hoare. Notes on data structuring. In O.-J. Dahl, E. W. Dijkstra, and C. A. R. Hoare, editors, *Structured Programming*, pages 83–174. Academic Press, 1972.
7. Ivar Jacobson, Grady Booch, and James Rumbaugh. *The Unified Software Development Process*. Addison-Wesley Longman Publishing Co., Inc., Boston, MA, USA, 1999.
8. Jeff Kramer. Abstraction - is it teachable? 'The Devil is in the Detail'. In *CSEE&T*, page 32. IEEE Computer Society, 2003.
9. Thomas Kuehne. What is a model? In Jean Bezivin and Reiko Heckel, editors, *Language Engineering for Model-Driven Software Development*, number 04101 in Dagstuhl Seminar Proceedings. Internationales Begegnungs- und Forschungszentrum (IBFI), Schloss Dagstuhl, Germany, 2005. http://drops.dagstuhl.de/opus/volltexte/2005/23.
10. Object Management Group. UML 2.0 Superstructure- Public Specification-. OMG document formal/05-07-04, August 2005.
11. The Joint Task Force on Computing Curricula. Computing curricula 2001 computer science - final report. IEEE Computer Society, Association for Computing Machinery http://www.sigcse.org/cc2001/, 2001.
12. The Joint Task Force on Computing Curricula. Software engineering 2004 curriculum guidelines for undergraduate degree programs in software engineering: A volume of the computing curricula series. http://sites.computer.org/ccse/, 2004.
13. Jörg Pleumann. Erfahrungen mit dem multimedialen, didaktischen Modellierungswerkzeug DAVE. In Gregor Engels and Silke Seehusen, editors, *DeLFI 2004: Die e-Learning Fachtagung Informatik, Tagung der Fachgruppe e-Learning der Gesellschaft für Informatik e.V. (GI) 6.-8. September 2004 in Paderborn*, volume 52 of *LNI*, pages 55–66. GI, 2004.
14. Jack J. Woehr. An interview with Donald Knuth. *Dr. Dobb's Journal of Software Tools*, 21(4), April 1996.

Best Practices for Teaching UML Based Software Development

Ludwik Kuzniarz and Miroslaw Staron

School of Engineering, Blekinge Institute of Technology,
Ronneby, Sweden
{Ludwik.Kuzniarz, Miroslaw.Staron}@bth.se

Abstract. Software development is the core activity performed within software engineering. The Unified Modelling Language (UML) has become a de facto standard language for expressing artefacts used and produced within software development process. As a result of that there is an expanding activity related to teaching the process of software development and the language at both higher education institutions and in software industry. The aim of the education in UML is to prepare software developers to effectively use UML and modelling at their work. Therefore guidelines on a proper way of teaching and learning processes and notations are foreseen. The paper elaborates on experiences and lessons learned from the course on UML based software development delivered as part of software engineering curriculum. In the paper we identify a set of best practices for teaching modelling and UML. The best practices are based on the experiences gathered from multiple course deliveries over a period of five years.

1 Introduction

Since its formal introduction *object oriented software development* (OOSD) has been widely adopted by both researchers and practitioners. At early stages the effective application of OOSD was limited by the lack of proper notation for expressing the artefacts used and produced throughout the OOSD process. To address this difficulty the Unified Modelling Language (UML, [1]) has been introduced. The language has been gaining wide acceptance and became de facto standard modelling language used within OOSD due to its generality, standardization and growing tool support.

Development teams in software industry use UML based OOSD approach due to the eminent advantages of visual modelling. The usage poses a requirement that the developers should be educated or trained both in OOSD and UML. To meet the demands education curricula at higher education institutions have been modified and updated. A number of OOSD and UML retraining courses are being developed and delivered. In order for the courses to focus on effective, holistic and deep student learning [2, 3] such courses should be well designed and executed. Furthermore, they should meet "local" constrains such as background and experience of participants as there are indications that (especially in the case of commercial retraining courses in industry) many individuals attend such courses just to find out that the benefits from participation are rather limited. These were basically caused by the fact that the courses were not properly designed and conducted.

J.-M. Bruel (Ed.): MoDELS 2005 Workshops, LNCS 3844, pp. 320–332, 2006.
© Springer-Verlag Berlin Heidelberg 2006

We identified a target reader of this paper as a teacher and practitioner who wants to teach UML based software development in a modern, proper and effective way, to design and to deliver an appropriate course. The research question considered in this paper is: *how to teach both UML and OOSD to novice and experienced developers?* As an answer to the research question we formulate eight good practices on how to develop an OOSD with UML course based on our experiences gained form delivering such a course at Blekinge Institute of Technology (BTH) and from the needs identified at our research contacts in industry.

The paper is organized as follows. First, we present the most relevant related work in the field in Section 2. In Section 3 we present the context in which the course has been developed and delivered. The context is considered in the subsequent section where we present best practices that we identified. Each identified practice is formulated as a general statement followed by a reference to the course with comments how it has been identified and used. Finally, in the last section we re-examine the practices and underline special role some of them play.

2 Related Work

The issues of teaching modelling for students is also discussed in [4]. The author of that paper show how graph theory formalisms can be used to teach modelling (using UML as an example) in graduate level courses. Although using graph theory in teaching could be perceived as a best practice, the authors do not consider the semantics of the graph structures and therefore introduce the danger of teaching modelling on a different level of abstraction than required in industry.

The issues related to teaching software development process in courses containing projects was already discussed in [5]. In this paper we support the claims of the author of that paper that teaching software processes should be done in courses which contain project activities.

One of the issues which we consider in this paper is using students as subjects in software engineering experiments. The issues related to that are presented in [6]. The authors of that paper show the challenges in considering different perspectives (teacher's, experimenter's and student's) while performing experiments with students. We used their experiences in our work which led to identification of this particular best practice (c.f. [7]).

A set of good practices related to introducing experiments to curricula in software engineering can be found in [8]. We used these practices in the course of considering whether experimentation is a good practice.

3 Software Development Course

Basic idea behind the Software Engineering (SE) curriculum at BTH is to prepare the graduates to be able to develop software systems in a professional way according to recent developments in software engineering technology. Our OOSD course [9] is a basic course in SE curriculum at BTH. Other courses (including projects which students do with industrial partners during their third year of study) require knowledge that the students are supposed to gain in this course. Thus one of the primary demands for the course is that it should be up-to-date – with respect to contents and the teaching process. Another demand is that it should be complementary with other courses within the entire program.

3.1 Overview of the Course

The course is given primarily for the first year students of the SE program but is also accessible for the students of other programs. The prerequisite to the course are the basic skills in object oriented programming. The objective of the course is provide the student with the knowledge and skills to perceive and solve problems in a systematic way utilizing the object-oriented paradigm; particularly using models expressed in UML as core development assets. It was desired that after completing the course the student will have knowledge and skills to be able to apply object oriented approach to the construction of software using UML as a modelling language and appropriate modelling tool. In particular to analyze the problem, design a logical solution and implement it. The focus in the course is put on awareness of development process and on proper and effective usage of models in order to create the working software product.

3.2 Structure of the Course

The course consists of the following study activities: lectures, exercises, labs and projects. Lectures are the source of information on the notions, techniques and processes related to the subject while exercises are a forum for discussion on concrete issues related to the topics covered on lectures. There is a strict mutual dependency between those two study activities. Students are given a set of small problems, have a chance to present their solutions, and have comments on them. The questions are followed by a general discussion on the possible approaches to solve the issues, their advantages and drawbacks. During labs which are placed in computer rooms student can get acquaintance with UML tools and have the possibility to get assistance from teachers on his/her individual project. Labs are assisted by a teacher who helps the student with technical problems concerning the functionality of the tool and with the problems related to performing the task for the project. During the project the student is supposed to develop a small size system using the process presented during the lectures.

The course is delivered as 5 study points course what means that participants are supposed to spend approximately 200 hours on it (i.e. equivalent to five weeks full time work). This influenced the overall work load assigned to the course activities and influenced the scope of the project. The task for the project is to develop a small size system. The development is structured into two interactions. In the first iteration a (simple) basic version of the system is to be developed while the task for the second is to create an extended version. Within iterations the development process introduced on the lectures has to be followed. Students produce a set of artefacts grouped into design report which are handed to the teacher for inspection, comments and correction. The teacher also plays the role of customer who wants the student to "produce" software that will fulfil his needs. Each student receives initial description of the problem (a simple requirements specification) and then requests a meeting with the customer if something seems unclear and needs to be discussed.

It was found that the having two iterations in the project was very important. In the first iteration students usually make many errors; they try to make short-cuts. But it is in a way desired that they learn on their mistakes. And in fact the second iteration goes rather smoothly and they see the advantages and profits from following the development process.

The organization of the course consists of several activities which are intertwined and should be considered together. These are presented in Table 1.

Table 1. Activities in the course

Activity	Units	Description	Aim
Lecture (L)	12	Provide theory to be applied during exercises and labs.	Provide material and information to be used in other activities.
Exercise (E)	5	Tutorial-like exercises–discussion on small problems related to lectures	Highlight issues from lectures on practical problems.
Lab (P)	5 (4+1) 1	Time for students own work on practical task – a mini project.	Provide assistance for students doing the projects
Report (R)	5 (4+1)	Deliveries of lab reports–each group have fixed time for individual comments	Provide students with individual feedback on their projects.

Each of the activities is aimed at different purposes. Lectures are mostly aimed at transmitting knowledge, while exercises and labs are focused on providing the students with the possibility to use the knowledge in practice. The way in which material is lectured and subsequently used during exercises determines the sequencing of the activities. The basic material is provided during the first lectures before any other form of exercises. Sequencing of the activities is shown in Table 2.

In principle the practical exercises and labs are given every other week so that the students have enough time to solve the problems, read upon them and, if necessary, turn for help to teachers.

The remarks on the course that have been made so far can be considered as a preliminary overall best practice which we have identified. It relates to the overall design of the course so that it meets the requirements and ensures proper quality of education and basically relate to any course. Further, more specific best practices are in the subsequent section.

---

[1] Four mandatory moments and one additional for high pass.

Table 2. Sequence of activities in the course

Week	Sequence	Comment
1	L1 – L3	L1-L3 cover material for Ex1, La1
2	E1, P1, L4 – L7	L4 – L7 cover material for E2 & P2
3	R1, E2, P2	R1 needs to be before star-ting next exercises and labs.
4	L8 – L10	Lectures cover material required for E3, P3, E4, P4
5	R2, E3, P3	
6	L11	Summary
7	R3, E4, P4, L12	
8	R4, E5, P5	
9	R5	

4 Best Practices

The course introduced in the previous sections has been delivered for five years. Initial course was based on overall requirements for the course from the curriculum but it has been constantly modified and adjusted based on the experiences from the course activities, observations, feedback from the participants, and our experience from researching in the UML-related topics. The best practices are intended to answer the questions what can be considered and taken into account when designing a course on UML based software development or for improving of the existing such a course.

4.1 Tailoring of Development Process

Standard development processes introduced and advocated by organizations or method specialists experts, due to their wide applicability, can be considered rather as frameworks to be instantiated in a particular environment. Moreover, they are not suitable for direct usage on introductory courses. So proper instantiation (or tailoring) of them is necessary. As a matter of fact, what we found more appropriate, a special dedicated development process for the course should be developed. Such a process should take into account the knowledge of participants, placement of the course in the context – education curriculum at academia or local environment of a company, course restrictions and format as well as requirements from real developments processes the participants are already familiar with.

In the case of the OOSD course at BTH a special didactic process named Sample Development Process has been elaborated. The created process is based on the recommendations from standards - Unified Software Development Process (USDP) [10, 11] and Rational Unified Process [12-14]. The idea behind the student oriented process was to extract key ideas preserving the "spirit" of the standard processes and focus on the basic ideas thus minimizing the burden of learning the rest for students. The approach is in line with (and in particular was stimulated by) other texts on USDP [15-20] which attempt to give a "light" introduction to USDP. Our tailored process has the following characteristics:

- It is iterative – it is arranged as a sequence of iterations (arranged by use cases),
- It is incremental – within each iteration a working version of the system is produced,
- It is UML-based – all major artefacts are expressed in UML.
- It is use case driven - iterations are supposed to produce a system realizing a set of use cases.

The process is arranged as a sequence of iterations. The goal of each iteration is to produce a working version of the system. During each iteration there are sequences of development phases and within each phase a number of artefacts are produced. The details of the process can be found in [17] when the activities and their relationships are discussed in more detail.

4.2   Defined Artefacts and Creation Procedures

All development activities are aimed at producing a set of artefacts based on already existing artefacts. One of the basic questions that are to be answered by a specific development process is what artefacts and in what sequence should be created. Definition of artefacts together with their purpose and mutual relationships is a starting point.

In the process that was designed for the course the following artefacts were defined:

- Use Case Diagram – for providing a graphical representation of the functionality of the system, relationships between functionalities and actors interacting with the system,
- Use Case Description – for description of the interaction between the system and the actor that uses the system,
- Domain/Conceptual Model – for presenting the concepts from the problem domain important from the perspective of the developed system,
- System Sequence Diagram – for specification of the steps identified in the use case description expressed as messages exchanged between the actors and the system,
- Contract for System Operation – for specification of the operations that model messages, which later serves as a specification of the interface of the system,
- Interaction Diagram for System Operation - for specification of a collaboration that provides functionality of a given system operation.
- Design Class Diagram – for defining the static view of the system which includes classes used to implement the functionality in the context of a solution domain (i.e. programming language),
- State Diagram for a design class – for presenting the behaviour of the design class (produced for a class having non-trivial state machines).

These artefacts are produced in a certain order and are mutually dependent and influential. Fig. 1 presents the sequencing of the artefacts within a single iteration. Unidirectional arrows indicate the sequence of creation of artefacts; bidirectional arrows indicate that the artefacts should be updated continuously based on each other.

These artefacts are produced in a certain order and are mutually dependent and influential. Fig. 1 presents the sequencing of the artefacts within a single iteration. Unidirectional arrows indicate the sequence of creation of artefacts; bidirectional arrows indicate that the artefacts should be updated continuously based on each other.

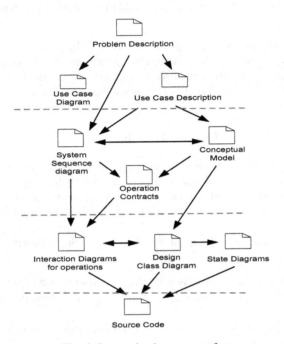

Fig. 1. Sequencing between artefacts

In the lecture and further in the project activities we stress the understanding of the role of the artefact in the process, how it contributes in achieving the final goal which we found to be of substantial help in learning of the development process.

4.3 Consistency Awareness and Management

Artefacts produced in the development process describe properties of the "things involved" – both from real world and the software. An important property of all the artefacts should be that they are mutually consistent. Basically it means that properties of a "thing" – modelling element - expressed on one artefact should not contradict the properties of the properties of the same "thing" expressed on another artefact. Consistency is about mutual relationship, agreement and logical consequence among all the artefacts used and produced within a development process. Consistency should be explicitly introduced. Proper sequencing of the artefacts is important from the perspective of consistency between artefacts. We introduce the notion of consistency in our process based on the relationships between artefacts shown on Figure 1. Each artefact should be consistent with its predecessors and successors. Some even informal rules at least for checking consistency should be introduced. It would be beneficial if some advice on how to create new artefact such that it remains consistent with the existing artefact could be formulated.

A number of consistency rules are formulated and used throughout our sample process. Here is a sample of pairs of categories of artefacts and example checks:

- Use case description and system sequence diagram: each step in a use case description should have a corresponding message in the system sequence diagram for this use case,
- System sequence diagram and conceptual model: messages (modelled as system operations) used in System Sequence Diagram should be defined for the class encapsulating the system in the Conceptual Model,
- Contracts and Conceptual Model: elements used in the pre and post conditions of the contracts should be defined in the conceptual model (contracts should be defined in the context of conceptual model),
- Interaction diagram for operation and design class diagram: links used in the interaction diagrams should be instances of the existing associations defined in the design class diagram,
- State diagrams and interaction diagram for operation: the sequence of messages that is defined for the interaction diagram for the operation in interaction diagram should be a subsequence of a sequence of messages acceptable by state machines for classes that take part in this interaction.

Awareness of preserving consistency between artefacts is of high importance from the practical point of view. If there are some inconsistencies in the design then sooner or later they will be revealed – most likely by programmers implementing the design, during tests or in the worst case while using the system – and the later the more serious consequences could be. So development process should include elements relating to checking consistency and ensuring consistency. At present this is mainly manual activity but to be really effective extensive tool support would be required based on formalization of the consistency rules.

4.4 Effective Usage of Models and Modelling

In every software development activity, the main goal of the development process is running code. The question of how to achieve that goal in a safe and effective way should be posed and answered during the course. The answer should be in a development process. We advocate and show that modelling is a proper way to achieve that goal and models are proper means to produce the code in an effective and safe way. We show that models in the process are used for different purposes – for improving understanding the problem and the solution as well as precise specification of the code which has to be produced. The purposes of the models dictate the elements (e.g. diagrams and elements presented in them) which should be used in models. The intention is to show that we model *all that we need but nothing less* (i.e. we advocate the Occam's razor principle). The students learn that models serve a purpose deeper than just documentation. All models must lead to final product – working version of the system. Another principle that the students learn is that *if the model is not used anywhere, it should not be created.*

We also show what support for the creation and maintenance of models can be obtained from a modelling tool in order to improve efficiency of modelling. Finally try to show the students by indicating and discussing errors in their design the value of abstraction and separation of concerns in early detection of pitfalls that otherwise would lead to serious implementation problems. We encourage students also to use the tool for performing simulation on models which will allow for earlier error detection and also to generate as much source code as possible (not only the "skeleton" code). For that reason we tested and evaluated tools from two different vendors and chose the one which had better fitted the course – had better support for creation and maintenance of the set of artefacts that are used in the sample development process. Therefore the tool can be said to be specifically chosen by the participants as the tool which provides the best help in their learning process. The evaluation relates to another best practice – experiments in the course.

4.4 Constant Feedback from Participants

In order for the course to be effective it requires to be delivered on the right level – the level that the participants of the course can comprehend – and on the right pace – the task that participants have to perform should be manageable. Both of those elements should be estimated when creating the course and later adjusted. The adjustment should be based on the feedback during the course – on the observations made on the understanding of the delivered material and progress of work within course activities as well as on discussion and suggestions from the participant during the course evaluation meeting. We found out that two such meetings are useful. The first takes place after first few course activities – and this allows to introduce "on the fly" necessary urgent improvements specific to the particular course group - if needed, while the second takes place after the course when more deep evaluation of the course and suggestion for future realizes is discussed. Exercises we have on the course play also an important role. During the discussion on the small problem we gave to the students it was possible to find out what particular problems the students of the particular edition of the course have and to adopt appropriately the lectures.

4.5 Industrial and Professional Relevance

Providing Industrial relevance is an important factor that should be taken into account when designing the course [21].

First, the participants should be prepared for real-world software development in industry. Second, the professionals in industry should be able to utilize the knowledge of new technologies that is introduced into companies with newly graduated employees. Thus the content of the course should be relevant for the industry. In particular, the problems that are lectured on the course should be *relevant* – i.e. similar to real-world problems – whenever possible. This situation is presented in Figure 2.

For example in the case of our course it was found that if the models are to be used effectively for code generation the code generation process needs to be well understood by developers. Therefore a lot of effort has been put on making the students aware of how the tool generates the source code from their models. For example the subjects used during exercises are also inspired by the needs identified in our industrial case studies (e.g. [22]).

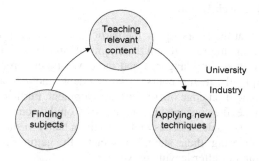

Fig. 2. Industrial coupling of the course

4.6 Conducting Experiments During the Course

A recent best practice which we identified and introduced in last three course deliveries was the conduction of experiments related to research carried out at the software engineering research lab at BTH. The experiments are aimed at evaluating usability of certain constructs in UML (namely stereotypes) for increasing understanding of UML models and thus improving quality of models [23]. The experiments are not mandatory for the course but they usually attract almost all students since the experiments:

- allow students experience new modelling elements in UML designs which are not lectured on the course,
- provide students with basic experience in empirical methods in software engineering (these methods are then required from the during their master year),
- stimulate the interest of students on practical issues related to using models in industry (since the experiments are aimed at evaluation of stereotypes from the perspective of their usage in industry; the experiment was also replicated in industry [24]),
- stimulate their interest in the subject since similar problems that are the object of the experiment appear also as examination questions, and
- give them feeling of contribution to the research carried out at their university which is appreciated by them.

Although there are some costs (from students' perspective) of taking part in the experiment the benefits are obvious and usually result in increased learning outcome – students are better motivated to study and as a consequence better prepared for the examination in the end.

Another example of experiment which was conducted during the course was an empirical comparison of two UML tools. One of the tools was later adopted for usage in the course – Telelogic Tau G2 [25]. Yet another experiment we performed was a comparison of performance of C++ and Java programmers in the context of manual translation of a toy-size design into source code. In that case students had real influence on the course as the choice was based on objective measured performance and subjective opinions.

4.7 Transfer of Research Results

It is also important that the course gives the participant awareness and raises interest of new upcoming technologies or recent developments in the area. In the case of this course it is both the modelling language and the development process. Using recent research results explicitly in the course gives students motivation that they learn things which are on the front edge of software development. Furthermore, since this is the introductory course, the concepts that are lectured on the course might be adopted by the time the students graduate. Thus motivates them better to study as they see it as a possibility of increasing their status in society by getting chances for better employment opportunities after leaving university.

We use the results of our research as part of the course content – i.e. we transfer experiences from research to education. In our course we introduced proper and effective usage of advanced UML elements based on our empirical studies – for instance where and how introduce stereotypes, how they can help, what benefits can be obtained (transferred from [23, 24]). Another example is a more efficient and advanced (or non–standard) usage of capabilities included in modelling tools – we encouraged only using them as much more than diagram editors - as model management environments. We encourage students to create automatically various artefacts using our custom add-ins to the tool in compliance with the emerging ideas of Model Driven Software Architecture (e.g. [26, 27]) inspired by our recent research results in it.

5 Conclusions

The research presented in this paper was motivated by increasing popularity of both object oriented software development paradigm and the usage of UML in the course of software development processes. It is a contribution to the discussion on how UML and modelling should be introduced to the developers. The paper starts with presentation of teaching of UML based software development at Blekinge Institute of Technology. It presents lessons learned during multiple deliveries of the course and formulates best practices for creating and conducting of this course. The practices are based on problems encountered and observations made during the course deliveries. The practices are basically of two basic types – pedagogy wise and subject wise. The identified practices address the posed research question – how to teach UML and OOSD. These practices can be used as a basis for formulation of guidelines for construction of dedicated (for a specific audience) courses on the concepts behind UML and software development process. The observations made can be adopted in migration to teaching Model Driven Development (MDD) as these kinds of courses are based on essentially similar principles – extensive usage of models.

Two of the practices are worth to be especially emphasized. The first practice is the consistency between all artefacts in the entire process – introducing the awareness of that, formulating appropriate rules and consequently checking it. Consistency between different models used and produced within software development process is an important relationship between the artefacts as it materializes the statement that all artefacts represent non-contradicting and uniform views of a single system. Consistency checking is also extended to incorporate checking the consistency between requirement specifications and the models.

The second practice is of the pedagogical type and concerns realization of the students' projects. The project should have two iterations – the first is focused solely on learning, quite often on the mistakes made, the second is a more mature solution based on experiences gained in the first iteration and aimed at testing the skills and final evaluation of the students.

Our further work includes further research into the practices. In particular we intend to investigate the impact of these practices on students' perception of the course in a qualitative and quantitative ways.

References

1. Object Management Group: Unified Modeling Language Specification: Infrastructure version 2.0. Vol. 2004. Object Management Group (2004)
2. Ramsden, P.: Learning to teach in higher education. RoutledgeFalmer, London ; New York (2003)
3. Prosser, M., Trigwell, K.: Understanding learning and teaching : the experience in higher education. Society for Research into Higher Education & Open University Press, Buckingham [England] ; Philadelphia, PA (1999)
4. Tamai, T.: How to Teach Software Modeling. 27th International Conference on Software Engineering. IEEE, St. Louis, Mo, USA (2005) 609-610
5. Filho, W.P.P.: Process Issues in Course Projects. 27th International Conference on Software Engineering. IEEE, St. Louis, Mo, USA (2005) 629-630
6. Carver, J., Jaccheri, L., Morasca, S., Shull, F.: Issues in Using Students in Empirical Studies in Software Engineering Education. 9th International Software Metrics Symposium. IEEE Computer Society, Sydney, Australia (2003) 239-251
7. Kuzniarz , L., Staron, M., Wohlin, C.: Students as Subjects in Software Engineering Experimentation. Third Conference on Software Engineering Research and Practise in Sweden. Lund Institute of Technology, Lund, Sweden (2003) 19-24
8. Höst, M.: Introducing empirical software engineering methods in education. Software Engineering Education and Training, 2002. (CSEE&T 2002). Proceedings. 15th Conference on (2002) 170-179
9. Kuzniarz , L., Staron, M.: Object-oriented software development. Vol. 2005 (2005)
10. Kruchten, P.: The rational unified process : an introduction. Addison-Wesley, Reading, MA (2000)
11. Kruchten, P.: The rational unified process. Addison-Wesley, Reading, Mass. (1999)
12. Kroll, P., Kruchten, P.: The rational unified process made easy : a practitioner's guide to the RUP. Addison-Wesley, Boston (2003)
13. Larman, C.: Applying UML and patterns: an introduction to object-oriented analysis and design and the unified process. Prentice Hall PTR, Upper Saddle River, NJ (2002)
14. Rational: Rational Unified Process documentation. Vol. 2002. Rational Corp (2000)
15. Robillard, P.N., D'Astous, P., Kruchten, P.: Software engineering process with the UPEDU. Addison Wesley, Boston (2003)

16. Kuzniarz, L., Reggio, G., Sourrouille, J.L., Huzar, Z.: Workshop on Consistency Problems in UML-based Software Development. In: Kuzniarz, L. (ed.): <<UML>> 2002. Blekinge Institute of Technology, Dresden (2002) 1-160
17. Kuzniarz , L., Staron, M.: Inconsistencies in Student Designs. The 2nd Workshop on Consistency Problems in UML-based Software Development. Blekinge Intitute of Technology, San Francisco, CA (2003) 9-18
18. Arlow, J., Neustadt, I.: UML and the unified process : practical object-oriented analysis and design. Addison-Wesley, London ; New York (2002)
19. Favre, L.: UML and the unified process. IRM Press, Hershey, Pa. (2003)
20. Jacobson, I., Booch, G., Rumbaugh, J.: The unified software development process. Addison-Wesley, Reading, Mass (1999)
21. Glass, R.L.: Facts and fallacies of software engineering. Addison-Wesley, Boston, MA (2003)
22. Staron, M., Kuzniarz, L., Wallin, L.: A Case Study On Transformation Focused Industrial MDA Realization. 3rd UML Workshop in Software Model Engineering, Lisbon, Portugal (2004)
23. Kuzniarz, L., Staron, M., Wohlin, C.: An Empirical Study on Using Stereotypes to Improve Understanding of UML Models. The 12th International Workshop on Program Comprehension. IEEE Computer Society, Bari, Italy (2004) 14-23
24. Staron, M., Kuzniarz, L., Wohlin, C.: An Industrial Replication of an Empirical Study on Using Stereotypes To Improve Understanding of UML Models. Software Engineering Research and Practice in Sweden. Department of Computer and Information Science, Linköping, Sweden (2004) 53-62
25. Telelogic: Telelogic Tau G2. Malmo (2004)
26. Mellor, S.J.: MDA distilled : principles of model-driven architecture. Addison-Wesley, Boston (2004)
27. Miller, J., Mukerji, J.: MDA Guide. Vol. 2004. Object Management Group (2003)

MoDELS 2005 Doctoral Symposium Summary

Jeff Gray

University of Alabama at Birmingham,
Department of Computer and Information Sciences,
Birmingham AL 35294, USA
gray@cis.uab.edu

Abstract. The MoDELS Doctoral Symposium brought together nine doctoral students and five mentors to spend a day discussing student research presentations. A truly international representation among students and mentors provided a diverse opportunity to offer suggestions and advice regarding the vision and direction of the student dissertation ideas. This summary offers an overview of the activities that occurred at the Symposium.

1 Introduction

The Doctoral Symposium at the MoDELS conference took place at the Half Moon Resort in Montego Bay, Jamaica, on Tuesday, October 4th 2005. The Symposium provided an international forum for doctoral students to interact with other students and faculty mentors. The Symposium brought together doctoral students working in areas related to modeling and model-driven engineering. Participating students were provided the opportunity to present and to discuss their research goals, methods and results within a constructive and international atmosphere.

The Symposium was intended for students who already settled on a specific research proposal with some preliminary results, but still had enough time remaining before their final defense so that they could benefit from the Symposium discussions. Due to the mentoring aspect of the event, the Symposium was open only to those students and mentors participating directly.

Among the nine students selected to participate in the Symposium, six students offered a formal presentation and three students discussed their work through a poster presentation. The participating students, along with the titles of their presentations and their affiliation, were:

- *Preening: Reflection of Models in the Mirror*
  Nelly Bencomo, Lancaster University, UK
- *Transformation-Based Structure Model Evolution*
  Fabian Büttner, University of Bremen, Germany
- *Software Hazard Analysis for X-By-Wire Applications*
  Erendira Ibarra-Alvarado, University of Sussex, UK
- *Enhancement of Development Technology for Agent-Based Software Engineering*
  Andre Karpištšenko, Talinn Technical University, Estonia

J.-M. Bruel (Ed.): MoDELS 2005 Workshops, LNCS 3844, pp. 333–336, 2006.

- *Aspect-Oriented Modeling Research*
  Mark Mahoney, Illinois Inst. Technology, USA
- *SelfSync: A Dynamic Round-Trip Engineering Environment*
  Ellen Van Paesschen, Vrije Universiteit Brussel, Belgium
- *A Framework for Composable Security Definition, Assurance, and Enforcement*
  Jaime Pavlich-Mariscal, University of Connecticut, USA
- *Ontology-based Model Transformation*
  Stephan Roser, University of Augsburg, Germany
- *Modeling Turnpike: a Model-Driven Framework for Domain-Specific Software Development*
  Hiroshi Wada, U. Massachusetts-Boston, USA

The Symposium organizers worked hard to provide useful guidance for completion of the dissertation research and initiation of a research career. The mentors comprising the organizing committee included the following:

- Aditya Agrawal, MathWorks, USA
- Jean Bézivin, University of Nantes, France
- Betty Cheng, Michigan State University, USA
- Emanuel Grant, University of North Dakota, USA
- (Chair) Jeff Gray, University of Alabama at Birmingham, USA
- Jörg Kienzle, McGill University, Canada
- Ana Moreira, Universidade Nova de Lisboa, Portugal
- Kerry Raymond, DSTC, Australia

2 Summary of Student Presentations

Each student prepared an extended abstract that also appears in this workshop reader. This section offers a brief summary of the student presentations and poster discussion.

Nelly Bencomo's doctoral research represents the design and implementation of a set of metamodels for specifying a family of reflective middleware. The metamodels are used to capture the core concepts of the middleware design and the existing relationships. The initial metamodels have revealed a range of techniques to generate the appropriate components required by the middleware.

A presentation by Fabian Büttner introduced a transformation catalog for UML class diagrams that have OCL constraints. The problem addressed is how to evolve the static class models without rendering the associated OCL invalid. Each transformation must be verified as transformation steps that preserve the OCL.

The doctoral work of Erendira Ibarra-Alvarado is focused on a comprehensive safety approach for developing automotive software systems focusing on X-by-Wire applications. In her work, the automotive application is modeled in UML with various safety assurance analysis techniques available.

Andre Karpištšenko discussed his initial work on integrating existing and emerging tools to provide a development platform for time-aware multi-agent systems; specifically, the integration of Real-Time UML (RT-UML) with Agent UML (AUML). The focus is on modeling techniques at the early stages of development.

Mark Mahoney spoke at the Symposium about his work on modeling reactive object behavior using statecharts and scenarios. The specific contribution of Mark's research is to realize that some of the properties in a Live Sequence Chart are crosscutting in nature and can be addressed by an aspect-oriented approach.

Hiroshi Wada's research centers on a generic framework that provides integration of arbitrary domain-specific modeling languages. In Modeling Turnpike, the core concepts from a specific domain can be represented in various notations and transformed to a final implementation.

A poster discussion was offered by Ellen Van Paesschen, whose work involves a dynamic approach to round-trip engineering with models. The heart of her approach uses a prototype-based language (Self) to provide a two-phased mechanism for rapid prototyping.

Another poster was presented by Jaime Pavlich-Mariscal. Jaime's research considers strategies for modeling alternative security concerns. The focus is an aspect-oriented approach to offer separation of the concerns between the modeling and code artifacts.

A third poster presentation was given by Stephan Roser, who discussed an approach toward model transformation that takes into consideration ontologies to derive the transformation. An application area of the proposed work may enable better integration during enterprise modeling.

3 Summary of Mentor Advice

At the end of the Symposium, each mentor was allotted several minutes to offer words of general advice regarding doctoral research and career advancement. This section provides an overview of the collective guidance offered by the mentors.

Doctoral research can be classified as a journey that requires a passion to be developed for the love of discovery. Along the way, many hurdles will need to be overcome that will require much patience. It is not unusual for a young researcher to be so zealous that they become depressed when the research does not progress at the speed they envisioned. Because there is more to life than research, the students were encouraged to also enjoy this special time in their life during their doctoral studies by developing new relationships and exploring activities outside of the laboratory. Socially and professionally, the network of contacts and friends that are established throughout the doctoral studies will serve as a lifelong source of support and opportunity.

The importance of a literature search was mentioned by several mentors. It was pointed out that the skill of exploring related research is not simply for the initial phases of the PhD, but rather an activity that will be useful throughout a researcher's entire career. A characteristic of a good literature search is that it does more than simply enumerate references; a good literature search provides a comparative description that offers a discussion of the advantages and disadvantages of the related work. Strategies for compiling a literature search include keeping a database of papers that were considered along with annotations of important contributions of each paper. To a doctoral student in the early phase of their research, the criticality of the literature search is essential to understand what has already been done and what can be leveraged as possible extensions.

It was suggested to the students that they always be able to define their research problem concisely, as well as the associated questions on why the question is important. The key challenges of the problem need to be understood and explained well to others, in addition to the approach and method taken to offer a new contribution. The importance of being able to validate the results of the research is a critical part of evaluating the impact of the contribution and proving the merit of the approach to others.

As researchers, the students were reminded of the necessity of publishing the results of their work. Several reasons were provided to highlight the need to publish. First, publishing provides feedback from research peers that may be useful to influencing the direction of the dissertation. Second, writing throughout the PhD process also eases the burden of having to write a large dissertation at the end. Writing helps to provide structure to incubating ideas and also offers a historical account of the decisions and justifications made along the way. Third, the current competitive climate for research positions (both in industry and academia) has seen junior candidates for entry level research positions with multiple journal papers and dozens of other publications. To be competitive, a doctoral student must establish a pattern consistent with a researcher active in publishing results.

4 Conclusion

The fruitful exchange among mentors and students at the Symposium provided mutual benefit toward addressing promising research ideas for future exploration. Among the mentors, it was agreed that there are many future stars among the student participants and that it will be exciting to watch all of their careers unfold. It was suggested that the Doctoral Symposium be offered as an annual event at the MoDELS conference such that the future of the modeling research community can be fostered from the candid interaction that is provided by such a mentoring opportunity. Additional information about the workshop, including pictures of the activities, can be found at: http://www.cs.colostate.edu/models05/doctoralSymposium.html

Preening: Reflection of Models in the Mirror a Meta-modelling Approach to Generate Reflective Middleware Configurations

Nelly Bencomo and Gordon Blair

Comp. Dept, InfoLab21, Lancaster University, Lancaster, LA1 4WA, UK
nelly@acm.org

Abstract. This paper outlines some partial results of my PhD research on how to use Model-Driven Engineering to systematically generate reflective middleware family configurations.

1 Introduction

Meta-level architectures and the concept of reflection are useful for modifying programming systems dynamically in a controlled way. A number of experimental reflective middleware platforms have been developed and used in industry. At Lancaster University [6], we have investigated the role of reflection [4] in supporting both customisation and dynamic re-configuration of middleware platforms. To complement the use of reflection, we also investigate the use of component technologies, and the associated concept of component frameworks [5] in the construction of our open middleware solutions.

Challenging new requirements have emerged when working with dynamically re-configurable component frameworks with (un)pluggable components. Middleware developers deal with a large number of variability decisions when planning configurations at various stages of the development cycle. These factors make it error-prone to manually guarantee that all these decisions are consistent. Such *ad hoc* approaches do not offer formal foundations for verification that the ultimately configured middleware will offer the required functionality.

Our main research topic focuses on whether Model-Driven Engineering (MDE) techniques can be successfully used to address the challenges described above and what are the implications of its application. MDE is a new paradigm that encompasses domain analysis, metamodeling and model-driven code generation. We believe that Model Driven techniques provide a key solution when systematically generating configurations of the Middleware families.

2 Partial Results and Research Challenges

We have already specified a *kernel* or set of UML meta-models that embraces the fundamental concepts. All middleware family members regardless of their domain shares this minimum set of concepts. On top of this, we propose a set of so called extensions (caplets and reflective extensions) that captures the extensibility of the

J.-M. Bruel (Ed.): MoDELS 2005 Workshops, LNCS 3844, pp. 337–338, 2006.
© Springer-Verlag Berlin Heidelberg 2006

approach [2]. Three reflective extensions are now supported (Architecture, Interface, and Interception). In outline, different middleware configurations are generated from models that are written in terms of these meta-models. The models are sufficiently abstract that a number of different concrete configurations of components can be generated from them. The concrete configurations that are generated are determined by the following dimensions of variability:

(i)   *deployment environment*: refers to the resource capabilities of the hardware/software environment in which the system will be deployed

(ii) *QoS*: allows the abstract-to-concrete mapping to be influenced by non functional consideration such as mobility, dependability, or security

(iii) *(re)configurability*: refers to the degree of reflective support required at runtime.

Achieving our goal requires that we deal with a number of research challenges:

– the variability dimensions described crosscut each other [1]. *How do we represent the crosscutting concerns identified (i.e. aspects) in the proposed meta-models?*

– a key area of future work is to investigate how to maintain the UML models at runtime and keep them causally connected with the underlying running system in order to support reconfiguration. *What should a runtime UML model look like?*

– we propose the use of our suit of orthogonal reflective extensions as basis for different reflective implementation mechanisms for supporting dynamic AOP to address the problem of adaptation at run-time [3]. *How can we model the synergy between AOP and reflection?*

Answers and solutions to these questions and problems would lead to new formal mechanisms to generate families of systems bringing together the advantages of MDE, reflection, and Aspect Oriented Software Development (AOSD) [7].

References

1. Bencomo N., Blair G.: Raising a Reflective Family, Models and Aspects - Handling Cross-cutting Concerns in MDSD, ECOOP, Scotland, (2005)
2. Bencomo N., Blair G., Coulson G., Batista T.: Towards a Meta-Modelling Approach to Configurable Middleware, 2nd ECOOP Workshop on Reflection, AOP and Meta-Data for Software Evolution, ECOOP, Scotland (2005)
3. Bencomo N., Blair G., Coulson G., Grace P., Rashid A.: Reflection and Aspects meet again, 1st Aspect Oriented Middleware Development, Middleware 2005, France (2005)
4. Maes, P.: Concepts and Experiments in Computational Reflection, Proc. OOPSLA'87, Vol. 22 of ACM SIGPLAN Notices, pp147-155, ACM Press (1987)
5. Szyperski C.: Component Software: Beyond Object-Oriented Programming, Addison-Wesley, (2002)
6. Middleware: http://www.comp.lancs.ac.uk/computing/research/mpg/reflection/index.php
7. AOSD Community: http://aosd.net/

Transformation-Based Structure Model Evolution

Fabian Büttner

University of Bremen, Computer Science Department, Database Systems Group

Models have become more and more important in software development. The Model Driven Architecture (MDA) currently addressed by a large number of people, research groups, and tools documents this emphasis on having models as central artifacts in software engineering.

Typically, a model undergoes many changes in its lifetime, in the same way as an end product (software) does. If it does not, the model might have been a throw away artifact which is no longer connected to the software developed from it. To prevent having throw-away models, we believe that one needs strong tool support for the evolution of models which allows us to continuously develop and refine existing models.

In our work, we formulate a catalogue of refactoring-like transformations to static structure models which are given by UML class diagrams and attached OCL constraints. Changing static structure model elements may render existing OCL expressions invalid. Thus, each transformation has to be accomplished by a number of change rules for existing OCL expressions. Furthermore, there typically exist states (represented as object diagrams) of the model as well. Such states may exist as analysis artifacts, for example to refine use case descriptions. It is therefore important to investigate each model transformation w.r.t. its capability to represent existing states under a changed model. We have to distinguish between state preserving model transformations and those which are not, or only partly state preserving.

In our work, each model transformation is organized as a set of *transformation steps*. Each of these steps describes a single change to a model in terms of its metamodel representation, providing an operational characterization of the transformation. Furthermore, each transformation is classified w.r.t. the context under which it is state preserving. If a transformation is state preserving, a corresponding state transformation is provided as well.

On the tool side we are currently implementing the complete catalogue as an extension of the USE ("UML Specification Environment") tool. This extended version allows us to interactively change a model while keeping OCL constraints and states in sync. An evolution browser documents all changes through the life cycle of a model.

There is related work in many areas: refactorings and design patterns aim to provide automatic changes and solutions to typical design problems to programmers. For models, there are several approaches to employ graph transformations to define model transformations. Other transformation languages follow a relation-based approach. There also exist a number of model transformation language proposals as a respond to the QVT RFP of the OMG. Due to the paper format, we consequently do not include any references except our own previous work. The final work will of course include a detailed discussion of related work. We have already studied a couple of transformations to UML class diagrams in [BG04b, BBG]. Particular aspects of class diagram semantics are discussed in [BG04a].

J.-M. Bruel (Ed.): MoDELS 2005 Workshops, LNCS 3844, pp. 339–340, 2006.

The catalogue under development will contain a selection of carefully chosen transformations that are essential to the evolution of structure models, particularly on the analysis level. This includes changing the multiplicity of association ends, changes to the generalization hierarchy, moving attributes along associations, splitting and joining classes, and other transformations. The idea is that as many as possible of the corrections, transformations, and other changes to be made during the lifetime of a model can be made consistently and automatically within the USE tool (i.e., without manually rewriting existing OCL constraints or throwing away existing states).

All transformations of our catalogue are (or will be) implemented in the aforementioned extension to the USE tool. Each transformation is motivated by a single change to a class diagram. Each of these changes is realized by a number of transformation steps. These steps are provided mainly by UML collaborations showing how an instance of the UML metamodel (for class diagrams) and the OCL expression trees (i.e., instances of the OCL metamodel) have to be modified. We like to emphasize that our steps are formulated in a simple, operational formalism given by standard UML collaborations and state machines.

At the time of writing, the transformation catalogue is partly implemented in USE. We have gained much feedback on our transformations by experimenting with several models. In particular, the transformations for changing the multiplicities of association end, replacing generalizations by compositions, and moving attributes along associations are already applicable. Implementing the collaborations in Java was really simplified by the help of our 'dynamic dispatcher' [BRLG04] component (a very slim implementation of multi-methods tailored for applying the visitor design pattern). The way the transformations are implemented follows closely the way they are presented in our work, giving some first evidence that the transformations, organized in transformation steps, are sound and consistent. A more formal discussion will be included in our final work.

References

[BBG]   Fabian Büttner, Hanna Bauerdick, and Martin Gogolla. Towards transformation of integrity constraints and database states. In Danielle Martin, editor, *Proc. 16th International Conference and Workshop on Database and Expert Systems Applications (DEXA 2005)*, to appear. IEEE, Los Alamitos.

[BG04a]   Fabian Büttner and Martin Gogolla. On Generalization and Overriding in UML 2.0. In Nuno Jardim Nunes, Bran Selic, Alberto Rodrigues da Silva, and Ambrosio Toval Alvarez, editors, *UML'2004 Modeling Languages and Applications. UML'2004 Satellite Activities.*, pages 67–67. Springer, Berlin, LNCS 3297, 2004.

[BG04b]   Fabian Büttner and Martin Gogolla. Realizing UML Metamodel Transformations with AGG. In Reiko Heckel, editor, *Proc. ETAPS Workshop Graph Transformation and Visual Modeling Techniques (GT-VMT'2004)*. Electronic Notes in Theoretical Computer Science (ENTCS), Elsevier, 2004.

[BRLG04]   Fabian Büttner, Oliver Radfelder, Arne Lindow, and Martin Gogolla. Digging into the Visitor Pattern. In Frank Maurer and Günther Ruhe, editors, *Proc. IEEE 16th Int. Conf. Software Engineering and Knowlege Engineering (SEKE'2004)*. IEEE, Los Alamitos, 2004.

Software Hazard Analysis for X-by-Wire Applications

Ireri Ibarra-Alvarado[1], Richard K. Stobart[1], and Rudi Lutz[2]

[1] Dept. of Engineering and Design, University of Sussex, Falmer, BN1 9QT, U.K.
[2] Dept. of Informatics University of Sussex, Falmer, BN1 9QH, U.K.
{eii20, r.k.stobart, rudil}@sussex.ac.uk

One of the latest technologies in the automotive industry is "X-by-Wire", where mechanical components are replaced by electronic functions typically controlled by software. X-by-Wire impacts on the overall vehicle safety for example: by eliminating the steering column, the likelihood of it intruding into the passenger compartment during a collision decreases. X-by-Wire also provides the driver with convenient features such as variable steering ratio for ease of manoeuvrability.

As a result of the lack of standardisation of the current modelling tools and the different approaches the tool vendors follow for code generation [1], amongst other software issues in the development of real-time embedded systems for vehicles, there is a need to adapt the current software development practices to give a competitive answer to the demands in the automotive market.

The objective of this research is to develop a set of guidelines on how to perform hazard analysis where models of both system and controls are developed in UML (Unified Modeling Language) following the ROPES (Rapid Object-Oriented Development Process for Embedded Systems) process; embedding with this hazard analysis procedures in the development process itself. By using UML we establish a common language to be used by the different stakeholders involved in the project.

The first phase of the proposed safety lifecycle starts with a PHA (Preliminary Hazard Analysis) which involves an initial risk assessment in order to identify safety critical components and functions and then reflect them in the requirements. PHA is performed on the UCD (Use Case Diagram) and CD (Class Diagram) to check that they contain enough information to roughly match the system requirements. This procedure is implicit to a degree, in the analysis process to build the diagrams and design reviews, in order to produce a highly abstract set of diagrams to be used in the next phase of the development lifecycle, which is the System Safety Analysis, where it is planned to use HAZOP (Hazards and Operability Study).

HAZOP was born in the process industry; its purpose is to find hazards arising from the interaction of components in a plant, which is achieved by analysing flows of substances using a set of guidewords to conduct the discussion. The general approach of this work is to use the guidewords in DEF STAN 00-58, which were modified from the original ones to fit systems containing electronics, with a very clear interpretation for each attribute, in analogy, examining information flows.

For the SSA (System Safety Analysis) phase a HAZOP study is performed on the master CD, here we anticipate that we will verify that it adheres to the requirements. If flaws are found at this stage, these constitute potential faults which are being identified and corrected. However two main things are evaluated with this strategy - the first is how close the model is to the requirements, and the second is the completeness and accuracy of the requirements from a safety perspective. These

J.-M. Bruel (Ed.): MoDELS 2005 Workshops, LNCS 3844, pp. 341–342, 2006.
© Springer-Verlag Berlin Heidelberg 2006

feedback paths make it difficult to differentiate the initial stages of the safety lifecycle.

In the DSA (Detailed Safety Analysis) that corresponds to the low level system design phase it is planned to have a much more detailed CD and Statecharts and to use a different hazard analysis technique than HAZOP. We have to bear in mind that not all hazard analysis techniques will be suitable to match the type of information provided by each diagram.

The case study is a Steer-by-Wire system, during the HAZOP analysis, performed in the SSA phase; we focused on the master CD, using the requirements list as the basis to determine if the information there was mapped adequately to the master CD. Two things are important to note here:

- A HAZOP study is not a design review. The master CD must be mature enough to be used in the HAZOP, making sure that it represents the designer's most refined representation of the system. Although informal design reviews were previously carried out between some members of the HAZOP team, a different perspective was brought up in the HAZOP meeting, such as a design change that needed to be considered for safety reasons, e.g. supplying additional information in the master CD such as redundancy for sensors and actuators.
- The master CD at this stage represents a combination of hardware and software, and the hardware at least needs to be represented as accurately as possible, since it constitutes a major design decision even at this early stage.

There were a total of 10 changes in the class diagram that resulted from the HAZOP study, they account for additions and deletions of inheritance and association relationships, and addition of classes. The nature of these changes in the CD, address specific safety concerns that were either not seen during the design reviews or that the requirements did not explicitly state.

HAZOP appears to be a useful technique for the initial phases of the safety lifecycle, due to its inherent level of abstraction. Nonetheless, in a later phase a more detailed safety analysis will be performed using a different technique, such as FMEA (Failure Modes and Effects Analysis) expecting that it will allow the quantification of the probability of failures.

References

1. Furst, S. Autocoding in Automotive Software Development, Qualification Aspects of ACGs. in IEE Automotive Electronics Conference. 2005.
2. Leveson, N., SAFEWARE 1995, USA: Addison Wesley.
3. MoD, Defence Standard 00-58: HAZOP Studies on Systems Containing Programmable Electronics. 2000.
4. Rumbaugh, J., Jacobson, I. and Booch, G., The Unified Modeling Language, Reference Manual. Second ed. 2004: Addison-Wesley.

Enhancement of Development Technologies for Agent-Based Software Engineering*

Andre Karpištšenko

Tallinn Technical University, Ehitajate tee 5,
19086 Tallinn, Estonia
andre@lap.ee

1 Background

Modern systems are software-intensive and must meet increasingly demanding requirements in order to cope with significant degrees of uncertainty, dynamic environments, and to provide greater flexibility. Agent-based development metaphors and technologies provide well suited structures and techniques to handle such complexity. However, when developing complex open systems, the tools provide insufficient support for effective specification and implementation of such systems.

With the official release of UML 2.0, the fundamental definition of behavior will offer means for modeling interactions and for specifying systems independently of where the system/environment boundary is drawn. This would suggest that the utilization of Model Driven Architecture (MDA) offers a content platform for modeling multi-agent systems. However, as critics of MDA suggest, it is distinctly nontrivial – many would argue impossible – to support and evolve semantically correct platform-specific models for complex platforms such as J2EE or .NET. Drawing the parallel with inherently complex multi-agent systems, additional means of modeling have to be considered.

2 Purpose and Possible Impacts

The focus of this doctoral work is on the effective modeling practices in the early stages of software development. The purpose is to improve the modeling possibilities of time-aware multi-agent systems (TA-MAS) to enable formal analysis of composite system behavior.

From the perspective of agent-orientation, the work could create possibilities to automatically control and verify agent-oriented implementations against their model specifications. This would facilitate the engineering of complex systems, as the problems associated with the coupling and interaction of components are significantly reduced and the problem of managing control relationships among the software components is reduced. This thesis is also expected to contribute to the behavioral modeling aspects – elaborate the list of behavioral features that can be analyzed in early stages of the software process, and methods applicable for this analysis.

---

* Due to paper format (extended abstract) no references are included here.

J.-M. Bruel (Ed.): MoDELS 2005 Workshops, LNCS 3844, pp. 343–344, 2006.

3 Preliminary Results

Due to the early stage of the doctoral work, the majority of results are "work in progress". For this reason this paragraph is organized as an overview of the relevant topics with a glimpse of the ongoing work.

3.1 Modeling Time-Aware Multi-agent Systems with UML

The existing trend in practical applications has led to (partial) merging of two domains – multi-agents and real-time embedded systems. For modeling real-time systems there are widely acknowledged Real-Time UML Profiles (RT-UML). However when it comes to modeling agents, the formalizations and standards are still evolving. A well known modeling language is AgentUML (AUML) which heavily relies on UML.

As RT-UML puts a lot of attention to concurrency and communication issues, which are inherent characteristics of multi-agent systems, the doctoral work is on merging the relevant parts with the existing AUML. As the authors of AUML have stated, that UML is not relied upon, but reused, open-source AUML tools are preferred for ease of modification. Integration with RT-UML is required, as current timing constraints and the underlying time model, defined in AUML do not satisfy the needs of real-time systems.

The first group of prototype models will include a model of an ant colony simulation and in the near future models will be developed for agents collecting information (e.g. for digital maps) in heterogeneous computing network with dynamically changing topology (e.g. ad hoc sensor networks, currently such an experimental environment is being built in Tallinn University of Technology).

3.2 Meta-programming of Domain-Specific Agents

As discussed in the background section of this paper, UML based models of TA-MAS might prove inefficient in practice. Since attention to methods, tools, and models that directly support domain-oriented programming is crucial, a study of alternative modeling tools is planned in parallel with the work on UML profiles.

The focus is on modeling/programming environments for domain-specific languages with full support from the IDE. The variety of languages and formalizations required for designing multi-agent systems suggest that seamless interoperability is a must for successful code generation and the maintenance of TA-MAS.

The current possible candidate environments, for defining domain-specific languages and models, are currently MetaEdit+ metaCase tool by MetaCase and Meta Programming System (focused on textual representation of model) by JetBrains. The motivation for using existing frameworks for design and implementation of languages is to shift focus of research work from tool development to agent domain specific characteristics. As a result of experimentation with existing tools, concrete modeling requirements inherent to agent domain can be specified.

Research within this doctoral work is expected to result in a prototype modeling language for TA-MAS with possible candidates for target format (code generation) being KRATT or JADE agent frameworks.

Modeling Reactive Systems and Aspect-Orientation

Mark Mahoney

Illinois Institute of Technology,
Chicago, IL, USA
mahomar@iit.edu

This paper describes the research I am currently performing as a PhD student at the Illinois Institute of Technology with my advisor Dr. Tzilla Elrad. The focus of my research is Aspect-Oriented Modeling and reactive systems. In particular I am interested in the modeling of reactive objects using statecharts and scenarios.

One of the limitations of object-oriented software development is that it does not have an efficient way of expressing crosscutting concerns. A crosscutting concern is one that cannot easily be modularized into a single unit such as a class. Rather, it is spread out or tangled with the implementation of other concerns. The goal of Aspect-Oriented Software Development (AOSD) is to separate crosscutting concerns from core concerns. The focus of my research is to tackle one of the most important parts of Aspect-Oriented software design- modeling. Currently, the modeling techniques that address crosscutting concerns in reactive systems lack the expressiveness to model interactions between core and crosscutting concerns effectively. In particular, my research focuses on modeling class behavior with statecharts and scenarios.

The goals of my future work are to further examine the use of statecharts and to explore scenario based languages for addressing crosscutting concerns. With respect to the statechart work I have begun, I am looking into other contexts such as ubiquitous computing and how crosscutting concerns are handled in those environments. On a parallel track, I intend to continue exploring Aspect-Oriented Modeling by researching techniques to model crosscutting concerns in scenario based languages like Live Sequence Charts (LSC)[1]. LSC's allow one to model user concerns in a formal language similar to UML use cases and sequence diagrams. Tools have been developed to verify these models are consistent and complete. I will be exploring the use of Aspect-Oriented use case research and scenarios.

I plan to continue working with state based systems. I am currently researching aspects as they apply to ubiquitous computing and variability. I am interested in discovering if statecharts controlling separate machines may be combined into one statechart with orthogonal regions for the purpose of coordination and control. These distributed statecharts would travel to different orthogonal regions of different machines based on the location of the device. For example, an airplane may have a statechart that describes its current state (ascending, descending, etc). Each air traffic control tower across the country may require that as a plane flies through its airspace it add its statechart to the tower's statechart in an orthogonal region. The tower can then reinterpret events from each plane to control the airspace. For example, an air traffic control tower in Washington D. C. may reinterpret a 'descent' event as a threat, whereas that same event may be reinterpreted to an indication of landing in another tower's statechart. I intend on altering the AOSF to handle distribution and movement of statecharts.

J.-M. Bruel (Ed.): MoDELS 2005 Workshops, LNCS 3844, pp. 345–346, 2006.
© Springer-Verlag Berlin Heidelberg 2006

I have just begun to research the effect of crosscutting concerns on scenario-based languages. A scenario, like a use case, models a typical interaction a user has with a system to provide some useful result. One particular scenario based language, called Live Sequence Charts (LSC), deals with reactive systems. Scenario-based descriptions of behavior are not immune to crosscutting concerns. I am researching ways to address crosscutting concerns in scenarios by proposing some additions to the LSC language and an accompanying tool called the Play-Engine. The proposals I have made would allow one to *see* the effect of applying crosscutting concerns to different scenarios.

My early work focuses on mapping concepts in the AOSD world to LSC's. I have been able to equate an LSC's pre-chart to the idea of a 'pointcut' and a main chart to an 'advice' in Aspect-Oriented Programming (AOP) languages. Further, in order to increase the amount of quantification in the models I have proposed extensions to the LSC language to allow regular expressions in the names of participating objects and the messages that flow between objects.

There are still some mappings needed to be worked out. Most AOP languages allow the developer to specify that an advice be applied before, after, or around a pointcut. More work is needed to be done to sort out the semantics of a similar mechanism in the LSC language. I plan on investigating whether there is any benefit to creating separate types of LSC for core and crosscutting concerns. If a separate model is created for aspect LSC's it may allow more flexibility in quantifying join points by being able to include more than one pre-chart using the logical operators AND, OR, and NOT.

I also plan on researching whether state machine generation is possible using LSC's and the proposed extensions to the language. Another alternative I am considering developing an executing environment similar to the Play-Engine that deals with my proposed extensions. Lastly, I intend on examining the relationship between LSC's and a recent work [2] on AOSD and use cases. I believe LSC's may be a more appropriate tool than sequence diagrams in the proposed process since they allow for verification and validation and serve as executable test cases.

References

1. Harel, D, Marelly, R. 2003. Come, Let's Play: Scenario-Based Programming Using LSCs and the Play-Engine. Springer-Verlag
2. Jacobson, I. Ng, P. Aspect-Oriented Software Development with Use Cases. Addison-Wesley. 2005.

SelfSync: A Dynamic Round-Trip Engineering Environment

Ellen Van Paesschen[1] and Maja D'Hondt[2]

[1] Programming Technology Laboratory
[2] Software and System Engineering Laboratory,
Vrije Universiteit Brussel,
Pleinlaan 2, 1050 Brussel, Belgium
{evpaessc, mjdhondt}@vub.ac.be

Abstract. Model-Driven Engineering (MDE) advocates the generation of software applications from models, which are views on certain aspects of the software. In order to minimize the delta between these views we propose a highly dynamic Round-Trip Engineering (RTE) technique where the elements of the various views are one and the same. We combine Extended Entity-Relationship diagrams with an object-oriented prototype-based language in a two-phased technique that allows for the rapid prototyping of the modeled applications. Run-time objects are included in the RTE process resulting in advanced constraint enforcement. Moreover support is provided for straightforward role modeling.

1 Introduction

In *Model-Driven Engineering* (MDE) software applications are generated from models, which are views on certain aspects of the software. The goal of this research is to minimize the "distance" (the delta) between different views. We consider the following three views:

- A domain analysis view represented by a data modeling diagram
- Implementation objects, related to object-oriented programs at *code-time*
- Population objects, derived from implementation objects, containing actual data for running the application

During *Round-Trip Engineering* (RTE) these views need to be synchronized continuously [1],[5],[10]. We want to provide a highly dynamic approach to RTE, where the elements of the data modeling view and the corresponding implementation objects are one and the same. This contrasts with other approaches, which usually employ a synchronization strategy based on transformation [10],[24] (see Section 4). Moreover we want to include population objects in the RTE process.

An interesting academic case study in this context is *role modeling* [19]. In this case the distance between the data modeling view and a corresponding implementation is significant: from a modeling perspective roles are subtypes of the persons performing them but in the code a person object performing a role is more specialized than the role object itself [16], [9].

J.-M. Bruel (Ed.): MoDELS 2005 Workshops, LNCS 3844, pp. 347–352, 2006.

2   Our Approach

We propose a two-phased approach that continuously synchronizes between a data modeling view and a view on an object-oriented implementation [14], [16], [15]. For the data modeling view we selected the *Extended Entity-Relationship* diagramming technique [3] while the object-oriented implementation is developed in the prototype-based language Self [20].

EER Modeling. EER diagrams consist of the typical data modeling elements, similar to *Class Diagrams* in the *Unified Modeling Language* (UML): entities (classes in the UML), attributes and operations[1] in entities, and association and inheritance relations between entities. The associations can be 1-to-1, 1-to-many, and many-to-many. The EER notation we use combines existing approaches [3], [6] but is merely a consequence of our choice of development platform.

There is an almost religious discussion between the (E)ER and the UML communities as to which approach is better. Typical claims are that (E)ER modeling is more formally funded but that the UML is more open [17]. In our work, however, the use of EER does not exclude the transfer of our conceptual results to an UML-based context. We describe Round-Trip Engineering on the data modeling level in terms of entities, attributes and operations, and association and inheritance relations. These EER modeling elements have equivalent modeling elements in Class Diagrams of the UML.

Self. The object-oriented implementation language we employ is the prototype-based language Self. Prototype-based languages can be considered object-oriented languages without classes. As such, a *prototype* is used for sharing state between objects and new objects can be created by cloning a prototype. Self introduces another concept, *traits*, which share behavior among objects and let objects inherit from them, similar to classes. For more details on the language we refer to [23].

Part of the motivation to select Self is based on its reflective and dynamic character that is crucial in Round-Trip Engineering. Class-based languages such as Java and C++ that apply static typing and have few or no reflection facilities do not allow for synchronization at the level of the run-time population objects. Moreover they do not support role modeling in a straightforward manner [9]. The fact that in Self parents are shared and can be modified dynamically caused us to prefer Self to a dynamically-typed class-based language such as Smalltalk. Role modeling can be simulated in Smalltalk but not as natural as in Self [16].

2.1   A Two-Phased Approach

Our approach constitutes two typically but not necessarily subsequently executed phases, which we present in detail in [14]. In the first *active modeling* phase a user draws an EER diagram while corresponding Self implementation

---

[1] We extended the standard EER diagram with operation slots in addition to attribute slots.

objects — prototypes and traits — are automatically created. In reality, the Self objects *are* the modeled entities: drawing a new EER entity automatically results in a graphical EER *entity view* being created on a new Self object. Hence, we support incremental and continuous synchronization *per entity* and *per object*: changes to an EER entity are in fact changes to a view on one object and thus automatically propagated to the object via Self's reflection mechanism. Similarly, changes to an object are automatically propagated to the corresponding EER entity.

The second phase of our approach is an *interactive prototyping* process[2]. This phase allows a user to interactively create and initialize ready-to-use population objects from each implementation object created in the previous phase.

3   Tool Support and Validation

SelfSync is a tool that implements the two-phased approach described in Section 2.1. First, we extended Self with a drawing editor for EER diagrams. Next, we added a new EER "view" on Self objects with the help of the Morphic framework and realized a bidirectional active link between EER views and implementation objects. As explained in Section 3.1, SelfSync supports (1) enforcing constraints on population objects steered from the data model, (2) advanced method synchronization between data model and implementation, (3) changing populations of objects steered from the data model and (4) a natural synchronization between modeling and implementing during role modeling.

3.1   Validation

Constraint Enforcement. After the interactive prototyping phase we ensure that the multiplicity constraints imposed by a one-to-one or one-to-many relationship between two entities are satisfied at all times. When two entities are in a relationship in which the first one has a single reference (one or zero) to the second one, the uniqueness of this reference is enforced in the population objects in two ways. We first ensure that all population objects that have been derived from the first entity refer to at most one population object that has been derived from the second entity. Secondly, we also ensure that only one population object derived from the second entity refers to population objects derived from the first entity. If two entities are in a one-to-one relationship, this is enforced in the two directions.

Dependencies between entities and weak entities in an EER diagram result in another kind of enforcement of population objects derived from these entities. In this case we ensure that when a population object is deleted, all population objects that refer to it and have been derived from a weak entity that depends on the entity from which the deleted population object is derived, are deleted

---

[2] Note that a *prototype* is a special object in prototype-based languages for supporting data sharing of several objects whereas *prototyping* is the activity of instantiating and initializing a program into a ready-to-use, running system.

also. Note that for the enforcement to be actually performed, the population objects that are candidates for deletion are not allowed to be referenced by any other population object.

Method Synchronization. The EER diagram used in SelfSync is extended with operations. These operations are linked to the method bodies of the corresponding methods in the implementation objects. First, the method bodies can be edited in the EER diagram, which is automatically synchronized with the actual method bodies in the implementation objects, and vice versa. Second, we also support the possibility to "inject" behavior before or after one or more selected operations in the EER diagram. This is a simple *visual* version of Aspect-Oriented Programming [13], where the join points are selected in a diagram instead of described by a pointcut. This new piece of code is again automatically added at the beginning or end of the method bodies of all selected operations in the EER diagram. These *code injections* maintain their identity: at any point in time the layers of different code injections of an operation can be consulted. Each of these injections can be removed locally or in all operations where this specific injection was added.

Object Generations. Changing a method in an implementation object, more specifically in the traits has repercussions on all population objects that have been derived from it. Since we allow changing method bodies by manipulating the corresponding operations in the EER diagram, SelfSync supports behavioral evolution of entire existing generations of population objects, steered from the EER diagram.

The Role Modeling Concept. SelfSync was successfully extended with a role modeling concept to represent the fact that one entity can dynamically adapt the behavior of another entity. To tackle the paradox of roles being both sub- and supertypes [19] we introduced the concept of *warped hierarchies* [16]. Modeling roles by means of our extension to the EER diagram results in corresponding implementation objects being automatically created with the structure of warped hierarchies. In the corresponding population objects, an arbitrary number of roles can be added or removed dynamically thanks to multiple inheritance and dynamic parent modification. The technique is based on meta-programming and Self's state inheritance mechanism called *copy-down* [23].

4   Existing Approaches

Round-Trip Engineering. The state-of-the-art in RTE includes application such as Rational XDE [22], Borland Together [24], and FUJABA [21]. One of the leaders in this domain is Borland's Together. In this commercial tool set the synchronization mechanism between UML Class Diagrams and implementation is realized by the *LiveSource* technology. More specifically, the implementation model (i.e. the source code) is parsed and rendered as two views: a UML Class Diagram and in a formatted textual form. LiveSource is in fact a code parsing engine. The user can manipulate either view and even the implementation model. However, all user actions are translated directly to the implementation model and then translated back to both views. Population objects are not included in the RTE process. There is no real support for constraint enforcement or for manipulating operations in the Class Diagram. Role modeling as described above is rather hard in a Class Diagram [9], [19]. Other related work in RTE, is mostly concerned with characterizing RTE rather than providing concrete tool support [1].

Role Modeling. We summarize the four approaches that are most relevant to our approach described in [16]. For more approaches we refer to [19]. The category concept [7] is defined as the subset of the union of a number of roles (types). As in our approach the Entity-Relationship diagram was extended: relationships are not defined on entity types, but on categories. In [2] roles are considered temporal specializations: statically, a manager is a specialization of a person. However, when a particular person object becomes a manager, its type is changed from person to the subtype employee thereby inheriting all aspects of its new role. In this way reversed specializations, similar to warped hierarchies, are realized temporarily. [18] also separate between static and dynamic type hierarchies: state sharing, behaviour sharing, as in Self, and subset hierarchies are combined into a new specialization modeling concept. In [12] delegation is used to implement dynamic roles that "import" state and behavior from their parent objects.

The role modeling concepts in the approaches described above provide suitable alternatives but were – to the best of our knowledge – never integrated in an object-oriented RTE modeling environment that supports automatic synchronization between the modeled roles and a corresponding implementation.

EER and Object-Orientation. Since the late eighties, it has been encouraged to combine (E)ER models and object-orientation (OO) [4]. Various approaches and techniques exist for translating EER into object-orientation [8],[11]. Such mappings can be used in the domain of object-relational (O/R) mappers [25]. These tools generate an object implementation from a data model such as (E)ER, and possibly support synchronization of both models. Some of them generate code to enforce constraints on relationships and dependencies between implementation objects, based on the data model. However, these applications do not consider behavior (operations) at the level of the data model.

References

1. U. Assman. Automatic roundtrip engineering. *Electronic Notes in Theoretical Computer Science*, 82.
2. C. Bock and J. Odell. A more complete model of relations and their implementation: Roles. *JOOP*, 11(2):51–54, 1998.
3. P. P. Chen. The entity-relationship model - toward a unified view of data. *ACM Trans. Database Syst.*, 1(1):9–36, 1976.
4. P. P. Chen, B. Thalheim, and L. Y. Wong. Future directions of conceptual modeling. In *Conceptual Modeling*, pages 287–301, 1997.

5. S. Demeyer, S. Ducasse, and S. Tichelaar. Why unified is not universal? In *UML'99, Fort Collins, CO, USA, October 28-30. 1999, Proceedings*, volume 1723 of *LNCS*, pages 630–644. Springer, 1999.
6. R. Elmasri and S. B. Navathe. *Fundamentals of Database Systems*. Addison-Wesley World Student Series, 3 edition, 1994.
7. R. Elmasri, J. Weeldreyer, and A. Hevner. The category concept: an extension to the entity-relationship model. *Data Knowl. Eng.*, 1(1):75–116, 1985.
8. J. Fong. Mapping extended entity relationship model to object modeling technique. *SIGMOD Record*, 24(3):18–22, 1995.
9. M. Fowler. Dealing with roles. Technical report, Department of Computer Science, Washington University, 1997.
10. A. Henriksson and H. Larsson. A definition of round-trip engineering. Technical report, Linkopings Universitet, Sweden, 2003.
11. R. Herzig and M. Gogolla. Transforming conceptual data models into an object model. In *ER'92, Karlsruhe, Germany, October 1992, Proceedings*, volume 645 of *Lecture Notes in Computer Science*, pages 280–298. Springer, 1992.
12. A. Jodlowski, P. Habela, J. Plodzien, and K. Subieta. Dynamic object roles – adjusting the notion for flexible modeling. In *IDEAS*, pages 449–456, 2004.
13. G. Kiczales, J. Lamping, A. Menhdhekar, C. Maeda, C. Lopes, J.-M. Loingtier, and J. Irwin. Aspect-oriented programming. In *Proceedings of the 15th European Conference on Object-Oriented Programming (ECOOP'01)*, pages 220–242. Springer-Verlag, 1997.
14. E. V. Paesschen, M. D'Hondt, and W. D. Meuter. Rapid prototyping of eer models. In *ISIM 2005, Hradec Nad Moravici, Czech Republic, April 2005, Proceedings*, pages 194–209. MARQ, 2005.
15. E. V. Paesschen, W. D. Meuter, and M. D'Hondt. Selfsync: a dynamic round-trip engineering environment. In *Proceedings of the ACM/IEEE 8th International Conference on Model-Driven Engineering Languages and Systems (MoDELS'05)*, October 2-7, Montego Bay, Jamaica, 2005.
16. E. V. Paesschen, W. D. Meuter, and M. D'Hondt. Role modeling in selfsync with warped hierarchies. In *Proceedings of the AAAI Fall Symposium on Roles, November 3 - 6, Arlington, Virginia, USA*, 2005 (to appear).
17. K.-D. Schewe. UML: A modern dinosaur? In *Proc. 10th European-Japanese Conference on Information Modelling and Knowledge Bases, Saariselkä (Finland)*, 2000. IOS Press, Amsterdam, 2000.
18. M. Snoeck and G. Dedene. Generalization/specialization and role in object oriented conceptual modeling. *Data Knowl. Eng.*, 19(2):171–195, 1996.
19. F. Steimann. A radical revision of UML's role concept. In A. Evans, S. Kent, and B. Selic, editors, *UML 2000, York, UK, October 2000, Proceedings*, volume 1939 of *LNCS*, pages 194–209. Springer, 2000.
20. D. Ungar and R. B. Smith. Self: The power of simplicity. In *OOPSLA '87, Orlando, Florida, USA*, pages 227–242, New York, NY, USA, 1987. ACM Press.
21. Fujaba: http://wwwcs.uni-paderborn.de/cs/fujaba/.
22. Rational: http://www-306.ibm.com/software/awdtools/developer/rosexde/.
23. Self: http://research.sun.com/self/.
24. Together: http://www.borland.com/together/.
25. Toplink: http://www.oracle.com/technology/products/ias/toplink/index.html.

A Framework for Composable Security Definition, Assurance, and Enforcement

J.A. Pavlich-Mariscal, S.A. Demurjian, and L.D. Michel

Department of Computer Science & Engineering,
The University of Connecticut, Unit-2155,
371 Fairfield Road, Storrs, CT 06269- 2155
jaime.pavlich@uconn.edu,
{steve, ldm}@engr.uconn.edu

The objective of this research is to develop techniques that integrate alternative security concerns (e.g., mandatory access control, delegation, authentication, etc.) into the software process. A framework is proposed to achieve composable security definition, assurance, and enforcement via a model-driven framework that preserves separation of security concerns from modeling through implementation, and provides mechanisms to compose these concerns into the application, while maintaining consistency between design models and code. At modeling-time, separation of concerns (e.g., RBAC, MAC, delegation, authorization, etc.) is emphasized by defining concern-specific modeling languages. At the implementation-level, aspect-oriented programming (AOP) transitions security concerns into modularized code that enforces each concern. This research assumes the use of an underlying object-oriented language with aspect-oriented extensions, and infrastructure to implement the applications and support secure access to the public methods of classes, e.g., Java with AspectJ or C++ with AspectC++.

The closest related research are [1] that proposes a metamodel to define security languages, and [4] that proposes an approach to validate access control policies. None of these approaches emphasizes aspect-oriented security enforcement code generation or method-based permissions, which are some of the main foci of our research.

The main research tasks required to realize the framework are:

1. Identify a broad set of Security Concern Models (e.g., RBAC, MAC, delegation, authorization, parameters of security models, etc.) that are both quantifiable units and composable. The main criteria to identify a composable concern is to determine if its properties can be expressed as formal method preconditions.
2. Design a means to integrate the Security Concern Models into a design model (UML) to capture security requirements as part of the software process. This may involve extending existing UML capabilities, proposing new UML diagrams, and/or integrating with other security modeling techniques.
3. Develop a formal model to represent security and non-security concerns that captures a design state for use in static analyses of the security properties of the framework.

J.-M. Bruel (Ed.): MoDELS 2005 Workshops, LNCS 3844, pp. 353–354, 2006.

4. Design formal rules that will govern the mapping of each Security Concern Model to AOP enforcement code, including the composition of multiple concerns and application code.

The central contribution expected from this research is a complete framework that integrates security with the software process, preserves the separation of security and non-security concerns, and yields applications that are the composition of application and enforcement code. Specific contributions include:

- Visual and non-visual modeling extensions to UML that represent and integrate all of the Security Concern Models into the software process.
- Strong assurance that the AOP code generated for every individual Security Concern Model, and for their composition with one another, is secure.
- A formal model to capture security and non-security application concerns, a design state, leveraged to prove assertions regarding security consistency and completeness of individual Security Concern Models and their composition.
- Detailed algorithms that map Security Concern Models (and their composition) into composable AOP enforcement code that preserves separation of concerns.

As of this writing, the status of the research plan outlined above is as follows: A new UML artifact was proposed, the *role-slice diagram* that allows a software/security engineer to capture the Security Concern Model for RBAC [2]. An initial formal model was proposed[3] for security and non-security concerns via a functional notation based on structural operational semantics. Algorithms were designed for mapping a role-slice diagram to AOP security enforcement code [2, 3] via model composition to manage role hierarchies. A software prototype is being built, and will be utilized for experimental validation of the research.

References

1. David Basin, Jürgen Doser, and Torsten Lodderstedt. *Model driven security, Engineering Theories of Software Intensive Systems*. 2004.
2. J. A. Pavlich-Mariscal, T. Doan, L. Michel, S. A. Demurjian, and T. C. Ting. Role Slices: A Notation for RBAC Permission Assignment and Enforcement. In *Proceedings of 19th Annual IFIP WG 11.3 Working Conference on Data and Applications Security*, 2005.
3. Jaime A. Pavlich-Mariscal, L. Michel, and Steven A. Demurjian. A Formal Enforcement Framework for Role-Based Access Control using Aspect-Oriented Programming. In Lionel Briand and Clay Williams, editors, *ACM/IEEE 8th International Conference on Model Driven Engineering Languages and Systems*, Montego Bay, Jamaica, 2005.
4. Eunjee Song, Raghu Reddy, Robert France, Indrakshi Ray, Geri Georg, and Roger Alexander. Verifiable composition of access control features and applications. In *Proceedings of 10th ACM Symposium on Access Control Models and Technologies (SACMAT 2005)*, 2005.

Ontology-Based Model Transformation

Stephan Roser and Bernhard Bauer

Programming of Distributed Systems,
Institute of Computer Science, University of Augsburg, Germany
{roser, bauer}@informatik.uni-augsburg.de

1 Introduction

Today, model-driven development is getting more sophisticated and is used for modeling enterprises and developing application systems. To develop more and more complex systems efficiently, the trend is to intelligent infrastructure services. Since current interoperability solutions operate essentially at a syntactical level, technologies have to be developed enabling interoperability based on middleware, and development platforms have to be enriched with machine-understandable semantics. Our approach of 'Ontology-based Model Transformation' will contribute to these challenges by lifting syntactical metamodel description into ontologies.

Software methodologies are typically characterized by modeling languages and a software process. Like described in [2] and also realized in many approaches, methodologies have to be tailored to software development projects, comprising the choice of appropriate modeling languages. By enriching model-driven development with ontologies a mutual understanding for conceptual integration can be achieved [1]. Model transformations specified between ontologies, will lead to interoperable model transformations independent of methodologies' tailoring to specific projects. The specification of multiple model transformations will be reduced to few ontology-based model transformations. One specification of an ontology-based model transformation can be used to generate multiple transformations for specific environments.

2 Ontology-Based Model Transformation

In the Model Driven Architecture (MDA) a model is a representation of a part of the functionality, structure and behavior of a system. A specification is said to be *formal* when it is based on a language with well defined structure ('syntax') and meaning ('semantics'). Most metamodels have, despite of well defined syntax, descriptions of their semantic concepts which is not machine understandable. Taking the idea of the semantic web, where the word semantic means machine understandable to modeling, metamodels have to be grounded using ontology metadata, enabling machines to understand the meaning of metamodels' concepts. We lift the syntactical model description into ontologies describing the concepts of the model in a machine understandable form. Model transformations are defined on top of those ontologies.

Ontology-based model transformation achieves an increased level of abstraction by the following:

J.-M. Bruel (Ed.): MoDELS 2005 Workshops, LNCS 3844, pp. 355–356, 2006.
© Springer-Verlag Berlin Heidelberg 2006

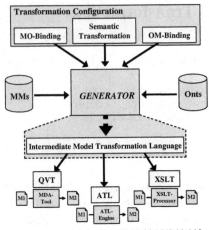

MM: Metamodel; Ont: Ontology; M1: Model 1; M2: Model 2

Fig. 1. Overall approach of ontology-based model transformation

- **Semantic Transformation:** A *semantic transformation* is a transformation specification describing a transformation between two ontologies. A semantic transformation is specified between a source ontology and a target ontology, but it can also be bidirectional.
- **Syntax-semantic Binding:** The *syntax-semantic binding* specifies the connection between syntax (metamodels) and semantics (ontologies).
- **MO-Binding:** *Metamodel-ontology Bindings* specify how semantic information can be derived from model elements.
- **OM-Binding:** *Ontology-metamodel Bindings* specify how ontology elements are expressed in models.

Figure 1 shows the overall approach of ontology-based model transformation. A combination of one semantic transformation, one MO-Binding and one OM-Binding form a *transformation configuration*. A transformation configuration is the basis for an automated generation of common model transformations. A generator for model transformations takes a transformation configuration as well as appropriate metamodel- and ontology-definitions as input and outputs a model transformation specified in an *intermediate model transformation language*. The generated model transformation is input to arbitrary MDA-tools performing model transformations.

3   Conclusions and Outlook

Since the approach presented is based on ontologies, more sophisticated ontology techniques can be applied. A challenge will be to combine ontology-based model transformation techniques with ontology technology like ontology mappings, semantic rules languages, inference machines, etc.. Ontology-based model transformation will provide input for interoperability solutions, like semantically enriched middleware platforms or semantic-based development platforms. This will contribute to interoperability in enterprise modeling, by providing basic technology for the development of generic and standardized model transformations and methodologies.

References

1. B. Elvesæter, A. Hahn, A-J. Berre, T. Neple: Towards an Interoperability Framework for Model-Driven Development of Software Systems, INTEROP-ESA'05, 2005.
2. S. Roser, B. Bauer: A Categorization of Collaborative Business Process Modeling Techniques, SoS4CO Workshop in 7th CEC Conference, IEEE, 2005.

Modeling Turnpike: A Model-Driven Framework for Domain-Specific Software Development*

Hiroshi Wada and Jun Suzuki

Department of Computer Science,
University of Massachusetts, Boston
shu@cs.umb.edu, xs@cs.umb.edu

This Ph.D. research investigates a generic model-driven development (MDD) framework that supports various domain-specific solutions (i.e. modeling, programming and development processes to directly deal with domain concepts), and empirically evaluates a series of techniques to develop such a framework. Steps towards creating the proposed framework include investigating a generic foundation to handle arbitrary Domain Specific Languages (DSLs); strategies, principles and tradeoffs in different DSL designs (e.g. DSL syntax and semantics); building blocks for modeling and programming domain concepts; transformation strategies from domain concepts to the final (compilable) source code; development processes to leverage the proposed framework well; model-driven approaches for maintenance and tests; and performance implications of major functional components in the framework.

This project proposes and investigates a new MDD framework, called Modeling Turnpike (or mTurnpike). mTurnpike allows developers to model and program domain concepts in arbitrary DSLs and to transform them to the final (compilable) source code in a seamless manner [1]. Leveraging the notions of UML metamodeling and attribute-oriented programming, mTurnpike provides an abstraction to represent domain concepts at the modeling and programming layers simultaneously.

At the modeling layer, domain concepts are represented as a *Domain Specific Model (DSM)*, which is represented as a set of UML 2.0 class and composite structure diagrams with UML profile. At the programming layer, domain concepts are represented as a *Domain Specific Code (DSC)*, which consists of attribute-oriented programs. By hiding the implementation details of those semantics from program code, attributes increase the level of programming abstraction and reduce programming complexity, resulting in simpler and more readable programs.

mTurnpike transforms domain concepts from the modeling layer to programming layer, and vise versa, by providing a seamless mapping between DSMs and DSCs. After mTurnpike generates a DSC, programmers write method code in the generated DSC in order to implement dynamic behaviors for domain concepts. mTurnpike transforms a DSM and DSC into a more detailed model and program by applying a given transformation rule. mTurnpike allows developers to define arbitrary transformation rules, each of which specifies how to specialize a DSM and DSC to particular implementation and deployment technologies.

---

* This research is supported in part by OGIS International, Inc. and Electric Power Development Co., Ltd.

J.-M. Bruel (Ed.): MoDELS 2005 Workshops, LNCS 3844, pp. 357–358, 2006.
© Springer-Verlag Berlin Heidelberg 2006

This project addresses several research issues as follows. 1) To handle arbitrary domain concepts at the modeling and programming layer, mTurnpike adopts a *language-in-language* design strategy to define DSLs in which different specialized languages are defined on top of a generic and customizable language (i.e. UML and Java). This design strategy improves the versatility of mTurnpike. 2) To provide higher abstraction to programmers through DSCs. Programmers write method code in DSCs before generating final source code. This means that programmers can focus on coding application's business logic without handling the details in implementation and deployment technologies. 3) To transform domain concepts at the modeling layer to the final source code, a transformation mechanism that handles both a model and code is required. mTurnpike allows developers to define transformation rules in a declarative manner. Declarative transformation rules are more readable and easier to write and maintain than procedural ones. This framework design contributes its ease of use and maintainability. 4) To improve the separation of concerns, mTurnpike maps domain concepts between the modeling and programming layers in a seamless and bi-directional manner. This mapping allows modelers and programmers to deal with the same set of domain concepts in different representations (i.e. UML models and annotated code), yet at the same level of abstraction. This means that modelers do not have to involve programming details, and programmers do not have to possess detailed domain knowledge and UML modeling expertise. This separation of concerns can reduce the complexity in application development, and increase the productivity for developers to model and program domain concepts.

The future directions of this project include the following issues. 1) To support multiple DSLs at a time, i.e. DSLs for a vertical domain and a horizontal domain, a future work will address generating compilable code through combining DSMs and DSCs written in multiple DSLs. 2) To clear the tradeoffs and selection criterions between languages to describe domain specific concepts. mTurnpike currently employs UML to define DSMs at the modeling layer, but there are several modeling languages to describe domain-specific concepts other than UML. Tradeoffs between them are not still clear. 3) To support code transformation from a DSC (i.e. method code that programmers add) to final code, a future work will investigate general code transform method (e.g. code transformation mechanism leveraging EBNF). 4) To improve maintainability, a future work will address a mechanism to debug a DSC directly and traceability between a DSM and the final code. 5) A set of preliminary performance measurements reveals mTurnpike's forntend has several bottlenecks. A future plan will address performance improvements on them.

Reference

1. H. Wada and J. Suzuki, "Modeling Turnpike Frontend System: a Model-Driven Development Framework Leveraging UML Metamodeling and Attribute-Oriented Programming," In *Proc. of the 8th ACM/IEEE International Conference on Model Driven Engineering Languages and Systems*, October 2005.

Author Index

Lecture Notes in Computer Science

For information about Vols. 1–3767

please contact your bookseller or Springer

Vol. 3814: M. Maybury, O. Stock, W. Wahlster (Eds.), Intelligent Technologies for Interactive Entertainment. XV, 342 pages. 2005. (Sublibrary LNAI).

Vol. 3813: R. Molva, G. Tsudik, D. Westhoff (Eds.), Security and Privacy in Ad-hoc and Sensor Networks. VIII, 219 pages. 2005.

Vol. 3810: Y.G. Desmedt, H. Wang, Y. Mu, Y. Li (Eds.), Cryptology and Network Security. XI, 349 pages. 2005.

Vol. 3809: S. Zhang, R. Jarvis (Eds.), AI 2005: Advances in Artificial Intelligence. XXVII, 1344 pages. 2005. (Sublibrary LNAI).

Vol. 3808: C. Bento, A. Cardoso, G. Dias (Eds.), Progress in Artificial Intelligence. XVIII, 704 pages. 2005. (Sublibrary LNAI).

Vol. 3807: M. Dean, Y. Guo, W. Jun, R. Kaschek, S. Krishnaswamy, Z. Pan, Q.Z. Sheng (Eds.), Web Information Systems Engineering – WISE 2005 Workshops. XV, 275 pages. 2005.

Vol. 3806: A.H. H. Ngu, M. Kitsuregawa, E.J. Neuhold, J.-Y. Chung, Q.Z. Sheng (Eds.), Web Information Systems Engineering – WISE 2005. XXI, 771 pages. 2005.

Vol. 3805: G. Subsol (Ed.), Virtual Storytelling. XII, 289 pages. 2005.

Vol. 3804: G. Bebis, R. Boyle, D. Koracin, B. Parvin (Eds.), Advances in Visual Computing. XX, 755 pages. 2005.

Vol. 3803: S. Jajodia, C. Mazumdar (Eds.), Information Systems Security. XI, 342 pages. 2005.

Vol. 3802: Y. Hao, J. Liu, Y.-P. Wang, Y.-m. Cheung, H. Yin, L. Jiao, J. Ma, Y.-C. Jiao (Eds.), Computational Intelligence and Security, Part II. XLII, 1166 pages. 2005. (Sublibrary LNAI).

Vol. 3801: Y. Hao, J. Liu, Y.-P. Wang, Y.-m. Cheung, H. Yin, L. Jiao, J. Ma, Y.-C. Jiao (Eds.), Computational Intelligence and Security, Part I. XLI, 1122 pages. 2005. (Sublibrary LNAI).

Vol. 3799: M. A. Rodríguez, I.F. Cruz, S. Levashkin, M.J. Egenhofer (Eds.), GeoSpatial Semantics. X, 259 pages. 2005.

Vol. 3798: A. Dearle, S. Eisenbach (Eds.), Component Deployment. X, 197 pages. 2005.

Vol. 3797: S. Maitra, C. E. V. Madhavan, R. Venkatesan (Eds.), Progress in Cryptology - INDOCRYPT 2005. XIV, 417 pages. 2005.

Vol. 3796: N.P. Smart (Ed.), Cryptography and Coding. XI, 461 pages. 2005.

Vol. 3795: H. Zhuge, G.C. Fox (Eds.), Grid and Cooperative Computing - GCC 2005. XXI, 1203 pages. 2005.

Vol. 3794: X. Jia, J. Wu, Y. He (Eds.), Mobile Ad-hoc and Sensor Networks. XX, 1136 pages. 2005.

Vol. 3793: T. Conte, N. Navarro, W.-m.W. Hwu, M. Valero, T. Ungerer (Eds.), High Performance Embedded Architectures and Compilers. XIII, 317 pages. 2005.

Vol. 3792: I. Richardson, P. Abrahamsson, R. Messnarz (Eds.), Software Process Improvement. VIII, 215 pages. 2005.

Vol. 3791: A. Adi, S. Stoutenburg, S. Tabet (Eds.), Rules and Rule Markup Languages for the Semantic Web. X, 225 pages. 2005.

Vol. 3790: G. Alonso (Ed.), Middleware 2005. XIII, 443 pages. 2005.

Vol. 3789: A. Gelbukh, Á. de Albornoz, H. Terashima-Marín (Eds.), MICAI 2005: Advances in Artificial Intelligence. XXVI, 1198 pages. 2005. (Sublibrary LNAI).

Vol. 3788: B. Roy (Ed.), Advances in Cryptology - ASIACRYPT 2005. XIV, 703 pages. 2005.

Vol. 3787: D. Kratsch (Ed.), Graph-Theoretic Concepts in Computer Science. XIV, 470 pages. 2005.

Vol. 3785: K.-K. Lau, R. Banach (Eds.), Formal Methods and Software Engineering. XIV, 496 pages. 2005.

Vol. 3784: J. Tao, T. Tan, R.W. Picard (Eds.), Affective Computing and Intelligent Interaction. XIX, 1008 pages. 2005.

Vol. 3783: S. Qing, W. Mao, J. Lopez, G. Wang (Eds.), Information and Communications Security. XIV, 492 pages. 2005.

Vol. 3782: K.-D. Althoff, A. Dengel, R. Bergmann, M. Nick, T.R. Roth-Berghofer (Eds.), Professional Knowledge Management. XXIII, 739 pages. 2005. (Sublibrary LNAI).

Vol. 3781: S.Z. Li, Z. Sun, T. Tan, S. Pankanti, G. Chollet, D. Zhang (Eds.), Advances in Biometric Person Authentication. XI, 250 pages. 2005.

Vol. 3780: K. Yi (Ed.), Programming Languages and Systems. XI, 435 pages. 2005.

Vol. 3779: H. Jin, D. Reed, W. Jiang (Eds.), Network and Parallel Computing. XV, 513 pages. 2005.

Vol. 3778: C. Atkinson, C. Bunse, H.-G. Gross, C. Peper (Eds.), Component-Based Software Development for Embedded Systems. VIII, 345 pages. 2005.

Vol. 3777: O.B. Lupanov, O.M. Kasim-Zade, A.V. Chaskin, K. Steinhöfel (Eds.), Stochastic Algorithms: Foundations and Applications. VIII, 239 pages. 2005.

Vol. 3776: S.K. Pal, S. Bandyopadhyay, S. Biswas (Eds.), Pattern Recognition and Machine Intelligence. XXIV, 808 pages. 2005.

Vol. 3775: J. Schönwälder, J. Serrat (Eds.), Ambient Networks. XIII, 281 pages. 2005.

Vol. 3774: G. Bierman, C. Koch (Eds.), Database Programming Languages. X, 295 pages. 2005.

Vol. 3773: A. Sanfeliu, M.L. Cortés (Eds.), Progress in Pattern Recognition, Image Analysis and Applications. XX, 1094 pages. 2005.

Vol. 3772: M.P. Consens, G. Navarro (Eds.), String Processing and Information Retrieval. XIV, 406 pages. 2005.

Vol. 3771: J.M.T. Romijn, G.P. Smith, J. van de Pol (Eds.), Integrated Formal Methods. XI, 407 pages. 2005.

Vol. 3770: J. Akoka, S.W. Liddle, I.-Y. Song, M. Bertolotto, I. Comyn-Wattiau, W.-J. van den Heuvel, M. Kolp, J. Trujillo, C. Kop, H.C. Mayr (Eds.), Perspectives in Conceptual Modeling. XXII, 476 pages. 2005.

Vol. 3769: D.A. Bader, M. Parashar, V. Sridhar, V.K. Prasanna (Eds.), High Performance Computing – HiPC 2005. XXVIII, 550 pages. 2005.

Vol. 3768: Y.-S. Ho, H.J. Kim (Eds.), Advances in Multimedia Information Processing - PCM 2005, Part II. XXVIII, 1088 pages. 2005.